Banking for Students

Banking for Students

M W Downey

Pitman

PITMAN PUBLISHING LIMITED
128 Long Acre, London WC2E 9AN

A Longman Group Company

© M W Downey 1986

First published in Great Britain in 1986

British Library Cataloguing in Publication Data
Downey, M W
  Banking for students.
  1. Banks and banking
  I. Title
  332.1   HG1601

ISBN 0-273-02320-9

All rights reserved. No part of this publication may be reproduced, stored in a retrieval system, or transmitted, in any form or by any means, electronic, mechanical, photocopying, recording and/or otherwise, without the prior written permission of the publishers. This book may not be lent, resold, hired out or otherwise disposed of by way of trade in any form of binding or cover other than that in which it is published, without the prior consent of the publishers.

Printed and bound in Great Britain at The Bath Press, Avon

To Margaret

Publisher's note

For ease of grammatical expression and presentation the author has resorted to masculine third person, singular pronouns and adjectives in this text. He intends no discourtesy to female readers, who are asked to substitute appropriate female pronouns and adjectives where required.

Contents

Preface

1 Money – Its Nature, Origins, Functions and Types — 1
1.1 Evolution of money — 1
1.2 Functions of money — 4
1.3 Characteristics of a good money system — 8
1.4 Shortcomings of money as an indicator of value — 10
1.5 Forms of money in modern society — 12
1.6 Money and near money — 14

2 Money Supply and Monetary Policy — 18
2.1 Credit creation and its effects on the economy — 18
2.2 Major government methods in the control of credit creation — 22
2.3 Money supply and the level of bank and economic activity — 24
2.4 Factors which bring about changes in the money supply — 33
2.5 Main objectives of government economic policy — 36
2.6 Techniques available for implementing monetary policy and their effect on banks — 40

3 British Banking System — 47
3.1 Early beginnings — 47
3.2 Banking in the eighteenth and nineteenth centuries — 49
3.3 Banking in the twentieth century — 51
3.4 Merchant banks — 53
3.5 British overseas banks — 56
3.6 Foreign banks — 56
3.7 Consortium banks — 57
3.8 National Giro Bank — 57
3.9 Savings banks — 58
3.10 Bank of England — 59
3.11 Analysing a bank's balance sheet — 67

4 Financial Markets — 75
4.1 Mechanism of the city — 75
4.2 Short-term money market — 76
4.3 Parallel markets — 81
4.4 Capital market — 83
4.5 Foreign exchange market — 96
4.6 Financial futures market — 97

5 Savings, Investment and Interest Rates — 99
5.1 The nature of savings in the economy, major savers and their role in the economy — 99
5.2 Major forms of saving — 106
5.3 Interest rates in theory — 123
5.4 Market interest rates — 135
5.5 Government influences on the market for interest rates — 138
5.6 Money market influences on interest rates — 141
5.7 Effects of interest rate changes — 141
5.8 Relationship between the balance of payments, exchange rates and interest rates — 146

6 Wholesale Money Markets — 151
6.1 Local authority market — 152
6.2 Finance house market — 154
6.3 Eurocurrency market — 155
6.4 Certificates of deposit market — 158
6.5 Interbank market — 158
6.6 Intercompany market — 159
6.7 Financial futures market — 160

7 Cheques, Negotiability and the Legal Implications of the Various Banking Instruments — 164
7.1 Definition of a cheque — 164
7.2 Development of the cheque as a method of payment — 164
7.3 Origin of cheque crossings — 169
7.4 Different types of negotiable instrument — 172
7.5 Parties to a bill of exchange, their rights and responsibilities — 177
7.6 Conversion and its consequences — 180
7.7 Conversion and safe custody — 181
7.8 Agents, their unlawful acts and the effects of these on banks — 182
7.9 Negotiability — 183
7.10 Acceptance, endorsement and discharge of a bill of exchange — 184
7.11 Statutory protection for various holders of a bill of exchange — 187
7.12 Presentation of a bill for payment — 188

viii Contents

    7.13 Position of the collecting banker with regard to statutory protection 190
    7.14 Position of the paying banker with regard to statutory protection 194
    7.15 Revocation of a banker's authority 195
    7.16 Material alteration of a bill of exchange 197
    7.17 Forgery 197
    7.18 Dishonour of a bill of exchange 198

8 Banking Services to Personal, Business and Corporate Customers **203**
    8.1 Cash 203
    8.2 Cheques 204
    8.3 Credit cards 207
    8.4 Credit clearing 209
    8.5 Foreign currency and travellers cheques 213
    8.6 Eurocheques and cheque cards 214
    8.7 Mail and telegraphic orders 214
    8.8 Banker's draft 215
    8.9 SWIFT 215
    8.10 International money orders 215
    8.11 Banking services 216
    8.12 Marketing the banks' services 233

9 Understanding the Basic Principles of Bank Lending **236**
    9.1 General principles of lending 236
    9.2 Credit scoring 240
    9.3 Circumstances in which a security may be required for a bank loan 242
    9.4 Some important definitions and principles 243
    9.5 Various types of security that can be used to back a bank loan 243
    9.6 Effect of the Consumer Credit Act 1974 on banks 259

10 The Banker and Customer Relationship **263**
    10.1 What is a banker? 263
    10.2 What is a customer? 264
    10.3 Opening up and operating a bank account 265
    10.4 Basic legal relationships between banker and customer 275
    10.5 Obligations of banker and customer 282
    10.6 Considerations of the different types of bank customer 283
    10.7 A banker's legal liabilities 297
    10.8 Wills 302
    10.9 Personal representatives 304
    10.10 Trustees 304

11	**The Banker's View of a Customer's Balance Sheet**	**307**
	11.1 Introduction	307
	11.2 Nature and composition of final accounts	307
	11.3 How a banker looks at the final accounts of a business	317
	11.4 Bankers' use of future financial projections	327
	11.5 The business as a going/gone concern	329
	11.6 Effects of a bank advance on the business balance sheet	332

Index   **337**

Preface

This text has been specifically written for people studying Elements of Banking 1 and 2 of the BTEC national diploma and certificate courses and the preliminary section of the Institute of Bankers' banking certificate. Incorporated in the text are a series of self-assessment exercises which students or teachers can use to assess progress through the course. At the end of each chapter are assignments, either in BTEC or traditional style to be used as learning exercises, or to assess satisfactory learning by the student.

Chapters have been structured so that students following the Elements of Banking 1 course can read as much of the chapter as is necessary for their syllabus. Elements of Banking 2 students will find it useful to read the first part of the chapter as revision before study of the area which is relevant to their syllabus.

This book will also be useful to those students following A level economics, the Institute of Bankers' Stage 2 diploma and any courses where a knowledge of the UK financial system is necessary.

I would like to acknowledge my gratitude to the following persons: my wife and daughters for their patience and understanding during the period of time that I spent writing this book; my colleagues at work for all of their help and assistance during the preparation of the text and the many exercises; and the staff in the clearing banks in Chichester, the Bank of England and the Bank Education Service for the provision of information and the supply of many of the examples of bank forms.

1 Money – Its Nature, Origins, Functions and Types

1.1 Evolution of money

It is very difficult to know exactly when money was first used in the world, as records do not exist. Most certainly it can be assumed that before it came into popular use people used a **barter** system, under which people exchanged one good for another.

Barter has never died out despite certain, very basic disadvantages. For example, the system operates every time someone exchanges goods in the playground. Barter also operates on an international scale, under 'swap' arrangements, where one country exchanges wheat for tractors, for example.

There are four inherent disadvantages to barter and the introduction of a monetary system aims at removing them.

(1) The first disadvantage is that the person seeking to barter must find someone else with the goods he wants, and who also wants to exchange the goods he has. This is known as a **double coincidence of wants**. If he is unable to do this, no exchange can take place.

(2) Secondly, a disadvantage exists in that goods produced are not all the same and many are perishable. Even with mass production, cars coming off the assembly line may all appear to be the same, but one only has to compare one person's experience of a new car with someone else's of a similar new car to see that similar objects are not the same. We shall find that each car has its own individuality. In the exchange of natural goods the variation between each unit is considerable. One sheep is not the same as another, nor is one cabbage the same as another. This leads to the **absence of an acceptable standard** as one person's view of what they are worth differs from another person's view.

(3) Thirdly, certain goods are not easily divided into smaller parts. Suppose a farmer wants to breed pigs and is prepared to exchange sheep for pigs. What would be the outcome if he wanted to give one sheep for three pigs while the pig farmer wanted to give only two pigs for one sheep? The diplomatic exchange rate would be somewhere between two and three pigs per sheep, but what use would part of a pig be for breeding? This example is a simplification, but it does explain the **lack of divisibility** of some goods so that no acceptable bargain can be struck.

(4) The fourth disadvantage to barter is the **lack of portability** of some

goods. Animals can move on their own and are more portable than inanimate objects. Imagine carrying around iron bars or even large quantities of bricks or sand or cement. Therefore, anything that is to act as money needs to be portable.

One can see that with these disadvantages barter was doomed to having a limited life. However, despite them, money is thought to have developed out of religious and social custom rather than directly out of barter. It can be seen that commodities that came to be used as money developed out of those things related to items for ransom, religious, ceremonial or decorative purposes. Early money was often some useful substance. Many things have served as money at one time or another including slaves, gunpowder, jawbones of pigs, stones, shells, cigarettes in prisoner of war camps and even tobacco in prisons in Britain today. Despite this variety Professor J K Galbraith sees the historic association between money and metals as one which 'is more than close', for he believes that 'for all practical purposes for most of the time money has been more or less precious metal'.

The earliest use of coins was in India, and is referred to in Hindu epics. The date appears to have been some time before the eighth century BC. It was at that time that Herodotus referred to the use by the King of Lydia of metal of a predetermined weight as a form of money. It was after Alexander the Great that the custom was established of depicting the head of the sovereign on the coins. This was more as an act of gratification of the ruler than a means of guaranteeing the weight and fineness of the metal. However, the use of precious metals gave rise to the development of public and private fraud. Public fraud occurred as rulers seized the opportunity to add more base metals into the coins and so produce more money. Private fraud took place as people privately filed off bits of the metal as gold dust which could also be used to pay off a debt. Strangely enough it was not until 1609 that coins began to be weighed and exchanged for actual value by weight; this occurred first of all in the city of Amsterdam. This, according to Galbraith, is one of the earliest links of money with the history of banking.

The development of coinage in the United Kingdom goes back to times before the Romans. Most of the documentary evidence about early currencies in the British Isles is found in Caesar's *De Bello Gallico*, where he refers to iron bars and rings being used as money. Certainly early coins known as staters circulated in the south of England around 75 BC. Bars of iron similar to crudely fashioned sword blades, have been found buried in ancient British camps which date from the first century BC. The Romans' most popular coin circulating in Britain around 30 BC–AD 5 was the silver denarius which formed part of the scanty supply of silver and bronze coins. It was the denarius from which the 'd' in our pre-decimalisation £.s.d. was derived. Later silver and bronze coins copied the Roman style. The development of coins that we have in circulation today is shown in the table opposite.

The development of banknotes as we know them today is closely

Table 1.1 Development of present coins

Coin	When introduced	Metal
Penny, halfpenny	c. 410–1066	Silver
Penny, halfpenny	Edward VI (1547–1553)	Base
Penny, halfpenny	Elizabeth II	Bronze
Florin	Edward III	Gold
Ten pence	Elizabeth II	Cupronickel
Sovereign	Henry VII (1483–1509)	Gold
Crown	Henry VIII (1509–1547)	Gold
Shilling	Edward VI (1547–1553)	Silver
Five pence	Elizabeth II	Cupronickel
Pound	Elizabeth I (1558–1603)	Gold
Pound	Elizabeth II	Base
Fifty pence	Elizabeth II	Cupronickel
Twenty pence	Elizabeth II	Cupronickel

connected with the history of banking. However, the invention of paper money can be attributed to the Chinese. The Emperor Hien Tsung began to use paper money made from mulberry bark and decorated with dragons and chrysanthemums. These were found to be safer and easier to carry around than coins. They were termed 'flying money' because they could be hidden in saddle-bags and quickly sent on long journeys by using relays of horses.

Banknotes were first issued briefly in Sweden in 1660 but their introduction into Britain was by stages, and arose from the development of banking. In the UK, as we shall see in Chapter 3, banking started with the goldsmiths. As people began to deposit their money or valuables with the goldsmiths they were issued with a receipt which gave them the right to withdraw their deposits. At first these receipts were made out to the name of the people who had deposited them. This meant that they, or someone they nominated, could be the only persons to be paid back. As time went by, the goldsmiths realised that it would be more convenient to make their receipts repayable to **bearer**. By the year 1729 printed receipts were produced. In the early years, these banks, as some goldsmiths were eventually called, issued their own notes. One bank, which had a privileged place in banking, the Bank of England, also issued notes but these were different. In 1695, it first printed banknotes ranging in denomination from £10 to £100. At this level it can be seen that these notes were not meant for ordinary people to handle. Each note had a bearer's name and the cashier's name. A great deal of forgery went on and in an attempt to stop this an Act was passed in 1709 limiting note issuing powers to organisations with no more than six partners. Since the Bank of England was excluded from this Act, it had a privileged position. During the reign of George III (1760–1820) gold coinage was more or less replaced by banknotes. The lowest denomination of Bank of England notes was still £10 but some private country banks, those operating outside of London, provided £1 notes. The practice of note issuing expanded considerably, with not only banks but all manner of tradesmen issuing notes, some for very small amounts. Forgery was considerable so in 1775 an Act of Parliament banned notes of less than £1 and in 1777 the smallest note allowed was £5.

In order to give these notes acceptability and stability they needed to be linked with gold. This would enable them to be taken back to the place of issue and exchanged for gold. Notes of this type are known as convertible notes, and this property of convertibility is the origin of the statement on our present banknotes 'I promise to pay the bearer'. Originally people could claim gold for their notes. This meant, of course, that banks needed to have a store of gold to meet the sudden demands of the holders of their notes. Over the years the Bank of England became the main note issuer in England and Wales, and by 1844 Sir Robert Peel brought in the Bank Charter Act which restricted the authority of unstable banking enterprises. It gave the Bank of England a monopoly in the issue of banknotes, the quantity of which was to be determined by the amount of gold in store; it was also allowed to issue £14m worth of notes against securities and not gold. This is known as the **fiduciary issue**. Only country banks already issuing notes could continue to do so, and the level was restricted to the total number of notes already being printed. No new banks could issue notes, and if any existing note-issuing banks became insolvent or amalgamated they had to give up their note-issuing powers. Today the only bank to issue notes in England and Wales is the Bank of England. In Scotland, the banks can issue notes but for every one of their own notes in circulation a Bank of England note has to be held to cover this issue.

Self-assessment exercises

1 What disadvantages are there to barter and how did the introduction of money remove them? Why was money introduced?
2 When were coins first thought to have been used?
3 What were the original problems created by the use of precious metals for coins? What measures were developed to remove these problems?
4 Who invented the use of paper money? Why was it used?
5 To whom is the development of banknotes in the UK attributed?
6 What was the early meaning to the words printed on a banknote 'I promise to pay the bearer'?
7 What actions were taken by the authorities to stop forgery of banknotes?
8 What is the fiduciary issue?

1.2 Functions of money

If we were to ask the question 'what is money?' we would find difficulty in answering. We would probably resort to an explanation of the major jobs that money performs in our society. In fact if we look at a number of textbooks about money we shall find that the authors either state that the best way to define money is to look at its functions or they actually give their definition by describing its functions. We can conclude from this that money's functions are very important, but just what does it do? We are all very much aware of its major function – that of a means of exchange – but most textbooks mention four functions and others even give five. Professor J K Galbraith defines money by highlighting its main function when he states that money is 'What is commonly offered or received for the purchase or sale of goods, services or other things'. These functions can be seen as:

1 Money acts as a medium of exchange.
2 Money generalises purchasing power.
3 Money acts as a store of value.
4 Money acts as a unit of account.
5 Money acts as a standard of deferred payment.

1.21 Medium of exchange

Anything that is a medium is a means by which communication takes place. Exchange means giving up something in return for something else. Thus when we say that money is a medium of exchange we mean that it is the instrument by which we give up one thing to gain another. Sometimes money is given up for goods; sometimes we give up goods to receive money. But another kind of exchange occurs when we exchange our time and talents by working for someon else and receiving a money payment which we then exchange for our own choice of goods and services. The statements below show how barter takes place and how money can enter into the transaction.

Barter can be shown as

CORN

IS EXCHANGED FOR

SHOES

When money enters the scene, this becomes:

CORN

IS EXCHANGED FOR

MONEY

WHICH IS EXCHANGED FOR

SHOES

In the first statement the person with corn is locked into a bargain which commits him/her to shoes. In the second statement the seller takes the money and the next step is a free choice. Instead of shoes he/she could have had fish or shirts or any other goods or service.

1.22 Generalises purchasing power

This gives the individual consumer the choice to spend money wherever and whenever desired. With barter, we have seen that trading has restricted people to the goods on offer. With the use of money, once we have sold our time, talents or goods, we have in our hands a commodity that will be accepted for the purchase of almost all goods and services provided we have sufficient of it.

1.23 Store of value

When our money was precious metal some people would store it away for future spending. This we know as saving. We in Britain today cannot store bullion but can hold precious metals in the form of coins. Indeed, in France where bullion can be stored, it is said that every French peasant farmer has his store of gold. In Britain people store their money in other ways. The most common is by means of a deposit account with a bank, building society or finance house. This means the actual money we pay, if we pay coins and notes in, ceases to belong to us in its physical form and all we have is a credit balance against our names. Indeed, we may ourselves have paid in this balance in a non-physical form by means of a cheque or bank giro credit.

Some people store up their wealth in other things such as antiques, works of art, land or property, stocks or shares. These are known as **assets**. They do present a particular problem to the holder for if he wishes to use this stored wealth as a medium of exchange then, unlike some bank or building society deposits, he has to convert these assets back into some liquid form so that the transactions can take place. In order for money to act as a good store of value two conditions must exist to some degree or other. First of all, by storing this money up in whatever form we may wish, we are postponing its present spending on goods and services for some future spending. We have to be certain that when we come to spend this money the goods or services will be available. If we feel that the goods will be in short supply in the future then we will buy them now. Indeed, if shortages are thought likely in the future, even more than our present needs may be purchased. This was seen in the 1970s when anticipated shortages of sugar, bread and toilet rolls caused panic buying and hoarding. We could say that this was saving, but planned saving in goods needed from future spending. The second feature which encourages saving is if the money is going to retain its value. In other words, we do not want to put money to one side only to find that because of prices rising faster than the interest we receive we can no longer buy the goods or services. However, experience over the past years has shown us that this is not an absolutely fixed condition. During the 1970s prices rose by leaps and bounds. This might suggest that people would not be very keen to save, particularly as the interest received on savings was less than the increase in prices but, strange as it may seem, there were times during those years when saving reached record levels. What this tells us is that there are other factors which determine savings as well as the rate of interest or the level of inflation (rising prices). However, rather than there being less desire to save, the nature of the savings may change. Certain items may keep their value better – gold, antiques, or land – so that savings are put into these rather than bank or building society deposits.

1.24 Unit of account

In most shops one can see price labels indicating the price to be paid for a particular item. Rarely does one see these prices quoted in terms of other goods to be offered but usually in terms of units of money to be exchanged. Thus in the United Kingdom potatoes can be exchanged for say 10p a lb or a dress for £19.99. In the USA or Germany these labels would be in dollars or marks whatever might be the currency of the country. In large tourist centres or near boundaries we can see labels showing the price in a number of currencies.

If we use an old fashioned term we can say that a bill is an account. Indeed accounts are being sent to people and businesses daily. The units in which these accounts are quoted happens to be the money system of the country. Here we can say that money is acting as a unit of account. In recent times two new units of account have been created in a worldwide context so that nowadays we can receive a bill under certain circumstances in international terms. The first of these is called a 'Special Drawing Right'. This was created by the International Monetary Fund in 1969 and one simple example of its use is seen in the bill presented for sailing through the Suez Canal. When one reaches Alexandria either at the start or end of the passage through the Canal then the bill is presented in terms of SDRs (as they are called). Of course, there is an exchange rate with all the major currencies so that the amount can be converted into a national currency and paid. The second international unit of account was created in 1978 and is called a European Currency Unit or ECU. This is part of the monetary system of the European Economic Community (EEC). Originally debts and money transferred between governments were quoted in terms of the ECU. As for the SDR there is a pound, German mark and French franc value which is not always constant. In recent times individuals within the EEC have started presenting bills in terms of ECUs. Accounts in banks are now set up in ECUs and cheques in ECU values are being cleared. We must remember that these new units of account do not exist in physical form like other currencies. All we are doing when paying bills in these units is instructing a bank to add one amount to an account and to deduct it from another account. There is no need to have actual coins and notes in SDRs or ECUs.

1.25 Standard of deferred payments

To defer anything is to put it off until a later date. Thus a deferred payment is a payment which is put off until later. This is having goods now and paying the bill in the future. When this happens we are said to have been given credit.

A standard is a held belief or value which one tries to live up to. Therefore, what is being stated here is that money is a measure or value upon which a system of credit is based. We would be foolish to think that credit would not operate if there was no money system. I am sure that when barter was used there were deals made whereby goods were exchanged for services, or goods which were to be supplied over a period of time. For example, a shoemaker might have made a pair of shoes over a number of weeks or months being paid in loaves of bread during that time. Money, however, enables a system of credit to be used more often and for very large amounts. Further, with money the lender can be compensated more easily for any loss which might be sustained.

Self-assessment exercises

1 What is meant when it is said that money is 'a medium of exchange'?
2 Which two factors are required to be present for money to be a store of value?
3 An ECU is said to be a unit of account. What is an ECU and how does it perform this function?

1.3 Characteristics of a good money system

In the book *The Restaurant at the End of the Universe* by Douglas Adams, when Arthur Dent and Ford Prefect returned to the space travellers after their wanderings around earth, they found that the people had tried to develop some form of commercial system. They had as a basis of their monetary system the leaves they found in the trees. We instinctively know that this is not quite right and if we go on to consider why this is so we would soon come to the realisation that leaves do not display many of the characteristics of what can be called a good money system. These are:

(1) First of all, one could say that to that society these leaves were **acceptable**. To what extent they were acceptable is open to question. However, this is a most important feature of any money system. If people are not prepared to accept whatever is being offered in return for goods and services, then the whole system is likely to collapse. If large quantities of a particular forged note flooded the market and this becomes known, then the acceptability of the note disappears. Buyers and sellers would think twice before accepting any notes of this type, good or bad.

(2) Secondly, these leaves display another aspect of a good money system, that is they are **recognisable**. We can easily identify a leaf when we see one. With money this recognition goes deeper than basic identification. Recognisability refers to its acceptability in payment of a debt. As we have already seen in the development of money, early coins were of precious metal and so were valuable in themselves. This meant that official recognisability was not needed; however, as coins began to have the sovereign's image stamped on them this helped to further their recognisability. With the development of base metal coins, some form of official recognisability had to be given and it was from that that legal tender was developed. This legal tender is a statement by the authorities as to what is legally acceptable in terms of coins in the payment of a debt. With notes, they were claims to valuable items deposited with goldsmiths and would be redeemable as and when the holder of the notes wanted them. These notes were said to be convertible so that gold would be redeemed by the holder. With the issue of non-backed notes, again state recognition of acceptability was necessary.

(3) Thirdly, the unit which is used in a money system must be **scarce**. This is an economic idea which relates the supply to demand up to the point where the demand is saturated. At this point the commodity is no longer scarce. From this aspect we can see how foolish it was to take leaves as money. In the winter, leaves would only be available in evergreen parts of the world and in other parts of the world they would be scarce or completely absent. On the other hand, in late spring and summer leaves would be so plentiful that supply would swamp demand.

(4) This leads us to the fourth characteristic of a good money system. For anything to act as money it must be **durable**. This means it must be able to last over time. One of the disadvantages of using any natural product is that over time it decays. Thus one might think that the answer to abundance and scarcity would be to store away the leaves from the summer to provide for the shortage in the winter, but lack of durability would prevent this. The leaves would decay so that when they were wanted they would be of no use.

(5) There is also another disadvantage related to the use of leaves, namely

that each leaf is different, even from the same tree. We know that one 10p is the same as every other 10p and also a £5 note is very much the same as every other £5 note. This is because they came from the same source and have the same features. They are said to be **homogeneous**. This is another economic concept and it is a necessary feature so that people do not display preferences for what should be exactly the same money unit. Thus we do not prefer one pound note to another, nor do we prefer one 50p piece to another. With leaves this would be different. Some leaves are bigger than others, some a more interesting shape or colour than others. We would have people selecting some and rejecting others. This would not make the money system very easy to operate.

(6) The sixth feature of a monetary system is that it must be **divisible**. This proves to be yet another disadvantage to the use of leaves. We might think that with the different sized leaves from various trees, we could develop a system whereby so many rose leaves were equal to one sycamore leaf and so many sycamore leaves were equal to a horse chestnut leaf ... but this only involves three types of leaves. What kind of system would be necessary to cover all the leaves in existence? Even if we standardised on one type of leaf, the lack of a completely standardised size of leaf would make a system of divisibility impossible to devise.

(7) The seventh characteristic of a good money system is that it must be portable. We can imagine trying to carry around large quantities of leaves. Even our own system of money falls down on this characteristic when one looks at coins and even large quantities of small denominations of notes. As a result, non-cash transfers of money have been developed.

(8) The final characteristic is that a money unit must be relatively stable. We have already seen that even our system of money has variations in value over time. In other words, what we can exchange for money in terms of goods and services is not the same amount from one year to the next. In the last ten years the amount of money needed to buy the same goods and services has gone up considerably.

1.4 Shortcomings of money as an indicator of value

At one time it used to be stated that money performed the function of being a measure of value. In other words it was able to measure the value of goods and services we buy. However, if we consider this closely, we can see that this is not really correct. What is being said is that if a book costs £7 then the value of the book is £7. However, someone interested in the subject of the book, its age, or its author, might be prepared to pay more than £7, whereas someone not interested in the book may feel that £7 is an excessive price to pay. This shows that value to individuals varies considerably and that this value is **subjective**. Almost everyone has a favourite article. There are often many particular reasons why these articles are special to us. In some cases, however, although they may be priceless to us, the actual value is very small. Although these articles can be said to have no **intrinsic** value (no value in their own right) they have a high subjective value. We mentioned a book that cost £7, what does this price measure? If we look at the situation again we are really being told, by looking at the price label, that if we offer this price to the shopkeeper he will probably agree to the sale. If he does then money in some form will be handed over. Here money is acting as a medium of exchange. We can, therefore, say that the price is really the measure of value in exchange and that in this case money is acting as a measure of value.

When society wishes to say how much anything is worth – how valuable it is – it tends to put this in money terms. Thus we say Mr X is a millionaire – meaning in excess of £1 000 000. We also say 'My house is worth over £50 000'. Here what we are describing is the money we would probably receive if we were to sell the house. This is another example of valuing items in terms of money. How does one value the money itself? We talk about the value of money, and know that in the 1970s the value of money declined considerably. How was this value measured? It cannot have been in money terms for it does not help to say that £1 is equal in value to £1. There was a time in Britain when a £1 note could be exchanged for a pound's worth of gold. Thus money could be valued in terms of what it could be exchanged for in gold or another monetary unit. Although we cannot exchange our notes for gold today, we can exchange them for other currencies which is useful when we go on holiday or wish to buy foreign goods or services. But how do we value money in Britain? The clue is to be found above. We said that the £1 could be exchanged for gold. It cannot be done today, but the £1 can be exchanged for goods and services. This is how it is possible to see a rise or fall in the value of money. What we could have bought for £1 in 1970 was considerably more than what £1 will buy today. We can see that the value of money is falling by the level of prices; if prices are rising we have to give more money to the shopkeepers to purchase a particular item or service. This situation of rising prices is called **inflation**.

Periods of low inflation (2–5 per cent) are not a problem for countries. It is periods of very high inflation that people fear, for these cause many economic problems and very often the actions taken to reduce inflation result in very unpopular outcomes such as unemployment and lack of industrial growth. Obviously during a period of falling prices the value of money rises. When the value of money is falling rapidly one of the problems encountered is that money loses its popularity. This was seen in Germany in the 1920s when considerable inflation pushed prices up to millions of deutschemarks and goods became more popular than the actual money itself.

Self-assessment exercise

Why is it wrong to say that money acts as a measure of value?

1.5 Forms of money in modern society

When looking at forms of money in a modern society we must include those assets which perform the functions of money. This does not mean that they must perform all of the functions completely – some assets may perform very well but others may only carry out one or two of the functions of money. Since a major function of money is its use as a medium of exchange, we shall use this function as our major reference for those assets we use as money.

The use of coins and notes as money may be jointly regarded as cash transactions. We might be tempted to think that cash is a major part of what we call the money supply. However, cash only accounts for about 20 per cent of all transactions in the UK. We would not deny that cash acts as a medium of exchange, however, there is a limit as to its use, particularly the use of coins. We cannot pay off a debt of any amount with coins. In order to make cash acceptable as a payment, the authorities have set down regulations which are known as **legal tender** – that is the amount one may legally offer in payment of a debt and which must be accepted. This is as follows:

Table 1.2

Gold (dated 1830 onwards if not below least current weight)		Any amount
Notes/coins	£1	Any amount
	50p ⎫	
	20p ⎬	Up to £10
	10p ⎭	
	5p	Up to £5
	2p ⎫	Up to 20p
	1p ⎭	

Cash can also act as a store of value but I doubt if very many people store their cash away in large amounts. We no doubt have small amounts of cash in 'piggy banks', jars or bottles, and indeed some people who do not trust banks store their notes in various places they consider safe. However, for most of us our money is stored in banks or other institutions where we may receive interest and almost certainly security. Cash also acts as a unit of account. We know that the price label on an article will be in our country's currency and we can exchange coins and notes for that article. However, legal tender makes the use of coins somewhat limited. The use of cash as a standard of deferred payments is also possible, though it is not the only method one can use. If we are given credit then we can use cash to pay off this debt over a period of time.

In a modern society money is also to be found in bank deposits where it acts as a store of value. People now maintain some, if not all of their wealth in this form. Such deposits also perform the function of medium of exchange, most commonly by means of a **cheque**. The cheque shows that the payer has funds available in a bank or other institution. The cheque is not money, it is merely an instruction to a banker to transfer funds from one person to another. Sometimes the money being transferred is not that of the issuer of the cheque but has been provided by the bank in the form of an overdraft or loan. In this case, as we will see in Chapter 2, this money has been created. There are other ways in which our bank accounts can be transferred as well as other ways in which credit can be given to pay off a debt. We can instruct our bank to pay out of our bank account by means of **bank giro**, **standing orders** and **direct debits**. These are also instructions to our banks to take money out of our account and transfer it to someone else. Of course the actual coins and notes do not transfer, but a figure is merely deducted from our account and is added to the shopkeeper's or other person's account.

The use of **credit cards**, to pay off a debt, affords us the facility of goods before we need to meet the payment. When our account comes from the credit card company, we are given time to pay. If we pay within this specified time, no charges are made, but if we put off payment we are charged interest. Another type of paper which can be used to pay off a debt is a **postal order**. These are not cheques since they represent the actual money which has been paid to the Post Office. Anyone can purchase them. The maximum value of a postal order is limited, but if you have a debt within this limit, then a postal order can be sent to pay the bill. By means of a system of recording and crossings, postal orders can be a safe and convenient way of paying out money.

Long before we used cheques in the UK a system had developed, particularly in foreign trade, whereby traders could extend credit to their customers, but gain an advantage of liquidity should they require it. This credit system was evidenced by a piece of paper called a **bill of exchange** (*see* Fig. 7.6). As well as having evidence that he is owed money, the holder can do one of two other things with the bill. He can use it to pay off any debts he may have for this value. This is done by endorsing the bill to the other person. The actual endorsement can be merely signed with one's name on the back; this is known as endorsement in blank. If the name of the person to receive the bill is written on the back as well as the giver's signature, this is known as endorsement in specific. The bill may change hands a number of times before it falls due. Secondly, the holder may have the bill encashed before the original debtor needs to pay; this is known as discounting. This is really a way of borrowing money with the bill acting as security. More is said about discounting of a bill of exchange in Chapter 4. So we can see that a bill of exchange can perform at least three of the functions of money – a medium of exchange, a store of value and a standard of deferred payments.

A very specialised store of value and one which is used in a restricted market is that of the Treasury bill. This is part of the government's debt. The government, in carrying out its functions on behalf of the citizens of the country, does not receive sufficient funds from taxation or earnings, therefore, it needs to borrow. This borrowing is either for a long term or a short term. Treasury bills represent short-term borrowing, the money is required to provide the government with funds to meet payments due before the income from taxes comes in. We say that this borrowing is assisting in the government's liquidity. The Bank of England, on behalf of the government, sells Treasury bills every Friday. The government is promising with each bill to pay back the money within ninety-one days from issue. Thus the institutions which buy these bills, mainly the discount houses, are really storing up value for a short period. In Chapter 4, we will see in detail how this system of Treasury bill discounting operates.

Self-assessment exercise

Show, by means of a diagram, how well the modern forms of money fit the characteristics of a good monetary unit system.

1.6 Money and near money

So far we have discussed what can be used as money in payment of a debt. We have seen that bank deposits are classed as money and that the use of cheques, standing orders or bank giro can transfer some of these bank deposits from one customer to another. But there are some types of deposits in building societies and finance houses which are not necessarily transferred by cheque. How do we classify these? This is where there is some difference of opinion. The *Dictionary of Modern Economics* sees these as 'near' money and this view is also held by Valentine and Mason in the *Basics of Banking* and by Cox in *Elements of Banking*, but if we look at the definition of 'near money' in the *Dictionary of Banking* by F E Perry, it is stated as 'a term sometimes applied to bills, cheques, promissory notes, postal and money orders or anything which is not banknotes, coin or bank deposits'. Cox goes on to change this definition to include, in a broad view of near money, bank deposits which are subject to longer notice of withdrawal than seven days as it takes time to turn these into a position of ready funds and medium of exchange. Therefore, Cox includes some bank deposits in his definition of near money; Perry completely excludes them.

One way of looking at a definition of near money is to say that it is those items which possess, as their major function, that of being a store of value, but they can eventually be converted into a form which will act as a medium of exchange. Thus with most of the items mentioned above, there is a time factor involved. Certain bank deposits, ironically, need to have notice for withdrawal, although the bank will waive this notice for small amounts or emergencies. The same applies to building society, share and deposit accounts. Some can be cashed immediately without forfeiture of interest, others are locked into a time agreement and cannot be encashed before that time. If we look at the definition of near money in this way then we can see that we can bring all of the definitions we have seen so far together. From the point of view of Perry, anything other than coins, notes or current accounts are near money and from Cox's definition, all the things he lists can, given time, be turned into cash and, until this is done, they are a store of value – that is performing the major role of near money.

One final point of relevance to this classification comes when we look at the government's various definitions of the money supply. These go through various stages from the simple definition of **M0** (*see* Chapter 2, Section 2.31) to the complex **private sector liabilities 2**. The government sees the need to keep the money supply under control in order to check any tendency to inflation. One of its problems has been in finding an adequate and realistic definition of the money supply so that this control can be successful. However, we have seen that cash and current accounts form the major part of the function of a medium of exchange. Since near money can eventually become cash or current account deposits, a very basic definition is not adequate for the government's use when trying to control inflation. Hence the reason for the various stages of definition until we reach private sector liabilities 2 when most forms of near money are included.

There has been a considerable growth in near money over the past fifty years. Why has this happened? There is no one reason for this. In the first place, incomes have risen, not only in money terms, but also in real terms. People have now more money to save. If we add to this the fact that people wish to place these savings in accounts which are safe, convenient and profitable, then the availability of various types of savings provides a reason for the growth of near money. Competition between the various types of savings institutions is very much in evidence. There are now many different ways to save with different rates of interest and different forms of availability. The latter are seen in the development, over recent years, of joint deposit/cheque accounts between the banks and the building societies. This means that the money can be safe, earn a slightly higher rate of interest and be available when banks are closed. For these reasons near money has grown over the years.

Self-assessment exercises

1 How would you define the term near money? Give examples.
2 Why do you think the ability to identify near money is important in the measuring of the money supply?
3 Why has the use of near money grown over recent years?

Assignments

1   In the fourteenth century, in Utopia, most of the goods and services were exchanged by means of barter. The King felt this was hampering the development of the country so he called three of his advisors and asked them what they thought should be done. They all agreed that some form of money unit should be introduced to replace the barter system but disagreed as to what this should be.
   The first one said, 'King, we in Utopia are good at producing sheepskin coats so we should use these as money.'
   The second said, 'These are no good, what we want is something that we don't have to work for. In Utopia there are plenty of small round stones. Why don't we use these?'
   The third said, 'These are no good either, what we want to use is the silver from our silver mines – produce round discs of various sizes and these can then be exchanged for the goods and services.'
   From the above say:
   (a) What disadvantages to barter the advisors gave to the King?
   (b) How each item suggested would be suited to use as money?
   (c) What would need to be done to encourage the use of the one finally selected?
2   How well do the modern forms of money fit the functions that money must perform?
3   Below are five basic transactions that could have taken place in the UK today.
   (a) Mr and Mrs Lones paid their monthly mortgage repayment to the Cornerstone Building Society.
   (b) John Bowne purchased a stacking HiFi system from a discount warehouse but did not wish to reduce his low current account balance further.
   (c) Mavis Wright purchased her weekly groceries but did not have sufficient cash when reaching the checkout.
   (d) William Rush purchased his daily packet of cigarettes and newspaper at the usual shop on the way to the railway station.
   (e) James Owner opened up a bank account by paying some money in that had been left to him by his grandmother. He now wants to purchase, for cash, a motorbike from the local dealer but he will not accept his cheque.

Tasks
(i) State which forms of money are likely to be used in each of these transactions.
(ii) Some forms of money have not been included – describe those that are missing.
(iii) Give your definition of 'near money'.
(iv) What do you understand by the term 'legal tender'? Why is it necessary?
4 How do you account for the greater use of near money in the UK in recent times? What effect do you think this use has had on the banking system?

2 Money Supply and Monetary Policy

2.1 Credit creation and its effect on the economy

We have seen in Chapter 1 that the total money supply in an economy is not just the coins and notes in circulation, in fact, many millions of transactions take place without a coin or note being exchanged. All that really happens is that balances are transferred from one account to another. Basically these balances occur as deposits in current accounts and are mainly transferred by cheques, standing orders, direct debits and other credit transfers. Instructions to a bank to use the above create a chain reaction which has a basic effect on the economy as a whole. This chain reaction can be seen in Fig. 2.1.

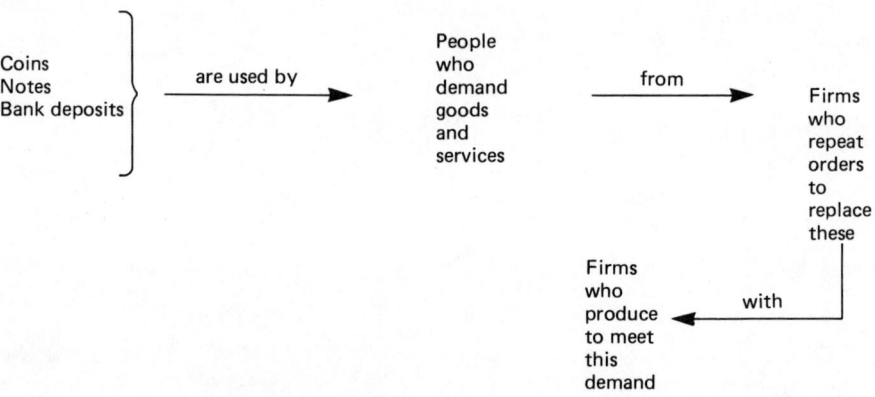

Fig. 2.1 Basic money supply and its effect on demand

We can see from Fig. 2.1 that demand from consumers creates economic activity in the form of production, which in turn creates employment and income. However, this system does not operate smoothly. Sometimes output is not able to meet the level of demand. Consumers may then do one of two things. Firstly, they may cause the prices of the existing goods and services to rise. A good example of this is seen in the shortfall in the supply of tickets for a concert of a famous 'pop' group. Since so many fans want to see this concert, if the seats are restricted then the ticket price will rise, on the 'black market'. If an economy experiences a general rise in prices, it is said to be experiencing **inflation**.

Secondly, consumers may seek to satisfy their demand from other sources by buying foreign produced goods. This might mean an increase in the country's import bill and, if there is no counter increase in exports, the balance of payments (that account which considers our trading abroad) might suffer. This could mean any surplus being reduced, the account falling into deficit, or an existing deficit growing larger. This simple explanation of the possible effects of an increase in demand because of a change in the money supply provides a clue to some of the major economic policies of governments – more about these later in this chapter.

We need to consider the components of the money supply further. Coins and notes in our society have already been discussed. We now need to consider bank deposits. Deposits in banks and other financial institutions are basically of two types as far as customers are concerned. The funds are either available immediately or after some period of notice. As regards the financial institutions, deposits are either costly as interest has to be paid on them, as time deposits in the bank, or they are non-interest bearing as is the case with the current accounts.

At the same time, we must remember that sometimes we can draw more funds from a current account than there is on credit – this is when an overdraft facility is granted. At other times, a bank manager grants a loan and this amount is added to the current account, and at the same time a new loan account is opened which is automatically in debit to the amount of the loan. Generally the money is spent by the drawing of cheques, without the use of 'physical money'. Perhaps some customers would like their loan in coins and notes, but this would usually be for a small sum in relation to the total size of loan. A bank manager, when granting loans, can be said to be creating this money. How is this done? The answer lies in the fact that people do not wish to have all of their bank deposits turned into coins and notes. They prefer to transfer these funds by means of instructions to bank managers who then alter figures accordingly. This is demonstrated by a simple example below for which, firstly, we must make a number of assumptions.

(1) A bank will keep 30 per cent of all cash deposits as a reserve against their customers' demands for coins and notes. We know that in fact banks do keep cash in their tills but the size is nowhere near this 30 per cent, but we will use this figure to make our calculations easier. (Later we will see the components of this reserve in reality.)

(2) The first payment into our 'bank' will be cash. Nowadays payments into banks are mainly by way of balance transfers. More and more people are receiving their salaries and wages as cheques or credit transfers (where the payment due is added to their account on the instruction of their

employer). Banks obtain their cash mainly by purchasing it from the Bank of England and this, along with cash payments by customers, allows them to meet the weekly demands for cash from customers. Now for the example of credit creation.

The Micawber Bank

Mr Micawber, rather than 'waiting for something to turn up' decided to open up a bank which would operate from his front room. He persuades Sam Weller to become his first customer and to deposit £1000 in cash. Mr Micawber knows that he has to keep £300 in cash as a reserve to meet Sam's demand for coins and notes. Therefore, his balance sheet would look like this:

Micawber Bank

Balance Sheet as at the 1st ....

Liabilities	£	Assets	£
Deposits	1000	Cash reserve	300
		Short-term assets	700
	1000		1000

Now Mrs Barkis comes to him and asks for a loan of £1000. Mr Micawber knows that Mrs Barkis, if given a cheque book, will spend most of the money in this way, but to be on the safe side and to keep to the regulations of the authorities he will keep £300 in cash for every £1000 he lends Mrs Barkis. If he agrees to the loan he will open up a current account in favour of Mrs Barkis and credit the £1000 to it. At the same time he will open up a loan account in her name for the same amount; this will be debited. His balance sheet will now appear as follows:

Micawber Bank

Balance Sheet as at the 2nd ....

Liabilities	£	Assets	£
Deposits	2000	Cash reserve	600
		Short-term assets	400
		Advances	1000
	2000		2000

Now suppose Mr Copperfield comes into the bank and asks to borrow £1000. Mr Micawber will go through the same procedure as above, but after this loan the balance sheet will appear thus:

Micawber Bank

Balance Sheet as at the 3rd ....

Liabilities		Assets	
	£		£
Deposits	3000	Cash reserve	900
		Short-term assets	100
		Advances	2000
	3000		3000

Next Mr Snodgrass comes into the bank and requests a loan for £300. Mr Micawber has to keep £90 in reserve, and as he has £100 as a short-term asset he can consider the request favourably. So now the balance sheet looks like this:

Micawber Bank

Balance Sheet as at the 4th ....

Liabilities		Assets	
	£		£
Deposits	3300	Cash reserve	990
		Short-term assets	10
		Advances	2300
	3300		3300

The Micawber Bank has now £3300 of deposits and the original deposit, all but £10, is now acting as a reserve against the demands of the depositors for coins and notes, and, in addition the bank has created £2300 extra spending power for its customers. In other words, the original deposit of £1000 has now become £3300 or it has multiplied 3.3 times. This latter is called the **credit creation multiplier** and it can be calculated by the following formula:

$$\frac{\text{Deposits}}{\text{Reserve}}$$

Thus with our example above this can be shown as:

$$\frac{£1000}{300} = 3.3$$

If the reserve had been 20 per cent then the credit creation multiplier would have been:

$$\frac{£1000}{200} = 5.0$$

Self-assessment exercise

What would have been the credit creation multiplier of the Micawber Bank and the final balance sheet position if the reserve had been (a) 12.1/2 per cent (b) 10 per cent?

2.2 Major government methods in the control of credit creation

When we consider this ability of banks to create money and are aware that this extra money could cause problems regarding inflation, then we must realise that if the government wishes to control inflation, it must be able to control credit creation. In order to do this the UK government has, over the years, developed a number of measures that it can introduce to help control the money supply.

2.21 Directives

These are instructions issued by the Bank of England to head offices of the banks giving an outline of the current economic conditions and the nature of what current credit policy should be to help solve any current economic problems. Sometimes these directives might be to restrict lending. At other times, the instruction might be to extend lending further to encourage greater activity in the economy.

2.22 Reserve requirement

As we have seen an increase or decrease in this can restrict a bank's ability to lend. However, it must be stated that this measure has rarely been used in the UK to control the money supply, being regarded rather as a control necessary for prudent banking so that banks are able to meet the cash needs of their customers.

2.23 Special deposits

These are calls by the Bank of England on banks to deposit funds with this Bank. As we will see in Chapter 3 banks have to keep a certain level of deposits with the Bank of England to enable them to clear cheques. The special deposits are in addition to these, and are aimed at reducing the banks' ability to lend this money to the general public by lending it to the government. The banks receive interest on these deposits so that the cost to them is not too great. When the government feels that the economy can stand these funds being back in the banks' possession, it will release them.

2.24 Open market operations

This is the entry into the open market by the government broker to buy or sell government securities. These actions have the effect of increasing or decreasing the banks' deposits. Thus the less deposits they have the less they have available to lend to their customers. If, on the other hand, deposits increase then the banks can lend more.

2.25 Interest rates

By influencing the level of interest rates the government can make money dearer or cheaper to borrow. The UK government has, in the past, influenced the interest rate in the money markets in two ways. These have been:
  (1) Directly – this was up to 1981 when, through the Bank of England, it fixed the rate of interest used by the other financial institutions by means of what became known as the **minimum lending rate** (MLR). The government fixed the level of MLR from time to time, and the other institutions altered their rates in line with this. Thus if the government wished to control borrowing it increased the MLR, other institutions increased their interest rates in line with this and borrowing became expensive so that, it was hoped, borrowing declined. When the government wished to encourage borrowing it reduced the MLR so interest rates in general fell and people were encouraged to borrow more.
  (2) Indirectly – this is where the government allows the market freedom to fix its own interest rates, but if it feels that these are inconsistent with overall economic policy then it will indicate to the market what a realistic level should be. This is the policy of the present government.

2.26 Supplementary special deposits

As mentioned, the Bank of England makes calls for special deposits when it feels these are necessary. These special deposits reduce the banks' ability to lend money to the public and they, in effect, alter the assets side of the banks' balance sheets. On the other hand, calls for supplementary special deposits control the banking world's demand for deposits so affecting the liabilities side. The operation of this scheme is as follows. The authorities fix the rate of growth for certain types of deposits. If a bank exceeds this rate of growth then the excess is subject to a call for supplementary special deposits. These deposits go into the Bank of England and are frozen until the Bank is ready to release them. The call is not a standard percentage regardless of the excess, but rises with its size. The more a bank exceeds the growth rate the greater the size of supplementary special deposit. At the same time, these deposits do not receive any interest with the result that, as they are usually levied against those deposits on which the bank has to pay interest, they are punitive to the banks. This scheme operated in the 1970s but by 1979 it was seen to be ineffective as the banks were able to arrange their affairs to bypass the regulations.

2.27 Funding

This relates to the changing structure of the government's debt. The government raises funds by selling securities with a varied life span from three months to thirty years plus. At any one time there are a great number of these securities held by individuals and institutions as they are an attractive form of saving. However, as far as the banks are concerned, they also represent the ability to keep certain funds liquid to meet the need for a reserve. These latter are short-term government securities. If the government changes the structure of the debt in the country, this can have an effect on the liquidity position of the banking world. For example, the government may replace short-term debt with long-term debt. Banks may now find that their sources of liquid assets have dried up, and must seek alternative forms of reserve assets. This might result in a reduction in the money available for lending indicating that the government has successfully curbed credit in the economy.

Self-assessment exercises

1 Which of the government's policies directly affect the banks' asset structure?
2 Explain the system of interest rate control operated by the present-day government.
3 What are the differences between special deposits and supplementary special deposits?

2.3 Money supply and the level of bank and economic activity

As explained in 2.1, the level of and changes in the money supply can have an effect on various aspects of our economy. We must now explore this concept of money supply further to discover how it is measured, how changes can affect economic activity and the factors which bring about these changes.

2.31 Measuring the money supply

It is a very simple matter to say that we are going to measure the money supply but in fact the actual procedures set up by the government are very complicated, and governments have had to use various measures in order to try and discover an acceptable way to measure this statistic. If we look at the various measures in very general terms we will see that they all comprise the following components:

Coins + notes + deposits + various monetary instruments

There should be no difficulty in identifying the coins and notes in circulation since the authorities have control of these. However, regarding deposits there are many variations and types. First of all, there are deposits in banks, building societies and finance houses. Some of these are available to depositors immediately, others cannot be withdrawn without some form of notice being given. Therefore, these latter are not part of the present money supply but are available in some days' time. Also some consumer spending has been funded by banks in the form of loans and overdrafts. Overdrafts are taken out for an agreed limit, but these limits are not always taken up. Therefore, if overdrafts are included in the money supply it may make the figure less accurate. Deposits in banks are not always in pounds but may be in other currencies and are likely to be used for transactions outside the UK. They, therefore, do not affect total demand at home in money terms immediately, but could do so at a later date.

Because of these variations the government has developed eight ways to measure the money supply which we will call definitions. Seven of these show a development from a very narrow definition to a wider one. The eighth, **domestic credit expansion** (DCE), measures the money supply in a different way. Now to look at these measures in greater detail.

(1) M0 – this is called M nought or Little M0. It first appeared as a government measure in 1983 and was officially adopted as the Narrow definition of money supply in April 1984. It consists of:

Coins and notes in circulation, plus banks' cash in tills and deposits with the Bank of England (except those held as part of the liquidity ratio).

These latter are known as operational deposits.

The authorities can operate direct control over these by limiting the coins and notes in circulation, and by issuing instructions to the banks to make special deposits. It is believed that by operating this policy the government can cause other measures to fall into line. The reason why this aggregate was adopted was because the Chancellor was looking for a reliable indicator of monetary conditions. One of the reasons why this was selected was that it contains no interest bearing assets, and, therefore, should respond unambiguously to changes in short-term interest rates. The Treasury believes that it is useful in signalling changes in short-term interest rates. Another reason is that it has been found to be a good guide to possible inflation occurring one to two years after a rise in M0. This has helped to reinforce the theory, outlined later in this chapter, that changes in the money supply are responsible for inflation.

It is, however, a strange choice of monetary aggregate for the Treasury to use, since deposits in banks are excluded even though the current accounts of these deposits are regarded as almost perfect substitutes for coins and notes. It is strange too that the banks' deposits with the Bank of England are not included as they are part of the private sector's liquidity. With the increase in non-physical money – more and more cheques are being used and more and more workers are being paid by credit transfer – it seems strange for the authorities to use an aggregate which ignores these items and is concerned mainly with cash which makes up 90 per cent of M0. The *Economist* suggests that since M1 is less affected by the swing away from cash, and since it includes both cash and current accounts, this aggregate should be used, or if a less distorted statistic is required, M1 should be used less interest-bearing components (i.e. deposit accounts) to produce a non-interest bearing M1 or NibM1.

(2) M1 – this was the narrow definition of money used by the government until it was replaced by M0 in 1984. It consists of:

Coins and notes in circulation + sterling sight deposits held by the private sector.

Sight deposits can be withdrawn at any time but also included in this aggregate are non-current accounts which cannot be used as a payment, consisting mainly of large deposits held by banks, companies and other large organisations. Although they are available for withdrawal immediately they are seen as short-term investments, earning good interest rates, and not part of the depositor's cash store. The size of these has been growing over the years, in 1975 they comprised 13 per cent of M1 and in 1983 25 per cent. It is felt that M1 is now no longer a good guide to money available for spending.

(3) M2 – this is also a recent statistic being introduced by the government in 1982. It is known as the **transactions balances** aggregate and consists of:

Coins and notes in circulation + private sector current accounts and other deposits of less than £100 000 with the banks that can be withdrawn in less than one month.

It is believed to be a better guide in two ways than M1 to the country's money held for everyday transactions.

(a) It excludes wholesale sight deposits. These are deposits of the big banks amongst themselves within the interbank market and, as we saw with M1, these latter are thought to be short-term investments rather than part of the depositor's cash reserves.

(b) It includes bank deposits up to £100 000 which though not withdrawable immediately could be available with little difficulty in a short period of time. There is a view that this makes them as convenient as current accounts for the purposes of everyday transactions.

Originally M2 only included bank deposits and not the deposits of other institutions such as building societies, however, these were added to the statistic in 1983. Although M2 is shown as a Bank of England statistic it is not one of the main measures used.

(4) Sterling M3 – this aggregate is used by the government as part of its wider definition to monitor the money supply on a monthly basis. It sets a target for this and then monitors the progress each month to see that it is staying within these targets. Up to 1984 it consisted of:

M1 + UK private sector time deposits + public sector sight deposits and time deposits.

Since 1984 it has been adjusted to exclude public sector bank deposits. This was aimed at bringing it into line with other monetary and liquidity aggregates, and with the practice of other countries. The authorities believe that this is an element of the statistic which has no economic significance since the level of public sector bank deposits is so small. As Table 2.1 shows

Table 2.1 Growth of M3 (seaonally adjusted)

	1980–1	1981–2	1982–3	1983–4
Including public sector deposits	19.4	12.8	11.2	9.7
Excluding public sector deposits	19.9	12.8	11.0	9.7

the removal has had little effect on the overall situation.

The authorities have used this aggregate as their broad measure of money supply for many years, one of the advantages is that there is a clear relationship between the banks' holdings of assets and any changes in £M3. Thus by looking at the growth of banks' asset holdings we can gain insights into the growth of £M3. These assets consist mainly of lending to the public sector. This is part of the **public sector borrowing requirement** (PSBR). Other sources include bonds and national savings. The more the public sector borrows in the latter the less it needs to borrow from the banks. These bank assets also include lending to the private sector. Sterling M3 can grow as a result of:

– lending to the private sector

– the public sector selling less debt to the public and raising more money by sales to the banks.

These are known as counterparts to £M3, and by looking at these we can identify where the necessary controls in the growth of the money stock need to be applied. Thus if lending to the private sector were the cause in the growth of the money supply, then some form of credit control policy is required. If it is due to an increase in the PSBR with large quantities going to the banking sector, then the government needs to look to its own spending. However, there is a danger of looking at the various items which go to make up £M3 as if they were independent, which is not the case. For example, if the government were to cut its expenditure and consequently PSBR were to fall because of a cut back in aid to companies, these companies would possibly resort to banks for loans so that lending to the private sector would increase and there would be no fall in £M3. Also, it should be realised that an increase in PSBR does not automatically increase the money supply, as this government debt may be taken up by the non-banking sector with the result that there is a syphoning off of money from the banks as the securities are paid for by cheques drawn on the banks.

Sterling M3 has recently become misleading as people have moved some of their bank deposits which are included in the statistic to the building societies, whose deposits are not included. This reduces the size of £M3 but it does not, in reality, reduce the funds available to the public for spending purposes. It can also behave in a perverse way, growing when interest rates are raised to control money supply growth, because money is drawn into interest-bearing deposits.

(5) M3 – this is the same as £M3 but it includes foreign currency deposits of non-bank residents. This was replaced by £M3 in the 1970s as the broad measure for monetary control, although it is still compiled in official statistics and used as an overall guide to monetary policy.

(6) Private sector liquidity 1 (PSL1) – so far the aggregates discussed have included cash plus various types of bank deposits. However, these do not give an accurate view of the money supply in the UK today. Reflection will show that the public keep funds in other institutions and in other instruments which are traded on the money market; some of these are as available to the public for spending. These money market instruments include Treasury bills, certificates of deposit, bank bills and deposits with local authorities. Since 1980 the Bank of England has published statistics of two aggregates known as private sector liquidity 1 and private sector liquidity 2. The first includes:

£M3 less deposits of more than two years maturity plus the private sector's holdings of the money market instruments.

(Deposits of more than two years' maturity are excluded since they have limited liquidity.)

(7) Private sector liquidity 2 – this is an even wider monetary aggregate. It consists of all the items included in PSL1 plus deposits with the building societies, national savings bank deposits and national savings securities. It does not include those deposits which are for more than one year, since they cannot be realised quickly without considerable loss to the holder and, therefore, have limited liquidity. Although PSL2 has much to recommend it, it does not reflect the pressure on the money supply from PSBR as well as £M3; this latter, therefore, is regarded as a more reliable statistic of the money supply. However, neither are very sensitive to changes in interest rates, so they are backed up by M0 in the overall monitoring of the money supply situation in the UK.

(8) Domestic credit expansion – this is the final aggregate used by the authorities. It was introduced in 1969. By looking at its composition we can see the usefulness of this aggregate in comparison with the others.

DCE = the increase in sterling bank lending to the private sector and overseas residents

Plus the public sector borrowing requirement *less* any sales of government debt to the non-bank private sector.

Another way of calculating this is to take:

The increase in the money stock (£M3) and adjust it by the current balance of payments.

If the balance of payments shows a deficit (meaning more money has flowed out of the country than has flowed in), then this is deducted. If it is in surplus because of an opposite flow then this figure is added. The way in which these flows affect our money supply can be seen in a particular example. Suppose we import more goods from abroad than we export. Purchasers will have to pay for these goods at some time. They will arrange for their bank balances to be reduced to meet these payments so that a net outflow causes a reduction in the amount of money held at home.

Self-assessment exercise

Try to explain how a surplus on the balance of payments will increase the money stock within a country.

We can see that the usefulness of DCE lies in its relationship with the balance of payments, and that it differs from the other aggregates by this relationship. It is particularly useful to the government when it is trying to improve, or prevent a worsening of, the balance of payments by adopting a monetary policy.

2.32 Changes in the money supply and its effects on the economy

Economists have, for many years, seen a relationship between the money supply and the level of prices in an economy. Evidence from previous years has shown that an increase in the money supply causes an increase in the level of prices. For example, when Europe experienced an influx of precious metals and stones from the New World in the sixteenth century, there was a period of increasing prices. Similarly, when Henry VIII debased the coinage so increasing the amount of money in circulation there was an increase in the level of prices, or inflation as this is known. Each time gold was discovered in South Africa, Australia and California there was a worldwide increase in the level of prices. On a national level, the UK in the 1970s experienced inflation and, although the total rise could not be blamed by an increase in the money supply, it was helped by the policy of the government which caused this money supply to increase.

In the light of their experience early economists developed the classical quantity of money theory. This theory is expressed as a relationship by way of a formula:

$$MV = PT$$

This is known as the Fisher equation and the components are as follows:

M = the money supply
V = the velocity of circulation of money

(this relates to the rate at which the money in circulation moves from hand to hand)

P = the general price level
T = the total number of transactions that have gone on in the period in question

The relationship of these components can be seen in the following example.

Assume that in the 1850s in a backwoods valley in the USA there are four families living there – Jones, Friedlander, Portier and Wazieks. They are mainly self-sufficient but a certain amount of barter goes on amongst them. The eldest son of the Jones's, Reuben, goes to the 'big city' and there one of the things he sees is money being used to buy and sell things. When he returns home he brings a silver dollar and starts a chain of events that are shown in Fig. 2.2.

This can be explained as follows. Reuben Jones goes to the Friedlander family and persuades them to accept the silver dollar for a racoon hat he rather likes. He tells them that they could also use the dollar to buy any goods they want from any of the other families. Kurt Friedlander goes to Pierre Portier, sees a pair of moccasin shoes he likes and persuades him

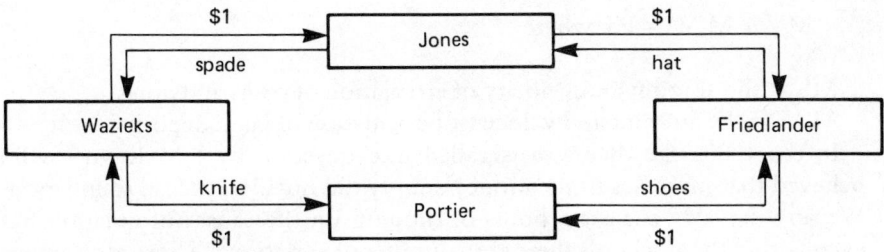

Fig. 2.2 How money flows in a community

to sell them to him for a dollar. Pierre has always admired Josef Waziek's knife and he persuades him to sell it to him for the dollar. Josef knows his father's spade is wearing out and that the Jones's have one to spare. He buys it from them for the one dollar. The dollar has now gone full circle. From these transactions we can see that the components of the Fisher equation give the following values:

$M = \$1$
$V = 4$ since it changed hands four times
$P = \$1$ this was the average price for each article
$T = 4$ since there were 4 transactions

This can now be stated as:

$MV = PT$
$\$1 \times 4 = \$1 \times 4$
$= \$4 = \$4$

Had there been only two transactions then the result would have been:

$\$1 \times 2 = \$1 \times 2$
$= \$2 = \$2$

The relevance of this theory lies in the fact that if $2 had been introduced into this society and had circulated four times and there were only four transactions, then the price level would have been $2 also. Thus an increase in the money supply would have caused inflation to have entered the community.

Self-assessment exercise

What would have been the effect on the price level in the community above if the price of the spade in the last transaction had been 50c?

This theory was later extended to account for the fact that the money supply was made up of cash and bank deposits and that these have a differing velocity of circulation. So the equation became:

$$MV + M'V' = PT \text{ where}$$

MV = the amount and velocity of circulation of coins and notes
M'V' = the amount and velocity of circulation of bank deposits

In the 1930s the theory was called into question by J M Keynes who believed that increases in the money supply did not always lead to inflation. We now have two basic schools of thought on the causes of inflation but even within these schools there are a number of variations. Those economists who follow basically the classical school are known as **monetarists** and those who follow the theories of Keynes are known as the **Keynesians**. After the Second World War the theories of Keynes came to the fore in government policies, but there were always people who followed the classical economists. These theories were refined to take into account the criticisms of Keynes with the ideas of one of the major 'new' monetarists, a professor of Chicago University, Milton Friedman. People following this theory have become known as **neo-classicists**, and those following Friedman as **Friedmanites**. These monetarist theories are founded on the following precept.

Suppose there is an increase in the money supply, say by banks lending more money, the result will be that the public will have more access to loans and overdrafts. Initially, their current account balances will increase so that their cash position will improve. However, on average, people tend to hold a certain ratio of cash balances to assets. These assets include stocks and shares, land, antiques, etc. With the increase in cash balances this ratio will be disturbed and, in order to return to it, it will be necessary to purchase more assets – that is to transfer some of the surplus cash to assets. Since the supply of these assets, in the short term, is fixed, then all that will happen is that the price of these assets will rise. With a fixed yield from these assets, any increase in their prices will cause this yield, in percentage terms, to fall. This will bring down the general level of interest rates which will encourage more borrowing and increase the demand for goods and services as people obtain more funds. Producers will find it more profitable to increase their output. Thus as a result of an increase in the money supply, the level of output in the economy will rise. This effect will appear about six to nine months after the initial increase in the money supply. Monetarists believe that because of this apparent impression of well-being government will be lulled into a false sense of security regarding the economy.

However, the effects do not end here. With the increased output, profits of some businesses will rise so that certain factors of production are able to earn a higher income. This will certainly be so for the owners of the factors of production. Other factors will seek to receive higher rewards and even though there may be no justification for this they will use their power to gain payments to redress any imbalance. This will apply particularly to labour. Owners who cannot pay increased rewards out of increased income will try to pass them on as higher prices so that inflation begins to emerge in the economy. This phenomenon will appear some twelve to eighteen months after the initial increase in the money supply. Inflationary expectations of people will continue to fuel the inflation so that increasing prices begin to feed upon themselves. This analysis has led monetarists to their view that 'inflation is everywhere and always a monetary phenomenon'. Monetarists, to answer the criticism that inflation can occur even when the money supply is not rising have redefined inflation as 'a sustained increase in the price level' and not just an increase in prices in a temporary sense.

This neo-classical analysis answered a number of criticisms by the Keynesians to the classical theory. Neo-Keynesians generally contend that influences can occur that result in inflation being caused by non-monetary factors, such as those experienced in the 1960s and 1970s in North America and Western Europe. Neo-Keynesians also believe that full management of the economy is better effected by the use of both fiscal and monetarist policies.

Self-assessment exercises

1 Define 'inflation'.
2 Define 'assets' as seen by the monetarists.
3 Explain, in your own words, how monetarists see the emergence of inflation.

2.4 Factors which bring about changes in the money supply

We have seen, so far, that changes in the money supply can affect the economy, and that the government tries to control these changes and so influence the economy in some way. We must now consider these changes in greater detail.

2.41 Changes in the quantity of coins and notes

We know that cash transactions are a relatively small part of the total transactions in the economy, however, the quantity of coins and notes supplied can affect the workings of the economy. In most countries the cash supply is regulated by the authorities who take it upon themselves to see that sufficient liquidity is available at all times, and that there is no danger of an over or under supply of funds. As there is a general need for the money supply to go up, then the level of cash in an economy will also go up to a level which is believed to be acceptable. There is also a need for seasonal adjustment of this cash supply, for at certain times of the year a country's inhabitants seek to spend more cash. Thus in Britain, the period before long public holidays, such as Christmas and Easter, will see a build up of cash held in the banks' vaults. After these holidays the authorities will reduce the amount of cash by not replacing notes that are removed, or not issuing as many coins. If, however, a country were to increase its cash supplies without reference to need, it would run the risk of building inflation into its economy. Because this is a well-known danger, it is unlikely to happen.

2.42 Changes in the level of bank deposits

These consist of money that has been deposited in banks and, as we have seen earlier in this chapter, the level of these can affect the ability of the banking sector to grant loans. These are affected by:
(1) The level of the national income.
(2) The desire to save and the level of interest rates.
(3) Government action to counteract growth in these deposits, like the introduction of schemes such as supplementary special deposits.

These factors are not totally independent. They all interact to affect the level of deposits in a country at any one time. The size of the national income depends upon the resources available and the use made of them. As we will see later in this chapter, one of the aims of government is to try and achieve steady economic growth without causing other economic problems. The measurement of this growth is by computing the size of the national income from one period to another. Thus if we add up all incomes from all sources, such as, wages, salaries, rents, interest payments and profits we can discover the total of all incomes for the community. As these incomes are earned by producing goods and services, if we add up the value of these goods and services produced we should come to the same figure as that for incomes. Finally, we can see that incomes are spent so if we add up all of this expenditure then once again it should come to the same calculation.

Thus incomes = production = spending

In very simple terms we have outlined the three ways in which the authorities calculate the national income every year. This is a very basic way of looking at the economy for we know that not all income is spent. Some of it is saved by individuals. Not everyone earns enough to be able to save but saving does go on. Generally, the higher our individual income the more we are able to save. This is also true for communities as a whole. The level of savings in a poor country is much lower than that in a rich country. We can also see that as the UK's national income has risen over the years so has its savings, not only in amount but also as a proportion of that income. One of the factors that can influence the level of savings in the short term is the level of interest rates. As we will see in Chapter 5 this has an important influence on the way people save individually. Generally, the higher the rate of interest the more will be saved. But this is not the only factor which influences saving. The need to protect oneself from events that may happen to affect earning ability, such as sickness and unemployment, will also affect savings' levels. The extent to which the state provides welfare benefits will also affect our desire to save, as will our expectation of the level of future inflation. Finally, government action on credit affects the levels of bank deposits. As our earlier example of the Micawber Bank showed a bank loan has the effect of increasing bank deposits generally. All of these act together to determine the level of savings and, consequently, bank deposits in the economy.

Self-assessment exercises

1   Why does the government find it necessary to increase the number of notes and coins in circulation at certain times of the year?
2   What is the possible effect on the money supply if people save less and spend more?
3   Explain what could happen to the level of deposits in a bank if interest rates were to fall and, at the same time, the Bank of England sent a directive to banks' head offices encouraging them to lend more money to small businesses.

2.43   Growth in the public sector borrowing requirement (PSBR)

The public sector consists of central government, local authorities and public authorities. The public sector is involved in a great deal of expenditure in carrying out its various activities on behalf of the nation. In order to finance this it has three major sources of income: taxes and rates, income from sale of the goods or services it provides and borrowing. This borrowing is of two types:

(1) Short term that assists the public sector in maintaining its cash flow position. This is necessary because current expenditure goes on continuously but the required funds do not flow in as smoothly. For example, income tax collected on the PAYE system may be paid by the employee on a regular basis, weekly or monthly, the employer collects this and it is transmitted to the Inland Revenue only twice a year. Rates are either collected twice a year or over monthly intervals. In order to obtain short-term funds in between these intervals the public sector sells short-term debt, such as Treasury bills and local authority bills or borrows on overdraft from the banks.

(2) Long-term borrowing in the form of securities which enables this sector to finance capital projects, such as new plant and machinery, offices, roads, schools and hospitals.

Sales of both of these types of debt can be to the banking sector or the non-banking sector. If the latter purchase this debt then, as demonstrated in the calculation of £M3, this is not seen as affecting the growth in the money supply as the result may be a syphoning off of money from the banks to the authorities who indulge in compensatory expenditure. The money supply remains the same. When debt is bought by the banking sector then the growth in the money supply may be affected. This is because, as mentioned the debt becomes part of the reserves of the banks and, eventually, results in the banks lending more money. Of course, not all public sector debt becomes part of these reserves immediately. Such items as Treasury and local authority bills can become so, but longer-term securities enter this category only when they have a year left before maturing.

Self-assessment exercise

(Revision). Explain why a loan to a customer creates a deposit for a bank.

Thus we can see that if the public sector's need for more funds arises from sales of securities to the banks then these will, in time, become the means by which the money supply can be increased through bank lending. In Britain in the 1970s the PSBR rose considerably with the effect that governments from 1975 tried to reduce their own expenditure in order to reduce the pressure of inflation which had become a feature of this decade.

Self-assessment exercises

1 Define 'public sector' and say why, and in what ways this sector needs to borrow.
2 Explain fully the effect on the money supply of an increase in the sale of Treasury bills to the banks. Show how this could affect a bank's balance sheet.

2.5 Main objectives of government economic policy

So far we have talked in general terms about government's economic aims and policies. We will now look at these aims in greater detail. In 1958 the Radcliffe report laid down four main aims of government economic policy. These are:

2.51 Full employment

This does not mean 100 per cent of the work force in employment at any one time. According to Lord Beveridge in *Full Employment in a Free Society* (1944), this level of employment will never exist because of a number of underlying factors which will always mean that some people are looking for work. This is why the government of the 1950s and 1960s were content with unemployment at a level of 2–3 per cent. Since the 1960s unemployment levels have risen dramatically in Western countries, causing governments' concern. Not all the governments of the world pursued these low levels of unemployment, for example, while the UK had 2–3 per cent unemployment, the USA and West Germany had up to 7 per cent at times and yet they showed better economic performance and growth. The view of some economists is that a country has a natural unemployment level relating to the current economic conditions, and it is wrong for governments to seek levels which are outside this level. Since 1979 the UK government has sought to combat inflation even though its policies have set into motion factors which have caused unemployment to reach levels at times in excess of 12 per cent.

2.52 Stable prices

Originally, governments aimed at keeping prices steady and trying to stop them reaching great heights. The UK government at the present time has sought and succeeded in bringing down inflation from the high levels it reached in the 1970s. These levels were on occasions in excess of 20 per cent. It is considered that inflation damages the economy. First of all, it distorts the normal market forces which operate, so making it difficult to identify whether price changes are the result of changes in demand, in supply, or because of general inflationary movements. In addition, high inflation introduces the risk of uncertainty in the economy and puts certain groups (like fixed income earners) at a disadvantage.

2.53 Growth in output

Growth in output can lead to increased national income so that people, in general, are better off. Since 1941 the government has carried out an annual statistical exercise which measures the size of the national income. From these statistics it can identify if output has grown in real terms, which areas have grown, which have declined and where readjustment is necessary.

2.54 A satisfactory balance of payments

The balance of payments refers to the flow of funds into and out of a country. These flows come from buying (imports) or selling (exports) goods, buying and selling of services and the flow of money into and out of the country for investment and depositing in banks and other financial institutions. If the flows in are greater than the flows out then the balance of payments is in surplus. If the flows out are greater than the flows in then the balance of payments is in deficit. During the 1960s and 1970s the UK's balance of payments was regularly in deficit, so successive governments had to take steps to ease the situation. Since 1975 the earnings from North Sea oil have helped to such an extent that deficits have been turned into surpluses.

One of the problems with a balance of payments deficit is that it can cause foreign holders of our currency to lose confidence in the currency's ability to maintain its value, so they proceed to sell it. A massive rush against the pound can cause its external value to fall to such dangerous levels that the government is forced to act to stop the slide and to reverse it. To do this the government may be forced to buy pounds that are for sale by using our reserves. As these are limited, we may have to borrow from the International Monetary Fund (IMF) (which is there for this purpose). If the borrowing is substantial, included in the deal will be suggestions for economic policies to be pursued by the government to put right the economy and remove the causes of the deficit. Sometimes these policies are not very popular with the electorate with the result that governments may find themselves in difficulties.

2.55 Major economic policies

In order to achieve these economic aims governments have at their disposal three major policy methods. These are:

(1) Fiscal policy – this relates to the manipulation of taxation and government expenditure. If government wishes to achieve growth in the economy it can increase the demand for goods and services by reducing taxes and/or increasing its own spending. Firms experiencing increased demand for their products will increase production, take on more workers, demand more raw materials and increase capital equipment. Other things being equal, the national income will increase, unemployment decline and the level of growth rise. This is only one example of how fiscal policy can be used to achieve an economic aim. It can be used to achieve others.

(2) Monetary policy – this relates to the way in which the government controls the level of economic activity through the control of the money supply. We have seen earlier in this chapter the major monetary policy instruments (*see also* Section 2.6), the monetarists' explanation of how inflation

occurs and the ways in which government measures money supply so that it can control it more effectively.

(3) Physical policy – this relates to the use of direct controls in the economy to achieve certain economic aims. For example, this may be a prices and incomes policy which will, if successful, reduce the rate of inflation. The policy may include some specific statement as to by how much prices and incomes may rise in a given period. At the same time, it may also include the setting up of organisations to monitor these rises.

Generally, overall economic management includes aspects of all three of these policies. The difference between the various parties, when in power, is the emphasis they place on a specific policy. For example, the Labour government under Mr Callaghan used all three with specific emphasis on fiscal policy reinforced by monetary and physical policy. The latter took the form of a voluntary agreement by the unions to limit pay rises for a concession of more say in overall economic and social policies – this was called the social contract. On the other hand, the Conservative government of Mrs Thatcher has set its main policy on monetarism and uses fiscal policy as a back up for this. The different emphasis of various governments' economic policies once again shows the differences between Keynesians and monetarists.

Finally, it has been the experience of governments that policies used to achieve certain economic aims can make other aims go wrong. In our example in 2.32 where the government sought to achieve growth in the economy by reducing taxes and increasing its spending, it achieved this but at the expense of inflation and a balance of payments problem. The present government, in pursuing its policy of reducing inflation, has caused unemployment to reach levels only experienced in the depression of the 1930s. Governments must try and achieve those aims they feel to be most important, with the hope that other objectives will not be affected adversely. It is a fact of political life that governments have to return to the electorate every five years for re-election, so their policies cannot realistically be planned for any longer period. However, some economic aims need a longer period to reach fulfilment. It is sensible if governments plan for this and put their position to the electorate. This has been the position of the Conservative government since 1979.

Self-assessment exercises

1 Explain why it is difficult to identify full employment.
2 What is inflation? Why has it become a major preoccupation of the Western world since the 1970s?
3 How does a country measure growth in output? Why do countries seek to achieve growth?
4 What components make up the flows on a balance of payments?

40 Banking for Students

5   What are the dangers to a country experiencing large balance of payments deficits?
6   Using similar analysis as in 2.55 show how fiscal policy can be used to reduce the level of inflation.
7   Explain the basic differences between the monetarist and Keynesian schools of thought.
8   Explain how inflation might occur in an economy with unemployment and also reduced output if the government were to reduce taxes and increase its own spending.

2.6   Techniques available for implementing monetary policy and their effect on banks

So far we have seen the nature of the money supply, how it is measured, why we need to control it and considered its position together with other economic policy methods available to manage the economy. Earlier in this chapter we looked at, in general terms, the measures governments may adopt to effect control of the money supply. We now need to look at these in greater detail and, at the same time, to consider their effect on the banking system.

2.61   Directives

These are instructions issued by the Bank of England to head offices of other banks. Generally, they outline the current condition of the economy and what the Bank considers the required credit policy to suit this condition. The banks are then entreated to fall in with this credit policy in the interests of the economy as a whole. Montague Norman, when Governor of the Bank of England in the 1920s, called this moral suasion since the authorities are calling upon the moral conscience of the banks to keep in line with official policy. In previous years these directives have sometimes been in specific terms stating accepted levels for the growth of credit, **quantitative measures**, or they have stated to whom lending should or should not be extended, **qualitative measures**. Over the past years the authorities have tended to restrict the use of such measures to quantitative measures. When the government indicates control of the credit level it is known as a **credit squeeze** and where it advocates an increase in credit, a **credit expansion**.

2.62   Reserve requirements

As stated, by increasing or decreasing the banks' reserve requirement government can affect the banks' ability to lend. Changing the reserve has an effect on a bank's balance sheet as this affects the size of the assets it has to hold as a reserve. Thus more assets to be held in reserve means that less assets are available to lend to the general public. A reduction in the reserve releases assets held for this purpose, and these become available to the general public for loans and overdrafts. In the UK this measure has been used only once as a monetary control; that was in January 1980 when the reserve requirement was reduced from $12\frac{1}{2}$ per cent to 10 per cent as the authorities thought that the money supply was going to fall because of the transfers of employees' taxes from their employers' accounts to the Inland Revenue, so reducing bank deposits overall. Generally, the use of the reserve requirement is regarded more as a prudential control to ensure that the banking world will be able to meet its customers' demands for cash. To this end, the system of fixing the reserve has changed so that no longer is a set reserve fixed for all banks to maintain. Now there are discussions with each individual bank to establish a realistic reserve depending on the deposits it holds and the demands for cash expected from its customers. A clearing bank dealing with the general public in the retail market would need a higher level of reserve than a merchant bank dealing in the wholesale market.

2.63 Special deposits

These are calls by the Bank of England for the banks to make an additional deposit of their funds, over and above those deposits they keep in their 'ordinary' accounts with the Bank. Calls for special deposits are a major measure in reducing the deposits available for the banks to lend to their customers. The effect of these calls or their repayment is to affect the asset structure of a bank – after one of these calls, a bank must show the special deposit as an asset on its balance sheet. However, since its total assets/liabilities have not changed it must adjust the other assets to maintain the same balance. Since it cannot reduce its reserve and would not wish to reduce those assets which give good returns or help diversify its activities, its only course of action is to reduce its lending to the general public. Thus the government achieves its aim. Recalls, therefore, have the opposite effect.

2.64 Open market operations

Government can influence the size of deposits available to the banks for lending by the use of such operations. In these cases, the government's broker enters the market to buy or sell government securities, with the ensuing effect. If the broker enters the market and sells securities a number of people will be tempted to buy them, because they are secure and give a relatively good rate of return. They will purchase these by drawing cheques on their bank accounts, and funds will be transferred from banks to the Bank of England. The banks, having less deposits, will be able to offer fewer advances to customers, with the result that credit in the economy is reduced. This is shown in the following simple example which shows the accounting position of the Utopia Bank plc:

Utopia Bank plc

Simplified consolidated Balance Sheet as at ....
(before open market operations)

Liabilities	£m	Assets	£m
Deposits	10000	Reserves	1000
		Short-term assets	2000
		Advances	7000
	10000		10000

Suppose the Central Bank now sells £1000m of securities

Utopia Bank plc

Simplified consolidated Balance Sheet as at ....
(after open market operations)

Liabilities	£m	Assets	£m
Deposits	9000	Reserves	900
		Short-term assets	1800
		Advances	6300
	9000		9000

This example shows that £700m less has been made available to the public in the form of advances.

If the government broker enters the market to buy securities the effect will be the opposite, as the funds flowing back into the banks as deposits will be available for lending. Since 1971 the government has tended to use this measure purely as a means of raising revenue, because it is aware of the banking world's concern about the unfair competition they were placed under by the effect of the sales of this debt on interest rates.

2.65 Influencing the level of interest rates

One of the factors which affects the desire and ability to borrow is how much this borrowing is going to cost – the rate of interest charged. If rates are low more people are willing to borrow. If they are high there is a fall in the level of borrowing. This does not always hold true, for there have been times when interest rates have been low and borrowing has been high, and at other times high interest rates have not curtailed the level of borrowing. The need or wish to borrow does not rest on the level of interest rates alone. However, past evidence shows that where interest rates have been increased there has been a significant reduction in the level of borrowing and *vice versa*. Governments, therefore, have measures at their disposal to push up or bring down interest rates.

In recent years there has been a movement away from such direct influence when the government-stated interest rate was the standard to which all other interest rates were tied. If the government put up this rate all other rates went up too. If it came down all other rates came down. Now the government prefers the market to set its own interest rate levels within a certain, undeclared band, regarded as necessary to the well-being of the economy. If the market rate strays outside the band the government indicates this fact to the market, and also the level it would wish interest rates to return to. One indicator the Bank of England uses is the rate charged to those financial institutions who wish to rediscount eligible bills. Another is the rate offered by the government for the purchase of its own short-term debt. This is an **indicative** rather than a **prescriptive** method of regulating the level of interest rates.

Despite the government's wish to see greater competition between the financial institutions regarding interest rate levels, there is a tendency for the market to keep together so that a shift by one bank of its interest rates in any direction is followed very soon by similar shifts by the other financial institutions in the same direction. One particular feature of this movement in interest rates effected by the government has been seen in recent times. This is the fact that high interest rates produce high profits for banks; this appears to be strange as, in theory, high interest rates should reduce the desire for loans and so the profits made by banks. This might tell us something about how effective control of interest rates is in economic management. One factor of interest to us is the fact that the recent government has used interest rate changes as a major tool in the control of monetary growth.

2.66 Supplementary special deposits

The basic system that operated in the UK from 1975 to 1979 affected the banking world to the extent that those banks who failed to keep their deposits within the required growth level faced a penalty of borrowing some of their money at a cost and having to lend it for nothing. Obviously, this affected the profitability of banks. This technique of monetary control was shortlived simply because it reduced competition amongst the banks, distorted competition between the banks and other financial institutions and diverted credit flows into uncontrolled channels. This latter is known as **disintermediation**.

One way this was effected was by 'bill leak'. Many firms, seeking loans, being unable to raise these through the banks issued commercial bills. The bills on acceptance (guaranteed by another financial intermediary) could be sold to the non-bank public. By this means the company received its funds, public liquidity was increased by holding these short-dated bills and the money stock was increased by this amount just as if the banks had loaned the money. Bill leak grew substantially with the introduction of the supplementary special deposits scheme, from £710m in the third quarter of 1978 to £2700m in the second quarter of 1980. This meant that the effectiveness of this scheme, called the Corset by the City, was reduced. At the same time, when this was not in operation banks increased their interest-bearing deposits in anticipation of the re-introduction of the scheme, with the result that even though there was a restriction on the rate of growth, by means of the increased deposit base they could increase further deposits by a greater amount. These ways of getting around the regulation, coupled with the abolition of exchange control in 1979 allowing individuals and banks to open foreign bank accounts and borrow from abroad, caused the authorities to abandon this form of direct control.

2.67 Funding

In Sections 2.2 and 2.5 we saw the effects of government borrowing both on the general public and on the banking world. The effects of funding techniques, which also deal with government borrowing, depend upon who buys these securities and their maturity date. If they are bought by the public then bank deposits fall, so reducing the level of bank lending. Sales of debt to the banks, if of the short-term variety, increase a bank's reserve assets very quickly. If for a longer term they appear as assets on the balance sheets of banks, but only become reserve assets at some point very near to their maturity. This could be four years or twenty-four years away. As we have seen the changing of a bank's reserve affects the size of the deposits it can hold and, as it can create or reduce deposits by lending, then sales of these securities can have a direct effect on a bank's ability to lend.

We have, so far, dealt with those techniques which have been used in the past to control the money supply. It would be relevant for us now to look at the form of monetarist techniques that have been operated by the present government. Monetarists believe that money supply growth should be kept in line with the expected growth in the economy as an excess of money supply will only lead to inflation. It is for this purpose that part of the government's medium term financial strategy (MTFS) is the setting of monetary growth targets which are rolled forward in six monthly intervals. These are regularly monitored and assessed in the light of events, and if, during or at the end of the period, they are seen to have been achieved and they are realistic for the next six months, they are rolled forward again. If, however, the target is no longer suitable for the economic conditions then new targets are fixed and rolled forward for the next six months.

At the same time, the authorities feel that the PSBR also needs to be kept in check as excessive growth can cause problems with the money supply. The government aims to keep this borrowing within set limits and so there is constant monitoring of the government's spending to see that it remains within the budget and that borrowing does not get out of hand.

This overall policy was introduced by Sir Geoffrey Howe when he was Chancellor of the Exchequer and is aimed at bringing down inflation to more acceptable levels. These policies, with the indicative approach to interest rate levels, represent a major part of the present government's economic policy. It must be remembered, however, that other techniques could be used if the government considered that these would assist it in achieving its aims.

Self-assessment exercises

1 Explain the difference between directives and a request for special deposits from the banks by the Bank of England.
2 How does open market operations differ from funding policy?
3 Why has the use of open market operations been curtailed in recent years?
4 Write an article for a Japanese magazine, which produces articles in English, explaining the official interest rate policy of UK governments from 1975 to 1985.
5 The following is a balance sheet for the Smalltown Bank plc before a 3 per cent call for special deposits by the Bank of England:

Smalltown Bank plc
Simplified consolidated Balance Sheet as at ....
(before a call for special deposits)

Liabilities	£m	Assets	£m
Ordinary shares	100	Reserves	125
Deposits	1000	Short-term assets	240
		Advances	650
		Property	85
	1100		1100

Show the balance sheet after this call has been carried out.
6 What do you understand by the term disintermediation? Why did the supplementary special deposits scheme cause this to increase?

Assignments

(1) The Micawber Bank started business with a cash deposit of £5000. At the end of the first week the balance sheet looked like this:

Micawber Bank plc

Simplified Balance Sheet as at ....

Liabilities	£m	Assets	£m
Deposits	50000	Reserve assets	5000
		Advances	45000
	50000		50000

If it received no more cash deposits how would you explain the increase in deposits?

(2) The following is taken from the financial page of a newspaper:

'The narrow definition of Money supply, M0, for the month of November has risen by 11 per cent, well outside the government's target. At the same time the broader definition, £M3, has also exceeded the target but has only risen 9.5 per cent.'

This statement shows that the growth in the money supply is not as the government would wish it to be. What measures can the government adopt to try and bring the money supply back into line? What effects would these measures have on the banks and their customers?

3 British Banking System

3.1 Early beginnings

Elementary banking activities are thought to have been carried out over 5000 years ago. There is evidence from inscriptions in ancient Babylon that the temples accepted deposits and gave loans. In ancient Greece deposit and lending activities flourished. However, banking in Britain has its origins in the Middle Ages. Financial relationships were, at this time, regulated by the 'law of Moses' which forbade anyone benefiting from another's misfortune. Lending money at interest was seen as breaking this law, known as the usury law, so strict observance restricted lending. It was, therefore, left to those people who interpreted this law widely to carry out the function of money lending. Many money lenders were Jews and, eventually, as a result of prejudice and bad feeling they were evicted from England. This left the business of banking to a group of Italians who became known as the Lombards, and who gave their name to Lombard Street in the City of London where they congregated. It is from these people that the name 'bank' originated, as the benches these money changers and lenders would sit upon were called 'bancos'. It also explains the origin of the word 'bankrupt', for if one of these dealers were to dishonour a deal then his bench would be broken so that he could not carry on any further business.

These Lombards were either large and powerful businessmen carrying out banking on an international scale, or they were smaller businessmen who traded as pawnbrokers. The traditional sign of a pawnbroker of three brass balls was the coat of arms of the Lombards. During the long protracted religious wars of the fourteenth and fifteenth centuries the credit structure of Europe was greatly affected. The result was that a large number of bankers were made bankrupt and their collapse caused a vacuum in the availability of good strong rooms. In London one of the obvious places seemed to be the Tower of London where the Royal Mint was housed, so people began to deposit their money there. At the outbreak of the Civil War, Charles I found his supply of funds cut off by his adversaries. He, therefore, commandeered £130 000 of bullion which was on deposit in the Tower. This caused a great outcry from the City merchants, who, after a day-long negotiation persuaded the King to release the gold bullion in return for a loan of £40 000. However, faith in the security of the Royal Mint was shaken and an alternative place was sought in which to place deposits. This was provided by the goldsmiths who had well-secured vaults in which to keep their precious metals and artifacts. By the time of the Restoration of the monarchy the goldsmiths were already carrying out a number of the functions of banking, namely accepting deposits, keeping running cash balances (very much like current accounts), honouring drawn notes (the forerunners of cheques), buying and selling bullion and some foreign business. Their interest on loans was often very high, sometimes as much as 25 per cent and, as they did not pay much on deposit, their profits were enormous. It was, however, from the goldsmiths that early banks developed. Indeed up until 1971 when Martins Bank was taken over by Barclays, the goldsmith's sign – a grasshopper – was to be seen in the coat of arms of this bank.

At first, a deposit was evidenced by a receipt very much like a warehouse receipt that is issued today which entitles the holder, on production of it, to the return of the items deposited. The earliest existing evidence of a goldsmith's receipt is one issued by Hoare in 1633. After 1640 there was considerable growth in this type of business, with receipts being replaced by promissory notes which gave the depositor the ability to withdraw, on demand, a sum equivalent to the amount deposited. The difference between a promissory note and a receipt was that the holder of a receipt was entitled to the return of the actual money deposited, whereas with the promissory note as long as an equivalent amount was returned it did not have to be the same money. These notes eventually circulated between merchants in payment of debts. In 1670 the word bearer was added so that transfer could be made easier by simply passing notes from hand to hand. Although this gave them negotiability (*see* Chapter 7) this was not legally recognised until 1704. There also developed a practice whereby a depositor wishing to pay off a debt could provide a written note to the creditor, he could then take this note to the goldsmith and receive payment from the deposit. These 'drawn notes' became the early forerunners of the cheque. By the end of the seventeenth century the practice had developed whereby deposits were placed with an agreement by the depositor to give the 'bank' a period of notice of withdrawal – in fact the birth of our present deposit accounts. The goldsmiths soon discovered that the money deposited was likely to be held by them for some time, with the result that they could lend this to other people without running the risk of the customer immediately requesting the return of his money. Thus by this time the basis of a banking system was established, namely:

(1) the depositing of cash – redeemable on demand or after a period of notice;

(2) the transfer of balances between one bank account holder and another;

(3) the on-lending of cash in excess of that likely to be recalled by depositors.

The development of banks in the City of London became known as town banking. Outside the City banks originated not only from goldsmiths but also from mercers, grocers, tax collectors and lawyers who were able also to offer customers security for their deposits. This development became known as country banking.

3.2 Banking in the eighteenth and nineteenth centuries

This may be regarded as the period of the private bank. Under an Act of Parliament in 1709 these were allowed to exist and issue their own bank notes provided they remained partnerships of no more than six partners. These, therefore, remained small and, as it happened, in the City of London were no threat to the Bank of England which was a joint stock bank. Country banking began to grow after 1750 when there were 20 of these firms to the extent that in 1820 there were 600. Most of them used a London agent either as a broker or a private banker to handle transactions in the City. These provided the country bankers with cheque clearing facilities and a channel of funds amongst each other.

As we have seen in Chapter 1 there was a surge of note issuing by all kinds of people including tradesmen. Because the system was small scale, fragmentary and relatively unstable, there were a large number of bankruptcies in the banking world. Between 1809 and 1830 commissions of bankruptcy were issued against 300 country banks. In 1825–6 there were as many as eighty such commissions. The authorities became concerned and realised the need to regulate the operations of banks. One of the answers to this problem was to allow banks to become bigger and encompass the idea of joint stock banking. The start of joint stock banking can thus be traced to when the Banking Act 1826 allowed the formation of these type of banks with note issuing powers outside a sixty-five-mile radius of London. This still gave the Bank of England a monopoly in joint stock banking inside the City. In 1833 another Banking Act was passed which allowed joint stock banking within this sixty-five-mile radius provided the banks concerned gave up their note issuing powers. This reduced the monopoly of the Bank to that of note issuing only. In 1844 the Bank Charter Act was passed which continued the regulation of banking by the authorities. Its major provisions were:

(1) The issue of notes by the Bank of England was to be fully backed by gold or silver except for an issue of £14m, which has become known as the **fiduciary issue**. The silver backing was to be no more than 20 per cent of the backed notes.

(2) The note issue of the remaining seventy-two banks was to be restricted to the circulation immediately before the Act.

(3) No other banks were to issue notes.

(4) A note issuing bank would lose this right if it opened a branch in London or amalgamated with another bank.

(5) As banks gave up their note issuing powers, the Bank of England could increase its fiduciary issue by two-thirds of the lapsed bank's issue.

International financial business was growing rapidly at this time. There was a marked increase in the acceptance and discounting of foreign bills, and by 1830 this type of bill had largely replaced the home bill in the London market. British banks were now being formed to operate in the Empire and other foreign countries.

Before 1844 the bank rate – the Bank of England's interest rate – was used experimentally as a means of controlling credit. In 1847, 1857 and 1866 this was used more formally, and there developed the system which existed up to 1971 of the Bank's bank rate being at the centre of interest rate control within the banking system.

The forerunners of the big banks were already established by 1844. These were:

(1) London and Westminster Bank opened for business in 1834 with two branches.

(2) Barclays Bank had had an office in Lombard Street since 1736 although the origins of one branch can be traced back to the Gurney Bank of East Anglia.

(3) Lloyds Bank started in Birmingham as a partnership in 1836.

(4) National Provincial was founded by a timber merchant in Gloucester in 1834.

(5) Midland Bank developed as the Birmingham and Midland Bank in 1836.

The mid-nineteenth century was still the period of the unit (one branch) bank. In 1880 there were 160 banks operating in England and Wales. The next stage in the history of banking was the appearance of the large joint stock bank with many branches. Even though joint stock banking was permitted after 1826, there was still an obstacle to its development in that the members were not entitled to limited liability. This was granted to trading companies in 1855 but was not extended to banks until 1862. This encouraged the development of these joint stock banks which grew by increasing their branches and amalgamating with other banks. In the last thirty years of the nineteenth century there was a rapid decline in the total number of private banks, and this trend continued well into the twentieth century as seen in Table 3.1. These figures show us the relative decline in the private bank and the reduction in the number of joint stock banks but also the relative increase in the number of branches of the latter. Between 1890 and 1918 the English banking system began to consist of very large banks with nationwide networks.

The banking crisis of 1890 saw the Bank of England take the lead in

Table 3.1 The numbers and branches of private and joint-stock banks 1844–1934

	Private Banks		Joint Stock Banks	
	Number	Branches	Number	Branches
1844	207	443	118	1621
1904	35	196	65	4384
1934	3	4	13	10127

Source: A hundred years of joint stock banking
Crick and Wadsworth

averting panic by raising a guarantee fund for one bank Barings, so developing its role as guardian of the UK banking system.

3.3 Banking in the twentieth century

Commercial banking in this century has experienced a number of changes. These are:

3.31 Greater amalgamation

A reduction in the number of banks has occurred but there has been an increase in the number of branches. This development was seen as necessary to provide for the needs of the increasing scale of industry plus the necessity for banks to maintain large reserves after the Barings crisis. By 1914 there were only sixteen members of the London Clearing House.

In 1891 the Birmingham and Midland Bank absorbed the Central Bank of London, and in 1898 the City Bank was absorbed to become the London, City and Midland Bank, the forerunner of the Midland Bank. Barclays Bank was formed by the amalgamation of fifteen banks in 1896. Other amalgamations proceeded in such number that there were fears that a money trust would be created. In 1918 the Colwyn committee, although not fearing the creation of a monopoly situation by amalgamation, felt it was necessary for government to intervene if only for strategic reasons. The banks gave an undertaking that they would refer proposed mergers to the authorities for approval, so that formal regulation was not felt to be necessary.

The next spate of mergers came in 1968 when a government body gave the signal to the banks that the authorities would not object to this. This occurred in a report of the Prices and Incomes Board in 1967 which was investigating the price position of the banks and the lack of competition amongst them. It stated: 'the Authorities would not obstruct some further amalgamation if the banks were willing to contemplate such a development and we think that a further reduction in the number of independent banking units would not necessarily affect very significantly the degree of competition'.

In January 1968 it was announced by the National Provincial Bank and the Westminster Bank that they were to merge to form the National Westminster Bank. Soon after it was announced that the Royal Bank of Scotland, Glyn Mills and William Deacons Bank would merge to form the Williams and Glyns Bank. A proposed merger of Barclays, Lloyds and Martins Banks was referred to the Monopolies Commission and was not recommended, however, the take over by Barclays of Martins Bank was allowed to go through. In recent years there have been amalgamations between banks and other financial institutions such as finance houses and discount houses. It is even being considered allowing connections between banks, jobbers and stockbrokers in the interests of the way in which this market has developed over the years.

3.32 Greater competition amongst each other and other financial institutions

Banks in the past, although not competing in the area of interest rates, have always maintained interbank competition in other services. Since 1970 this competition has become even fiercer with the banks offering varied savings schemes, different bank charges, varied services to different parts of the community (business, students and senior citizens, for example), variation in the number of branches and the services offered by these branches. In addition, banks have found that they have had to face more competition from other financial institutions. In the 1960s this came from the merchant banks and finance houses competing for deposits and borrowers. The 1970s have seen competition from foreign banks and building societies. At the same time, banks have tried to alter their image to attract a wider range of customer. Before the Second World War banks were regarded as staid institutions – with their wood panelled banking halls giving a mausoleum-type atmosphere – only for people with large sums of money or who came from a certain class or background. Since the war the banks have tried to maintain their reputation for safety and security, but have changed their image with modern banking halls, open plan offices and a much more 'human' face to the public. The aim was to appeal to the lower income groups who, because of increased prosperity, were finding they needed the services of banks. In addition, banks developed new services to appeal to all classes of persons.

3.33 Greater regulation and supervision by the authorities

As we will see later in this chapter in Section 3.9 there has been considerable change in this control over the years. This is outlined in greater detail elsewhere, but the main aims have been to introduce greater competition between the banks and the money markets generally, to reduce direct government intervention but to maintain some form of control, to make the financial system safer (particularly after the banking crisis of 1973/4) and to bring us into line with EEC regulations.

Banks continue to develop and change to meet the needs of the domestic and international financial markets. This evolution will need to continue if banks wish to survive into the future.

Self-assessment exercises

1 What early evidence is there of banking activities?
2 Describe the origins of banks in the UK.
3 Explain the difference between town and country banking in the eighteenth century.
4 In what ways did the 1844 Bank Charter Act regulate the banks?
5 How would you describe the period of banking in the nineteenth century?
6 What factors halted the continued amalgamation of banks in this century?

3.4 Merchant banks

There are about fifty firms in the UK who come within this category and they include such names as Barings Bros and Co. Ltd, Hambros PLC, Kleinwort Benson Ltd, N M Rothschild and Sons Ltd, J Henry Schroder Wagg and Co. Ltd and Warburg (SG) and Co. Ltd. Their names give a clue to their origin. Several of these were foreign merchants who, as well as trading abroad, took on the business of banking. Throughout the nineteenth century these firms were heavily committed to this foreign trade, sometimes trading on their own behalf or sometimes acting for others, on occasions providing finance for these ventures. With the eventual departure from the gold standard in 1930 they found their traditional role contracting so they turned their attention to industrial issues at home, and this trend has continued strongly since 1946. Today they are responsible for the following activities:

3.41 Accepting deposits

Although these banks accept deposits from the general public, indeed in the 1960s there was evidence of strong competition with the clearing banks in this field, their major customers come from the wholesale money markets, particularly corporate concerns. They offer sight and time deposit facilities as well as money transmission services similar to the clearing banks.

3.42 Provision of credit to companies and other large scale borrowers

This is an extension of the banking services provided to corporate customers. They have become experts in the field of company finance, knowing the risks and assessing the profitability so that companies receive the benefit of this experience. They are not alone in this field as the clearing banks also offer these services and are in competition with the merchant banks.

3.43 Financial advice

As we have seen they have become experts in understanding the financial needs of businesses. Some of these merchant banks also act as **issuing houses** providing a range of services to companies seeking finance from the issue of securities, either for the first time, or as a subsequent issue following other sales to the general public. This service ranges from simple advice as to how to go about the business of selling securities so that the company can carry this out for itself to a comprehensive service whereby the issuing house takes over the whole issue, completes the administration, issues the prospectus, checks the applications for shares, allots the shares and issues the certificates to the new owners. They will even underwrite the issue so that the company will be guaranteed that the issue will provide the necessary funds.

In addition, merchant banks give advice on other sources of finance available to companies, such as government funds for venture capital, or financial institutions that have been set up to finance industry and commerce. They also give advice about possible mergers and take over bids made for or by the company. If a large loan is required, merchant banks are prepared to act as intermediaries setting up consortia, bringing in a number of financial institutions to take on part of the loan.

3.44 Acceptance business

Within the well established and largest of the merchant banks are sixteen who operate as **accepting houses**. Some articles and textbooks refer to merchant banks particularly with reference to this function. However, some merchant banks do not carry out this function so it is preferable, in the author's view, to refer to them all as merchant banks and to regard acceptance business as one function of some merchant banks. These firms are often those whose origins go back to foreign trade. In order to qualify for membership of the Acceptance Houses Association they must meet the following conditions:

(1) Have a substantial part of their business consisting of accepting bills to finance trade of others. This acceptance is a guarantee, by the acceptance house, that should the named person on the bill default on payment then the acceptance house will meet the payment.

(2) The bills, when accepted, must command the finest rates on the discount market.

(3) The acceptances are freely taken by way of rediscount at the Bank of England. In order to fulfil this condition the merchant bank has to continually satisfy the Bank of England that it has adequate capital and liquidity. These bills are now classed as 'eligible bills' as they represent acceptances by those banks which the Bank of England is prepared to discount.

3.45 International operations

As we have seen these banks had their origins in overseas trade, and generally they have not severed their links with these trading operations completely. In addition, they offer a wide range of financial services to foreign customers, be they individuals, companies, or foreign governments. They continue to accept foreign bills, they act as agents arranging loans for foreign customers acting for them on the London or international markets. They have become active in arranging medium-term credit for export since the end of the Second World War. Many have forged new links with financial institutions abroad.

3.46 Investment management

This is a particular service to holders of pension funds and to charities, although some offer advice and management services to individuals holding portfolios of securities. This is sometimes called **portfolio management**. With their knowledge of the markets (national and international), companies and finance in general, merchant banks are able to offer a very knowledgeable and efficient service. Some operate as managers for unit trusts funds, once again making use of their knowledge and expertise.

Self-assessment exercises

1 What were the origins of some merchant banks?
2 How do the deposits of a merchant bank differ from those of a clearing bank?
3 What are the services of an issuing house?
4 What do you understand by the acceptance of a bill of exchange by a merchant bank?
5 What is 'portfolio' management?

3.5 British overseas banks

These banks have their origins in trade and international relationships. They are now banks and banking groups who have their head offices in Britain, are British owned, but whose major area of operation, through branch networks, is found abroad. Over the years there have been mergers and take over bids amongst other banks so that the number of independent banks in this area has declined. Today there are three major groups:
  (1) Standard Chartered Banking Group
  (2) Hongkong Banking Group
  (3) Grindleys Bank

They tend to concentrate in specific areas in the world dividing up into four areas:
  (a) Latin and South America
  (b) Australasia
  (c) Middle and Far East
  (d) Africa

Because of their branch networks abroad they tend to have a large staff ratio and carry more cash balances. They have, since 1950, become very active in the money markets particularly with Eurocurrency and medium-term lending facilities. They also offer some degree of competition with the clearing banks for depositors. This may increase if Standard Chartered are allowed to enter the clearing house which is being considered at the present time.

3.6 Foreign banks

There are about 450 foreign-owned banks with branches in the UK. Most of them operate in and around the City of London, but some are to be found in areas where large ethnic groups have settled. Thus a number of Irish banks are found in and around Liverpool, and Pakistani banks are found in Bradford. Some of these banks are here because of the links this country has with parts of the world, like the Commonwealth, others because of the financial need of their nationals while resident here for a short time or on holiday. The number of these banks that have entered the UK market reflects the importance of London as a major international banking centre, and particularly as the centre of the Eurocurrency market. These foreign banks sometimes operate through subsidiaries and sometimes open up branches in their own names. In some cases they are merely representative offices where they do not actually transact banking business but are used to develop business relationships. As well as services to their own nationals, some of these banks operate in the retail and wholesale banking areas of the UK, while others enter the merchant banking sector and offer financial services to business. American banks feature strongly in this foreign banking sector but in recent years the Japanese have entered the market.

3.7 Consortium banks

Many companies and governments seek to borrow large sums of money to finance large capital projects. Such finance is not easily obtained from one source. As a result the concept of consortium banks developed to help further large international finance. In 1964 the first such venture was set up by the coming together of the Midland Bank, the Commercial Bank of Australia, the Toronto and Dominion Bank and Standard Chartered Bank. This no longer exists. A consortium bank is formed by a number of banks coming together to form a company in which no one bank has over 50 per cent of the capital of the new company.

Self-assessment exercises

1 Explain the difference between a foreign bank and an overseas bank.
2 For what reason did consortium banks come into being?

3.8 National Giro Bank

The National Giro Bank was set up in 1968 and is part of the Post Office corporation. It has the advantage of providing services at every post office counter. When it started as the National Giro it was seen as a money transmission service providing a simple, cheap and efficient money transfer service. It was aimed at the large section of the public that did not have bank accounts. Originally, it only accepted deposits and the settlement of debts by transfers from one account to another. It gave loans only to local authorities. In 1970 arrangements were made with Mercantile Credit, a finance house, so that giro account holders were able to obtain loans through this institution. In some cases the loans were made direct to customers. To qualify for loans of between £150 and £1000 the account holder had to have his salary paid directly into the National Giro account.

The money transfers are handled centrally by a computer at Bootle in Lancashire. It is possible for non-account holders to use this system to pay bills of account holders, and there is a facility for transfer between the banks and the National Giro. It now offers a wide range of services which include the provision of loans, overdrafts, deposit accounts, travellers cheques and foreign currency, hire purchase, bridging loans and budget accounts. It is now part of the London Clearing House.

3.9 Savings banks

Savings banks have their origins in the nineteenth century and were established to encourage saving by the poorer sections of the community. A Mrs Wakefield first developed the idea of savings banks on the broadest possible lines. In 1804 she opened up her Tottenham Benefit Bank which anyone could join by depositing anything from one shilling (5p), and receive interest on these deposits. For many years there were two major institutions operating as savings banks.

3.91 The National Savings Bank

This was originally called the Post Office Savings Bank and was established in 1861. It is now possibly the largest organisation of its kind. It offers a large number of savings opportunities to the general public. These are outlined in Chapter 5 and can be listed as follows:
  (1) Ordinary accounts
  (2) Investment accounts
  (3) National savings certificates
  (4) Income bonds
  (5) Deposit bonds
  (6) Premium bonds
  (7) Yearly plans

3.92 Trustee Savings Banks (TSB)

The true parent bank of the Trustee Savings movement was the bank set up by Dr H Duncan in the parish of Rothwell in Scotland. This bank prospered to the extent that, after three years, its deposits were £1164. Soon similar banks were started in many parts of Britain. However, because of legal difficulties the position of the trustees was in jeopardy. It was the Rt Hon George Rose who became the father of the Trustee Savings Banks system. This system encompassed trustees in charge of borrowing and managers who were responsible for management of the bank. Safeguards were incorporated into an Act in 1817. A really important provision was that which required the trustees to pay money they received, other than that which was needed for day-to-day transactions, into the Bank of England. to the account of the National Debt commissioners for reduction of the national debt. This money was to be kept in a separate account there.

For many years the Trustee Savings Banks, in their role as independent local banks, were primarily savings banks. On 3 June 1977, the Treasury appointed a committee, under the chairmanship of Sir Henry Page. The committee's terms of reference were to consider the future development of the national savings movement, the Department of National Savings and the Trustee Savings Banks in the provision of public savings, money transmission and other financial services. In addition, they were to consider a broadening of their structure and to make recommendations as to future development.

The Page commission recommended, as far as the Trustee Savings Banks were concerned, that they become one banking organisation catering mainly for personal accounts, organised on a regional and national basis with a strong central organisation freed from specific government controls.

Since 1977 these banks have offered current accounts, personal loans, mortgage loans and travellers cheques. Not all of these were offered from the beginning but have been gradually included. They have also begun to offer some facilities to the small business. In 1983 they were merged into one bank for England and Wales, one bank for Scotland, one bank for Northern Ireland and one bank for the Channel Islands. Although these banks form part of the monetary sector controlled by the Treasury, it is expected that they will come within the scope of the Banking Act 1979 some time in the future.

The Central Trustee Savings Bank was set up in 1973 to provide mainly those services which the head offices of the clearing banks operate for their branches, particularly in the area of clearing cheques and other credit transfers.

Self-assessment exercises

1 What is the National Giro?
2 Why did savings banks develop?
3 How did the Trustee Savings Bank movement start?
4 Up to 1977 what was the organisation and role of the Trustee Savings Banks?
5 Outline the major changes that have taken place in the TSB since 1977.

3.10 Bank of England

The idea of a national bank had been floated since the time of Cromwell. Sir William Petty saw such a bank as being responsible for the supply of coin money and for control of commerce. It was thought that this bank would be similar to the Bank of Amsterdam or the Bank of Hamburg. In 1683 a National Bank of Credit was set up in Devonshire House, Bishopsgate Street but it soon closed down. When William of Orange came to the throne in 1688 his preoccupation with his war with France, along with the civil wars that were being fought in Ireland and Scotland, caused him to have a shortage of funds. The Bank of England owes its existence to the needs of the king. A Scotsman, William Paterson, put forward a scheme to raise money 'upon a fund of perpetual interest' which was basically the introduction of the national debt. His scheme was to raise £1 200 000 to lend to the government at interest of 8 per cent. This money was to be subscribed by the public, who would form a company to produce notes up to the value of its capital. The company was to become known as the Governors and Company of the Bank of England.

A number of people were opposed to the proposal. In 1694 it was added on to an ordinary Finance Bill and has since become known as the Bank of England Act; however, its full title was:

'An Act granting to their Majesties several rates and duties upon tonnage of ships and vessels and upon beer, ale and other liquors for securing certain recompenses and advantages in the said Act mentioned to such persons as shall voluntarily advance the sum of £1,500,000 towards carrying on the war with France.'

The sum of £300 000 was raised by the sale of annuities, but there was no mention of the Bank of England by name, with the result that later the Bank became associated with 'beer, ale and other liquors'. The money raised by the taxes and duties from ships and alcoholic drink was to be used to pay the interest on the remainder of £1 200 000 to be borrowed.

In its passage through Parliament two clauses were added:

(1) The corporation was not to lend to the Crown or purchase Crown lands without the consent of Parliament.

(2) The corporation was forbidden to trade in goods, wares or merchandise.

On 21 April 1694 the Bill went to the House of Lords. Here there were proposals to remove any mention of the proposed bank, but on 25 April the Bill was passed. The early promoters had no conception of how the Bank would develop.

The attendance of the Commissioners in Mercers Chapel to receive subscriptions became a social event. It took twelve days for all of the money to be subscribed. The first Governor was Sir John Houblon, he and the directors took the oath of allegiance on taking up office, and this oath is still taken today by new governors and directors. From the first, the Bank issued bearer notes with a genuine promise to pay the bearer. Thus up to 1914 Bank of England notes were convertible into sovereigns and half sovereigns. The notes were not legal tender at first. Nowadays they are legal tender so that any request for conversion will only produce other Bank of England notes or coins.

When the £1 200 000 was paid to the Exchequer the Bank of England received wooden tallies as receipts. Thus began the national debt, still unpaid today, so that the Bank still holds these tallies. After 1709 the Bank of England charter was open to renewal on a regular basis. It was, however, so much part of the financial scene by then that its renewal became a matter of course. On 5 June 1724 the Bank opened in Threadneedle Street. In

1751 it formally took over the management of the national debt, and by 1766 it was the official banker to the government. In 1789 the Bank was attacked during the Gordon riots and, as a result, the Bank picket, a military guard, was mounted and this continued every night until 1974. In 1790 a code of rules and orders for staff was set up and these have been added to and strengthened over the years. In 1797 the government, once again, asked for support for a war with France. The Bank stopped paying out gold for notes and so began the start of a period of restriction which lasted twenty-four years. The politician and playwright, Sir Richard Sheridan, felt that this move brought the Bank into disrepute, he stated: 'there is an Old Lady in the City who has fallen on bad company'.

The 'bad company' was the Prime Minister. This nickname has stayed so that the Bank is often referred to as 'the Old Lady of Threadneedle Street'.

In 1844 the Bank Charter Act demonstrated the success of the currency school over the banking school. The former believed that the note issue should be fully backed by gold or as nearly so as possible. The latter believed in a more flexible note issue with this being expanded as and when necessary. The Act had two major effects on the Bank of England:

(1) It divided the activities of the Bank into two major departments – the banking department and the note issue department. To this day the weekly return published every Friday, shows the separation of these two activities even though there is no such physical division in the Bank into these two areas.

(2) The authorities wished to control the issue of notes and, as a result, although the Bank could issue unlimited quantities of notes it found that its unbacked issue was limited to £14 million. This was the start of the fiduciary issue which now exceeds £10 000 million.

In the 1840s, 1850s and 1860s the Bank of England found it necessary to resort to its use of the bank rate to control the level of interest rates in the country. This was the beginning of a function that the Bank has carried on up to the present day although, as we have seen, this has been refined and changed.

As the Bank developed it stopped regarding itself as an ordinary bank but as one with a 'national conscience' responsible for the financial monetary system of the country. In fact the Bank was operating what Montague Norman (Governor 1920–44) saw as 'moral suasion'. In 1939 Clement Atlee forecast that, should a Labour government come to power, they would take the Bank into public control. Thus in 1946 the Bank was nationalised. The Bank of England Act 1946 allowed for the government to offer 3 per cent Treasury stock for Bank of England stock in the ratio of four to one. This act of nationalisation did not really alter the role of the Bank but merely 'rubber stamped' what was already in operation. However, the Act did introduce some changes in the supervision of the banking world by the Bank.

This very brief history of the Bank of England shows us the development of some of its present day functions. These can now be seen in greater detail as follows:

3.101 Note circulation

The Bank is responsible for the printing, issue and withdrawal of notes and is the only note issuing bank in England and Wales. At the present time some £10 000 million notes are in circulation, of which £560m are £1 notes. From the end of 1984 no new £1 notes were issued, being replaced instead with the £1 coin. The £1 note was in use from 1914 when the sovereign was withdrawn. The notes had only a life of ten months while the coin is expected to have a life of forty years. At the same time the halfpence coin was withdrawn. The Bank prints about seven and a half million notes a day and destroys about the same amount. Two-thirds of the notes are issued through the Bank's branches and the remainder through the head office. The money raised by the sale of notes is used to purchase securities which earn interest and this sum, less the production and administration costs of the issue, is paid to the Treasury. In 1984 £1000m surplus was paid in this way.

Because of its expertise in note production, the Bank is also responsible for the production of notes for other countries and this activity helps to earn us foreign currency.

3.102 A banking function

The Bank acts as banker in three areas:

(1) To the government – this does not mean that all payments to and from the government are operated by the Bank. Although some departments of government maintain accounts with the Bank they also have accounts with other banks. These help them to operate payments to and from the general public more easily. The Bank of England is responsible for overseeing the consolidated fund, the fund that receives revenue from customs and excise, income tax and succession duty. It is used for the payment of certain public charges. It really is an amalgamation of all government expenditure and income from all sources.

The Bank also oversees the government's borrowing needs by arranging for the sale of the many gilt edged securities which are offered each year. These new issues form part of the national debt, and it is the job of the Bank to see to the issue of dividend payments and to the redemption of these securities as it is considered necessary.

(2) To the banking system – all banks and licensed deposit-taking institutions operating in the UK, whose eligible liabilities exceed £10 million,

must keep a certain balance with the Bank. At the present time this is a half a per cent of these eligible liabilities. This regulation is aimed at operating some form of monetary control on these institutions. This is seen as a non-operational non-interest bearing requirement. In addition clearing banks maintain higher balances so that they can settle their indebtedness to each other arising from their cheque clearing activities (*see* Fig. 3.1).

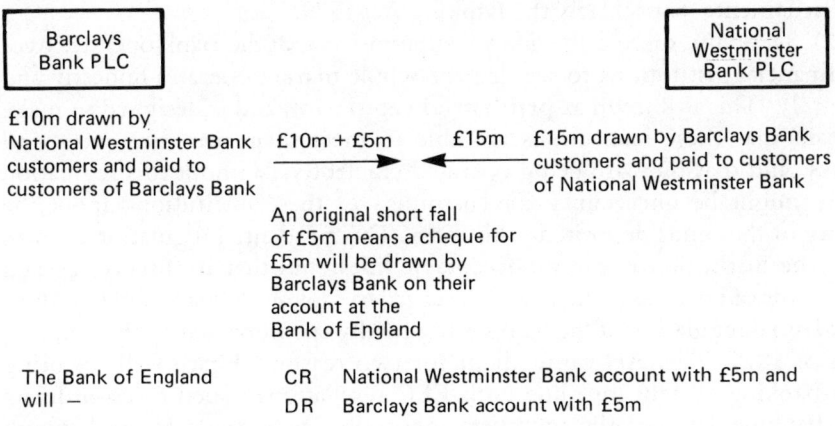

Fig. 3.1 Mechanism of clearing

On occasions in the past the Bank has made calls for extra deposits by these banks known as special deposits. These have generally answered the need to control the level of credit, as we have seen in Chapter 2. The Bank also holds deposits belonging to the central banks of other countries. These may be in bullion or in the form of currency deposits. These are held to facilitate international payments without the risk of transferring bullion or currencies from one country to another.

(3) To private customers – this is a result of its earlier operation as an ordinary bank. Since 1946 no new private accounts have been allowed unless opened by an employee of the Bank. It is believed that as time goes by these private accounts will disappear, so that eventually this service will be of only minor importance to the bank.

3.103 Operation of monetary policy

In general terms the Bank acts as advisor to the government on its economic policies, including the operation of its monetary policy. As explained in Chapter 2, the government seeks the Bank's advice on this and at the same time expects the Bank to be an instrument of its implementation.

3.104 Supervision of the financial system

As the Bank developed it became more of an institution exercising control over other financial institutions. This was felt necessary to aid the development of a safe and sound banking system. This supervision can be divided into two basic parts.

(1) First of all, there is the statutory regulation as laid down in Acts of Parliament – particularly the Banking Act 1979.

(2) Secondly, there is the general supervision that the Bank operates over all financial institutions to see that the whole market operates honestly and securely. This is known as **prudential regulation** and is designed to make certain that these institutions are able to meet their commitments at all times, and that they are being operated efficiently. Without this regulation there might be uncertainty for customers of these institutions about the safety of the funds deposited with them. This prudential regulation ensures that the institution is run on acceptable lines, and that it observes certain standards of business prudence with regard to capital adequacy and liquidity. Prudential regulation of the banks is not totally encompassed by the Banking Act of 1979. This Act came about for two reasons. First of all, to bring our banking system into line with EEC regulations issued to co-ordinate the banking laws of the members. Secondly, as a result of the banking crisis of 1973/4 when a number of unsupervised, fringe banks found themselves in serious difficulties and had to be bailed out by the Bank of England and the Big Four in what has become known as the 'Lifeboat'. This meant financial support to these institutions of around £1000m.

The Act lays down, with certain exceptions (National Giro Bank, building societies, and Trustee Savings Banks), that all institutions which accept deposits must be authorised. They fall into two categories.

(1) Recognised banks – those who can use the word bank in their title and are able to show that they provide a wide range of banking services or a highly specialised service, and that they enjoy a high reputation and standing in the financial community.

(2) Licensed deposit-taking institutions – all other deposit takers who must have a licence to operate. Only the Bank has the power to recognise banks, grant licences and to withdraw these authorisations. However, an appeal may be made to the Chancellor of the Exchequer by any institution in the case of withdrawal. Banks operating outside the UK using this word in their title can still use it in their operations here.

There are five aspects of a bank's operations that are of interest to the Bank of England and about which the Bank must have information at regular intervals. The Bank receives accounting and statistical information, and senior management meet regularly with officials of the Bank for discussion. These five areas are:

(1) The experience and competence of the management.

(2) The earnings or profitability of the bank.

(3) The nature of the bank's assets, particularly the riskiness of its loans and other assets.

(4) The sufficiency of the capital to cover the risks which are ordinarily attached to its business. This is a capital requirement and the Bank is interested in two measures. The first is the ratio between the bank's capital and its deposits and certain other liabilities. The second is the 'risks assets' ratio which is the relationship between its capital and the total value of its assets adjusted for risk weightings. These weightings are given by the Bank for each category of asset held by the bank. They vary from zero to two.

(5) The banks must ensure that they are holding suitable stocks of liquid assets so that they can meet their obligations as they fall due. The Bank of England has a system for liquidity which is based on a projection of potential cash flows into and out of the bank. Liabilities are classified into five life bands which are related to the length of time these deposits are held by the banks before they can be legally reclaimed by the customers. However, with deposits up to seven days banks will allow customers to withdraw without notice provided they forfeit the interest due.

     0 –   8 days
  8 days – 1 month
  1 – 3 months
  3 – 6 months
  6 – 12 months

Assets and liabilities are placed into such bands to show the extent of their mismatch so that a bank's liquidity needs can be identified. Assets which can be turned into cash immediately in the market are put into the first of these bands, but they are discounted to take into account any losses likely to be incurred by an immediate sale instead of waiting the full period.

The Bank of England is also interested in a bank's foreign currency items on its balance sheet and also any large commitments to any one customer at any one time. The Bank has to follow a course which allows for adequate regulation and, at the same time, gives the system sufficient flexibility to meet the need for efficiency and competition. It does not impose a uniform system of regulation on all institutions, but through negotiation with the senior management of a bank comes to an agreement for its operations which will seek to achieve capital adequacy and liquidity. This system recognises the different requirements of different banks operating in the financial markets. With the recent mergers and amalgamations in the City between banks and other financial institutions, the Bank of England is now considering supervision of these additional activities so that they fit in with the requirements for capital adequacy, liquidity and commitment to particular borrowers or lenders as do their traditional operations.

The 1979 Act also introduced a deposit protection scheme which aimed at protecting the small depositor in the event of the financial institution getting into difficulties. Institutions are required to subscribe to a fund an amount which is related to the size of their deposits. It is in effect a deposit insurance scheme. Should a bank fail then depositors of up to £10 000 will be paid out of the fund up to an amount equal to 75 per cent of their deposits. This scheme does not please the larger banks as they have to make the bigger contributions but the likelihood of their failure is less than the smaller banks so they see themselves as subsidising these banks.

In its general, non-statutory, supervision of the City, the Bank ensures, for example, by the regulation of relationships and the provision of adequate capital sources, that the general financial climate is such that industry will develop in a way that is compatible with current government policies.

3.105 International activities

The Bank looks after the gold and foreign currency reserves of the country. These have been amassed over the years from our international trading, and they belong to the state. In the past the Bank has used these reserves to keep the external value of our currency stable when this has been under pressure. For example, if the value of the pound is falling against the dollar because of either a loss of confidence in the pound or a demand for the dollar, then the supply of pounds exceeds the demand. The Bank of England employs agents throughout the world to buy up these pounds and so try to halt any further slide. In the opposite case, if the pound is rising this is because the demand for pounds exceeds the supply. The Bank enters the market selling pounds to halt this rise if possible. The Bank, in recent years, has been prominent in the assistance of those Third World countries which have had difficulties in repayment of loans to other banks and countries.

It is also a function of the Bank's officials to represent the UK government on occasions at meetings of international financial bodies such as the EEC and the International Monetary Fund.

Self-assessment exercises

1   How much did King William borrow to finance his war with France in 1694?
2   How was the money raised?
3   Why was the Act creating the Bank of England called the 'Beer and Ale' Act?
4   What was given as a receipt for the money loaned to the government when the Bank of England was created?
5   Complete a list of the major dates and events in the history of the Bank of England.

6   Why is the Bank known as the 'Old Lady of Threadneedle Street'?
7   How did the passing of the Bank Charter Act 1844 affect the operation of the Bank of England?
8   How does the Bank control the level of coins and notes in the economy?
9   What functions are performed by the Bank when acting as banker to the government?
10 What areas of a bank's operations are of interest to the Bank of England?
11 Explain the deposit protection scheme operated by the Bank of England.

3.11 Analysing a bank's balance sheet

A typical bank's balance sheet is shown in Fig. 3.2.

This is displayed in traditional style as is usual with banks. It shows liabilities on the left and assets on the right. In other accounting studies you will probably be taught a more modern linear layout for other businesses.

3.111 Bank liabilities

(1) *Capital* – shown as ordinary shares, reserves and preference shares. This is the same as in all other types of business and represents the shareholders' stake in the business. The size of these shares and reserves is important to a bank as their function is to support the borrowing of the bank in the form of its deposits. We are interested in the ratio of this capital to deposits, which for purposes of our balance sheet can be seen as:

$$\text{CAPITAL:DEPOSITS}$$
$$£1\,570\,000 : £29\,420\,000$$

which is $1:18.7$
   or 5.3%

This means that for every £18.70 of deposits there is £1 of shareholder's capital providing backing. Although this ratio is small, it is a cushion which can absorb the shock of any losses that the bank may suffer, thus protecting, in part, the deposits of its customers.

Another ratio that can be calculated is the free capital to deposits ratio. Free capital is defined as:

   capital less *fixed assets*.

Free capital represents that money which has been subscribed to the bank and is not covered by the value of the fixed assets.

For our balance sheet this is:

68 Banking for Students

Liabilities		£	Assets	£	%
Ordinary shareholders' funds			**Sterling assets**		
Ordinary shares		240	Notes and coin	400	
Reserves		1 320	Balances with the Bank of England	150	6.2
		1 560	Money at call	900	
Preference share capital		10	Treasury bills discounted	100	9.9
		1 570	Eligible bank bills discounted	300	
Loan capital		850	Other bills	60	
Proposed dividend		36	British government stocks up to one year		
Deferred taxation		34	to maturity	90	
Amounts due to subsidiary companies		600		2 000	49.0
Sterling deposits			Market loans	3 200	
Sight deposits	£8 090		Advances and investments	15 900	65.1
Time deposits	12 300			21 100	
Certificates of					
deposit	560	20 950	Market loans	6 000	18.5
Other currency deposits			**Other currency assets**		
Sight and time deposits	£8 080		Advances, bills and investments	2 200	6.8
Certificates of deposit	390	8 470	**Miscellaneous assets**		
			Fixed assets	£1 000	
			Others	2 210	
				3 210	9.6
		32 510		32 510	100.0

Fig. 3.2 Proforma bank balance sheet

capital − fixed assets
£1 570 000 − £1 000 000
= £570 000

Fixed assets include such items as buildings, plant and machinery.
This ratio is now:

£570 000 : £29 420 000
which is   1 : 51
or about   2%

Thus for our bank for every £51 of deposits £1 is backed by free capital.

(2) *Amounts due to subsidiaries* – these are deposits or loans to the bank by subsidiary companies. These will no doubt feature as part of the interbank market (*see* Chapter 6).

(3) *Deferred taxation* – this is an allowance for tax that is likely to be due to be paid by the bank on its profits. The actual amount will be negotiated with the Inland Revenue.

(4) *Proposed dividend* – until the shareholders agree the accounts and the dividend this cannot be paid, but a provision can be made for it and will have to be shown on the accounts as it is here.

(5) *Sight deposits* – for a clearing bank these are known as current accounts. They are an important part of the money transmission service which the banks provide. Generally these deposits do not earn interest although some institutions do offer a small rate of interest. They also take on a small amount on deposit from the wholesale market (*see* Chapter 6) on sight on which they pay some interest. At sight deposits mean that the customers can withdraw these deposits without giving notice. These are usually deposits of large amounts but are so small in relation to the whole of the sight deposits that they are not significant to the money transmission service. These sight deposits are in sterling and foreign currencies.

(6) *Time deposits* – these are called deposit accounts in the UK. This money is deposited for a specific time or subject to notice of withdrawal. Most of the deposits by private individuals are small and are on seven days' notice of withdrawal, corporate deposits are larger and a company may negotiate or be offered varying types of deposit accounts. Banks have also introduced deposit accounts linked with automatic borrowing rights, monthly income and regular savings schemes.

(7) *Certificates of deposit* – an example of one of these is shown in Fig. 3.3. This is evidence of a deposit which is made with a bank and is repayable on a fixed date. The deposit is evidenced by the issue of a certificate. These are made, in general, by corporate customers who have large sums available for deposit. The depositor can either hold this certificate until it matures or sell it to someone else. The development of the use of the certificate of deposit is outlined in Chapter 4. These items can appear on both sides of a bank's balance sheet: as liabilities when the bank accepts them as deposits,

NEGOTIABLE STERLING CERTIFICATE OF DEPOSIT
(Issuing Bank)

.... LIMITED
.... Address

Serial Number   £ ....
....   Maturity Date .... Fixed
                              LONDON, ... 19 ....
                      (Issuing Bank)
.... LIMITED CERTIFIES THAT
the sum of ....
POUNDS STERLING has been deposited upon terms that it is payable to bearer on surrender of this certificate, through an Authorized Bank,
                              (Address)
at ....
                              (Maturity date)
on the ....
fixed, with interest at the rate of .... (Words)...............

Fig. 3.3

assets when the bank buys them from businesses before they mature. Sometimes these certificates are described as negotiable certificates of deposit.

3.112 Bank assets

When looking at the various assets held by a bank we must consider the motives underlying their appearance on the balance sheet. Banks seek two basic objectives from their asset structure. These are **liquidity** and **profitability**. A bank must have assets which are reasonably liquid-cash or capable of being quickly changed into cash with a minimum loss in value. They hold these assets in order to meet the liquidity needs of their customers. It is not good practice for banks to accept deposits from customers on a short-term basis, then lend these funds out for longer periods and be unable to meet the needs of repayment by the original depositors.

At the same time, banks are owned by private shareholders who seek a return from their investment in the bank, or require the bank to generate funds to cover the costs of its operation. These profits come from the various bank loans. Ideally banks would like to hold assets which are both liquid and profitable but this is not possible. So banks keep a mix of assets which range from those that are liquid and earn only slight profits, to others which are not liquid but earn acceptable profits. This mix is shown on the balance sheet in the order of liquidity first to profitability last.

It is now time to look at the various assets.

(1) *Coins and notes* – banks hold these cash balances to meet the immediate demands of their depositors. Obviously, the amount is not constant as there are times of the year when more cash is needed than at others, for example, at Christmas and summer holidays. Banks with large amounts deposited in current accounts need a bigger cash reserve than banks with strong deposit accounts. Banks have developed, over the years, an ability to judge the right level of cash reserves to keep them at a minimum level which is safe, these reserves being in no way immediately profitable to the banks.

(2) *Balances with the Bank of England* – as we have seen earlier in this chapter the Bank of England is the banker to the banks. They hold these funds in the Bank for two major reasons. First of all, as part of the cash reserve to help maintain their liquidity; this is a requirement set down by the Bank itself. Secondly, so that banks in the clearing system can settle indebtedness amongst each other. As we have seen in Chapter 2, the Bank of England can, as part of its monetary control arrangements, make calls for special deposits from other banks. These are frozen, but they do not constitute a penalty on the banks as they receive interest on them related to the average return on Treasury bills. The size of these calls relates to the size of an individual bank's liabilities.

We can use these two assets to compute another valuable ratio. This is the **cash ratio** which uses the coins and notes in the banks' tills plus the ordinary balances with the Bank of England. For our balance sheet this is:

COINS AND NOTES IN TILLS
+ BALANCES WITH THE BANK OF ENGLAND
£400 000 + £150 000
= £550 000

Thus the *cash ratio* is:

CASH RESERVE : DEPOSITS
£550 000 : £29 420 000
1 : 53
or   1.8%

In other words the cash ratio is less than 2 per cent. This demonstrates that banks do not regard it as necessary to carry large sums of money in absolutely liquid form, and that this small ratio adequately covers the cash needs of their customers.

(3) *Money at call* – this is money on loan to the members of the London Discount Houses Association. The discount houses borrow this money on the understanding that, if the bank needs it the next day, the bank will call it back. Hence it is called 'overnight money'. If the bank does not

require it then the discount houses have it for another night. Banks enjoy a high degree of liquidity with these loans and, at the same time, a small amount of profitability. The discount house uses this money to discount commercial or Treasury bills.

(4) *Treasury bills* – these are ninety-one-day bills issued by the UK government through the Bank of England which enable government to meet short-term cash flow needs. They are promissory notes, undertaking to pay a given sum ninety days after issue. They are sold in two ways, either through the 'tap' where they are offered to certain government departments which are holding public funds, like the National Debt Commissioners, or by **tender** to the discount houses which buy these every Friday. The discount houses submit various prices at which they are prepared to buy these bills, and an employee of the Bank of England selects those prices which are the best for the government. The discount houses also offer to buy all the bills that are on issue. After sixty days the discount houses offer these to the banks, and they are now acceptable to the banks as they are only committing money for thirty days. The banks are not so ready to purchase them when they are new. More details are given about Treasury bills in Chapter 4.

(5) *Eligible bills* – these are the largest component of a bank's holding of bills of all kinds. They are mainly commercial bills which the bank has discounted. They also consist of a small proportion of local authority bills. They are classed as eligible bills as they are recognised for rediscount by the Bank of England (*see* Chapter 2). If they have been accepted by an acceptance house then these have the highest credit standing.

(6) *Other bills* – these consist of any other bills that a bank has discounted which are not eligible for rediscount by the Bank of England. These include some types of local authority bill.

Having discussed what are known as a bank's main liquid assets we can now calculate its **liquid assets ratio**. This is calculated as follows:

LIQUID ASSETS : DEPOSITS
£2 000 000 : £29 420 000
1 : 14.7
or 6.8%

(7) *Market loans* – these are loans to members of the London Discount Houses Association for a longer period than overnight. They also include loans on the interbank market. This latter is a market in which banks lend to each other on an unsecured basis without going through the traditional market of the discount houses. They also include the discounting of certificates of deposit.

(8) *Advances* – this is the largest item found on a bank's balance sheet. It includes all kinds of lending, from overdrafts to long-term loans to both the public and private sectors. These are the most profitable assets held

by the banks but they are the most illiquid. On the other hand, banks have to make such provision for some advances could turn out to be bad debts. The basic nature of bank lending can be seen in Table 3.2.

Table 3.2 Profile of bank lending in the UK (industrial detail)

	Loans and advances outstanding May 1985 £m
Extractive industries and mineral products	1351
Metal manufacturing	1049
Chemical industry	1505
Mechanical engineering	1706
Electrical engineering	2381
Motor vehicles	600
Other transport equipment	1204
Other engineering and metal goods	1698
Food, drink and tobacco	3522
Textiles, leather clothing and footwear	1564
Other manufacturing	4528
Total	21109

Source: Bank of England Quarterly Bulletin

The ratio of sterling advances to sterling deposits is:

ADVANCES
15 900 : DEPOSITS
        1 : 20 950
        7 : 1.3
or   75%

This tells us that 75 per cent of the deposits in a bank are out on loan to customers in the form of overdrafts or longer-term loans.

(9) *Investments* – these include the holding of gilt edged stocks, local authority stocks and bonds and investments in subsidiaries and associates. The first two of these have a sure return as they are usually tied to fixed interest rates. Thus a bank is able to forecast the return and use this money as a contribution towards its operating costs. At the same time, they represent reasonable liquidity as they can be traded on the Stock Exchange. There is a danger here of a capital loss, as the price of these securities might be low at the time when the bank wishes to sell them.

Investments in subsidiaries give the bank a wider interest in firms which are possible competitors, or help to widen the bank's sphere of operation.

(10) *Fixed assets* – these include the premises from which a bank is able to offer its services, and also the equipment which aids the efficiency and nature of these services. Obviously, they do not contribute themselves directly to a bank's profit, but they are very important to the bank in enabling

it to offer the services which do give profits. One thing that must be remembered is that the banks hold property, whose value is considerable, in the high streets of every town and city in the country.

Self-assessment exercises

1   Which liabilities of a bank represent the shareholders' stake in the business?
2   What is meant by 'free capital'?
3   What kind of deposits are held by a clearing bank?
4   Which assets are liquid to a bank?
5   Why does a bank need profitability?
6   Why do banks hold balances with the Bank of England?
7   What do you understand by 'overnight' money?
8   Describe and explain the difference between the various bills that have been discounted by a bank.
9   Why are advances important to a bank?
10   What kinds of investments are banks likely to participate in and why are they important?

Assignments

1   Construct a typical bank balance sheet reflecting the importance of liquidity and profitability.
2   Outline the relationship that exists between the Bank of England and the discount houses in the UK at the present time.
3   By means of research complete the following tasks:
   (a) The following are the names of various types of bank. Say which type.
   (i) Clydesdale Bank
   (ii) Hoare and Co.
   (iii) Williams and Glyns PLC
   (iv) Standard Chartered Bank
   (v) Kleinwort Benson Ltd
   (vi) Northern Bank Ltd
   (vii) Chase Manhattan Bank
   Explain briefly if and how they may be related.
   (b) Explain the difference between clearing and merchant (accepting) banks. Write about 200 words covering origin, services and number of branches.
   (c) Why do foreign-owned banks operate in the UK? Which countries in the world predominate in this area.
   (d) Why were savings banks started in the last century? Explain fully any role these types of bank may still have to play in the banking world today.
4   What do you understand by the terms retail and wholesale banking? Is it still relevant to use this classification at the present time?

4 Financial Markets

4.1 Mechanism of the City

The City of London has been described as the financial centre of the world. It brings together the people who supply funds and those people who demand funds so that both of these interests can be satisfied. To this end it is called a **mechanism** but it is no simple structure. It has developed into a complex arrangement of institutions, deposits and instruments of debt which are linked together so that at times it is only the nature of the transaction which identifies a particular market in which the institution is operating. We can illustrate this mechanism in the following diagram which shows us that there are three basic markets whose operation is linked in some way or another.

If we view this diagram as a series of cogs relating to each of the four groups, noting that the source of power is seated with the Bank of England

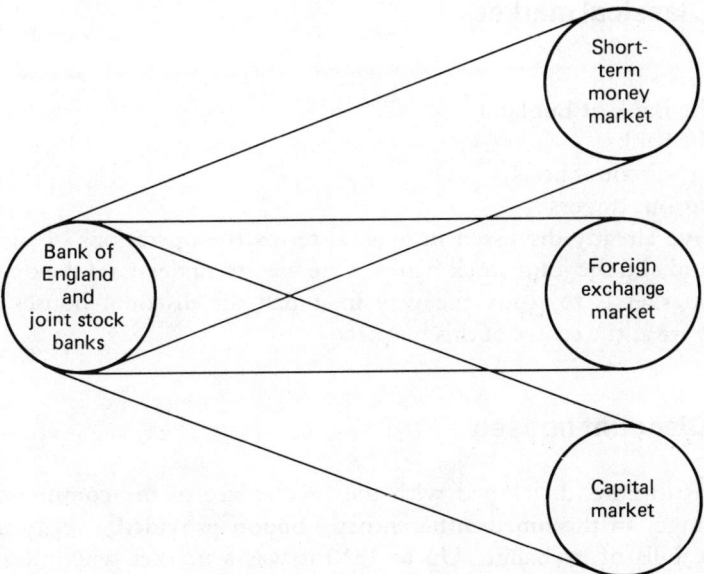

Fig. 4.1 Market mechanism of the city

and the joint stock banks, and if this power source is connected by driving chains to the other three markets, then we can see that they will operate at whatever speed this power source directs. If we imagine that the markets can be operated at different speeds depending upon the wishes of the Bank of England and the pressures it brings to bear on the joint stock banks and the other institutions, then we have a simple idea of how this mechanism works. We must appreciate that the Bank of England is not just an observer of these markets, like a referee of a football match, but that it is also one of the players. We also find that some of these institutions, like the finance houses and the merchant banks, to a greater or lesser extent, operate in different markets so that there is no simple division of the institutions into the three markets.

Now let us look at these markets in greater detail.

4.2 Short-term money market

This is not just one simple market but is made up of a number of markets which are divided up into two – the **classical** and **parallel markets**. These are markets in which large sums of money are borrowed and lent for relatively short periods of time. Figure 4.2 shows us the basic relationship that exists in these markets.

4.21 Classical market

This consists of:
 (1) The Bank of England
 (2) The banks
 (3) The discount houses
 (4) Various traders

We have already discussed in general terms the operations of the Bank of England and the joint stock banks. One way to understand the operation of this market is to study the way in which the discount houses work, for these are at the centre of this market.

4.22 Discount houses

These institutions developed with the greater use of the commercial bill of exchange. In the nineteenth century London provided a ready market for these bills of exchange. Up to 1810 it was a market where dealers in these bills acted as brokers, buying and selling on behalf of others rather than dealing on their own behalf. Until the development of a specialised

Financial Markets 77

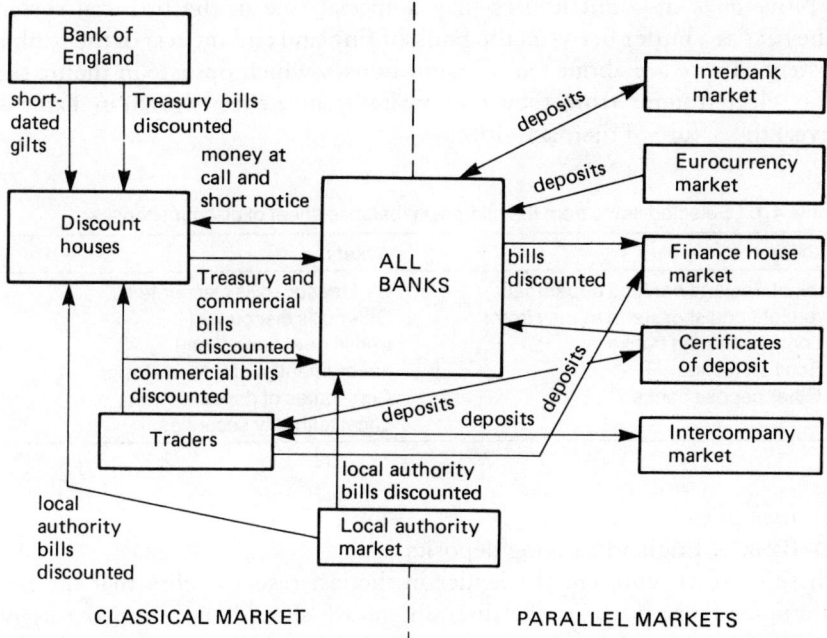

Fig. 4.2 Short-term money markets

bill market in London, both the town and country bankers found markets for their deposited funds only in the outright purchase and sale of these bills, with these bill brokers acting as intermediaries. Thus a trader who sought to encash a bill could use one of these discount brokers who would then negotiate with a bank for a sum of money below the face value of the bill. The broker would then receive a brokerage.

After 1810 there was a marked expansion in the bill business both with the country banks and merchants. In the case of the country banks it was as a result of their increase in number. With this increase in bill business the brokers began to discount bills themselves. As the brokers became known, the banks realised that there was another source for lending short-term funds – namely lending to these discount houses. It was not, however, until 1827 that the banks began to lend on call or short notice.

With the greater use of the cheque after 1853, when the Stamp Act provided for a fixed stamp duty on order cheques, the internal use of the commercial bill declined. In 1877 the government issued for the first time a Treasury bill. Growth in the issue of this debt instrument was rather spasmodic, but the discounting of this bill by the discount houses replaced the loss in business resulting from the decline in the use of the commercial bill.

Nowadays discount houses play a special role in the financial system. They act as a buffer between the Bank of England and the rest of the banking system. There are about ten discount houses which operate in the market. The selected items from their composite balance sheet shown in Table 4.1 reveal the nature of their activities.

Table 4.1 Selected items from the composite balance sheet of discount houses

Liabilities	Assets
Bank of England banking department	Uk Treasury bills discounted
Overnight and short-term money from:	Other bills discounted
London clearing banks	British government and
Scottish banks	government guaranteed stocks
Other deposit banks	Certificates of deposit
	Local authority securities

(1) *Liabilities*
(a) Bank of England banking deposits
These used to represent the lender in the last resort facility that the Bank of England provided to the discount house should they find themselves short of funds and be unable to meet the demands on them to discount Treasury bills and commercial bills. Nowadays, as we have seen in a previous chapter, the assistance given by the Bank of England is to rediscount eligible bills.
(b) Overnight and short-term money
Discount houses borrow overnight and for a short period of time from the banks. This is illustrated in Fig. 4.2. This short-term money is for various periods of time and is classified as overnight money, good money, privilege money and short fall money. The term of the loan is arranged with the bank, and often the only way we can identify which type is being borrowed is by the rate of interest charged. Generally, the longer the period of time of the loan the higher the rate of interest charged by the bank, although the difference between one period and another may be only a thirty-second of a per cent.
(2) *Assets*
It is in the use of these borrowed funds that we can see the functions of the discount houses.
(a) UK Treasury bills
As we have seen in Chapter 2 the government borrows large sums of money for both short- and long-term periods of time. Its short-term needs are met in the main by the sale of Treasury bills. These are ninety-one-day bills issued by the government in amounts ranging from £5000 to £1m. The government requires these funds to meet current expenditure when its income is not likely to come in until a later date. The issue of these bills

is carried out in two ways, firstly, by way of the 'tap'. This is not a sale on the open market but direct to government departments, savings banks, statutory insurance funds, the exchange equalisation account and certain overseas monetary authorities. Most Treasury bills are sold by 'tender' to the discount houses, some banks and a few bill brokers. Tendering occurs when the buyer puts in the price at which he is prepared to purchase an item. The seller can then choose the bid which is regarded as the best. In this case the discount house submits prices for various quantities of bills it wishes to buy with the price for each successive quantity of bills being lower than the previous one. These prices are below the face value of the bills, so they are being discounted. This tender takes place every Friday and, although the Bank of England is not absolutely certain of the prices it will obtain, it is guaranteed that the total issue will be taken up by the discount houses. The value of Treasury bills discounted over the past few years is shown in Table 4.2.

Table 4.2 Size of Treasury Bills discounted 1974–83

	£m
1974	535
1975	819
1976	563
1977	1052
1978	845
1979	709
1980	586
1981	99
1982	70
1983	31

Source: Annual Abstract of Statistics

(b) Other bills discounted

One of the ways that trade credit can be operated, other than by the invoice system, is to use a commercial bill of exchange. If this system of payment is agreed by traders then the debtor draws up the bill for the amount owed, payable to himself or his agent, and sends it to the creditor who, if he agrees to the amount and the conditions, signs across it in acceptance. The bill is then returned to the debtor who can then do with it one of three things:

    (i) Hold on to it until it falls due (matures), and then pass it through the banking system for collection.

    (ii) Use it to pay off a debt to a third party for a similar or higher amount. The bill would need to be signed on the back by the person transferring it. This is called endorsing the bill. In effect the original creditor is withdrawing any claim on the bill.

(iii) Take the bill to a discount house or bank for cashing should the debtor require cash before it falls due; the bill will then be discounted. (An example of discounting is found in Chapter 2.) Traders outside London find it expensive and time wasting to go to discount houses to have their bills discounted and, therefore, banks are prepared to offer this service.

Discount houses hold onto both Treasury bills and commercial bills until they have about thirty days left before they mature and then they offer them for sale to the banks. The banks are now prepared to buy these bills, as they are not committing money for so long a period. It is by the sale of these bills that the discount houses obtain funds to enable them to discount further bills.

(c) British government and government guaranteed stocks

These represent purchases of the other types of government debt by discount houses. They are prepared to do this as these stocks offer a fixed, and usually known, rate of dividend and are also reasonably secure. The discount house could sell them on the open market in the Stock Exchange should they so wish.

(d) Certificates of deposit

These were first introduced in New York in 1961. A bank issues a certificate in return for a fixed-term deposit, the holder of the certificate can have it discounted at any time before the end of the term by selling it to a third party, usually a discount house or a bank. When these certificates of deposit were first used in the UK they were for dollar deposits. It was not until October 1968 that banks were authorised to accept sterling deposits. The minimum deposit is £50 000 and the term is from three months to five years. When discounting of these certificates began, it was welcomed by the discount houses as developments were taking place which tended to reduce the sources available for their idle balances.

(e) Local authority securities

As we have seen in Chapter 2 part of the public sector borrowing requirement is borrowing by local authorities. These authorities sell bills and bonds which are bought by financial institutions, particularly banks and discount houses. These are popular as they are reasonably secure and provide a certain fixed income to the holder.

4.23 Position of the discount houses today

(1) Their existence depends upon being regarded favourably by other financial institutions. Both the Bank of England and the banks allow them to exist in order to fulfil roles which they themselves are not prepared to do.

(2) They mobilise idle balances and other short-term money for lending to industry, trade and the government. They have also shown an ability to adapt to changing circumstances.

(3) They operate in a delicate mechanism for controlling short-term interest rates, and help to even out unwanted fluctuations in bill and bond prices and interest rate changes.

(4) If they were removed there would be a considerable upheaval in the financial system, particularly the short-term money markets.

Self-assessment exercises

1 What is meant by 'discounting a bill'?
2 Name the types of bill that are discounted by a discount house.
3 List the services a discount house provides to the banks and the Bank of England.
4 Why are the discount houses important in the money market?

4.3 Parallel markets

These markets have developed in recent years and, as Fig. 4.2 shows, they consist of:

4.31 Local authority market

This developed after 1955 when central government gave the local authorities the power to enter the market to raise funds rather than, as previously, borrowing solely from the Public Works Loans Board. This market takes the form of the local authorities issuing bills and bonds which are bought by the banks and the discount houses in order to meet the local authorities' need for short-term funds.

4.32 Finance house market

To understand this market it would be useful to consider selected assets and liabilities of the finance houses. The table shows how these institutions

Table 4.3 Holdings of selected assets and liabilities of finance houses

Liabilities	Assets
Deposits	Hire purchase outstanding
Bills discounted with UK banks and discount houses	Other advances and loans
	Assets with the UK financial institutions (not banks)
Other borrowing	Securities other than trade investments
Unearned finance charges	
Issued capital and reserves	Trade investments
	Leased assets

operate as financial intermediaries accepting funds from one group of people, mainly depositors, to onlend for hire purchase, credit sales or leasing. Thus finance houses specialise in providing instalment credit to industrial and commercial businesses, and also to households.

Hire purchase and credit sales appear to be similar, but a basic difference exists in that the ownership of the asset bought on hire purchase remains the property of the finance house during the term of the contract until at some point towards the end it becomes the property of the customer. With credit sales, the legal ownership passes immediately the first payment is made and the borrower stands as an ordinary debtor in the eyes of the law in relation to the finance house.

Leasing has grown considerably, to such an extent that specialist companies have developed, generally subsidiaries of other financial institutions such as banks and finance houses. These usually borrow funds from their parent companies or from other financial institutions. We will learn more about the finance house market in Chapter 6.

4.33 Eurocurrency market

After the Second World War the world, and particularly Europe, was in need of dollars to help pay for rebuilding and development. At the same time, the Americans found that interest rate restrictions at home encouraged them to deposit their dollars abroad where they could obtain higher interest rates. Out of this demand for and supply of dollars arose the Eurodollar market. As the market progressed other currencies joined until today it consists of the major European currencies plus the Japanese yen, and it is now known as the Eurocurrency market; London is the centre of this market. A Eurocurrency deposit is a deposit of French francs by a German in a UK bank. It is a flexible market and has shown that it can easily adjust to changes and adapt to new practices should it so need. It is an international market as it covers not only Europe but also the Middle and Far East. It is a competitive market as institutions compete with one another for the funds of depositors or for the lending of this money to an international borrower. In recent years it has become part of the newly developed Eurobond market, whereby a company wishing to raise capital by the sale of bonds uses this market for the issue.

4.34 Certificate of deposit market

The development of this market has been explained previously.

4.35 Interbank market

In 1971 the government introduced new regulations controlling the operation of the financial sector. Within these regulations the banks had to keep 12.5 per cent of eligible liabilities as a reserve in the form of selected assets. If a bank fell below this reserve it had to arrange its affairs in such a way that it would return to the required reserve. This might mean that a bank had to borrow money, perhaps at a price that was more than it was obtaining from some of its advances. At the same time, some banks found themselves with more funds than they needed. Therefore, it was obvious that in these circumstances a bank with surplus funds would lend to a bank in need of funds. In the 1950s a minor market had developed for just this kind of support for smaller, fringe banks. In the 1970s this market developed, and its activities have become so important that its interest rate structure has considerable influence on the other markets. This is known as the London interbank offered rate (LIBOR). You will learn more of this in a later chapter.

4.36 Intercompany market

This is a small market which developed in the 1960s because of a series of government credit squeezes which made bank funds scarce to businesses. As a result, a self-help system came into being whereby a company with spare funds lent those to another company in need of funds. This market is small because companies are widespread and communication between them is difficult.

Self-assessment exercise

Describe each of the parallel markets in a separate sentence.

4.4 Capital market

This is the market that provides industrial and commercial firms with long-term finance for their capital development. This is termed by economists as investment, and is regarded as the provision of goods not for immediate consumption. The goods themselves consist of inventories (stocks of raw materials and finished products), capital goods (factories, machines and equipment) and residential housing. This market is shown in Fig. 4.3.

Before we consider the functions of the various institutions in this market it is important for us to understand the main types of finance that firms seek.

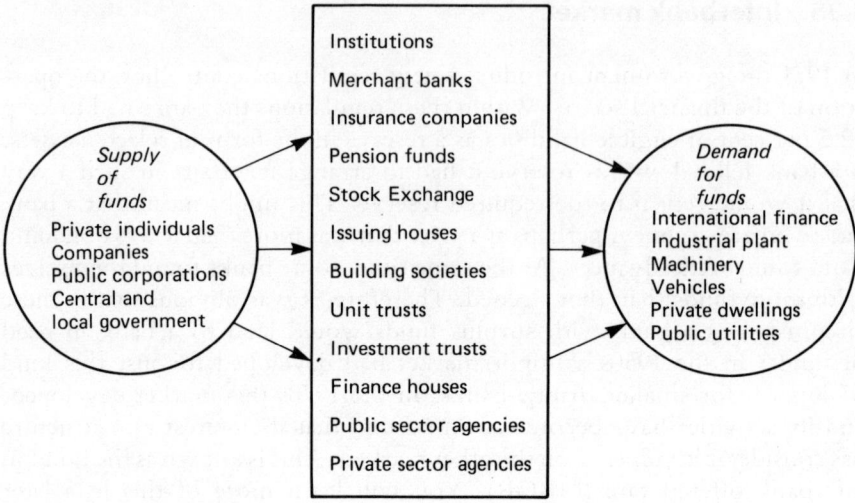

Fig. 4.3 Capital market

Self-assessment exercise

Define 'capital goods'.

4.41 Types of finance

These can be divided into five main areas:

(1) *Equity finance* – for most companies the initial funds are raised by the sale of shares. Should a company wish to raise more funds it can sell additional shares. This is generally by means of a **rights issue** whereby the existing shareholders are given the right to purchase these new shares usually in some proportion to their present holding. This enables them to maintain their financial interest in the firm. If all of these shares are not taken up by the shareholders then, in the case of a public limited company, they might be offered to the general public. Often companies use the service of merchant banks and other issuing houses to manage this public issue. On other occasions, a company may make a direct placing with a merchant bank and receive its money this way. The merchant bank will sell the shares on the market as and when it thinks it is a good time. The type of share on offer depends upon the state of the market – which security will be acceptable to the investing public. Sometimes ordinary shares are taken up and at other times the market only invests in preference shares.

Ordinary shares are the most common and generally the highest risk share sold. This is because they carry no fixed rate of dividend, and because these shareholders are the last to be paid out of profits. If there are no profits at all or if, by the time the other shareholders have been paid, there are no profits left they will receive no dividend for that year. However, these shares generally carry voting rights for their holders.

Preference shares, as their name states, give their holders some kind of preference over the other shareholders. This is usually a fixed rate of dividend on the share, expressed as a percentage. They are also paid their dividend before the ordinary shareholders. The rate of dividend is determined by the level of interest rates at the time of their issue and also on the anticipated profitability of the company. Another advantage to these shares is that, unless it is stated otherwise, the dividend payment is **cumulative**. This means that if any one year a dividend is not paid and in the next year profits are big enough, then double dividend will be paid. This build up of back dividends owed can cover a number of years. This privilege is not given to the ordinary shareholders. However, these shares do not carry any voting rights. They can also be made **participating** which means that if any profit remains after the ordinary shareholders have been paid, then these preference shareholders are eligible for an additional share of the profits.

In the case of public companies already quoted on the Stock Exchange new shares are issued as described above. There are, however, a number of ways that an issue can be arranged for a company which is seeking a listing for the first time. The first method is by means of a 'public issue' whereby the company offers a certain number of shares to the public at a stated price, sometimes this issue is underwritten by a merchant bank or issuing house. The second is by means of an 'offer for sale'. Here the shares are sold to the merchant bank or issuing house at a fixed price, then these institutions subsequently sell them to would-be investors. Usually the company issues a **prospectus** detailing the issue, its financial position and what it believes is its potential for the future. In the case of small companies, the issuing house may just place the issue with its own specific investing customers. Sometimes issues are put out to **tender** so that the investing public are invited to make their own price offer for the shares they wish to buy. In this way the company discovers the market's evaluation of its shares and is able to select only those tenders it wishes to take up. Another system has developed in recent years under a business expansion scheme set up by the government, as part of a policy to encourage enterprise by helping new businesses to start. The government regards this development as beneficial to the economic and technological development of the country. This scheme gives a tax advantage to investors in these new ventures whereby they can offset the price paid for the shares from their total taxable income provided they are held for five years. It is possible to buy these shares in what is known as the 'over the counter' (OTC) market. They are purchased from specific dealers in the City of London. They also make up part of what is known as the unlisted securities market. This is discussed under the Stock Exchange later in this chapter.

(2) *Long-term bonds* – this is the issue, by companies, of pieces of paper called **bonds**.

These bonds have a life of twenty to thirty years, generally carry a fixed rate of interest and are repaid when the time is up. This market has had a limited revival in recent years because of the fall in inflation and the subsequent fall in interest rates. This has been encouraged by the authorities as they see this borrowing as not having the same effect as bank borrowing. Recent tax changes have made certain types of bond very attractive. The first of these is the index-linked bond whereby interest rates are adjusted as the cost of living changes. The second is one whereby a low annual interest rate is paid but the bond is sold at a discount on its face value on redemption. There are other variations linked to these bonds, such as:

(a) Bonds issued with increasing rates of interest over time so that the cost to the company in the early years of the capital asset is not so high.

(b) A company will issue a series of bonds over time so as to meet the particular financial needs of a specific project.

(c) Switch arrangements between a bank loan and an issue of bonds. This is a variable bank loan which, if the long-term interest rate falls to a determined level, then the bank loan will be replaced with a bond issue placed with certain institutions.

(d) In the case of some Eurobonds the holder can opt to have the bond converted into another currency at a predetermined rate of exchange. This reduces the risk of loss from currency fluctuations.

(3) *Bank finance* – there are a whole variety of loans available to firms from the banks. As we will see in later chapters, the interest rate charged will depend upon a number of factors. Generally, these loans are at variable rates of interest depending upon the movements in market interest rates which are reflected in the banks' **base rate**. There are some occasions when the customer can be offered a fixed interest rate or may be given the choice of fixed or variable interest rates.

(4) *Leasing* – this is sometimes called 'off balance sheet finance'. Leasing is an arrangement between a business and a finance house or bank or specialised company whereby the latter buys a capital asset and then rents it out to the business. This type of finance has grown considerably in recent years.

(5) *Government finance to industry* – the government has an industrial development policy in which it aims to make the economic and industrial environment suitable for development. In addition to fostering good economic conditions generally, it can either provide finance in the form of loans, or it can adjust the tax system so that financial incentives are made available to the investing public or firms. In addition, the government may purchase shares in companies rather than provide loans. In particular, this applies to new developments, known as sunrise industries, that are seen to be in

need of government support. At the same time, in order to encourage the depressed regions, the government can give financial incentives to firms willing to set up in these regions.

Self-assessment exercises

1. What is a 'rights issue'?
2. How do ordinary shares differ from preference shares?
3. Describe the procedure for the issue of a new share by a public company.
4. Explain:
   (a) Capital bonds
   (b) Leasing
   (c) Government financial sources to industry.

4.42 Building societies

These are mutual societies that are owned by their customers rather than by external shareholders. They operate in the personal savings market and lend most of their funds to individuals who wish to buy their own homes. There are about 200 building societies with over 6000 branches. In recent years there has been a large number of mergers so that since the Second World War their numbers have declined, but at the same time the number of branches have increased. The assets of the building societies have increased considerably over the years reflecting the greater demand by the public for house ownership. These have grown five times in real terms from 1955 to 1980 and, at the present time, they stand at £86 million.

Building societies offer a variety of savings schemes in the form of shares and deposits (*see* Chapter 5), and use these funds to provide mortgages at variable interest rates repayable over periods of up to thirty years. They also hold large stocks of liquid assets which can be sold to cover any short-run excess of withdrawals and lending over new deposits. Up until 1983 the interest rate levels of the building societies was recommended by the Building Societies Association, but these arrangements were relaxed to give the societies more freedom in setting their own interest rates. This is in line with present government policy of encouraging greater competition in the economy. As can be seen in Chapter 5, there have been moves by the building societies in two main directions. First of all, they have come to work more closely with banks and, secondly, some of their activities can be seen to be in direct competition with the banks. In addition, the government is looking at a new legal framework for the societies to meet the changes that are occurring in the financial environment. The purpose is to extend the building societies' role from their original purpose so that, as well as offering mortgages, they can offer money transmission and conveyance services, and a wide range of quasi-financial services such as giving structural surveys on property, acting as agents for public utilities, acting as insurance brokers and offering stocks and shares for sale to the public.

Self-assessment exercises

1   What are the traditional services of the building societies?
2   What changes have occurred in the activities of building societies?

4.43   Insurance companies

These are a major part of the institutional investing market. About 850 companies are authorised to carry on one or more classes of insurance business in Britain. Of these about 175 are from overseas. About 350 companies belong to the British Insurance Association and these account for 95 per cent of the business. Life assurance is carried out by some 200 authorised insurance companies, and this is also available through a number of friendly societies.

This sector is divided into two main areas:

(1) General business – this provides insurance for policyholders against particular risks such as fire, accident or theft. The policyholder pays a regular premium and if loss is suffered then he is reimbursed. Insurance companies are able to pay these claims from the other premiums and from income earned from assets bought by the premium income.

(2) Long-term business – there are two elements to this provision of life assurance. First of all, there is cover in the event of death and, secondly, there is the savings element which can be incorporated into the contract. The various types of savings schemes offered by insurance companies are explained in Chapter 5.

The assets in which these companies invest vary and include government securities, mortgages, ownership of property and other loans. With general business insurance the demands tend to be short term, and so investments covering these have to be in similar liquid assets.

4.44   Pension funds

These also form part of the institutional investing market. As we will see in Chapter 5 there are three basic types of pension fund:
   (1) State retirement pension schemes
   (2) Occupational pension schemes
   (3) Personal pension schemes

The basic state pension scheme covers everyone but the additional state scheme, which is related to earnings, does not apply to everyone as some employees contract out. These usually belong to private occupational schemes. In some of these occupational schemes employees pay contributions out of earnings; in others they are non-contributory – the pension fund is built up by the employer. Occupational pension scheme funds are usually invested in various assets which in turn earn income for the fund. The most important assets held by these funds are company shares followed by government securities and then property. The state pension scheme operates on a pay as-you-go basis in that current contributions are used to pay current pensions. However, the National Debt Commissioners do place excess funds on short-term loan by purchasing Treasury bills through the 'tap'. Personal pension schemes are for self-employed persons and people who are employed but not in an occupational scheme. They are usually based on insurance policies with life cover as well as the provision of funds when the insured retires. As we have seen, the premiums paid in go into assets which will earn income for the insurance companies. There are three types of schemes:

(1) Insured schemes – this is where the funds are handed over to the insurance company who guarantees certain pension benefits.

(2) Managed pension funds – this is where the money is placed in one managed fund of an assurance company. Usually the level of benefits is not guaranteed.

(3) Self-administered schemes – this is direct investment of the fund into various assets. Usually the trustees of these companies hand over the fund to a group of managers – such as insurance companies or merchant banks.

Self-assessment exercise

State and describe the types of pension scheme that might apply in the following situations:
1   A sole trader greengrocer.
2   A 60-year-old civil servant who has worked in the one department for 30 years.
3   A tool-fitter who works for a small engineering firm with no occupational pension scheme.

4.45   Unit trusts

These are another branch of the institutional investment market. They enable the small saver to receive the benefit from investing in the stock market and, at the same time, spread the risk of the investment, and provide the saver with the benefit of expert management. This is achieved by the formation of a unit trust company which collects the funds from a large number of small savers into one single fund, and then places this in the hands of professional management. These small savers buy a number of units in the fund. Anything from £50 upwards may be purchased. The managers use the large fund within the terms of the trust deed to invest in various securities. The fund may be used to buy a wide range of securities, or it may operate in specific areas like commodities, or regions, or types of company. The saver pays an initial joining fee and an annual management fee for as long as he holds the units. The units can be sold back to the trust at any time although it is possible for the saver to lose some of the capital value of the units, as their daily price reflects the movements in prices of shares held by the fund. Savers receive annual income reflecting the performance of the shares held by the fund. Savers may join the scheme at any time as a buying price is always quoted. Thus the fund quotes two prices – one at which it will sell units to the public and one at which it will buy back units from the public. Obviously, the buying price is always higher than the selling price at any one time. Some unit trusts are very successful while others have only performed moderately or even poorly. Many management companies are subsidiaries of other financial institutions such as banks and insurance companies.

4.46 Investment trusts

These are companies whose objectives are to use the capital received from the sale of shares to invest in other companies. Many of these are quoted on the Stock Exchange and come under their own **investment trust** classification. The investors in these companies do not buy units but are shareholders. The value of the shares reflects the demand and supply of these shares, as well as the performance of the shares held by the fund. Another difference is that the management of the company is in the hands of a board of directors, although some directors hand over the investment management to investment advisors such as merchant banks.

4.47 Stock Exchange

The Stock Exchange is a centralised market for the buying and selling of 'second-hand' securities. These securities consist of stocks and shares of industrial and commercial companies, government securities known as gilt edged stocks, local authority and public sector securities and some authorised foreign company stocks and shares. It is a second-hand market as the securities traded are not new issues but those which are for resale.

Operation of the market

Deals on the Stock Exchange are carried out by jobbers and stockbrokers. Jobbers actually operate on the floor of the Exchange from areas that are called booths. They also have offices outside the Exchange. Jobbers usually deal in one area of shares, buying and selling these shares on their own behalf. When asked, jobbers quote prices at which they will buy and sell their securities. The buying (or offer) price is lower than the selling (or bid) price. The difference is called the **jobber's turn**. These prices do not remain static but vary during trading as the jobber's holdings of a particular share go up or down. If the jobber has to buy more than he can sell so that his holdings go up then he will mark down the selling price. This will tend to discourage the sellers of the security from offering any more. If, on the other hand, the share is being bought heavily by the public the jobber will find his stocks falling so that his selling price will be marked up. If all jobbers find the demand or supply for a particular share is the same then prices will rise or fall accordingly.

A stockbroker does not buy or sell shares on his own behalf but acts as an agent for a customer who cannot enter the floor of the Stock Exchange. For this service he receives commission. The stockbroker, on receiving an instruction from a customer to buy or sell a particular security, either goes to the Stock Exchange, if the business is in London, or has an agent act on his behalf. At first a note is made of the various prices quoted for this security by the different jobbers. The stockbroker aims to obtain the best deal for the client. If he is selling it will be at the highest price; if he is buying it will be the lowest price quoted. Once decided the stockbroker approaches the relevant jobber and makes the deal. At this point it is only a verbal agreement but it is quite safe as the motto of the Stock Exchange is 'My word is my bond' and no trader would go back on his word. In addition, particulars of the transaction may be written on a slip which is placed in a box so that the details can be posted in the Exchange and published in either the Official List or a Supplementary List the following day. At the end of the day's trading the dealers return to their offices and the paperwork for their various deals is begun. The transaction is written up by the broker's clerk in a journal or day book, and he fills out a contract note similar to the one shown in Fig. 4.4. This includes such details as: date, name and address of broker, particulars of the stock and the agreed price, commission (brokerage) payable, along with the transfer stamp duty, VAT and the date of settlement. The next morning the brokers' and jobbers' clerks meet in the Settling Room to confirm the transaction with one another.

Since 1979 shares bought and sold on the Stock Exchange have passed

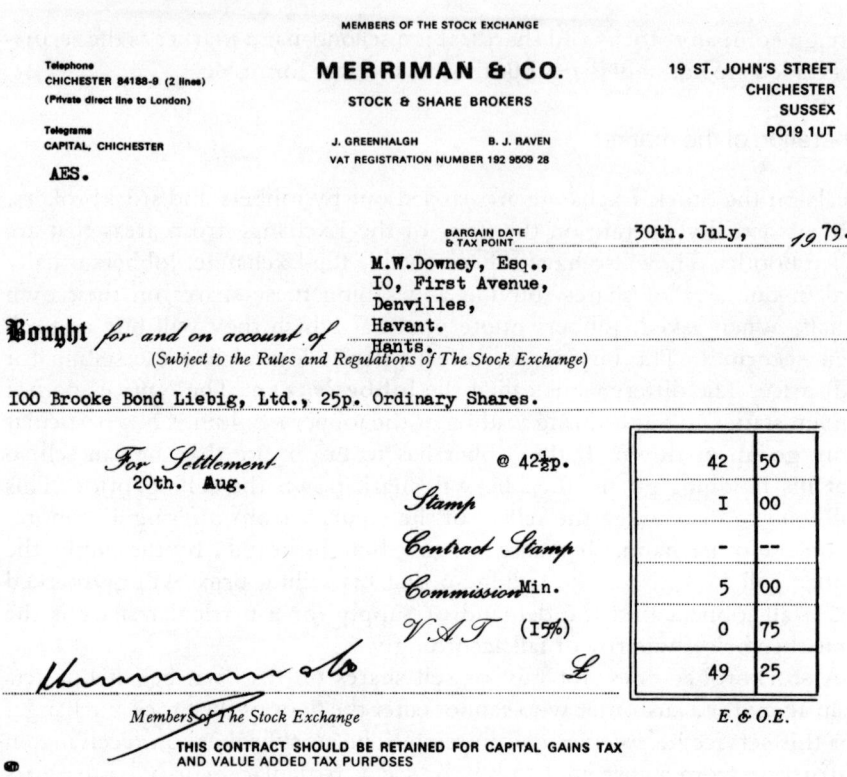

Fig. 4.4 Contract note for the purchase of shares

through a nominal account called the Stock Exchange Pool Names (SEPON LIMITED), sales are placed in this pool and purchases are drawn out of it. The seller of the shares is required by the broker to complete a **stock transfer form**, this is known as a **talisman** transfer; it is a special form and its full title is a transfer account lodgement for investors, stock managers and jobbers. An example of this form is seen in Fig. 9.5. On settlement date, which occurs about every two to three weeks, the transfer and payment of shares is put into effect.

This separation of the broking and jobbing functions of the Stock Exchange is known as a 'single capacity' system. At the present time moves are going on in the City to change this system, particularly the operation of a fixed commission charged by brokers on deals. If these go ahead the single capacity system may also disappear, as it may not prove commercially viable because of the lower broking commission and the greater competition which will enter the market. At the present time, the single capacity system benefits the small investor as he receives totally independent advice from his broker. If broking and jobbing firms merge there may be some danger of this independence being lost. Recent government moves to maintain accountability have been developed with the emphasis on self-regulation rather than external control.

The market often displays various facets of investors' thinking. For example, if investors feel that security prices are likely to rise in the future, possibly because of an improvement in the economy, then there will be a great deal of buying and consequently prices will rise. This is said to be a **bull** market. On the other hand, if the general mood is one of pessimism and investors think that security prices are likely to fall then they will sell so that in general share prices will fall. This is said to be a **bear** market. There are occasions when a new issue of a security about to be traded on the Exchange is bought by investors who believe that the value of the share will rise considerably when it is traded, with the result that they can sell at a profit. In this case the issue is said to have been **stagged**.

As well as dealings in the listed securities the Stock Exchange has developed in two other areas in recent years.

Option trading

This is a contract which gives the holder the right to buy or sell a security at some future specified date at a fixed price. It is not a contract to buy or sell the security but to buy or sell the option. Having gained the contract the holder can buy or sell the option to someone else through the Stock Exchange. For example, a person may arrange to buy ICI shares for £3.70 each in three months time and pay 50p for this option. In three months time the shares may have risen to £4.50 each so that even with the cost of the option the buyer will be able to buy at a discount of 30p per share; if he were to sell them he would make a capital gain. On the other hand, if the option were one to sell ICI shares in three months time at £3.60 and when the time came they were £3.00, then, depending upon the cost of the option, the seller may be in profit. It is possible to buy or sell the option at some price advantage.

Unlisted securities market

Mention has already been made of this market when we discussed equity capital earlier in this chapter. For a full listing on the Stock Exchange, a company must issue a prospectus which gives considerable information about its operation on a continuing basis. Because of the cost of these requirements some companies are not prepared to use the Stock Exchange. In 1980 the unlisted securities market was set up to counteract this problem. It allows companies to raise money by selling shares and for the formalised trading of these shares on the market without the onerous and costly requirements of a regular listing. As these companies are often new ventures a number of very successful enterprises has entered this market, although there have been one or two who have not been successful. 'Over-the-counter' deals whereby certain licensed dealers are able to sell shares directly to the investors have been discussed. There is concern about the lack of regulation of this market outside the Stock Exchange, although there are some self-regulatory bodies set up by the OTC traders themselves.

Self-assessment exercises

1 Name the activities of the Stock Exchange.
2 In traditional activities how does a jobber differ from a stockbroker?
3 How does a 'bull' market differ from a 'bear' market?
4 Explain how the pricing system operates on the Stock Exchange and how the prices on the Exchange fluctuate.
5 What is a traded option? How does the option market work?

4.48 Public sector agencies providing funds

Public Works Loans Board

This was established in its present form by the Public Works Loans Act 1875. Its functions derive from this Act and the Public Loans Act 1968. The Board consists of twelve commissioners who are appointed by the Crown for four years, each year three of these retire. The purpose of the Board is to make loans to the smaller local authorities who find raising money on the capital market difficult. These local authorities must use the loans for the purposes which lie within their borrowing powers. The funds for these loans come from authorisations made from time to time by Parliament. The rate of interest and the fees charged by the Board are fixed by the Treasury. In 1980 the staff of this Board and the National Debt Office were merged to form the National Investment and Loans Office.

British Technology Group (BTG)

This was formed in 1981 by the combination of the National Research Development Corporation and the National Enterprise Board. Its main functions are:

(1) To promote development and commercialisation of technology arising out of public sector sources. These sources include government research establishments and universities. The BTG protects and licenses inventions from these sources, provides funds for their development, seeks licences and negotiates licence agreements. In 1983 the BTG's portfolio contained 6000 British and foreign payments, 620 licences in Britain and overseas and 350 revenue earning inventions.

(2) To provide finance for the development of advanced technology in British industry. Although it provides finance it does not give grants. Its aim is to make a return on its investments so that each transaction is treated on a commercial basis. The finance may take the form of BTG subscribing to the share capital of the company, or direct finance to the project. In its joint venture projects it provides 50 per cent of the cash flow required for the project, but it expects some form of return on its investment by way of a percentage levy on sales. At the present time there are some 400 investments in British industrial companies by the BTG.

(3) To support the creation of growth in small firms – there are many start-up projects financed by the BTG in such areas as computer software, reinforced cement, robotics, underwater engineering and biochemistry.

(4) Support of industrial enterprise in the regions. This is a wider investment role supporting the traditional industries as well as the companies involved in technological innovation.

Development agencies

With the decline in the traditional industries in many regions the government has aimed at the development of new industries. The regions outside England have been particularly badly affected by this decline, the government, therefore, has set up development agencies in Scotland (1975), Wales and Northern Ireland to help promote industrial development. They encourage investment by overseas companies, provide equity and loan capital for industrial projects, provide government factories, have powers to assist small firms and undertake land reclamation.

Export credit insurance

This is provided by the Export Credit Guarantee Department for about one-third of the country's export trade. This includes both goods and services. The main risks covered are:
  (1) insolvency or protracted default by the buyer;
  (2) government action which prevents the British exporter from receiving payment;
  (3) new import restrictions;
  (4) war or civil disturbance in the buyer's market.

The insurance cover starts either from when the goods are shipped or from the time when the contract is made. The premiums for the latter are greater. Insurance may be supported by unconditional guarantees of repayment which are given to banks granting loans in sterling or foreign currencies to the exporter. If the contracts are for over £1m the ECGD will guarantee loans direct to overseas buyers so that they can buy on cash terms – the banks provide finance against these guarantees. For cash or near cash contracts of over £250 000 the ECGD is prepared to give support to performance bonds (*see* Chapter 8).

There is also a scheme to provide insurance for capital investment schemes by British firms where the contracts fail because of war damage, restrictions on remittances and expropriation.

4.49 Private sector agencies providing funds

Investing in industry (3is)

This is a holding company for the Industrial and Commerical Finance Corporation (ICFC) and a number of other organisations. It is owned by the Bank of England (15 per cent of the stock) and the clearing banks (85 per cent of stock). The 3is provides funds to large companies on a long-term basis, while small and medium firms receive loans and equity finance from the ICFC. At present the possible sale of some of the equity in the 3is to private investors is being considered.

Agricultural Mortgage Corporation

This was established by the Agricultural Credits Act 1928. Its share capital was provided by the Bank of England and the commercial banks. It also received a loan from the then Ministry of Agriculture and Fisheries for an amount equal to the share capital. Further funds were provided by the sale of marketable debentures which were then traded on the Stock Exchange. It operates in England and Wales only, there is a separate Corporation for Scotland. It provides funds to farmers who can mortgage up to two-thirds of their land for up to sixty years. The commercial banks act as agents for the Corporation in arranging business.

4.5 Foreign exchange market

This is the market in which a particular currency is bought or sold in terms of another currency. Its participants are:
  Bank of England
  Joint stock banks
  Merchant banks
  Foreign exchange brokers
  Foreign and overseas brokers

All of the big banks have foreign exchange rooms where currency dealings take place. There are foreign exchange markets in foreign centres all over the world and close links are maintained between these markets. Deals are made by telephone and telex and most transactions are through foreign exchange brokers acting for other people. Deals may be 'spot' in which currencies are sold at today's prices, delivery within two business days; or 'forward', contracts for the purchase or sale of currencies more than two days ahead. In the latter case the prices quoted are either at a **premium** or **discount**. If the price is at a premium, this is below spot making it more expensive. If the price is at a discount, it is above spot so that more of the currency may be purchased or more funds gained. This is usually for one year but some forward contracts for main currencies may be for longer periods.

4.6 Financial futures market

This was opened in 1982 and is operated through the London International Financial Futures Exchange (LIFFE). A contract for financial futures is an agreement to buy or sell a standard quantity of a specified financial instrument at a future date at a price agreed by the parties. These financial instruments may be a bond or a currency. There are seven contracts traded on LIFFE, these are:
  (1) Twenty-year gilt edged stock
  (2) Three months sterling deposits rate of interest
  (3) Three months dollar deposit rate of interest
  (4) Sterling
  (5) Deutschemarks
  (6) Swiss francs
  (7) Yen

The first three are related to movements in interest rates and the last four to movements against the US dollar.

This market allows people to hedge against movements in exchange rates or interest rates. It gives certainty, for with a fixed negotiated rate investors will know what they are liable for in the future. At the same time, people can trade in these future contracts so that a capital gain might be made, thereby allowing room for speculation. A safe move to make for a buyer is to make a contract to *sell* a futures contract similar to the one he made to *buy* in the future. In this way he neither gains nor loses. This move is known as closing your position. Participants in this market are the banks, stockbrokers, jobbers and money brokers. Dealing can only take place on the floor of the exchange and delivery is up to fifteen months ahead. There are proposals for an option market to be developed in these futures, and there is some disagreement between this exchange and the Stock Exchange as to where it will operate. The latter regards itself as the traditional options market institution.

Self-assessment exercises

1 Give a list of the projects helped by the British Technology Group.
2 How does the Public Works Loans Board differ from the Agricultural Mortgage Corporation?
3 Make a list of the types of projects and risks covered by the Exports Credit Guarantee Department.
4 What is the difference between the foreign exchange market and the financial futures market?

Assignments

1 The following is an extract from the financial section of a newspaper:
'There has been a considerable breakdown in the traditional barriers between the *classical* and the *parallel markets* in the *short-term money markets* in recent years. The widening of certain *institutions*' area of operation along with the amalgamation of different firms, has led to a great deal of competition for *deposits* and in the extension in the use of the various debt instruments. This has resulted in the *Bank of England* seeing it necessary to revise its system of overall *supervision in these markets.*'

Task 1 In one sentence explain each of the words/phrases in italics.
Task 2 Produce a table showing the institutions and debt instruments found in these markets and show how each are related.
Task 3 What important roles are played by the discount houses in these markets?

2 *Situation.* You are employed in a bank. Your manager has agreed to propose the following motion in a debate at the local branch of the Institute of Bankers:
'That this house believes that building societies should continue to offer only those services for which they are traditionally known.'
He has been called away to a conference just before the meeting and will not have the time to prepare his speech so he asks you to prepare it for him detailing the main points in support of the above proposition.
Task Carry out his request.

5 Savings Investment and Interest Rates

5.1 The nature of savings in the economy, the major savers and their role in the economy

5.11 Savings

For a lay person these are any money which is placed with a bank, building society or other similar institution. For a more precise meaning of savings we need to resort to an area of economics. Economists identify that people earn various types of income whether it be wages and salaries for work done, interest on money loaned, profits on business enterprises or rents from the hiring out of various equipment and land. The services people provide, such as land, labour, capital and enterprise are called **factor services** and the incomes earned from the supply of these are called **factor incomes**. From our total income, whether we be individuals or groups, we spend some or all of it on goods and services. If we do not use all of our income on consumption then that part of income which is not spent on consumer goods and services is classed as saving by economists. We can show this relationship in the form of an equation as follows:

$$Y - C = S$$

where Y = Income
C = Consumption and
S = Saving

For example, if an individual earned £8000 from employment and spent £7500 on goods and services then he has £500 left for saving.

Thus £8000 − £7500 = £500

We can put this equation another way:

$$Y = C + S$$

so that in our example we can see that

£8000 = £7500 + £500

Saving can also be said to be refraining from current expenditure since this excess money may be put into a bank to be available for our summer holidays, or for our old age, or to buy a car in the autumn.

Thus we need to see what can be done in the way of saving. Some people will keep their money in a bank. If they think they will need it urgently this could be in a **current account**. If they do not need the money quickly then a **deposit account** will be more attractive for whatever terms they feel suit their needs. Alternatively, building societies offer comparative services with, in some cases, more attractive returns and benefits. These are a well known area for savings as are the ordinary and investment accounts in the National Savings Bank. There are other, lesser known areas, which can be used by the general public. We will learn more about these later in this chapter.

Modern societies have developed very comprehensive systems which help to cover events which people will or are likely to encounter. Events which are certain to happen, for instance, it is an assured fact that we will either survive to our next birthday or we will die, are covered by **assurance**. If a person takes out an assurance policy which provides benefit if the assured dies before a certain date, or if they survive to this date, it is called an endowment policy and, for the person who survives, the money put into the policy is a form of savings. The contract can be such that the assured receives more money than the total put into it, as is so with a **with profits policy**. A policy which gives benefit only on the death of the assured is not really savings for the assured but for his next of kin.

At the same time, people at work, or those who are self-employed can make contributions into a fund to provide for a pension when they retire. This is in addition to their state pension, provided they have made the necessary contributions. However, current income is reduced by these payments in many cases so that less is available for current expenditure. Finally, people are encouraged to deal in stocks and shares, some directly through the Stock Exchange and others through the purchase of units in a unit trust plan. We shall see later in the chapter how these operate and how they represent saving.

Self-assessment exercises

1   What do you understand by the terms 'income' and 'factor services'?
2   Give a definition of 'savings' from the economist's point of view.
3   If Miss Redex earned £10 000 and spent £7500 what fraction of her income would she save?

5.12 Who saves?

We have already seen that saving comes from individuals and groups. To enlarge upon this further, we can see that savings come from individual private citizens, individuals as businesses (sole traders), people acting in their social groups such as sports clubs and from groups in businesses such as partnerships and companies. Included in the latter are private and public sector organisations. It would be useful at this point to look at the reasons why these different groups of people save.

Individuals

These see the need to save for a variety of reasons. First of all, they may wish to purchase a particular item which is costly and they do not have the funds at the present time to buy it. They can, therefore, save up until the necessary funds have been amassed. Secondly, they save money so that they will be better able to overcome some specific event that may occur, like sickness, unemployment, possible car repairs or replacement. Finally, if they have sufficient funds left out of income they may wish to place these in savings which will eventually increase their wealth by giving a good rate of interest or a capital gain. We have used the term investment previously when referring to this activity but as we shall see later this term also has a specific meaning to the economist.

Groups of individuals

These groups such as sports clubs, churches and interest groups save for some of the above reasons, but also to provide funds for the replacement of worn out assets, or to help develop further assets. For example, in the case of a sailing club it may wish to build a set of changing rooms onto its premises and a bank may not give it a loan until it has some funds of its own to put into the project.

Firms

These include all types in both the public and private sector. The decision to save may be to meet some future current expenditure but more than likely it will be to finance some future capital development, new machines, equipment, or premises. These decisions may be made by the owners themselves, in the case of sole traders and partnerships, or by the management who are acting on behalf of the shareholders. These latter may decide to save by not paying out profits as dividends. Naturally, they need to get the permission of the shareholders to do this. The motivation for this saving comes from the conceived profits that can be made by using the money to buy these assets. We shall see later how the level of interest rates affects these decisions to save and invest.

Before we leave this point it is necessary to consider what factors make the various areas for savings funds attractive. First of all, savers seek a rate of return on their money. This means that generally they expect the value of their money to go up. This does not mean only in money terms, but that its value in relation to the rate of inflation does not go down. If we study the savings market we can see that there are varying rates of interest offered to savers. Some funds, like current accounts in banks, receive no interest at all. This is because of the second requirement of savers – that, of liquidity, or the ability to get at these funds quickly should it be necessary. Here lies a conflict, for generally funds which give a good return are not liquid while liquid funds, as we have seen, are not profitable. Very rarely can we find a savings scheme which offers both to its savers. Thirdly, savers seek security for their funds. They are reluctant to place their savings into the hands of someone who is likely to steal or use them unwisely.

Regarding the need for savings to keep up with inflation, we would think that if they did not do this people would not save. The 1970s showed us the opposite when interest rates were below the rate of inflation but saving still took place and, indeed, reached levels which had not been reached previously.

Self-assessment exercise

What do savers seek from their savings?

5.13 Role of savings in the economy

Savings have been shown as helping to fulfil certain needs for various groups of people, from the point of view of building up funds for future expenditure. However, this is only one factor, the savings institutions themselves must be considered. Banks, building societies and finance houses, who accept these savings do not hoard them up and do nothing with these funds, they are lent to borrowers who seek to satisfy some of their present needs. In general terms borrowers seek a number of things also. First of all, they seek often to borrow this money for longer periods of time than that for which savers deposit it. Secondly, they seek to borrow at as low a cost as possible to themselves. Finally, some seek to borrow large sums of money to pay for large capital projects that will not reach maturity for a very long time.

If we now consider just what these needs are we can see that they may be classified as follows:

(1) Borrowing to buy goods and services for our everyday use, consumables – this borrowing may take the form of arranging an overdraft with a bank.

(2) Borrowing to buy consumer goods which last a longer time, consumer durables such as television sets, motor cars, dishwashers, boats and caravans – for the ordinary person this may take the form of a personal loan.

(3) Borrowing by businesses to purchase all kinds of capital equipment, such as plant and machinery, which help to produce other consumer goods and services. Capital goods are one aspect of what are called investment goods. Investment goods are defined as goods which are not wanted for immediate consumption. In addition to capital goods these include stocks of finished and semi-finished goods and residential housing. This classification helps us to identify two things. First of all, the use of the word **investment** in economist's terms which means something more than what it means in general use. Generally, when someone talks of investment they really mean saving whether it be a deposit in a bank, purchase of shares on the Stock Exchange, or shares in a building society. When an economist uses the word investment a very specialised meaning is implied. Investment goods include such items as plant and machinery, roads, schools and hospitals, stocks of raw materials and finished products and residential housing. We can see that the demand for these investment goods affects certain types of businesses producing these goods.

The second thing we can see from this is that some firms save for these investment goods, others borrow these savings and the savings of individuals to purchase investment goods now. Thus we can see the system whereby current savings are channelled to borrowers, and the institutions are part of this system. We should also note how important these investment goods are to an economy. If we do not replace or increase our capital goods then our ability to produce consumer goods and services declines, so that the population does not have these goods available in the future. As a result our standard of living declines. It follows from this that if we did not have savings we would not have the funds to lend to businesses for their capital goods needs. At the same time, employment in these capital goods industries would decline, the demand of the people in these industries would fall, the consumer goods industries would suffer from declining demand and so it would go on so reducing the income of the community and causing a further fall in the standard of living.

We can show this relationship between savings, investment, income and consumption in a series of diagrams. If we start with a simple economy this relationship can be seen in Fig. 5.1.

This shows the **circular flow of income** and how income flows from households to firms and back to households. In the diagram, factor incomes flow from households to firms by way of spending consumption (C). Households are able to spend from the incomes (Y) they earn from firms. These

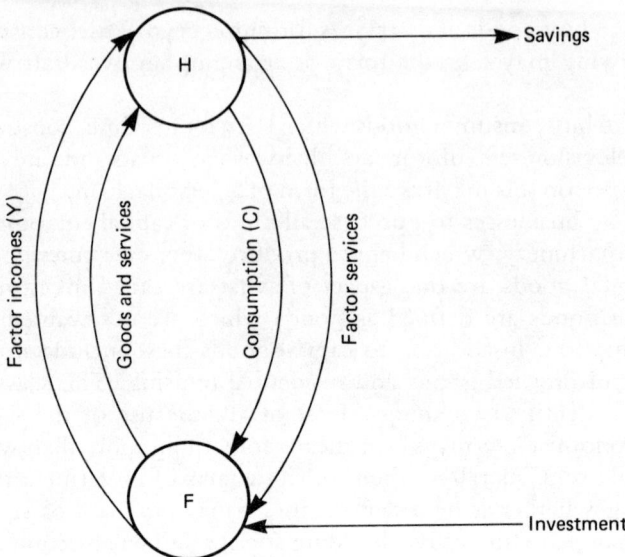

Fig. 5.1 The circular flow of income

incomes consist of wages and salaries, rents, interest, profits and dividends, that are earned by supplying factor services which include land, labour, capital and enterprise. These factor services are used to produce the goods and services which are bought by consumers. However, as we have seen, not all of our income as a nation is spent, some of it is saved. This is regarded as a leakage out of the circular flow. On the other hand, not all demand by firms is created by their income, some is caused by their borrowing for investment which in turn increases demand. Thus this investment is seen as an injection into the circular flow. If the leakages are equal to the injections then there is no real change in the circular flow. The economy is said to be in **equilibrium**. This can be seen in Fig. 5.2.

This shows that incomes equal £1000m. Households spend £800m and save £200m. If investment were to equal £200m then the economy would be in equilibrium with the total flows equalling £1000m. If, however, only £150m came back as investment then the equilibrium would be disturbed, for total demand would be only £950m while the country's ability to produce would be £1000m. There would be a shortfall in demand which would create unemployment. This would work its way through the economy so that eventually equilibrium would return at a lower circular flow. If saving were only £150m and investment were £200m then the opposite would be true. There would be a higher demand for goods and services so that increased incomes would be earned. Consumers would be able to save more so that equilibrium would return at a higher level of income.

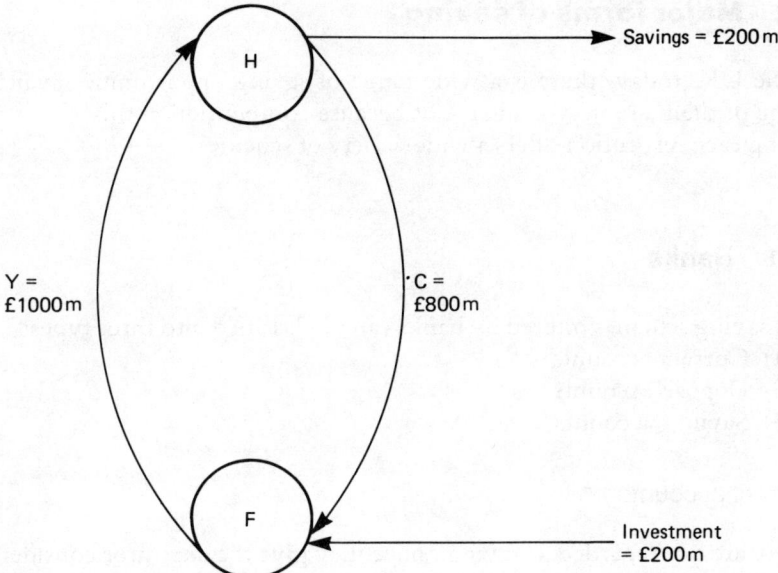

Fig. 5.2 The circular flow of income

Another important aspect of the role of saving lies in the provision of outlets. As long as people wish to save, institutions will exist to meet this need. These institutions themselves provide a number of benefits.

(1) They act as financial intermediaries facilitating the flow of funds from one group of people to another. The wishes of savers – liquidity, return and security – are different to the wishes of borrowers – low cost and long periods of repayment. Financial intermediaries are prepared to meet these diametrically opposed needs so that a flow of funds is maintained.

(2) They provide employment, and the importance of this sector can be seen by its contribution to the national income of the country.

(3) A highly developed financial sector, centred on London, has attracted foreigners who wish to use its financial services and, in payment for these, the country has earned much needed foreign currency.

Self-assessment exercises

1 Give a definition of 'investment' in the economist's terms.
2 Why are savings known as leakages out of, and investment known as injections into, the circular flow of income?
3 What important role is played by financial intermediaries in the savings market?

5.2 Major forms of saving

In the UK, today, there is a wide range of saving opportunities available. Some of them are very similar, but because competition in this area is very strong each institution offers a wide variety of schemes.

5.21 Banks

The saving schemes offered by banks can be classified into three types:
  (1) Current accounts
  (2) Deposit accounts
  (3) Savings accounts

Current accounts

These are not regarded as savings since they give the depositor considerable liquidity plus the use of money transmission services such as cheques and various types of credit transfer. In addition, very few banks offer interest on these accounts. At one time, these were subject to charges no matter how much money one had deposited in them. However, in recent years, banks have offered free banking to customers who kept their accounts at a certain credit level. The actual level depends upon the particular bank with one of the 'Big Four' the Midland, only requiring the account to stay in credit. Although these accounts are not meant for savings, some customers keep large amounts here when they could put the money to better use in a saving scheme. It might even be necessary for a manager to point this out to a customer.

Deposit accounts

These are the traditional savings accounts of the banks. Money placed in these accounts earns interest related to each bank's individual **base rate**. Withdrawal is, contractually, subject to seven days notice but the banks will often waive this for small amounts, or in cases of emergency but the customer will forfeit interest. This is calculated on a daily basis and is credited to the account each half year in November and May. Customers of banks and building societies are credited with interest less a deduction for tax at whatever the standard rate of tax is at the time. If the customer is liable for higher rates of tax, the additional tax due will be recouped by the Inland Revenue at the end of the financial year. A disadvantage is that customers who are not liable for tax have tax deducted and are not able to reclaim it.

Savings accounts

These were set up to encourage children to save, and to form an allegiance to one particular bank. The original schemes used to provide the young person with a money box into which the young person would put his savings. When he had filled it, the box would be emptied by the bank and the money credited into a deposit account in the young person's name. All manner of schemes now exist to attract children to save with banks, from giving away ceramic pigs of various sizes as savings grow, to the offer of a satchel full of 'goodies' if a young person opens up an account. Nowadays all manner of savings schemes are offered to the public in general, not just children, in competition with other institutions. Accounts are offered with varying rates of interest for varying terms; there are schemes for people of different ages with different amounts to save.

The attractiveness of savings facilities offered by banks lies in the fact that banks have a large number of other services to offer and that, in addition, these savings are deemed to be secure. The saver is known to the bank by the operation of a current account; and he will have the bank's relative expertise in the handling of his money.

5.22 Building societies

From early times building societies provided an opportunity for savers to build up funds for the purpose of owning a house, and this is still their main function today. Originally, these were terminating societies whereby a group of people paid into a fund, and as and when the money became available one of the members would receive funds to purchase a house. This continued until all the members were housed, then the society was terminated. This form of savings became attractive to other people who already owned houses since this money earned good rates of interest. This meant that unhoused members were housed more quickly, and that once housed the fund continued so that the word 'terminating' was dropped and, in some cases, replaced by the word 'permanent'. Hence the Leeds Permanent Building Society of today. This system of house purchase became popular so that since 1759 when the first one was set up in Birmingham the number of societies has grown rapidly. In order to attract funds societies offer two main types of account.
   (1) Share accounts
   (2) Deposit accounts

Share accounts

These are not the same as shares in companies. As Lord Dunedin said in a famous case when he referred to 'the so called shares' of building societies, though the name was the same there was nothing more than a faint analogy between them and the shares of a joint stock company. They are commonly called **paid-up** shares and their size often varies with some of the longer-term accounts which may require sums in excess of £500 to be placed in them. A deposit of £1 will open an ordinary share account. Some societies operate savings schemes in which the saver agrees to pay so much per month until sufficient funds have been saved to open up one of these higher deposit accounts. These generally carry higher rates of interest. There are now schemes where money can be deposited on terms from one month to five years with varying benefits for the longer terms. There is no legal limit to the number of shares a shareholder holds but the societies, themselves, place a limit on these holdings. There is a special income tax arrangement with the Inland Revenue so that tax is deducted from the interest before it is paid to the saver, or credited to the account. This is at standard rate so that the higher tax payer will be asked for the difference at the end of the financial year. Interest is paid every half year with some societies calculating it on a day-to-day basis and others on a monthly basis. Each share account is subject to its own conditions of withdrawal and these are governed by the society's rules. However, in some circumstances withdrawal notice may be waived for small amounts or in the case of urgency. Shareholders are entitled to attend the annual meetings of the society and vote on the election of the directors and the acceptance of the annual accounts.

Deposit accounts

Under certain building society Acts the societies are allowed to borrow money from individuals or corporate bodies. These are different from shares in that the depositors stand as creditors of the society and are, therefore, in a different legal position to shareholders. They do not have voting rights and, in addition, they receive a slightly lower rate of interest. The societies have a legal limit as to how much they can borrow in this way, calculated as being no more than two thirds of the amount due from mortgages. A society cannot legally accept deposits with less than one month's notice of withdrawal, but once again this can be waived under certain circumstances. Generally, the larger the deposit the higher the rate of interest received.

In recent years the activities of the building societies have grown. The situation today is one which appears to be a kind of 'love/hate' relationship with the banks. Some activities are carried out jointly with banks, while, at other times, they appear to be in direct competition with each other. The nature of these joint activities in offering financial services to the public can be seen in Table 5.1.

These agreements help both institutions to widen their services and so bring benefit to each. On the other hand, competition exists in the different

Table 5.1 Agency agreements between banks and building societies

Bank	Building Society	Services Provided	Name of Account
Barclays	Halifax	Deposit cheque	Account
Citibank	Leicester	Leicestercard	—
Co-operative	Abbey National	Cheque books Co-op visa card	Cheque Save
National Giro	Leicester	Use of Post Office outlets	
National Westminister	National Provincial	Access Card Use of automated teller machines Access Card	Money Management
Midland	Nationwide	Use of automated teller machines Cheque book	Flexacount
Standard Chartered	Bristol and West	Guarantee card Visa travellers cheques Barclaycard	Moneylink
Yorkshire	Leeds Permanent	Use of automated teller machines	Pay and save

services offered to the public and in the differences in what appear to be similar services. At one time, all banks closed on Saturday mornings but the building societies remained open. The public began to use building society accounts like current accounts and drew cash from them for Saturday spending. The banks retaliated by developing cash point services and, in some cases, opening on Saturday mornings, Barclays being the first. Some banks offer the wide range of services, while others only offer personal banking services which mean services other than the provision of cash over the counter. Cash can be obtained from the machine outside as well as inside the bank. In retaliation building societies are planning to offer automated teller machines, as these cash point machines are called. Another area of competition between the banks and the building societies is in the provision of mortgages. Traditionally the role of building societies, the 1970s saw the banks move into this area. Banks had provided mortgages on rare occasions prior to this, but long-term finance was not popular with the banks. However, with the development of new regulations banks saw an opportunity to develop this kind of business. Banks have also widened their savings schemes, once again to compete against the building societies for the limited funds of savers.

The attractiveness of building societies' savings schemes lies in the fact that savers are given preference when they apply for a mortgage or mortgage extension. A wider range of schemes is on offer, societies are open for more hours than the banks and the interest rates are higher.

It was mentioned in Chapter 4 that the government is looking into the position of the societies and has recommended that their services be extended. If they do move closer towards the bank, their legal standing must be altered.

Self-assessment exercises

1   Draw a diagram to show how the savings schemes of banks compete with those of building societies.
2   What is the difference between a shareholder and a depositor in a building society?

5.23   Pension funds

There are three different types of pension schemes to which people may be subject in one way or another. These are:
  (1) State retirement pension schemes
  (2) Occupational pension schemes
  (3) Personal pension schemes

State retirement pension scheme

The state operates a pension scheme available to all persons in the UK who have reached pensionable age. For men this is 65 years of age and for women it is 60 years of age. Claimants must either have retired or can be treated as having retired from regular employment. Men at 70 years of age and women at 65 years of age are treated as having retired even if they are still working and regardless of how much is earned. People who have retired before state pension age may have to pay voluntary insurance contributions if they are to qualify for a full state pension. A full state pension is only payable to those who have made the qualifying national insurance contributions. In 1978 a new state pension scheme came into operation and will mature after twenty years of contributions. Under this scheme, the retirement pension consists of a basic pension plus any additional earnings related pension. The Social Security Act 1975, which came into force in April of that year, introduced four classes of contribution. Class 1 relates to contributions of employed persons and is collected through the pay-as-you-earn income tax scheme. These are related to earnings so that contributions increase on a sliding scale the more a person earns. Classes 2 and 3 contributions are flat rate contributions. Class 2 relates to self-employed persons and class 3 to earners and others who wish to gain additional benefit or make up existing benefit. Class 4 also applies to self-employed persons but in respect of profits or gains made in the trade, profession, or vocation in which they may be engaged. In addition to employees' contributions, the employer also makes a contribution to the fund and then the state supplements this from its income from taxation. This is because the system is a pay-as-you-go scheme where present benefits are paid out of present contributions. Employers are free to contract out their employees from the state scheme provided that their own occupational pension scheme provided in its place is as good as the state scheme. Contributions of 'contracted out' employees are less than those for 'contracted in' employees.

Self-assessment exercise

Which class of state pension scheme contributions is applicable to the following:
1   A bricklayer, who operates his own building firm.
2   Mrs Johannes, who wishes to make up her contributions to earn a state pension in her own right but who only returned to full-time employment recently.
3   James Russ, who is employed as a capstan lathe operator for a local machine tools firm.

Occupational pension schemes

About half of the working population belong to occupational pension schemes whereby they receive a pension from their job as well as a state pension. There is a variety of schemes but the most common is one related to a person's pay at the time of retirement, and the number of years he has belonged to the scheme. Some schemes are non-contributory for the employee – such as the pension scheme for civil servants, in others the employee makes a contribution as well as the employer. At the present time, tax relief is given on contributions made to the funds. There are limits to the maximum benefits which can be paid out by these schemes. Some provide less than these maximum benefits. These maximum benefits are:

(1) Two-thirds pay after ten years' service.

(2) Cost of living increases are paid using the cost of living index or some other agreed index.

(3) A tax-free lump sum is paid on retirement if at normal retirement age. The maximum for this is one and a half times the final pay after twenty years of payment. If this option is taken then the pension is only half the final pay.

There are four possible schemes.

Final pay scheme – this has been outlined above.

Average pay scheme – the pension is based on the employee's pay for each year in the scheme. A graded scale of earnings is employed, and for each year the pay is in a particular earnings band the employee receives a fixed amount of pension. As the pay rises the amount in each band increases.

Flat rate scheme – an employee receives a fixed amount of pension for each year in the scheme.

Money purchase scheme – the contributions of the employer and employee are added together and the pension is worked out from these. Both contributions are a fixed percentage of earnings so giving the employer control over the total cost. The effect of this scheme is to give employees with varying amounts of service different levels of pension. It could well be that people on this scheme with long periods of service receive a higher pension than people on a flat rate scheme with similar service. The last three schemes outlined above are less common than the first. One of the dangers in all of these schemes is the fact that people who change their occupations regularly may lose their entitlement to benefits. Discussions are going on to try and introduce a system whereby benefits from one occupational pension scheme can be transferred to another scheme when an employee changes his job.

Non-state pension funds are usually accepted as one of the most tax efficient forms of saving. They offer three major advantages. First, payments in by both employers and employees are exempt from income tax. Secondly, the earnings of the assets, into which these funds are placed, are free of tax. Finally, the benefits from the pension fund, if paid out in a lump sum, are at the present time, free of all taxes.

Self-assessment exercises

1   R Kebab is in a final pay occupational pension scheme which pays 3/80 of his average final pay for every year of service in a lump sum, and 1/80 for every year of service as an annual pension. Given the following information calculate his annual pension and lump sum:
   (a) His average annual salary is calculated from his last three years' salaries which were £10 950, £11 750 and £12 820.
   (b) He had thirty-two years of service.
2   What are the advantages of non-state pension schemes?

Personal pension schemes

These were introduced as a result of the Millar Tucker committee which was convened in 1950 to look at the provisions for pension of the self-employed. Its recommendations were incorporated into the Finance Act 1956 and consolidated into Sections 226 and 229 of the Income and Corporation Taxes Act 1970. Subsequent finance acts have included additional provisions all aimed at improving the flexibility and tax position of such schemes.

Although called self-employed plans they are not restricted to these persons only. Perhaps the largest group of people who might be interested in such plans are those employed persons who are not covered by occupational pension schemes.

Therefore, they apply to three classes of person:
- self-employed
- partners in professional or business partnerships
- those people who are not in occupational pension schemes and would have to rely on the state retirement pension scheme only.

In October 1984 it was estimated that about two million workers can be classified as self-employed, about 9.5 per cent of the total work force. Those working full time or part time in organisations which do not have their own pension fund make up about 40 per cent of the work force.

The main aim of any personal pension scheme is to provide the highest benefit in pension at the time when the person retires. How this is achieved depends upon the type of scheme chosen. The different types of policy can be grouped into four types with a common basis of a **deferred annuity** system, whereby a single or regular payment is made. This continues up to retirement age which is usually between the ages of 60 and 75 years.

The four main types are as follows:

(1) *With profit policies* – where contributions are made and a guaranteed minimum pension is given but added to this is a reversionary bonus which increases the guaranteed amount. They usually include a terminal bonus reflecting the surplus gained over the life of the plan, although these are not always certain to be paid. These are very similar to endowment insurance policies. They are popular with people who look for security in their pension and are prepared to sacrifice more adventurous rates of growth.

(2) *Non-profit policies* – these give only a minimum amount of pension. They are a better return over the short period and are, therefore, only suitable for people who are near to retirement.

(3) *Unit linked policies* – with these schemes, contributions buy units in a pension fund. The pension received reflects the success or otherwise of the management of the fund which is reflected in the price of the units at a particular time. Thus if the fund is placed in a successful and profitable savings scheme the benefits paid out are considerable, but of course the fund may not be successful. In addition to the performance of the fund, the size of the benefits received may also be affected by the charges made for management of the fund and the annuity rates set down when the policy is started. Most unit-linked contracts are so funded that they provide a total pension fund which is used to provide benefits and cannot be withdrawn as cash in one lump sum at the end of the contract.

(4) *Deposit administration* – these are the newest type of personal pension plans and work like a bank deposit account. A company takes from the customer the agreed contributions, deducts a charge and then deposits the remainder into an account in the policyholder's name, this has interest added to it at regular intervals. Interest rates are variable depending upon the current market rates, but in some a minimum interest rate is guaranteed. The capital value of the contributions is also guaranteed not to decrease.

The money which is built up by these deposits is then put into a fund and used at retirement to work out the client's pension benefits.

Self-assessment exercise

State to whom personal pension schemes apply and describe them fully.

5.24 Insurance companies

We have already discussed how certain types of insurance policies are regarded as savings as well as providing some form of security should certain events take place. The savings opportunities provided by insurance companies can be broadly classified as follows:
  (1) Endowment policies
  (2) Annuities

Endowment policies

There are about 850 companies in Britain authorised to carry out one or more classes of insurance. Life assurance is handled by some 260 authorised companies and it is also available through some friendly societies. The size of this market gives us a guide to the extent of the competition that exists in this business and, therefore, to the fact that there are a great number of different schemes. Despite the wide variety of schemes, they all have a certain number of features in common. First of all, in their operation these, like other life insurance policies, are for a prespecified time and benefits are paid out if the insured dies within that period. The amount paid out is usually a guaranteed sum. They differ from other policies in that benefits are also paid out if the policyholder survives to the end of the policy term. As the policy benefits must be paid at some time, endowment contracts contain a substantial savings element. This is especially so if the insured reasonably expects to survive the term of the policy. The second feature is the variety of endowment schemes that are on offer. These are as follows:

(1) *Non-profit endowment* – these schemes give a guaranteed fixed amount in the event of the death of the insured, or at the end of the contract if he survives. One of the disadvantages is that high levels of inflation in the economy can reduce the value of the lump sum considerably.

(2) *With profits endowment* – by paying a higher premium than in the non-profit scheme the policyholder receives bonuses on maturity, or if he dies the bonuses which have been credited to date will be paid out on the insurance. As these bonuses are built up annually and are paid out of the profits earned by the insurance company, then the more successful the insurance company the bigger the returns for these policyholders.

(3) *Unit-linked endowment* – under these schemes part of the premiums go towards the purchase of units in a unit trust fund. When the policy matures the policyholder receives benefits which are linked to the value of the units. Often the policyholder has the choice of taking the units and cashing these at a later date when their prices may have risen, or having the cash at the end of the contract. Obviously, the success of the unit trust fund determines the value of the units at any one time. About 90 per cent of the premium is used to buy the units, the remainder is used for administration expenses and for a very modest temporary insurance cover. Schemes vary but the greater the number of units bought out of the premium the more basic the insurance cover. On the other hand, larger death benefits can be guaranteed provided less units are purchased. In the early years these funds were invested in authorised unit trusts, but now insurance companies have developed their own unauthorised unitised funds with greater specialisation in various types of securities such as ordinary shares only, or government stocks only, or in property only. The most popular is a **managed fund** which is a mixture of equities, gilt edged and properties.

(4) *Unit-linked whole life* – this is where unit linked policies have a whole life basis. Benefits are only paid on death whenever that occurs. Policyholders can sell their holdings of units without tax liability provided premiums have been paid for at least ten years. The cash value of the units is linked to the value of the securities held in the unit trust fund. As these vary from day to day so does the value of a unit in the fund.

(5) *Flexible endowment schemes* – most of these schemes are with profits policies with guaranteed surrender values, with bonuses paid and full benefits paid on maturity. Policyholders can only surrender these policies to the insurance companies after ten years. These differ from ordinary endowment schemes in that surrender of ordinary endowment policies before they mature means a considerable reduction in benefits. There are elaborate flexible schemes which allow the policyholder to surrender parts of the policy without ending the whole contract.

(6) *Guaranteed insurability policies* – these allow the policyholder to increase his insurance cover as his financial circumstances improve without having to have medical checks to guarantee health.

(7) *Pure and double endowments* – a pure policy gives benefits if the policyholder survives, but no death benefit if he does not. A double endowment gives double benefits on survival after the length of the contract.

Self-assessment exercises

1 What is the difference between life assurance and insurance?
2 What is the difference between non-profit and with profits assurance policies?
3 Explain the difference between pure and double endowment schemes.

Annuities

An annuity is a contract whereby the purchaser, having agreed to provide a lump sum or a number of payments, receives a guaranteed income usually for the rest of his life. An annuity is an insurance policy in reverse. In this kind of agreement the risk to the insurance company is not that the insured will die but that he will live a long time. This would mean that their payments to the insured could be rather heavy. The cost of the annuity depends upon the person's age, sex and the way in which the annuity is to be paid. A payment to be made at the beginning of the month or quarter is more expensive than at the end. This is because the company could make a payment and the person might die, whereas if the person dies and payment is at the end of the period no payment will be required.

There are four common forms of annuity:

(1) The most common type is the *immediate single life annuity*, where for a lump sum the person receives immediate payments at the end of each year, half year, quarter, or month. This is useful if you want to turn capital into income and feel that the income from use of the capital in any other savings scheme would be insufficient to live on, and there would be a danger of cutting into capital.

(2) Some policies have the payments put off until a later date – *deferred single life annuities*. Some offer to return the premiums if the policyholder dies before any benefits are paid out.

(3) Some agreements can be made so that benefits are paid for a fixed time regardless of the death of the purchaser. These are *annuity certain agreements*.

(4) Some agreements allow for payments to be made only if some particular contingency occurs – *contingent* or *reversionary annuities*. An example may be where payments are to the wife if she is still living at the time of the husband's death.

(5) Some agreements include benefits to both husband and wife while both are alive and continue at a lower level after the death of one of the partners. These are *joint life* and *last survivor annuities*.

Self-assessment exercise

In what ways does an annuity differ from an insurance policy? Explain fully.

5.25 Unit trusts

A unit trust is a mechanism which allows a large number of savers with small savings to pool their money in a single fund and to put this accumulated fund into the hands of professional management. It is a *trust*, with a trust deed, subject to strict rules and with a trustee to whom the management must answer. They are set up by management companies which advertise for investors and arrange for the placing of their money into various securities. Savers have to pay a management fee for the management services. Before they can advertise they must be authorised by the Department of Trade and Industry which ensures that the fund operates within the various legal requirements and that subscribers' funds are adequately protected.

The trust deed

As well as the rules of the unit trust the deed contains:
  (1) How the prices of the units are to be calculated.
  (2) What the managers can charge.
  (3) Some general investment principles, for example, that not more than 5 per cent of the fund will be invested in any one share, or that investment will be only in those shares listed on the Stock Exchange.

Protection under the law

Protection is given under the Protection of Fraud (Investments) Act whereby:
  (1) Unit trust management must have a reasonable amount of money behind it.
  (2) The fund must be in the hands of an independent large trustee.
  (3) The fund must operate strictly according to the rules set out in the trust deed.
  (4) The management will lose the benefits of authorisation if they fail to obey the rules.
  (5) Only authorised unit trusts can advertise for subscribers.
  (6) No unit trust may engage in door-to-door selling.

What it costs

Unitholders when buying units have to pay a unit price which includes payment to the management company for administration, plus the cost of the investment, plus the duty due on the investment. Two prices are quoted in the financial press for any one type of unit. The higher price refers to the price for which the unit trust company will sell the units to prospective purchasers. This is called the **offer** price. The other price is the one at which the company will buy back units from holders. This is a lower price and is called the **bid** price. Strict rules apply to their calculation. The management charges include an initial service charge and a management fee. Strict rules also apply to the composition and total of these two charges.

General aspects

There are over 800 unit trust schemes on offer in the UK today. These are operated by specific companies, or banks, or insurance companies with unit trust departments. Unit trust funds are either **general funds** in which investments are spread across a wide area of securities, or **specialised funds** in which specific areas are selected such as commodities, or areas of the world like USA or Japan.

Confusion could exist between unit trusts and investment trusts. The difference is very basic. Both use funds to invest in securities, but subscribers to the latter are shareholders in these companies. The holders of unit trusts do not occupy the same legal position.

Advantages and disadvantages of unit trusts

(1) *Advantages* – first, they allow small investors to participate in investment in companies without having large funds and, at the same time, they are able to spread the risk of losing this money over a wider range of securities than if they invested directly on the Stock Exchange. The wide range of securities held by the fund means every individual unitholder has a small interest in each one of these companies. Secondly, subscribers to units are able to gain the benefit of expert management of their investment. Thirdly, the system of buying and selling units is simple so that even the investor with a small sum of money can participate easily. Fourthly, there are tax benefits to unitholders under capital gains tax when they sell their units.

(2) *Disadvantages* – first, this form of investment is not as exciting as investing in the stock market oneself. Secondly, since control of your money is in the hands of managers, there is a possibility that you could lose an opportunity of selling the securities when they are at the top of the market and so making a 'killing'. Thirdly, there are many unit trusts available to the would-be investor and they are all not equally successful. It is a matter of choice and those chosen for you might be less profitable.

Self-assessment exercises

1 Give four examples of some of the clauses that may be found in a unit trust 'trust deed'.
2 What is the 'bid' price of a unit?
3 How do unit trusts differ from unit trust linked insurance policies?

5.26 National savings

Savings banks have their origins in the nineteenth century and were established to encourage saving among the lower income groups. With the development of our industrial society the new 'artisans' found that they had funds to spare, but, at the same time, they needed to provide for any unexpected contingencies.

The National Savings Bank developed from the Post Office Savings Bank established in 1861. It became the National Savings Bank in 1969 just before the Post Office became a public corporation. This organisation offers two basic accounts.

Ordinary account

This is a basic savings account which allows relatively easy access to the saver's funds. This facility is available to individuals, trusts, charities, clubs and friendly societies. The minimum deposit is £1 and the maximum holding is £10 000. Interest is paid on these accounts with a higher rate for amounts in excess of £500 and a lower rate for amounts below this. Interest up to £70 per annum is free of tax. Up to £10 may be withdrawn at any Post Office, but regular customers can withdraw up to £250 on demand from chosen Post Offices. The holders of these accounts also receive free standing orders and use of the paybill scheme.

Investment account

This is for people who wish to save money over a longer term and so receive a higher rate of interest. In addition to those groups able to hold ordinary accounts, this facility is also available to registered companies and other corporate bodies. The minimum deposit is also £1 but the maximum holding is £50 000. The higher rate of interest is calculated on a daily basis. Interest is paid in full but this is liable to income tax at whatever is the individual's rate of tax. Withdrawals require one month's notice in writing. To do this the customer collects a form from the Post Office, completes it stating the amount to be withdrawn and the method of payment and places the form in the pre-addressed, prepaid envelope for posting to the relevant office. The higher rates of interest make these accounts very attractive to non-taxpayers. If they were to put this money into bank accounts or building societies they would find that the interest would be paid net of tax, and they would be unable to claim it back.

Some of the remaining forms of national savings are available through banks as well as through the Post Office. These are:

(1) *National savings certificates* – these are a form of loan to the government, the certificate is a debt instrument being a receipt for the amount loaned. This form of saving is aimed at the longer-term saver as the longer the certificates are held the higher the rate of return. They are basically agreements to lend this money for five years, but there is a facility for the holder to cash these at a reduced rate of interest before the five years are up. Eight

days' notice must be given before they can be cashed. They can be purchased by individuals (singly or jointly), trusts, charities, clubs, or friendly societies. As the interest is free of income tax and capital gains tax, they are attractive to high level tax payers.

(2) *Premium savings bonds* – these are one of the most popular forms of saving in the UK. They were first introduced on 1 November 1956. Instead of earning interest, each bond offers the holder a chance of earning a money prize in a draw. The minimum purchase is £5(5 units) and the maximum holding is £10 000(10 000 units). Bonds are sold in multiples of five units. They can be purchased by individuals over 16 years of age. Bonds may be bought for children under 16 by parents, guardians, or grandparents. They must be held for three clear calendar months before being eligible for a prize draw. Every month holders have a chance of winning some 100 000 prizes representing, from 1 November 1984, 7.75 per cent of the value of the bonds eligible for prizes. Prizes are paid free of UK income tax. Withdrawals need at least eight working days' notice. A new prize structure was introduced in November 1985.

(3) *Index-linked national savings certificates* – one of the disadvantages of ordinary national savings certificates is that even if they are held for five years they represent a fixed return, so that during times of high inflation they might represent a significant loss in face value. The UK experienced high levels of inflation during the 1970s, and so the government, to make savings certificates more attractive, introduced national savings certificates where the rate of return was linked to the cost of living index, or more correctly the index of retail prices. This meant that the money placed in these certificates kept its value – in real terms it would be worth at the end of the five years as much as it was at the beginning. They are available to individuals (single or jointly), trusts, charities, clubs and friendly societies. The minimum holding is £10(one unit) and the maximum is £10 000 for one issue, other holdings may be held in other issues. Provided the certificates have been held for at least one year the repayment value is based on the index of retail prices and its recent performance from one month of purchase. A bonus of 4 per cent of the purchase price is paid on the fifth anniversary. A further bonus of 4 per cent is payable on the tenth anniversary of purchase. Interest is paid free of income tax and repayments free of capital gains tax. Eight clear working days' notice is necessary before withdrawal. Supplements are paid for previous holdings at various amounts as long as people still hold the certificates. One of the disadvantages of buying these certificates is that if interest rates are higher than the rate of inflation then the returns are lower than those that could be gained from other savings. For this reason, the government introduced supplementary payments.

(4) *Income bonds* – these allow savers the opportunity to save large sums of money with national savings and to be paid the income from this at regular intervals. They are available to individuals (singly or jointly), trusts,

charities, clubs, friendly societies, registered companies and other corporate bodies. The minimum holding is £2000 and the maximum £50 000. Bonds are sold in multiples of £1000. At the present time, the interest rate is calculated on a daily basis and is paid out on the fifth of every month after the bond has been held for six months. In order to keep the bonds attractive to savers, the rate of interest on these bonds can be varied at six weeks' notice. Income can be paid directly into a bank account, or to a National Savings Bank account, or can be sent to the saver direct by post. Interest is payable in full, but it is subject to income tax at whatever rate the holder is liable. Withdrawal is on three months' notice. After the first year, if three months' notice of withdrawal is given interest is paid in full. If the money is withdrawn before the first anniversary of purchase the bonds earn only half the published rate.

(5) *Deposit bonds* – these allow the saver the same opportunity as income bonds, but instead of paying out the interest it is allowed to build up over a period of time. They are available to individuals (singly or jointly), trusts, companies and voluntary bodies. The minimum purchase and holding is £250 and the maximum is £50 000. Bonds are sold in multiples of £50. Interest is calculated daily but is credited yearly on the anniversary of purchase. Again the rate may be varied at six weeks' notice but is kept at a level which is competitive with other market rates. Every year a certificate is sent to the holder on the anniversary of the day of purchase showing the current value of the bond. Interest is paid at full rate but is subject to income tax and capital gains tax at the individual's full rate. Withdrawals require three months' notice. If the bonds have been held for a full year they receive full interest on withdrawal. Bonds which are repaid before the first anniversary of purchase earn half the published rate. Withdrawals must be for at least £50 a time and the holder must leave at least £50 in value in the bond.

(6) *Yearly plan* – this allows savers to put aside regular amounts of money over twelve monthly periods. Payments are by standing order, and after a year of these payments the saver receives a yearly plan certificate. Further payments can be made to purchase additional certificates every year following. The minimum amount of saving each month is £20 and the maximum £100. These plans can be taken up by individuals and sole beneficiary trusts only. Interest is paid in full if twelve monthly payments are made and the certificate is then held for five years. They have the added bonus of being free of UK income and capital gains tax. Withdrawal is after two weeks' notice and by crossed warrant only.

(7) *National Savings Stock Register* – this allows the small investor to purchase government stocks and shares without going to a stockbroker, either through the Post Office or the National Savings Stock Register. This does not apply to all government stocks but only specific ones. The prices quoted for the purchase of the securities apply to their price on the market on

the day of purchase. The purchase on one day by an individual cannot exceed £10 000 but there is no limit to the amount that can be purchased over a period of time. The fees charged are very competitive with the other ways of buying these securities.

The attractiveness of national savings to savers lies in the great variety of schemes available, in the first instance. Secondly, they are seen as being very secure since they are linked to the government. Returns on these savings are very competitive with other forms of saving particularly where tax concessions are attached. As they are sold through Post Offices, they are readily available to the general public.

Self-assessment exercises

1   Complete a table showing the details of the various savings schemes for national savings to include:
   (a) Type of account
   (b) To whom available
   (c) Amounts to be invested
   (d) Tax position
   (e) Withdrawals allowed
   (f) Other details necessary
2   Why are investment accounts in national savings of interest to non-tax payers?
3   What is the difference between ordinary and index-linked national savings certificates? Under what conditions in the economy are the latter more attractive than the former?
4   How do deposit bonds differ from income bonds?
5   How do the attractions of savings in banks differ from those in the National Savings Bank?

5.27 Local authorities

Most of the income of local authorities comes from the rates charged on the property within their administrative areas. These are supplemented by government grants and any fees and charges that they may make. Any surplus from these sources over current expenditure goes towards capital expenditure. A short fall in funds for capital expenditure is met by borrowing. A local authority has three sources from which to borrow. First of all, it can borrow from the government for each local authority has a quota up to which it can borrow from the Public Works Loans Board. We have already discussed this body in Chapter 4. Secondly, they can borrow from the money markets and the banking world through the issue of bonds. These latter are part of the short-term borrowing needs of the local authority to meet any short fall in current expenditure against current income. In addition, some local authorities offer deposit facilities to the public which are at competitive rates compared with other savings institutions. They are usually term loans offering interest rates at a level which is slightly higher than other market rates. This money is often used by the local authority to finance a specific capital project which the local authority regards as necessary but cannot fund from other sources. In recent years borrowing by local authorities has been reduced as a result of government policies to cut the public sector borrowing requirement in order to bring inflation under control (*see* Chapter 2).

5.28 Finance houses

As we have seen in Chapter 4 the balance sheet of a finance house contains, on the liabilities side, an item 'deposits'. Some finance houses raise funds by inviting the public to deposit money with them. These are in direct competition with the longer-term deposits in banks, building societies and other deposit-taking institutions. They advertise in the press and by post for depositors, and offer attractive rates which are sometimes slightly higher than those in other savings institutions. Some offer other financial services. In the 1970s they became very active setting up in direct competition for savings with the banks and building societies. Nowadays, these latter institutions are equally competitive and, as we saw in Chapter 3, some finance houses are linked with banks. We have already seen that they are part of the short-term money market, and in Chapter 6 we shall see the exact nature of their role.

5.3 Interest rates in theory

Now that we have looked at the various savings opportunities it is, perhaps, useful at this point to consider what determines interest rates both in theory and in practice, and to see what influences the level of interest rates in the UK economy. In theoretical terms there are two basic theories about interest rates, these are not necessarily opposing, rather the second theory is seen as an extension of the first. These theories are:

5.31 Loanable funds theory

We should be aware of how important the rate of return is to both savers and borrowers. In fact this rate of return or rate of interest is the **price** that savers receive for the use of their money, and also what borrowers have to pay to use it. It is possible to say that the saver is being paid for relinquishing the use of his money. In any theory relating to price

Demand for money

Early economists saw that the demand for money came from a desire to use that money to buy goods and services. The demand from individuals and households came so that they could buy consumables and consumer durable goods and services. Perhaps the nearest they got to buying investment goods was in the purchase of their homes. With businesses, their borrowing was to meet both current and capital expenditure. To both of these groups, the cost of borrowing was seen as being important as the higher the rate of interest the less they would be inclined to borrow. Individuals and households are less inclined to borrow if they fear that they may be unable to meet the cost of the regular repayments. Businesses may fear that the return they expected from the assets bought with the money might not be adequate, so that over the life of the project a loss may be incurred. In these circumstances there is a reluctance to borrow. We can demonstrate this reaction to interest rates by use of what is called the normal demand curve.

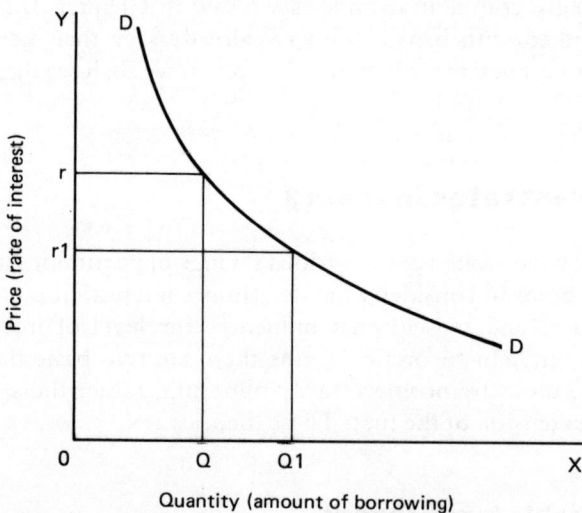

Fig. 5.3 Demand for loanable funds

You will note that we have called Fig. 5.3 the demand for loanable funds for this is what the early economists called this demand to borrow money. In the diagram the interest rate is r and the amount of borrowing is OQ. At the higher interest rate of r the demand for loanable funds is seen as being OQ. At the lower interest rate of r1 the demand for loanable funds has risen to OQ1. This reaction to changes in interest rates will be the same along the whole length of the curve.

Supply of money

Once again the early economists saw this not as a total supply of money but as a supply of money for people to borrow or, in other words, the supply of loanable funds. We saw in Chapter 2 that the supply of money meant something else. Savers supply the funds which can be onlent by the financial intermediaries. They save for a variety of reasons. The early economists saw the basic reaction of savers to interest rate levels as being important in determining these interest rates. They believed that if interest rate levels were high then more people would be prepared to save money. On the other hand, if they were low less money would be saved. This reaction of savers can be seen in Fig. 5.4.

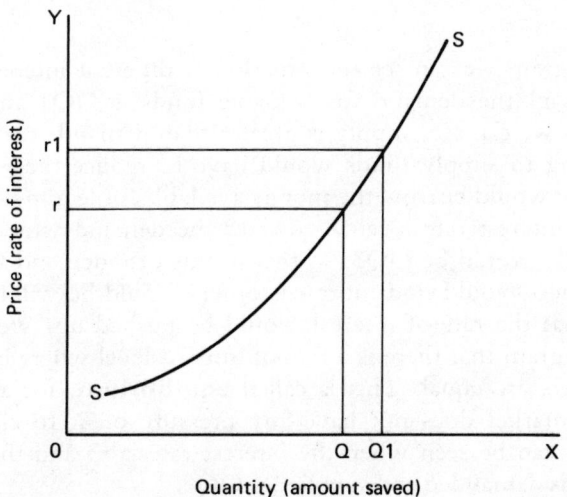

Fig. 5.4 Supply of loanable funds

In this diagram if the interest rate is r then the supply of funds is OQ, but at the higher rate of interest of r1 the supply has risen to OQ1. This shows the opposite reaction from people who are wishing to borrow loanable funds.

We have now seen both sides of the market regarding loanable funds – the reaction of those people who come to borrow loanable funds (demand) and the reaction of those willing to provide loanable funds (supply). In Fig 5.5 we can see just how these two sides react to one another.

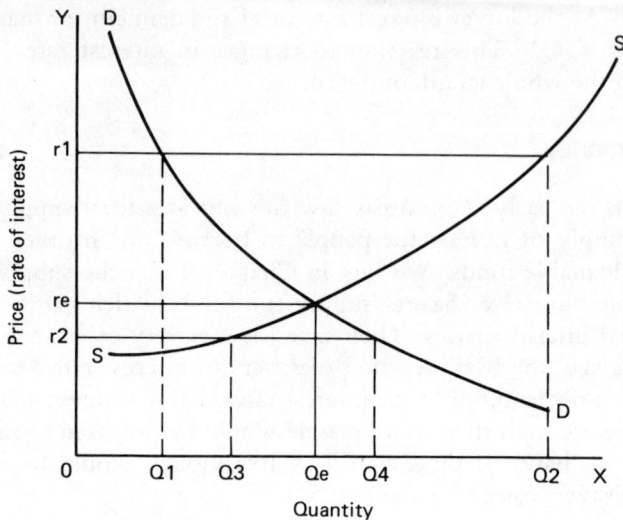

Fig. 5.5 Market for loanable funds

In this diagram we can see the situation at different interest rate levels. If the rate is r1 the demand for loanable funds is OQ1 and the supply OQ2 and, as we can see, supply is greater than demand. As a result those people willing to supply funds would have to reduce their interest rates so that people would borrow the money available for lending. On the other hand, if the interest rate level were at r2 the demand would be at OQ4 and the supply would be OQ3, so that in this case demand would exceed supply. Lenders would find more customers would be willing to borrow money so that the rate of interest would be pushed up. We can also see from this diagram that there is a rate of interest level where both suppliers and borrowers are equal. This is called **equilibrium**, for at this rate of interest the market does not have any pressure on it to change. In the diagram this can be seen when the interest rate is r3 and the quantity of loanable funds demanded and supplied is OQe.

The early economists then showed that if either demand for or the supply of loanable funds were to change then this would have an effect on the level of interest rates in the economy; for example, if there was an increase in the demand for borrowing with the result that a new demand curve came into operation. This can be seen in Fig. 5.6 where the demand curve shifts from DD to D1D1. If the supply does not change, we can see that at an interest rate level of r1 the demand for loanable funds will no longer be OQ but OQ1. The demand OQ1 exceeds now the supply of OQ. Suppliers of loanable funds find that more customers are seeking to borrow money so that interest rates rise, this rise only stops when equilibrium is restored, the interest rate level is at r2 and the quantity of money at OQ2.

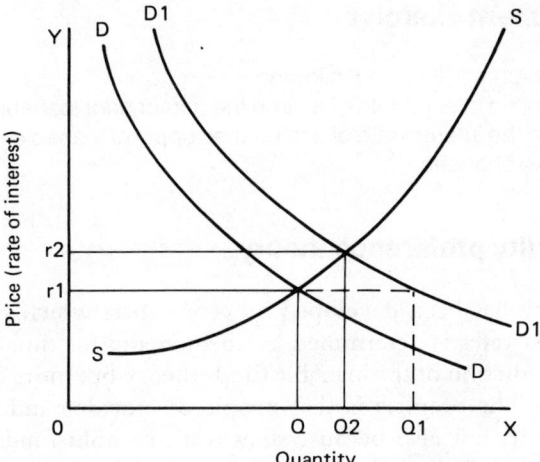

Fig. 5.6 Effect of an increase in the demand for loanable funds

On the other hand, if there was a shift in the supply of loanable funds then this could also have an effect on the level of interest rates. This is shown in Fig. 5.7. Here a rise in the supply of loanable funds is shown by a shift in the supply curve from SS to S1S1 with the result that at the interest rate of r1 the supply OQ1 exceeds the demand OQ. Institutions wishing to lend money find that they can only do this if they reduce the level of interest rates. Therefore, these will fall until equilibrium is restored at an interest rate level of r2, the quantity of money being OQ2.

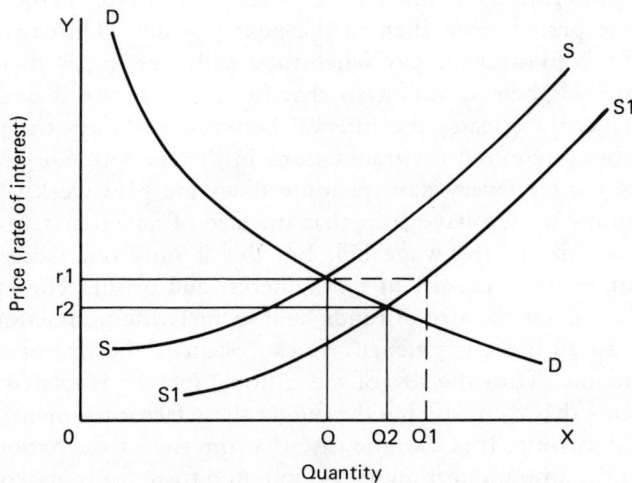

Fig. 5.7 Effect of an increase in the quantity of loanable funds

Self-assessment exercise

Draw graphs which will show the following:
1   The effect on the interest rate of a fall in the demand for loanable funds.
2   The effect on the interest rate of a fall in the supply of loanable funds.
3   Explain these changes.

5.32   Liquidity preference theory

Another theory has been developed by economists which shows how the level of interest rates is determined by the demand for money. This is not seen as a contradiction of the loanable funds theory but more of an extension of the theory. The premise is that people do not demand money purely for the use of it, but also because they want to hold funds in money or near money form. This will, in the view of J M Keynes, who expounded this theory, help them to remain liquid. Liquidity really means flexibility. Keynes saw this preference for liquidity arising from three motives as explained below.

Transactions motive

This is the money we need to hold to meet the every day transactions we encounter from day to day. As we saw at the beginning of this chapter, money circulates round the economy in a flow from households to firms and back again to households. If this flow was instant so that the money paid out was received at exactly the same time, then there would be no need to hold money for transactions balances. However, this is not the case. People are paid at one time, and then they need to spread their payments out over the period from then to the next pay day. Thus firms have to build up funds to meet the day when they will have to pay their workers. Workers spread their spending so that funds are returned over a period of time. Thus the greater the interval between pay days the greater the store of money required for transactions in that period. We need to hold less money for our every day spending if we are paid weekly than if we are paid monthly. We have seen that the size of any transactions balance relates to the size of the wage bill, but this is only one factor payment, other factor incomes consist of rent, interest and profit. The rate of flow of these also affects the size of funds held to meet the transactions motive. If we add up all these payments, we can estimate the size of a country's national income. Thus the size of the national income is related to the size of those items that comprise it – the bigger these factor payments the bigger the national income. It is also the case that the size of the national income determines the amount of money held in liquid form for transactions needs. If the national income rises people have more money and, other things being equal, they tend to spend more so that they need to hold more funds to meet this additional spending. Economists regard these changes in national income as being the main determinant in the level of transactions balances held, and see the level of interest rates as having no effect on the size of these transactions balances.

Precautionary motive

We have seen that people hold money balances because the flow between receipts and payments is not synchronised. What is uncertain, however, is the extent to which a short fall is likely to occur when payments out exceed payments in. On some occasions, we may meet demands on our money balances which we had not expected. A business is not certain when a creditor is likely to call for his money, or if an expense may suddenly increase. Individuals or households are not certain when, for instance, the car is likely to break down or a sudden expense may materialise. In order to meet any sudden demands for cash, people hold balances as a precaution against this uncertainty. Again the ability to hold these precautionary balances depends upon the level of income, with the higher income groups being able to hold a greater level of precautionary balances. Businesses may find that the return on using these idle balances is greater than the risk of being caught without the necessary liquidity, so they may reduce their balances to very low levels. The extent to which a firm carries out this policy depends upon the availability of short-term credit and its cost.

Speculative motive

This reason for holding money in liquid form stems from uncertainty about the future. Keynes related this uncertainty to the prices of bonds – fixed interest government securities. People react to what they think the likely events of the future will be. Thus if people think the prices of these bonds are likely to fall in the future they will sell them, as they do not want to be caught holding an asset which has reduced in value. They will, however, wish to purchase these bonds when they have fallen so low that they think future prices are likely to rise. By acting in this way people are said to be acting speculatively – that is speculating on the future prices of bonds – as the expected event may not occur and they may lose out. We can also see that by their action these speculators are moving in and out of liquidity. Holding bonds can be seen as being in an illiquid position for the holder does not have the flexibility of being able to spend the money should the opportunity occur – it takes time to turn them into cash. When they sell bonds they gain cash so they can be said to be moving from illiquidity to liquidity. On the other hand, the buying of bonds is a movement from liquidity to illiquidity. The very fact that speculators move into and out of bonds has an effect on their prices. When people sell thinking prices are going to fall, the supply of bonds generally exceeds the demand so that the expected fall in price occurs. If people think that bond prices are likely to rise then they purchase bonds, they move from a liquid to an illiquid position, with the result that demand exceeds supply so that prices do rise.

These changes in the price of bonds affect the return received on these bonds – the **yield**. For example, if a 10 per cent Treasury stock price falls from £100 to £50 then the yield to the new holder, who paid £50 is 20 per cent. This can be explained by the following. Every year the Treasury pays out on this bond £10 interest to the holder regardless of its price on the market. This is 10 per cent on the nominal value of the bond. Therefore, if you pay £50 for it you will still receive £10 gross interest per year. If we use a simple interest formula we can see that this represents a 20 per cent dividend:

$$\frac{£10}{£50} \times \frac{100}{1} = 20 \text{ per cent}$$

Thus if this price fall came about as a result of a movement from illiquidity to liquidity (people sold their bonds thinking prices would fall) then the speculative motive has affected the return on these bonds. If this return then becomes greater than that on other forms of savings, it becomes more attractive to those people who are seeking a return on their savings. They might move savings out of these lower savings areas into bonds. Institutions losing this interest would increase their level of interest rates to stop this outflow. We can see here that as a result of speculative action on the part of bondholders, interest rates in the community rise in general. The position is reversed if speculators buy bonds in anticipation of their price rise. The consequent price rise causes the yield on these bonds to fall. Holders who seek return on their saving may now find better returns elsewhere. Institutions gaining these savings may find they have additional funds coming in and, in order to be able to lend these, interest rates may come down. Thus as a result of speculative action the general level of interest rates falls.

The operation of this theory can be seen in the following diagrams. The total liquidity preference is the total of the transactions, precautionary and speculative motives. If we designate the following values to each, we can see how to bring them together.

Let L1 = the transactions motive
Let L2 = the precautionary motive
Let L3 = the speculative motive
Therefore, **Liquidity Preference**(LP) = L1 + L2 + L3

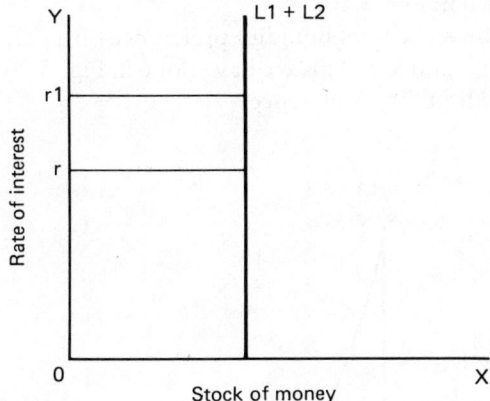

Fig. 5.8 Transactions and precautionary motives and interest rates

Keynes stated that L1 and L2 were not directly related to interest rates and this can be shown in Fig. 5.8.

This shows that the level of money for the transactions and precautionary motives is not related to the level of interest rates, so that no matter what the interest rate is this money remains at a fixed level. On the other hand, we have already seen that the speculative motive is related to interest rates as we show in Fig. 5.9.

As we can see, when liquidity for speculation is low then interest rates are

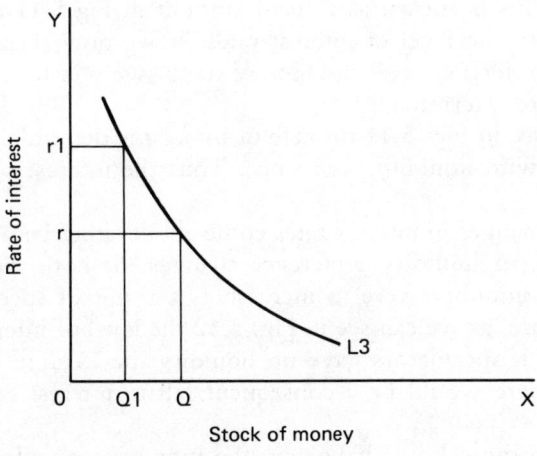

Fig. 5.9 The speculative motive and interest rates

high, and when it is high then interest rates are low. This helps to explain the example shown in Fig. 5.10.

If we wish to show the total liquidity preference on a graph, we need to combine Figs 5.8 and 5.9. This we have done in Fig. 5.10 where the line LP is the total liquidity preference.

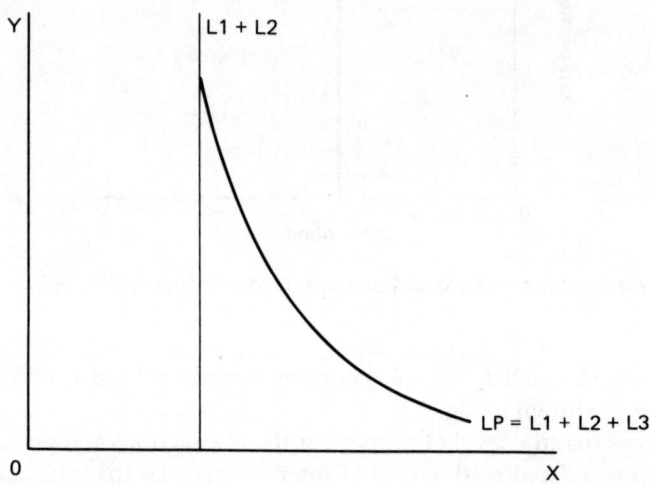

Fig. 5.10 Liquidity preference

The ability of a community to hold liquid funds is also determined by the total money stock in that community. As we have seen in Chapter 2 this supply is determined by the authorities and is, at any one point in time, fixed. This is shown as a fixed amount in Fig 5.11 not necessarily being related to the level of interest rates. If we now relate this demand for liquidity preference with the money stock, we will be able to see how interest rates are determined.

As we can see in Fig. 5.11 the rate of interest is determined by equating money stock with liquidity preference. Thus the interest rate in this case is r.

However, changes in interest rates come about either because the money stock changes, or liquidity preference changes, or both. For example, if the desire for liquidity were to increase as a result of speculators selling bonds, therefore, as we can see in Fig. 5.12 the level of interest rates rises. Alternatively, if speculators gave up liquidity the LP line would shift to the left and there would be a consequent fall in interest rates, as shown in Fig. 5.13.

We can also show how changes in the money stock affect interest rate levels.

Savings Investment and Interest Rates   133

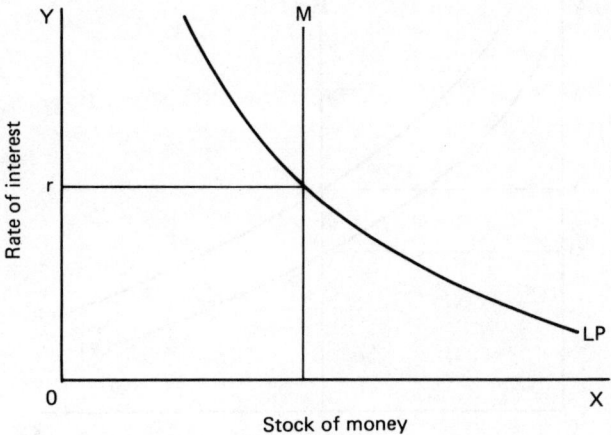

Fig. 5.11   Liquidity preference and interest rates

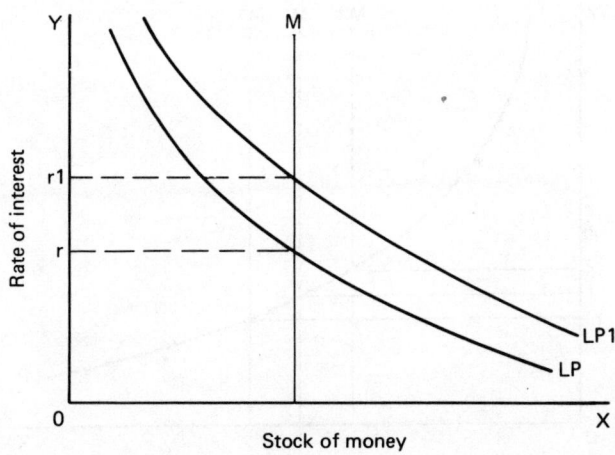

Fig. 5.12   Effect of an increase in liquidity preference on interest rates

In Fig. 5.14 if the stock of money is increased from M to M1 then this causes a fall in interest rates, as the financial institutions now have surplus funds and, in order to encourage borrowers, the interest rates have to come down. If the money stock were to fall from M to M2 then the opposite would happen with interest rates rising.

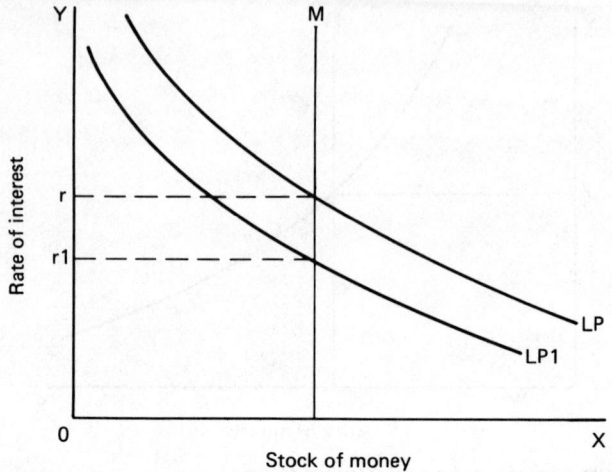

Fig. 5.13 Effect of a decrease in liquidity preference on interest rates

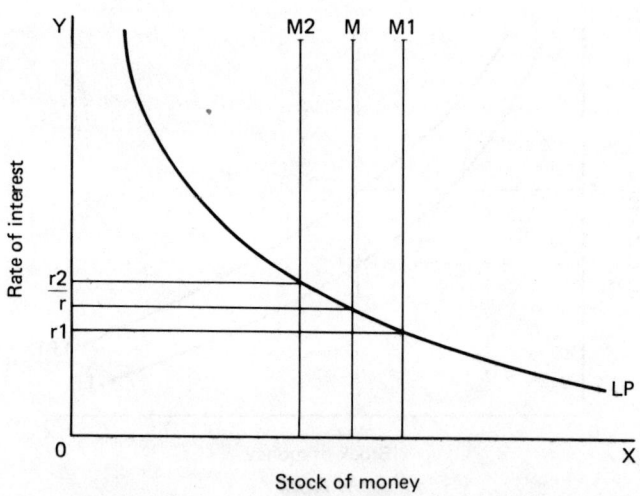

Fig. 5.14 Effect of changes in the money stock on interest rate levels

Self-assessment exercise

Draw a diagram and explain what would happen to interest rates if the stock of money were to rise and, at the same time, the liquidity preference were to fall at a greater rate.

5.4 Market interest rates

It would be wrong for us to think, from what has been said so far about interest rates, that there is only one interest rate in an economy. In the money markets we will see many different interest rates being offered to savers and charged to borrowers. These various rates are related as they tend to move up or down at about the same time. Studying the influences on one particular interest rate helps us to understand the influences which affect all rates. For example, we can quote one rate of interest for a deposit in a bank, a different rate of interest for a similar deposit in a building society, and yet another rate for such a deposit in a finance house. If we borrow, the rate charged depends upon a number of different factors. It is because different factors are taken into consideration depending on whether one is lending or borrowing that there are different interest rates on the market.

5.41 Factors which influence the rate of interest to borrowers

There are six basic factors which react with one another to determine the rate of interest charged to borrowers.

Time

Money is borrowed for either short-, medium- or long-term periods. These periods are not the same for all institutions. Fig. 5.15 shows some of these variations.

Time period	Banks	Building societies
Short term	2 years	—
Medium term	5 years	15 years
Long term	5 years +	20 years +

Fig. 5.15 Periods of time for borrowing from two of the major institutions

Generally the longer the period of time for the loan the higher the rate of interest, but this usually combines with other factors to affect the final rate charged to the individual.

Character of the borrower

This represents the risk the lender sees in giving this particular loan to the borrower. Some borrowers are more creditworthy, either because of their financial assets or because they have succesfully completed contracts to borrow in the past. An unknown or little known borrower, who has very few financial assets, or who has not been proved to be a good credit risk may find that the interest rate charged will be higher than to a borrower who fulfils any one of these criteria. It may be that a loan is refused.

Purpose for which the loan is to be used

Once again the lender assesses the risk, but this time in relation to the use to which the money is to be put. This is so that the lender can make certain that the loan plus the interest is likely to be repaid. The lender does not want the undue worry or trouble of having to try and obtain repayment from a defaulting borrower. Therefore, the greater the risk the greater the rate of interest likely to be charged.

Amount to be borrowed

This also affects the rate of interest to be charged for the loan. In some cases, the larger the amount to be borrowed the higher the rate of interest. In some cases, as it does not cost much more in administration costs to arrange a higher loan, the rate of interest is not significantly different for a larger loan.

Cost of arranging and running the loan

This is also taken into consideration when the rate of interest to be charged for a loan is calculated. The arrangements for some loans can be completed within a matter of minutes, however others may need to be considered over a period of time so that administration costs may be high. For example, analysing the past finances of a business before deciding whether or not to give a loan involves some clerical costs. If it is thought that the administration of the loan during its life will be costly, then no doubt the rate of interest charged will reflect this.

Lender's loss of benefit or alternatives

Another factor which is taken into consideration is loss of benefit that could have accrued to the lender had he not lent the money. By lending he has given up a certain amount of flexibility, perhaps he may lose the opportunity of securing a particular deal. It may be very inconvenient or even impossible to turn the loan back into cash should an urgent need for cash arise. Once having loaned the money, the lender may lose a subsequent opportunity to lend on a much more favourable basis. At the same time, the lender faces the risk that the loan may, by the time it has been repaid, be of less value in real terms because of inflation. Interest rates, therefore, reflect these dangers; they will, in some way, compensate the lender for this loss of flexibility and for any perceived possible loss of value.

It is by the interaction of all of these factors that the interest rate charged to lenders is determined.

5.42 Factors which influence the rate of interest paid to depositors

There are three such factors:

(1) *Time* – the period of time over which the depositor is prepared to let the institution have the money is an important factor regarding the rate of interest. Although we speak of short-, medium- and long-term periods for deposits, they are not the same as those for borrowing and are, if anything, somewhat shorter. As we will see in Chapter 9 the major aim of lenders is to maintain some form of liquidity. This means that they are unlikely to make money less available to themselves for long periods of time. A possible time scale for deposits is as follows:

> Short-term deposits – up to 1 year
> Medium-term deposits – up to 5 years
> Long-term deposits – 5 years +

These time scales are not official and are merely the classification I would give having observed the market for some years. As commercial practice is constantly changing there could be a change in this practice at any time. As depositors are giving up liquidity if they hand over money for long periods of time, they seek to be compensated for this by receiving a higher interest rate. In addition, they might even wish to be compensated for any loss in the value of their money because of the effects of inflation.

(2) *The institution* – anyone studying the money markets will soon see that depositors are presented with a bewildering array of interest rates for the different types of deposits offered by the many financial institutions. As we have already seen, commercial banks tend to offer lower rates of interest for deposits, although many of their longer-term, higher interest rate deposits are very competitive. We must realise that the competition for savers' funds does not come only from the home market, but also from international markets like the USA and the Continent. Thus savers might receive higher interest rates on their money if they were to put it in deposits abroad. To some extent also, institutions may be able to offer higher interest rates depending on the uses to which they put the money and the rates they charge when they onlend these deposits.

(3) *Amount deposited* – generally, the greater the amount placed on deposit the greater the rate of interest received by the depositor. In the 1960s the banks began to offer higher rates of interest on larger deposits placed in accounts for longer periods than the traditional seven-day deposit account.

This was when certificates of deposit were introduced. The banks, knowing that they had the money for a longer term, were able to place this to more profitable use and so offer the depositor a share in these profits.

Self-assessment exercise

Compare and contrast the factors which influence the interest rate paid to depositors with that paid to borrowers.

5.5 Government influences on the market for interest rates

In economics we see the influence of the free market on the forces of supply and demand in price determination. In the loanable funds theory, outlined in this chapter, we are using the same concept. In fact the free market for interest rates does not exist as the government exerts a direct or indirect influence on this market. In the past its influence was very much a direct one, both in the way in which it acted as one of the operators in the market, and in the way it used economic policies to influence the market. Nowadays economic policies are very much an indirect influence as the present government wishes to foster a free market. At the same time, it still operates as one of the 'players' in the market. Let us now look at these two areas. We have already seen in Chapter 2 that the government has a number of economic aims. In seeking to achieve its economic aims, it has in the past influenced public demand by making loans expensive by means of the interest rate mechanism. If interest rates are high borrowers are less inclined to borrow so that the demand for goods and services is not as great. The effect on the demand for loans of goverment causing interest rates to rise is illustrated in Fig. 5.16.

In this diagram the demand for loans is seen as the normal demand curve. If the government influences interest rates to rise from r to r1 then the demand for loans falls from OQ to OQ1. On the other hand, if the government reduces the interest rate from r to r2 then the demand for loans increases from OQ to OQ2.

We are not, at this point, interested in why the government seeks to influence interest rates, but we are interested in seeing how this influence is brought about. Up to 1981 we could say that the system of interest rate control was a prescriptive one where the government exerted a direct influence on the market rates. To understand this we must go back to the period before 1971. Prior to this we had operating in the UK a system of interest rate structure which was based on the **bank rate**. This was the rate the Bank of England used to charge the discount houses if they needed

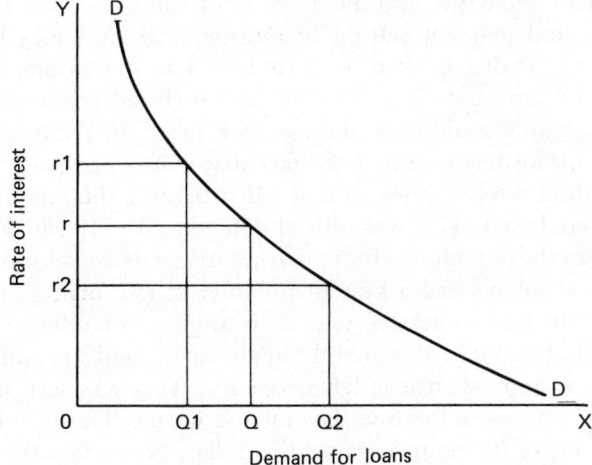

Fig. 5.16 Effects of changes in interest rates on the demand for loans

to borrow money under the lender in the last resort facility. All other institutions and particularly the banks used this rate as a base for their interest rates. This meant that very little competition in interest rates existed, with both depositors and borrowers finding the same prices for money in the market. This was regarded as a **cartel** by the authorities. At the same time, the banks felt the system was unfair as the authorities appeared to fix interest rates without any reference to commercial criteria.

In 1971 the authorities introduced new regulations known as **competition** and **credit control** with the aim of introducing more competition into the financial sector and revising the methods of credit control. Part of the underlying philosophy on competition was that there should be a market-orientated interest rate system. The authorities introduced the idea of each bank setting its own **base rate**. This was the rate on which they were to base their own interest rates. No longer were they to base these on a central rate or on the rates charged by other banks. This base rate was to reflect individual banks' own experience regarding the flow of funds. If funds were flowing in, they obviously had too high a base rate so it should be reduced. If a particular bank was experiencing an outflow of funds then its borrowing was too cheap so it needed to increase its base rate. The interest rate charged to discount houses was then fixed to the movement in interest rates in the market. Thus the system was meant to become a market-oriented system.

The term bank rate was used until October 1972 and then it was renamed the **minimum lending rate (MLR)**. From 1972 to 1978 a mixed system operated, at times the market was allowed to set the interest rate and at other times, when it was felt necessary in the interests of the economy, the government set MLR and all other rates followed suit. In addition, the hoped for independent setting of interest rates by banks never quite materialised, for if one bank moved its base rate it was not long before the other banks came into line. One thing which did result was that customers of the banks could now shop around more for competitive terms. By 1978 the authorities accepted the fact that it was necessary to lead the market regarding interest rates so that MLR became the rate on which all other rates were based. This was official policy until 1981 when the present government, in the pursuit of a more market-orientated economy, put MLR to one side and introduced a system for interest rate management which can only be called an indicative one. The minimum lending rate has not been removed altogether, it is merely in abeyance, and the authorities can resurrect this as and when it is felt necessary. This was seen in February 1985 when it was used for one day by the Chancellor to help stop the slide in the value of the pound against the dollar. Nowadays the authorities like to indicate to the market rather than dictate to it what the level of interest rates should be. Thus the Treasury sets a notional band for interest rates which are realistic for the economy in its present state. If interest rates move outside this band, either upwards or downwards, then the Treasury indicates to the market what it considers to be the correct level. This indication is inferred from the rate at which the Bank of England is allowed to rediscount Treasury bills when the discount houses seek to use the lender in the last resort facility. Indication may also come from the rate of interest the government is prepared to give to purchasers of short-term government securities. It is present government policy to influence short-term interest rates in the way we have seen above so as to influence bank lending and the growth of the money stock.

We can also see that the government, itself, operates in these money markets. We have seen in Chapter 2 that the government needs to borrow both in the long term and short term. In order to attract funds it needs to offer attractive rates of interest. One difference between the government and other borrowing institutions is that the latter are bound by commercial considerations, in their borrowing they must relate the cost of borrowing to the charges for lending. In some respects the government does not have the same considerations as it pays the interest on its borrowing from taxation. Obviously, if this debt servicing, as it is called, becomes a burden on the taxpayers the government could find itself in difficulty at a future general election. But the timescale between this borrowing and when it has to be accounted for may mean that it is no immediate problem to the government. For example, government, acting in direct competition with other institutions, might offer very attractive rates to buyers of its securities. This might result in the institutions being short of funds and, in order to attract more, having to put up their interest rates. In this way the general level of interest rates rises as a direct result of the government's action.

5.6 Money market influences on interest rates

In addition to the general level of interest rates in the market, banks' lending rates are also influenced by specific rates in the money markets. Thus rates charged to industries are in fact expressed as a margin over the money market rate. This rate is known as the **London interbank offered rate (LIBOR)**. This is the rate of interest charged by the banks when lending to each other. As we saw in Chapter 4 this is a recent development which has grown to be of considerable importance. It is now the practice for banks to use this LIBOR when calculating the interest to be charged to companies negotiating loans over longer terms. In addition, banks use this rate to calculate the profitability of their branches and district offices for the year. Now some well-known firms are able to negotiate their own rates when borrowing, these are known as **blue chip rates**. For other borrowers from the banks, the interest rate charged is related to base rates.

Long-term interest rates are left to be determined by the market but they are generally related to short-term interest rates. This is not always the case, however, as these interest rates can reflect the market's view of the future. If it is believed that the present rates of inflation are likely to come down in the future, then the long-term interest rate may reflect this. If the government is thought to want long-term rates to fall and it tries to secure this, then again interest rates could reflect this, so that we could have a situation where very long-term interest rates are lower than short-term rates. No doubt this situation is only a temporary one, for depositors may be tempted to switch funds if they can cancel long-term contracts. Thus market forces will come into play so forcing short-term rates down or long-term rates up, or both.

5.7 Effects of interest rate changes

5.71 On banks

The most obvious effect of a change in interest rates is on the bank's base rate which in turn affects the rates given to depositors and charged to borrowers. We have seen that an individual bank's base rate is affected by other factors such as other banks' rates, building society rates, rates in the USA. This was seen in 1983–4 when the government wished to bring interest rate levels down, but the high interest rates in the USA caused an outflow of funds so that it was necessary to allow interest rates at home to rise in order to halt this outflow. The 1970s showed how the banks' interest rates reflect the high levels of inflation, not always compensating the saver for the fall in value of his savings. Banks in the UK have been very profitable during these periods of high interest rates, so much so that the government introduced a 'windfall' tax on banks' profits at this time. It will be interesting to see if these profits are reduced during times when interest rates are lower.

5.72 On the competition for saving

We have seen in the past twenty years considerable competition for depositors' money. This is reflected in the wide range of opportunities offered to savers by the various financial institutions in the market. This is not only reflected in the interest rate given on these savings, but also in the wide range of accounts that can be opened. The effects of interest rate changes may be illustrated by the situation which occurred in 1984. As stated, it is the present government's policy to bring down the level of interest rates. As a result, these fell steadily from 1979. At the same time, the government sought to raise funds to meet its own expenditure needs. One of the ways it does this is through the sale of national savings certificates which give an added bonus of being tax free. This means that certain high tax paying groups find these attractive as they receive a much higher interest rate. In 1984 the twenty-eighth issue was particularly attractive to these groups, so much so that there was a large withdrawal of funds from other institutions to purchase these certificates. As a result, in August 1984 when building society deposits had dropped from around £600 million a month to £100 million, the societies were forced to put up their interest rates to attract funds necessary to meet the demand for mortgages. Of course, this meant an increase in interest rates for those seeking a mortgage. This had a rippling effect on interest rates in the market, the authorities were forced to withdraw the twenty-eighth issue and replace it with a less attractive issue in order to bring down interest rate levels.

5.73 On investment

We have already seen that to economists the term investment has a specific meaning. J M Keynes considered that the level of investment in a community related to two factors:
    (1) the marginal efficiency of capital (MEC); and
    (2) the rate of interest.

It is in the interaction of these two factors that the level of investment is determined. Before considering this interaction we need to consider these factors in themselves.

(1) Marginal efficiency of capital

Businessmen purchase capital assets not for their own sake but because they enable them to produce other goods and services for sale. Thus they expect to make some form of return from the use of these assets. They see these returns not as coming all at once but over a period of time, throughout the life of the asset. However, the actual money returned in the future may be worth more or less in real value depending upon the way that prices move over this time. Thus £1000 received next year after 10 per cent inflation is really only worth £900 at its present value in terms of the goods and services it will purchase. What we have done here is to discount the future income in terms of its present value. We are really saying that £1000 in a year's time is as good as having £900 at the present time in terms of the goods and services it will buy. Thus if a businessman held an asset providing him with £1000 per annum over the ten years of its life with 10 per cent inflation per year, he could discount these returns as follows:

Year	Actual return (£)	Present value of return (£)
1	1 000	900
2	1 000	810
3	1 000	729
4	1 000	656
5	1 000	590
6	1 000	531
7	1 000	478
8	1 000	430
9	1 000	387
10	1 000	349
TOTALS	10 000	5860

As we can see from the above, the present value of each successive year's income reduces the further away we move from the year of purchase. In this example it is a compounded deduction of 10 per cent per annum. The businessman obviously wants at least to recover the cost of the asset, and he uses this method of discounting in order to compare the present cost of purchase with the returns he is going to get over the years. *The marginal efficiency of capital is defined as the rate of discount that is required to bring the expected rate of return to a present value which will just equal the supply price of the asset.* By doing this the businessman is identifying the minimum amount of return he expects from the asset to make investing in it worthwhile. In the example above the businessman would think it worthwhile to carry out the project as long as the supply price did not exceed £5860. But the position is not as simple as this, for at any one time most businessmen will have a number of projects which they would like to carry out. These different projects will not yield equal rates of return – some will be more profitable than others. A businessman will probably list these in descending order of profitability, and obviously, the rational businessman will carry out these projects in that order. Thus any money borrowed will go towards the more profitable projects first and subsequent borrowings will be used for each successive less profitable project. This analysis led Keynes to show a businessman's marginal efficiency of capital as illustrated in Fig. 5.17.

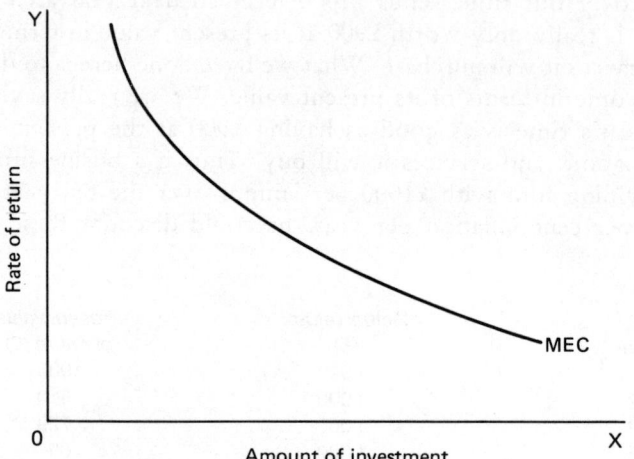

Fig. 5.17 Marginal efficiency of capital

Here we show the rate of return on the Y axis and the amount of investment on the X axis. This shows that the early levels of investment yield a higher rate of return than the later levels of investment in capital projects.

(2) Rate of interest and level of investment

We have already discussed what determines the rate of interest. We now need to see how this rate of interest reacts with the marginal efficiency of capital to determine the actual amount of investment that goes on in the community. At any one point in time, the rate of interest is fixed and so a businessman wishing to borrow an amount of money must do so at this fixed rate. This is shown in Fig. 5.18 as a horizontally straight line, r. If we superimpose on this rate the marginal efficiency of capital, we can use this to show how the amount of interest is arrived at.

In Fig. 5.18 with the interest rate being r, all those projects on the MEC line above this rate will earn a return in excess of this rate and are, therefore, profitable, those projects on the MEC line below this rate are not.

If the interest rate level rises from r to r1, there is less investment and this falls from In to In1. This is because some projects which were profitable are now no longer profitable at the highest interest rate. On the other hand, if the interest rate falls from r to r2, then those projects which were not profitable become profitable and investment rises from In to In2.

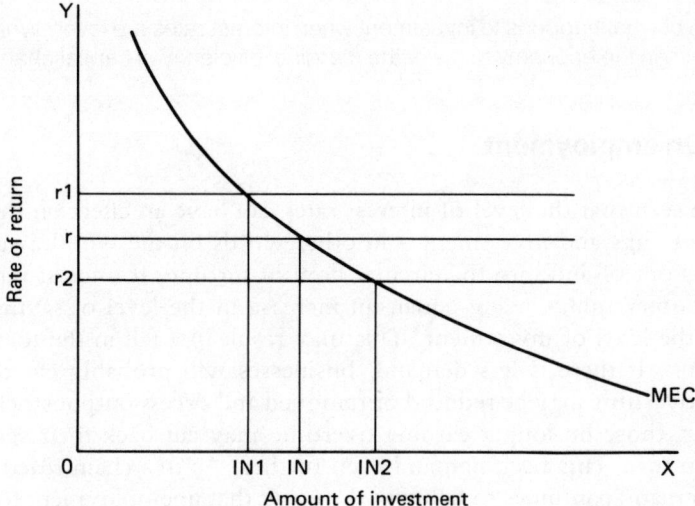

Fig. 5.18 Effects of changes in the rate of interest and the marginal efficiency of capital on the amount of investment

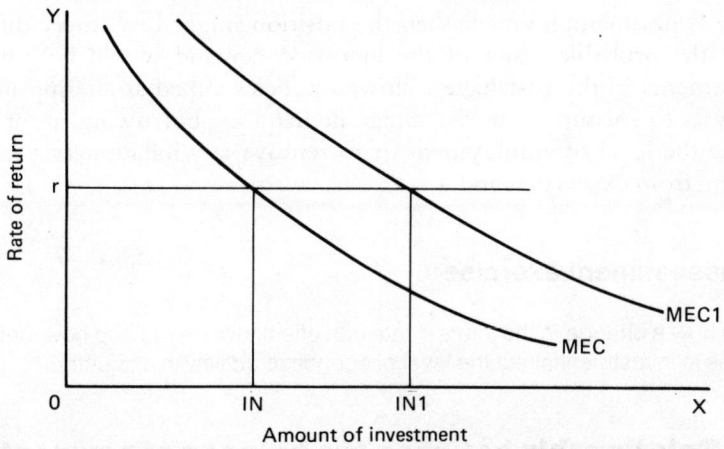

Fig. 5.19 Effect of changes in marginal efficiency of capital on the level of investment

We can see in Fig. 5.19 that an increase in the marginal efficiency of capital without a change in the interest rate will result in greater investment from IN to IN1.

Self-assessment exercise

Show on a similar diagram what would happen if the interest rate were to remain constant and the marginal efficiency of capital were to rise or fall. What does this tell us of what happens to investment when interest rates are level? What can happen in the economy to make the marginal efficiency of capital change?

5.74 On employment

We have seen that the level of interest rates can have an effect on the level of both savings and investment – in other words on the withdrawals and injections out of and into the circular flow of income. If interest rates rise there is, other things being equal, an increase in the level of savings and a fall in the level of investment. This may result in a fall in the total level of demand. If there is less demand, businesses will probably cut output. At first, overtime may be reduced or removed and excess output stockpiled. However, those no longer earning overtime may cut back their spending which, in turn, cuts back demand even further. As this chain reaction develops demand continues to fall with the result that unemployment follows. This is a classic example of how a recession in economic activity is caused. At the same time, a lowering of interest rates may encourage more borrowing which, in turn, encourages more spending so that this increased demand takes up any slack in the employment position of the community. Of course, if there is no unemployment then the position might be entirely different in that the probable result of the increased demand would be inflation. Governments in the past have followed policies aimed at altering interest rate levels to encourage or discourage demand for borrowing, in order to increase the level of employment or to remove any inflationary pressures resulting from excess demand.

Self-assessment exercise

Explain how a change in the interest rate can affect investment and how these changes in investment affect the level of economic activity in a country.

5.8 Relationship between the balance of payments, exchange rates and interest rates

A country's balance of payments identifies all the currency flows from external transactions. It includes the money flow from goods and services which are bought and sold by that country from other countries, and also any currency flows which are a result of investments, deposits, credits, or other borrowings. If the flows inwards exceed the flows outwards then the balance of payments is said to be in surplus. If the flows out exceed the flows in then the balance of payments is said to be in deficit. The official statistics show this as a balance by means of accounting methods which operate on a double entry basis. Thus a net outflow is matched by a decrease in our foreign currency reserves, or an increase in foreign borrowing, or both. A net inflow means either an increase in our reserves, or a reduction in debt commitment to external bodies, or both. As we have seen, a country seeks as one of its economic aims a satisfactory balance of payments position. Satisfactory does not mean an exact balance of flows for this is very difficult to attain. It might mean at one time a small deficit, and at another a small surplus. So long as the balance does not cause other problems, the government will not be unduly worried.

However, linked with foreign trade is the external value of our currency as seen in its exchange rate with other currencies. Generally, the external value of our currency is determined by the demand and supply of our currency in relations to other currencies. This is because we can regard the exchange rate as the price we have to pay to obtain these other currencies, or the price foreigners have to pay in terms of their currency to get pounds. Foreigners demand pounds for four basic reasons. These are:

(1) to purchase our goods and services;
(2) to hold as a reserve – a form of savings;
(3) to buy investment goods;
(4) to hold against a rise in value at some future date – this is a form of speculation.

Just as foreigners seek to hold pounds for these reasons so we seek to hold foreign currencies for the same reasons.

The total supply of a currency outside its natural country depends upon the previous transactions of the country in the world – its trade, and investment holdings by foreigners as a reserve and for speculation. The supply entering the world markets at any one time depends upon whether holders wish to give up their holdings. This depends upon their future expectations of trade with this country, or if they think the currency will keep its comparative value against other currencies. If they think there is a possibility of better trade with other countries, or that the pound will fall in value, they will sell it for other currencies. As with standard demand and supply analysis, movements in the demand and supply of a currency affect its external value. We can see in Fig. 5.20 how these movements affect the exchange rate value.

For example, where the demand for a currency is shown by the line on the graph as DD and the supply as SS, then the exchange rate is where these equate on the graph at $1.20. If the demand for the pound rises because British goods are in greater demand abroad, then there is a shift in the demand curve from DD to D1D1. With no change in the conditions of supply, the value of the pound rises in terms of dollars to $1.22. If, on the other hand, the supply of pounds increases because interest rates in the USA are higher than in the UK with the result that British savers seek to convert their pounds into dollars to deposit in America, then we can

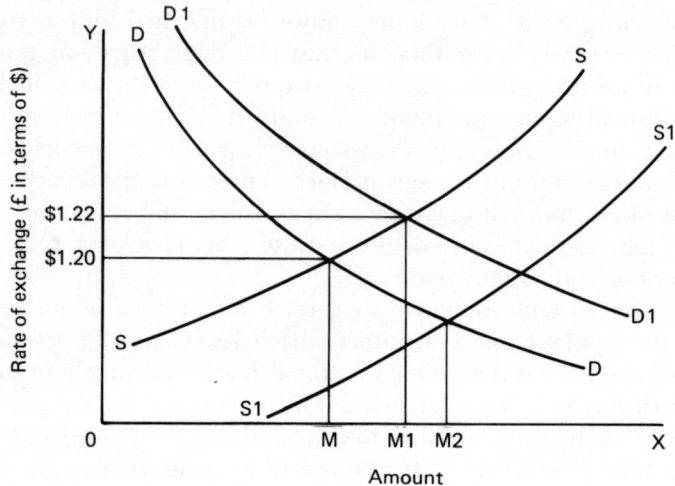

Fig. 5.20 Effect of shifts in the demand and supply of a currency on its exchange rate value

see, from the diagram that the value of the pound falls to $1.18. The UK government might have to allow interest rates at home to go up to stem the flow of funds out of the country and stop an adverse balance of payments situation.

The second example is what happened in fact in 1983–4. US interest rates were higher than in the UK and international transfers were so easily arranged that the flow of funds out of the UK was alarming, so much so that the government had to allow UK interest rates to rise, despite the fact that this was contrary to its declared policy. At this time, the balance of payments was in surplus as a result of North Sea oil income, although this surplus had been reduced by 1985.

When the pound began to fall again against the dollar early in 1985, this time because of the uncertainty of the world price for oil, the government did not increase interest rates immediately. It hoped that the fall in the value of the pound would work its way through to give exporters the advantage of improved price competition and so improve our economy. However, interest rates had to be increased when the pound fell dramatically over one weekend. To influence the market, the Chancellor used the minimum lending rate for one day only to cause these market rates to rise. This rise rippled through the economy to cause a general increase in the interest rate level.

Initially, any outflow of funds from a country may cause problems for the balance of payments, but the resulting reduced value of its currency makes its products cheaper for foreigners and so more competitive. At the same time, the cost of foreign products becomes more expensive so that imports may fall significantly. In the long run the outflow may be stemmed by events. Higher interest rates in the UK compared to the rest of the world may also produce the same effect. Funds flow in as foreigners seek higher returns on their savings. Our short-term balance of payments improves, perhaps sending a signal to speculators that our currency is worth holding, so increasing its demand. Other things being equal, increased demand may result in an increase in the value of the pound against other currencies, making our products less competitive and the price of other countries' products attractive. Thus, in the long run, the balance of payments surplus may be reduced or obliterated.

Thus we can see that changes in interest rates affect the relative attractiveness of saving in the UK, and consequently the attractiveness or otherwise of the country's currency. These changes also affect the healthiness or otherwise of the balance of payments.

Self-assessment exercises

1   Show by means of a diagram what would happen to the value of a country's currency if there was a fall in demand for its currency and, at the same time, British citizens were demanding more of this foreign currency to go on holiday abroad. Explain your diagram.
2   Why is it that when a country's currency falls in value against other currencies its exports become cheaper in price and its imports become dearer?
3   Under what circumstances could the benefit of a fall in price of a country's exports be lost?
4   Why would it be possible for a rise in import prices to cause a country's balance of payments to worsen instead of improve?

Assignments

1 *Situation* 'TIMELY ADVICE'
   You are employed in a small town branch of the Eastlands Bank PLC. Mr Horizon, a customer of the branch, has inherited £50 000 from an uncle who died recently. He has come to the branch to ask its advice as to where he could invest this money so that it will give a reasonable return but will also be secure. He has also calculated that he has about £600 a year out of his current income to put into some savings plan and asks your advice about this. Again he seeks security for this investment.
   Task Produce a written statement as to what you would recommend.
2 You are a student on a banking course studying 'Elements of Banking'. Your lecturer has asked you to prepare a talk to give to the rest of the class entitled

'Interest Rates in the UK today'. She asks you to:
(a) Prepare a table which can be used to illustrate your talk.
(b) Produce notes for the talk identifying the institutions, the different rates available and stating why these differences exist.

6 Wholesale Money Markets

We have seen in Chapter 4 the basic structure and details of the short-term money markets, that they are broadly divided into the classical markets and the parallel markets. The former consists of the banks, the Bank of England and the discount houses. The parallel markets consist of a number of separate, but related, markets which include the banks, discount houses, local authorities, finance houses and companies.

The classical market, as we have seen, dates back to the eighteenth century when use of the bill of exchange developed. This market became the method of settling interbank indebtedness among the clearing banks, helping also to smooth out the fluctuations in net payments between the government and the banks.

The parallel markets have developed since the Second World War for three basic reasons:

(1) To allow certain institutions to 'tap' other short-term funds which have developed. This was because the discount market did not provide a suitable way of settling interbank indebtedness between the secondary banks and the other financial intermediaries. These new markets which developed were able to compete successfully for short-term deposits by offering interest rates which were higher than in the traditional discount market.

(2) To allow the money market greater flexibility to meet the changing needs of the financial world. There have been considerable changes in this world with new markets operating on a worldwide perspective. New firms have entered the market as a result of the competition that started in the 1950s and has been fostered even up to the present time.

(3) To enable institutions to find a way round the restrictions of the classical system. This is one of the reasons why the interbank and intercompany markets developed. The former as a means of overcoming the regulations under competition and credit control, and the latter as a way of avoiding the various credit squeezes of the government.

The effect of the development of these markets has also been considerable. In their early days they operated somewhat separately, but since 1971 they have become more closely linked.

The discount houses are active in the parallel markets as they operate in the interbank market by borrowing and lending unsecured money. In 1968 they inaugurated the certificates of deposit market. The Bank of England operates in the local authority market by direct lending to some of these bodies.

We have come to use the term 'wholesale banking' in connection with these markets as they onlend some of their deposits in large amounts to corporate bodies. Indeed, as we have seen in Chapter 3, we have now come to classify banks in relation to the size of their retail or wholesale banking services, the former being services to households and small firms and basically involving small sums of money.

There have also developed alongside these markets firms of money brokers. These act as intermediaries bringing together borrowers and lenders. At first, they tended to operate in one market but over the years they have extended their business to encompass a wide range of markets.

These parallel markets consist of:

6.1 Local authority market
6.2 Finance house market
6.3 Eurocurrency market
6.4 Certificate of deposit market
6.5 Interbank market
6.6 Intercompany market
6.7 Financial futures market

Self-assessment exercise

In what ways has the development in the parallel markets affected the operation of the UK financial sector?

6.1 Local authority market

Local authorities consist mainly of county councils and district councils. At the present time, changes are being suggested for metropolitan county and district councils whereby these may disappear. Local authorities supply a considerable number of services to the population of their areas. To pay for these services they have four sources of income. These are:

(1) Grants from central government.

(2) Income from rates charged to the inhabitants in their administrative area.

(3) Income from the fees and charges they make for direct use of some of their services.

(4) Borrowing from various sources.

It is the fourth area that involves the local authority market. Their borrowing powers are regulated by various local government acts relating to different areas of the United Kingdom. The main purpose of borrowing is to finance **capital expenditure**, that is the purchase of plant, machinery and equipment. However, short-term borrowing is also required when a local authority has a temporary short fall in its current income over current expenditure. In 1955 local authorities were given permission to enter the market to borrow money. Up to that time their only source of borrowing was from the Public Works Loans Board (*see* Chapter 4). There are now a number of ways in which local authorities can raise money on the open market.

    6.11   Local authority bonds
    6.12   Market loans
    6.13   Local authority bills

6.11   Local authority bonds

These bonds are defined as instruments of indebtedness issued by a local authority as security for repayment of money borrowed. Of interest to the money market is the negotiable bond; these are registered and quoted on the London Stock Exchange. They are negotiable in a special London market which sees to their rapid transfer; they are held by many financial institutions. The bonds are for one to five years, can have a fixed or variable interest rate but are subject to Bank of England approval as to terms and when they can be issued. Usually the local authority has a ceiling placed upon it in relation to the number of bonds it can issue, often related to its level of outstanding debt.

6.12   Market loans

These are loans to the local authorities in the market like banks or finance houses. They are for large amounts with fixed or variable rates of interest. They are secured by a bond or mortgage which states the terms and conditions of the loan. If the loan is syndicated by a number of banks there is also a loan agreement. The bonds are not negotiable but are freely transferable on a secondary market which has developed. In recent years, there has been a marked increase in this type of borrowing from banks which require local authorities to accept variable rate agreements. A wide range of options have been developed mainly through the work of the London loan brokers, banks and other financial institutions. The interest charged on these loans is usually related in some way to the London interbank offered rate (see Section 6.5).

6.13   Local authority bills

Local authorities with an annual rate income of at least £3 million may issue local authority bills in order to help meet revenue expenditure which will be paid out of funds they are expecting to receive in the near future. These bills are bearer documents, are sold at a discount on the money market and are redeemable at their full value. They are usually issued in multiples of £25 000 lasting for a period of three months, but they can vary from two to six months. They are purchased by the discount houses, banks and larger commercial organisations. At the present time, bills may not be issued to finance capital expenditure.

The importance of this market obviously lies in satisfying the various demands of the institutions involved. In the first place, local authorities can tap a wider market for their financial needs, so receiving the right type of loan for their purposes. They are able to carry out activities which would not be possible if sources of funds were restricted. They have built up a wide range of expertise in debt management and knowledge of the market which is beneficial to their ratepayers. The financial institutions are able to acquire a financial asset which is reasonably secure, of acceptable liquidity and which is also profitable. For the Bank of England and the Treasury, supervision of this market allows greater freedom and flexibility in local authority finance.

Self-assessment exercises

1   List the major differences between a local authority bond and bill.
2   What are the advantages to be gained from allowing the local authorities to borrow from the open market?

6.2   Finance house market

As we have seen in Chapter 4 the finance houses act as financial intermediaries raising short- and medium-term funds and then onlending these for hire purchase, credit sale and leasing finance. This market developed after the Second World War because of the technological development in consumer goods, and a change in consumer habits whereby goods began to be purchased for credit rather than cash. The stringency of the war years, plus the expectation of continuing incomes helped to encourage people in the use of instalment finance. We can see how this market operates by looking at the way in which the finance houses acquire some of their funds. Table 4.3 shows the main sources of these to be assets. These institutions raise some of their deposits from the retail market in direct competition with the banks, building societies and other deposit-taking institutions. They do this to help compensate for loss of funds when foreign depositors remove their funds when they see the possibility of the pound falling in value on the foreign currency markets. Competition for retail funds became very fierce in the 1960s so much so that the banks sought to ally themselves with finance houses with the result that today many banks have some kind of association with a finance house, either as a subsidiary, or as part of its banking group.

Finance houses also raise funds on the wholesale money markets. They receive deposits from a number of institutions in these markets, either overnight, or up to one-year periods. They also raise funds by drawing bills of exchange on themselves and then having them discounted with the banking sector. They use as security the funds they are expecting to receive from their instalment credit and leasing contracts. This latter source allows the finance houses to meet any short fall in funds required for lending in relation to income from previous lending. The banks, at the same time, are in receipt of an asset which is reasonably secure, liquid and profitable. This market gives to the finance houses a flexibility to raise funds in whichever area is most beneficial to them at the time.

The government has found that it needs to regulate this supply of credit in the interest of controlling inflationary pressures on the economy. This is done by a measure known as the **regulator**, by fixing the size of deposit required for a hire purchase or credit sale and restricting the period of time in which the money can be repaid, the government has found that it can control the demand for this type of finance from the public.

Self-assessment exercises

1   For what reasons did the finance house market develop?
2   What are the major differences between a bill drawn on a finance house and a bill drawn on a trader?

6.3   Eurocurrency market

The Eurocurrency market consists of Eurocurrency deposits which are on-lent in wholesale amounts to governments, or central banks, and in some cases to large multinational firms. A Eurocurrency deposit is a deposit taken by a bank in a currency which is other than its own. Thus pounds sterling deposited in a French bank is a Eurocurrency deposit. Generally, these deposits are made by nationals of a country which is not the currency's origin. Thus a true Eurocurrency deposit is the deposit of US dollars in a French bank by a German company.

This market developed in the 1950s as a result of two factors. In the first place, the US balance of payments deficit, which at first was paid by the US government printing and supplying more dollars, caused the Federal Reserve Bank to operate regulation Q which caused a restrictive rate of interest to be paid on deposits in US banks. As a result, American savers sought deposits outside the USA where they could get higher rates of interest. The market further developed as inhabitants of European countries sought to get around restrictions in their own countries. This explains the development of the Eurodeutschemark business in Luxembourg and, in the late 1970s, the development of the Scandinavian business. Secondly, Europe was in need of rebuilding at the end of the war and, as the only market which was relatively untouched was the US one, it was only natural that the dollar was in demand to help purchase the goods and services for this rebuilding. In this way the increase in the supply of dollars circulating around Europe in the 1950s was met by a demand for these dollars.

Although it is referred to as the Eurocurrency market it extends further than Europe with centres in London (the main one), Luxembourg, Bahrain, Singapore, Hong Kong and Nassau. The main currency deposits are in dollars but it includes deutschemarks, Swiss francs, Canadian dollars, Dutch guilder, sterling (outside the UK) and Japanese yen.

Since 1950 the market has been one of the most important single developments of the financial world and is a major channel for international financial intermediation. Evidence of this growth is seen in the following figures:

Table 6.1 Growth of Eurocurrency deposits ($BN)

Year	Gross deposits	World money
1965	19.5	626.0
1970	91.1	1001.5
1975	347.5	2099.0
1978	682.3	3470.0
Percentage growth per annum	34.5	14.1

It is now an indispensable part of the international monetary system; a truly international market as demonstrated by the centres in which it operates and the currency deposits provided. It is one of the most free markets in the world as it crosses international boundaries and is not subject to any national regulation. There is, however, some unofficial supervision by the Bank for International Settlement and the Organisation for Economic Co-operation and Development. It is also the most competitive with international institutions vying with each other for deposits. Finally, it is the most flexible; as it is free from direct regulation it can change as and when conditions require.

6.31 Eurocurrency deposits

These are for large amounts and are placed by official monetary institutions, government agencies, international companies and private individuals. These deposits provide the depositor with:

(1) a good rate of interest;

(2) no costs with regard to the conversion and reconversion of currencies;
(3) an opportunity for currency speculation – the currency held may go up in value;
(4) funds being available for the purchase of goods or services in that currency;
(5) an ability to avoid any restrictive regulations at home.

6.32   Eurocurrency lending

Deposits are accepted by the banks which lend them on to banks or other commercial enterprises. The initial lending by the bank may not be to the ultimate borrower. For example, an American multinational may deposit deutschemarks in a French bank. The French bank may lend these to a Swedish bank which may lend them to a British bank which lends them to ICI which wishes to finance a project in Germany. The major lending banks in this market are largely the overseas branches of the big US banks. The types of loans are:
(1) fixed interest loans;
(2) loans at variable interest rates (roll-over loans);
(3) standby credits;
(4) syndicated credits.

6.33   Eurocurrency interest rates

These are influenced by supply and demand, the rate of interest for the currency and the relative strength of the currency in the world markets. Rates are quoted for a day, one year, or up to five years.

6.34   Growth of the Eurocurrency markets

One of the reasons for the high rate of growth in this market has been the rise in the size of international companies seeking cash balances in a variety of currencies. Another reason is the fact that this market is convenient for both lenders and borrowers, plus the fact that the price is attractive. Because the transactions are in wholesale amounts, interest rates tend to be lower. Another factor has been the free convertibility of the major world currencies added to a freeing of the movement of these currencies around the world. Finally, its flexibility has also contributed to its growth. This flexibility is seen in the way the market has assisted in removing some of the problems of the 1974 oil price crises, by recycling the external surpluses of the Organisation of Petroleum Exporting Countries (OPEC) to those countries suffering from oil balance of payments deficits. This action has been described as the market's 'finest hour'.

Self-assessment exercises

1 What are the major advantages of the Eurocurrency market?
2 Draw comparative bar charts illustrating Table 6.1.
3 What factors determine the level of interest rates in the Eurocurrency market?

6.4 Certificates of deposit market

As we have seen in Chapter 4 this market came to London in 1968 when the sterling certificate of deposit was introduced, the dollar certificate having been introduced in 1964 by way of the American banks. What developed was a second-hand market for these certificates. They are bought by the banks, discount houses and by some non-bank institutions if the latter have surplus funds to invest for an uncertain length of time. They prefer, therefore, to invest in certificate of deposit rather than a fixed term deposit, so maintaining their flexibility. However, most certificates of deposit are held by banks.

The major advantage of this market to the investor is that the certificates are negotiable so that they are regarded as useful liquid assets.

Self-assessment exercise

Why might a bank show certificates of deposits as both assets and liabilities on its balance sheet?

6.5 Interbank market

This is the market where banks borrow and lend to each other. This market developed very soon after the local authority market. Much of the lending was to the discount houses overnight, but some of the secondary banks found it advantageous to lend on a short-term basis to other banks. The market, as we know it today, really developed after 1971 when the clearing banks, which had not up to then participated in the market, found it necessary to enter. Up to that time the clearing banks found that they had adequate arrangements to meet liquidity and authority control by use of their 8 per cent cash ratio. In 1971 the new regulations on competition and credit control were introduced. These required all banks to maintain a reserve asset ratio of 12.5 per cent in relation to eligible liabilities. This reserve was a day-to-day requirement, so that if a bank fell below this level it had to re-arrange its affairs to return to the required reserve immediately. This meant taking on reserve assets to make up the difference. Banks soon found that they could go to other banks, which might have excess funds and borrow. Thus a system of self-help started in the 1950s was extended considerably in the 1970s.

These loans are secured and are for amounts in excess of £250 000. Much of the dealing is in short-term funds, usually overnight, but rates are now quoted for loans over the following timescales: overnight, seven days' notice of withdrawal, one month, two months, three months, six months, nine months and one year. These rates are usually quoted at levels higher than the rates on the discount market.

Nowadays this market is used by banks for three main purposes. Firstly, to help discover the future trends in rates of interest. The interest rate in the larger interbank market is the London interbank offered rate (LIBOR), which is determined by the supply and demand in the interbank markets. It ranges from overnight to one-year loans. The three-month LIBOR has become the benchmark for calculating some banks' internal rates of interest in order to establish the profit and loss figures for branches and divisions. Secondly, it is used as a base for roll-over sterling and Eurocurrency loans. These are loans at variable rates of interest. Thirdly, in 1979 it also became used by some banks to determine the interest to be charged to selected company customers on overdrafts. The interbank market is now a well-established and very large market for short-term funds and exerts considerable influence on the other parallel markets.

Self-assessment exercise

Why is the interbank market so important?

6.6 Intercompany market

This is the market on which companies borrow and lend large sums of money to each other. It was established in 1969 and it illustrates how something called 'disintermediation' can work. Disintermediation is the process whereby direct controls or other restrictions on banks can lead to a greater amount of lending, business being routed through uncontrolled institutions and markets. In this case, in 1969 a government squeeze on credit from banks meant that companies were unable to raise funds through bank finance. At the same time, companies with spare funds were depositing these with the banks which were not allowed to onlend them. As a result, a practice developed where companies in need of funds would contact those companies with spare funds and arrange to borrow. Because the banking system and its charges for handling loans was being bypassed, interest rates were slightly lower to the borrower and a little higher for the lender. Because this market is diversified and not easily organised, it is relatively small compared to the other parallel markets.

Self-assessment exercise

What do you understand by the term 'disintermediation'?

6.7 Financial futures market

Recent years have seen great movements in interest rates and exchange rates, even over short periods of time. These movements create risks for businesses with regard to costs and revenues so that some traditional fixed costs have come to be regarded as being variable costs. In order to protect against these risks, new financial markets have emerged dealing with financial futures. For some time, markets have been in existence in the UK dealing with future prices of commodities and in forward exchange contracts for certain currencies. In September 1982 the London International Financial Futures Exchange (LIFFE) was opened to provide dealing facilities in a range of seven futures contracts relating to interest rates or exchange rates.

6.71 A financial futures contract

This is a legally binding contract to buy or sell a specific financial instrument at a specified date in the future at a price which is agreed at the time when the contract is made. Thus a person can make a contract to buy or sell yen in three months' time at a fixed price in terms of dollars. If the price three months hence is lower than that stated in the contract then the seller gains and the buyer loses. The same applies when a person enters into a contract for a deposit for three months at a fixed rate of interest. Contracts may be entered into for:

(1) Financial instruments which are related to interest rates and also related to:

   (a) Three months sterling time deposits with a minimum value of £25 000.

   (b) Long-term sterling gilt edged securities notional stock 12.5 per cent £50 000 nominal value.

   (c) Three months Eurodollar time deposits minimum US $10 million.

(2) Financial instruments which are currencies trading against the dollar:

   (a) Sterling – minimum £25 000
   (b) Swiss francs – minimum 125 000
   (c) Deutschemarks – minimum DM 125 000
   (d) Yen – minimum 12.5 million

As the futures contract commits the seller and the buyer to take delivery of these financial instruments at the contract price, it is useful to be able to identify the characteristics of these instruments. These are:
(1) an identifiable and recognised value;
(2) a value that must be standardised.

6.72 Operation of the market

This is shown in Fig. 6.1. Members of the Exchange are drawn from banks,

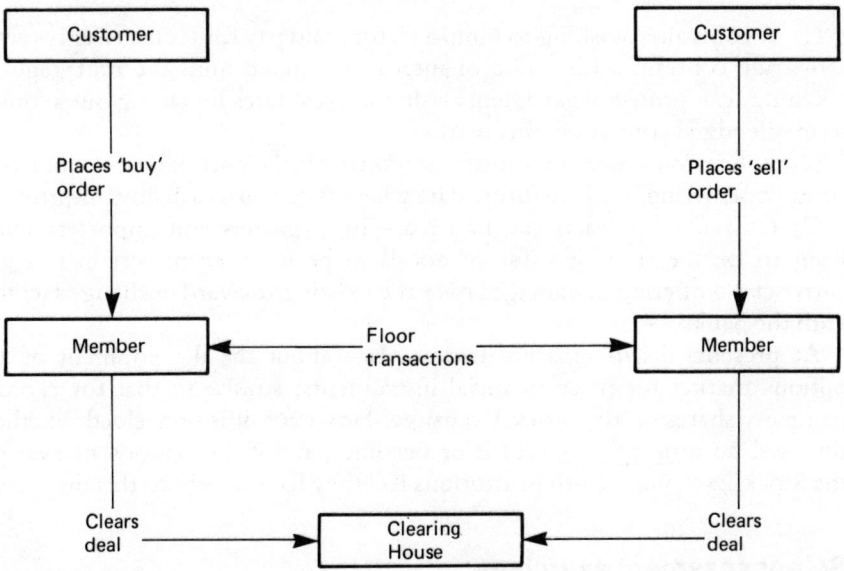

Fig. 6.1 Operation of the financial futures market

commodity brokers, investment companies and Stock Exchange firms. There are also some trading firms and individuals. A certain percentage are foreign companies and residents. Each member of the London Clearing House has to meet certain financial standards, measured in terms of minimum capital reserves. The market owns premises located at the Royal Exchange, and only members or their representatives have the right to trade on the floor of the Exchange. People wishing to use the Exchange must, as Fig. 6.1 shows, place instructions with a member.

Dealing on the floor is by 'open outcry'. For each contract members stand around a stepped pit quoting prices verbally, or in a busy market by hand signals. The details of any agreed transaction, price and number of contracts, are passed through the Exchange to the Clearing House by the buyer to the seller, and by the seller to the buyer. In this way the original parties do not have to rely upon the creditworthiness of the other party. There are strict regulations on their payments, on deals and on the limit of prices. The capital of the Clearing House plus its reserves act as a guarantee that it can meet unusual market conditions.

Self-regulation of the market is carried out by LIFFE and the International Commodities Clearing House Ltd which have taken on specific rights of control within their rules and regulations.

6.7 Some uses of a financial futures contract

(1) A company, wishing to build a factory and pay for it on a twenty-year mortgage contract with a rate of interest not fixed until the mortgage is taken up, can protect itself against rising interest rates by taking out a long-term gilt edged contract in this market.

(2) A firm may use the futures market to limit uncertainties about the cost of borrowing until the future date when its seasonal cash flow improves.

(3) Currency contracts can be used – by exporters and importers who want to fix the sterling value of goods to be invoiced in certain foreign currencies – offering advantages over the existing forward exchange facility with the banks.

At present, discussions are taking place about the development of an options market for these financial instruments, similar to that for certain company shares on the Stock Exchange. However, it is undecided whether this will become part of LIFFE or become part of the options market of the Stock Exchange. Both institutions feel they have a right to this business.

Self-assessment exercises

1 What is a financial future?
2 What instruments are traded on the financial futures market?
3 Give two examples of how a financial futures contract can benefit a businessman.

Assignments

1   MEMORANDUM
                      EASTLANDS BANK PLC
To: Chief Securities Clerk
From: The Manager
Subject: The City

At the Golf Club the other day I met Geoff Rider, secretary of the local Lions Club. He asked me to give a talk in September to his branch on the current position of the wholesale money markets in the City of London. Unfortunately, as you know I am away on a manager training course at the time when he wants me to give the talk and I have suggested that you might be prepared to give it instead. Let me have notes on the main points you would include in your talk and a report of how it went afterwards.

Tasks You are to act as this chief securities clerk and complete the tasks requested.

2   See table of various money markets.

London Money Rates
Interbank
Sterling certificates of deposit
Local authority deposits
Local authority bonds
Discount market deposits
Company deposits
Finance house deposits
Treasury bills (buy)
Bank bills (buy)
Fine trade bills (buy)

Tasks
   (a)   Using the above table explain the markets shown.
   (b)   Produce a diagram to illustrate the relative size of each of these markets.
   (c)   What is the relative importance of these markets as shown by the figures?

7 Cheques, Negotiability and the Legal Implications of the Various Banking Instruments

7.1 Definition of a cheque

By reading Sections 3(1) and 73 of the Bills of Exchange Act 1882 together we can see that a cheque can be defined as: 'an unconditional order in writing addressed by one person, to another, who must be a banker, signed by the person giving it, requiring the banker to pay on demand a sum certain in money or to the order of a specified person or to bearer.'

However, in the case of *Orbit Mining Co. Ltd v. Midland Bank Ltd* (1963) it was held that an order to a banker in the words 'Pay Cash or Order' was not a cheque but merely a mandate.

A facsimile of a cheque is shown in Fig. 7.1.

7.2 Development of the cheque as a method of payment

As the goldsmiths developed banking facilities, depositors found that they could issue instructions to these banking firms to pay funds out of their accounts. These became known as **drawn notes** and were the origins of the cheque as we know it today. An example of an early drawn note is shown in Fig. 7.2.

Some writers consider that there is controversy over the origin of the cheque as a method of payment. They believe that the key lies in the acceptance of the cheque as a bill of exchange which, in its early stages, was addressed by a depositor to a bank authorising payment to a creditor of the sum due. The cheque is thought to have developed for two reasons. First of all, as a natural extension of the work of the goldsmiths, and their desire to gain more business. Secondly, from an increasing desire by the public to avoid the risks and burden of transporting cash.

The use of the word cheque for these drawn notes probably arises from the fact that the Bank of England encouraged their customers to write their drawn notes on chequered paper. During the eighteenth century the use of the cheque as a means of payment increased, especially in and around London. It did not represent then, as it does today, the transfer of a claim on deposits in a bank, but merely a request to pay out coins and notes

Legal Implications of the Various Banking Instruments 165

OPEN CHEQUE

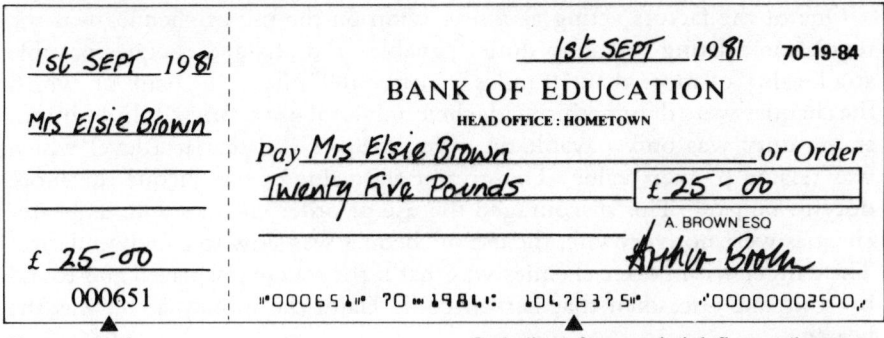

Cheque number

Code line of magnetic ink figures (known as E13B characters) these enable electronic sorting and computer recording (see Study Booklet Series 11)

CROSSED CHEQUE

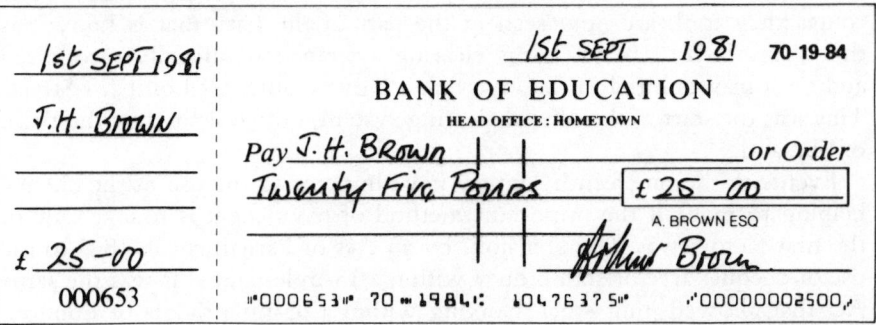

Fig. 7.1 Facsimile of a cheque (Reprinted by permission of the Bank Education Service)

        Mr Morris and Mr Clayton
          Pray pay the bearer hereof Mr Delloe on order ffour hundred pounds I say £400:
                                    o
                      for Yrs Nic Vanacker
      London the 16th February 1659

Fig. 7.2 An early drawn note

to the holder. It was more popular in town banking than in country banking where it remained insignificant until the second quarter of the nineteenth century. It was during the 1770s that the London private banks ceased issuing notes and used instead Bank of England notes and their own cheques.

One of the factors acting as a restriction on the use of cheques was the regulation relating to stamp duties payable on drafts and cheques payable at a locality of more than 10 miles (15 after 1825) from the bank on which the cheques were drawn; this made their universal use restricted. In addition, stamp duty was only payable on order cheques and this at a level which was related to their value. The greater the value of the cheque the more duty to be paid. This discouraged the use of order cheques and, as bearer cheques were not very safe, the use of cheques was slow to gain popularity. The danger with bearer cheques was that if they were misplaced and found by someone else, then that person could claim the money as he was the bearer.

Because the use of the cheque developed in and around London there became a need for some form of clearing system to be set up. What originally happened was that when a banker received a cheque for collection from a customer, a clerk was despatched to the relevant bank on which it was drawn to collect the money. Very soon these 'walks' clerks found that they could meet each other in a coffee house or some other meeting house, exchange their cheques and make up the differences with the money. (The routes they took are now seen in the part of the City that is known as the Walks today.) In 1773 this clearing system was officially recognised and a room was hired in the Five Bells, Dove Court, off Lombard Street. This was the start of the official clearing system, now operated by the Bank of England.

Events in the nineteenth century gave impetus to the use of the cheque helping to make it the important method of payment it is today. One of the first factors was the extension, by an Act of Parliament in 1825 to the use of cheques free of stamp duty within a 15-mile radius. It was the same Act that allowed joint stock banking within a 65-mile radius of London. In 1833 the cheque was given confirmed legality by another Act of Parliament. This Banking Act allowed joint stock banking into the City of London provided these banks gave up their note–issuing powers, but it did not allow them entry into the Clearing House. They were not admitted until 1854 and, up to that time, they had to present the cheques for collection to the banks upon which they were drawn, and were paid in coins and Bank of England notes. Another stimulus to the use of the cheque was the realisation by those banks which gave up their note-issuing powers that they did not go out of business, and that they could do more business if they replaced note issuing with the operation of a cheque system. In 1853 the Stamp Act fixed the duty on bearer and order cheques at one old penny. This encouraged the use of the cheque, particularly the order cheque, and from this time the use of the cheque grew at the expense of the inland bill of exchange. The growth in the use of the cheque at this time also reflects the growth in joint stock banking and the decline in private banks. In the early part of the twentieth century stamp duty was increased to two old pence and in 1971, with decimalisation, this was abolished.

The use of the cheque grew until the First World War, when a notable increase in the currency supply and a positive retreat from the use of the cheque saw a decline in bank clearing. The use of the cheque increased again after the First World War but following the economic crises of 1929–32 it declined and it was not until after the Second World War, in fact 1962, that cheque clearing regained the importance it had in 1928.

One of the important developments in the use of the cheque happened in 1965 with the introduction of the cheque guarantee card. Figure 7.3 illustrates this type of card.

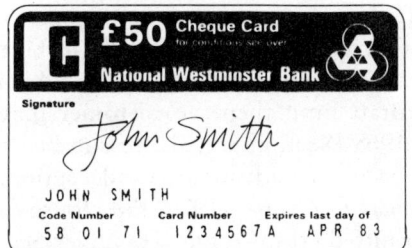
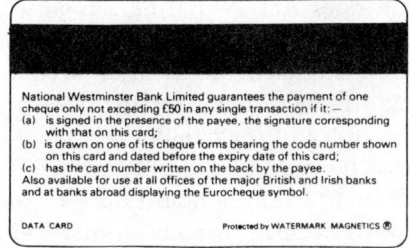

Fig. 7.3 Facsimile of a cheque guarantee card (Reprinted by permission of the Banking Information Service)

The first guarantee cards were for cheques up to £30, their effect was to make these cheques more acceptable. They now guarantee cheques up to £50 if drawn according to the regulations. It might be useful at this stage if we consider the nature and effects of these cards.

As a customer is given a cheque book and an accompanying cheque card, banks could find themselves liable for sums up to £1500. The greater use of cheques and the extent to which the banks have lost money by fraud have made the banks seek measures to reduce this risk. In addition to the original preventive measures, recent cheque cards have features which attempt to make them less susceptible to fraud. Banks only issue cards to new customers when they have established that the customer is someone who will conduct the account properly and that his integrity is proven. An exception is the issuing of cheque cards to students whose income and financial base may be small, but this is done in the hope that they will encourage customer loyalty.

The rights of the various parties to a cheque drawn backed by a cheque guarantee card are as follows:

(1) *Holder or payee* – these persons are guaranteed payment by the issuing bank provided that certain conditions as to the use of the card are observed. These conditions printed on the back of the guarantee card are:

(a) The cheque bears the same name and number as the card.

(b) It is signed before the expiry of the card, in the United Kingdom and Northern Ireland, the Channel Islands or the Isle of Man, in the presence of the payee by the person whose signature appears on the card.

(c) The card number is written on the back of the cheque by the payee.

(d) The card has not been altered or defaced.

It must be remembered that it only guarantees transactions up to £50 and that the practice of drawing more than one cheque for a transaction of over £50 in order to safeguard the cheques is technically not acceptable. Banks do, however, honour such cheques.

(2) *Banker* – the card belongs to the bank. If a customer misuses it the bank can demand its return. The banker is protected by Section 4 of the Cheques Act 1957 if he acts in good faith and without undue negligence in the event of the fraudulent misuse of a cheque and cheque card. If there are insufficient funds in an account, or a customer draws cheques which take the account over the agreed overdraft limit then the customer may be guilty of theft under the Theft Act 1968 (Section 16), the reason being that he may be regarded as gaining a pecuniary advantage by deception. Thus in Metropolitan Police *Commissioners v. Charles* (1976) the House of Lords decided that a customer had committed criminal offences under Section 16 when he drew twenty-five cheques against a cheque card totalling £750 during one evening to pay for gambling losses when his overdraft limit was only £100.

It is the duty of the customer to keep the cheque book and cheque card safe and not in the same place. If these are stolen it is up to the customer to inform the bank swiftly. If this is not done the bank has the right to bring an action against the customer for the recovery of any monies fraudulently spent. This also applies where a customer is found to have been negligent regarding the security of these items.

(3) *Customer* – as we have already seen a customer has the right to have his cheques honoured provided he follows the regulations relating to the use of his cheque card. Also if the cheque book or cheque card is stolen and the bank is informed right away, the customer suffers no loss as a result of any misuse of these items.

Self-assessment exercises

1   What is a drawn note?
2   What two reasons have been given for the increase in the use of the cheque in its early days?
3   How did the early use of the cheque differ from its use today?

4 What caused the restriction in the use of the cheque in the early 1800s?
5 How did the Walks in the City of London develop?
6 List the events in the nineteenth century which caused the cheque to be more widely used.
7 What is the purpose of a cheque guarantee card?
8 List the conditions which are attached to cheque guarantee cards.
9 How is a banker protected if these cards are misused?

7.3 Origin of cheque crossings and their current meanings

In English law a general rule is that the sending by post of a cheque or money is not payment if it is lost before it reaches the creditor, unless payment by this method has been requested by the creditor. In *Pennington v. Crossley & Son* (1897) a firm had been paying for goods for many years by cheques sent through the post. One cheque for £503 never reached the creditor, and was used by a stranger to open up a bank account, the money being paid out. It was held by the Court of Appeal that it was not possible to infer that the creditors had requested this form of payment and so the loss fell upon the defendants who were the drawers of the cheque. Thus in the light of this law it is safer to use cheques which have been crossed. If an open (uncrossed) cheque is stolen the thief can present it to the drawee bank and obtain cash for it, even if the cheque is made payable to a named payee or to his order, it is not difficult for a thief to forge the payee's signature. Thus it is best not to use open cheques unless specifically requested to do so, or if it is certain that they are to be delivered to the payee or his authorised agent. A way to safeguard any cheque is to use one of the many crossings which have come into use. Crossing a cheque gives an instruction to the paying banker to pay this amount into a bank account. Although this would not prevent a determined thief, it would make the commission of this fraud difficult either by allowing time for it to be discovered or by allowing recourse to the thief's account, unless a fictitious name was used. The only exception to this is under a 'holder in due course' situation, which is explained later in this chapter.

7.31 Origin of crossings

Crossings originated in the eighteenth century in the bankers' Clearing House as a way of making the system work more easily. Clerks of the collecting banks used to take cheques to the Clearing House to hand over to the paying banks' clerks. If these clerks were not there, the cheques were placed in the drawer of the paying bank and, so that the cheques could be identified, the collecting bank clerk wrote the name of his bank across the face of the cheques. Customers of the bank, hearing of this practice, felt it might be useful to safeguard their cheques if they wrote across them the name of the payee's bank. This became known as a **special crossing** as the cheque was said to have been specially crossed to that bank. If the payee's banker was not known the words '& Co' were written between two parallel lines. This was a **general crossing** and it meant that the cheque would be paid only if presented through a bank.

Legal recognition of cheque crossings came after the Cheque Acts of 1856, 1858 and 1876. These have been repealed and now the current provisions relating to crossed cheques are contained in Sections 76 to 81 of the Bills of Exchange Act 1882. We still have the double classification of general and special crossings. The basic difference is that a general crossing enables the cheque to be collected by any banker while a special means it can only be collected by the named banker.

Self-assessment exercise

Explain how crossings on cheques developed and the difference between general and special crossings.

7.32 Types of crossings

General crossings

Figure 7.4 shows the forms these may take.

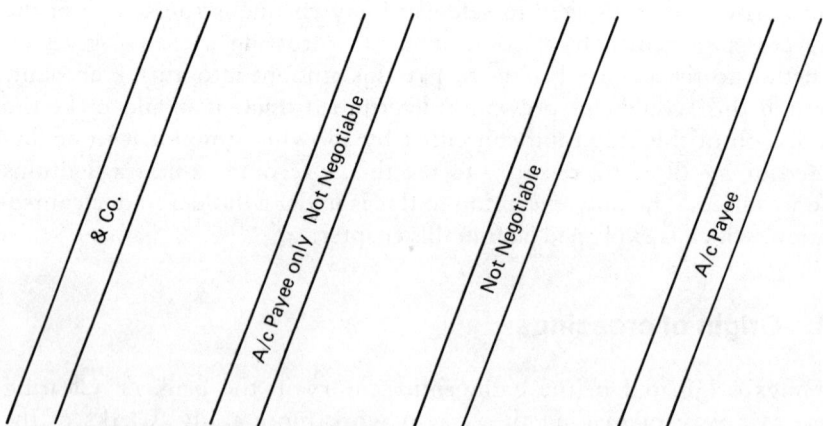

Fig. 7.4 Examples of general crossings

As we can see the cheque is crossed by drawing two parallel lines across its face and by writing any of the above words between the lines. We have already seen the effect of putting & Co in the crossing, the two blank lines have the same effect. When a cheque is crossed 'not negotiable' it is no longer a negotiable instrument. Thus anyone subsequently receiving such a cheque can acquire no better title to it than the person who is passing it on. The cheque is transferable but is so with this limitation attached to it. The full effects of negotiability are discussed later in this chapter. The use of 'A/c Payee' has no statutory standing but it is recognised by the courts who have ruled that if the collecting banker disregards this instruction by collecting for someone other than the payee, in the event of that person not being entitled to it, the banker may be liable for damages to the rightful payee. Thus the bank will not collect on these cheques unless they are for small amounts and the customer is one of long standing. Marking a cheque 'A/c Payee' and 'Not Negotiable' is one of the safest ways in which a cheque can be crossed. As we have seen, not negotiable makes the cheque no longer a negotiable instrument and this gives protection to the drawer of the cheque. A/c Payee gives clear instructions to the collecting banker to collect only on behalf of the payee, again protecting the drawer. This latter form of crossing was recommended by the Council of the Institute of Chartered Accountants in England and Wales in October 1957.

Special crossings

These are shown in Fig. 7.5.

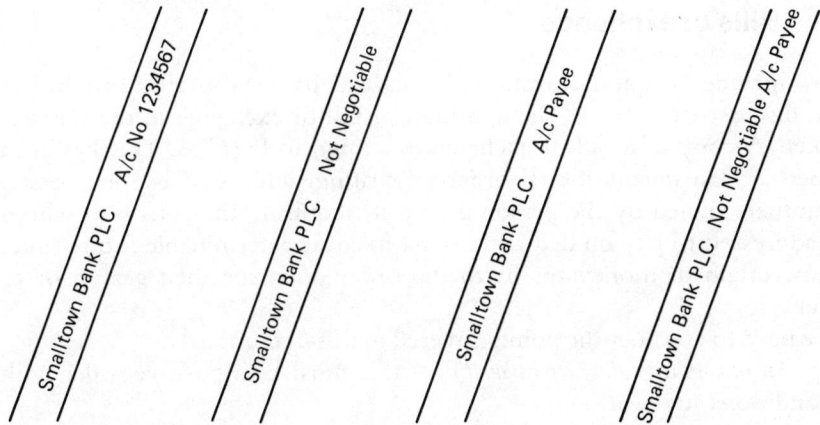

Fig. 7.5 Examples of special crossings

As we have seen a special crossing is when a cheque bears the name of a banker across its face. The words A/c Payee or not negotiable or both can be added as well. These have the same effects as those explained under General crossings.

If a cheque is uncrossed it can be crossed generally or specially, also the words not negotiable can be added to any other words in the crossing. A generally crossed cheque can be specially crossed again by adding the name of a banker. The Bills of Exchange Act 1882 makes it illegal to add to or alter a crossing, and it makes the crossing a material part of the cheque.

Self-assessment exercise

What is the safest form of general crossing and what is its effect?

7.4 Different types of negotiable instrument

Negotiable instruments can be described as anything which is used in business to enable payment of a debt to be made. Thus a cheque has already been described as a negotiable instrument and later in this chapter we will learn more about the legal aspects of negotiability. For the present, we need only consider the items which are identified in the commercial world today as being negotiable. Thus the list is not a closed one and, although there have been no recent additions, it is possible that new types of instrument could be introduced in the future. It would be up to the courts to decide if they were fully negotiable. The following are the principle negotiable instruments in use today.

7.41 Bills of exchange

These include cheques, commercial bills and bankers' drafts. In Chapter 4 we discussed the use of the commercial bill of exchange in the classical market. A copy of a bill of exchange is shown in Fig. 7.6. This has been defined as: 'an unconditional order in writing, addressed by one person to another, signed by the person giving it, requiring the person to whom it is addressed to pay on demand or at a fixed or determinable future time, a sum certain in money to, or to the order of, a specified person or to bearer'.

We need to consider the points covered in this definition.

(1) *An unconditional order in writing* – this must be a positive order with no conditions attached.

(2) *In writing* – this includes printing and typewriting. Use of a medium which can be easily rubbed out is not to be encouraged.

(3) *Addressed by one person to another* – this can include one person instructing another to pay a third party. In this event the person giving the instruction is called the **drawer**, the person instructed to pay is called the **drawee** and the person receiving the payment is called the **payee**. Sometimes the drawee and payee are one and the same person.

Legal Implications of the Various Banking Instruments   173

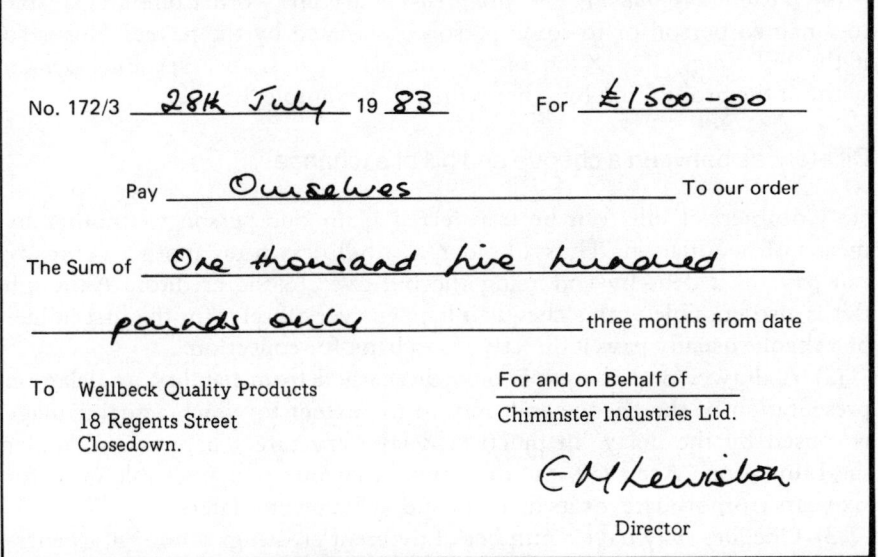

Fig. 7.6   Facsimile of a bill of exchange

(4) *Signed by the person giving it* – the drawer may sign the bill himself or it may be signed by an agent. If an agent signs it then he is made personally liable unless a clear indication is given that he is acting for someone else. This can be done by signing it 'per pro' or 'for and on behalf of' the principal. If it is signed by an agent without proper authority it is not a proper bill unless the action is ratified by principal later. This cannot be done if the signature is a forgery. If 'per pro' is indicated this shows that the agent has limited authority, and that the principal will only be bound if the agent is acting within that authority.

(5) *Requiring the person to whom it is addressed to pay on demand* – this can be on demand or presentation at sight where no time for payment is indicated.

(6) *Or at a fixed or determinable future time* – this may be a fixed time or determined by a period of time from when the bill is drawn, or when the drawee sees it (at sight). It can even be after some certain event takes place the time of which is not certain.

(7) *A sum certain in money* – this can include the addition of interest, some statement about instalments, or even some relationship to foreign currency exchange rates. If the words and figures differ the bill is still valid, and the words are what is accepted. However, the use of computers in modern banking systems might mean that where there are small discrepancies bills will be returned unless the amount is confirmed by the drawer.

(8) *To or to the order of a specified person or to bearer* – order bills are payable to a named person or to some person designated by the payee. This is so if the bill states 'Pay X on order' and also if it is to a specified person without the prohibition by other words, for example 'Pay X . . .'.

Differences between a cheque and bill of exchange

(1) Commercial bills can be transferred from one person to another by means of negotiation. Thus a holder of a bill drawn on another company can pay off a debt by endorsing the bill over to the creditor. Although this is also possible with a cheque it happens very rarely, for the first holder of a cheque usually pays it directly into a bank for collection.

(2) A drawer of a cheque is only discharged from liability by delay on presentation of the cheque and only to the extent to which actual damage is caused by the delay. In practice, delay very rarely happens so, under the Limitations Act 1939, the drawer of a cheque remains liable on it for six years from its date, or its date of issue, whichever is later.

(3) Cheques may have a number of different crossings while bills, generally, are not crossed.

(4) A person raising a commercial bill sends it to another party to have it accepted. Thus this latter person is liable on the bill. A cheque is never accepted by the bank on which it is drawn. Thus the rules relating to the acceptance of bills do not apply to cheques. If a bank is instructed to pay on a cheque and it is dishonoured the bank is not liable, all the payee can do is sue the drawer and any endorser.

(5) In certain circumstances where a bank pays an order cheque which has a forged or unauthorised endorsement then it may have discharged its liability. This is not so with a bill which is paid under the same circumstances; certain rights and liabilities still exist.

(6) The contractual relationship that exists between a banker and his customer is not the same as the relationship that exists between the parties to a bill.

A banker's draft is an instrument that is drawn by a banker upon himself. The Bills of Exchange Act 1882 allows the holder of this instrument the option of treating it as a bill of exchange or a promissory note, and as seen in *Slingsby & Others v. District Bank* (1932) it is not a cheque. A typical example of a banker's draft is seen in Fig. 7.7.

Self-assessment exercises

1 Draw up a bill of exchange showing the following transaction:
   A bill drawn by G Fawkes, Director of the Pyrotechnics Co. Ltd for £2000 payable to the Galaxy Fireworks Co. for acceptance by the Chinese Novelty Co., Leyton Street, Soho.

Legal Implications of the Various Banking Instruments 175

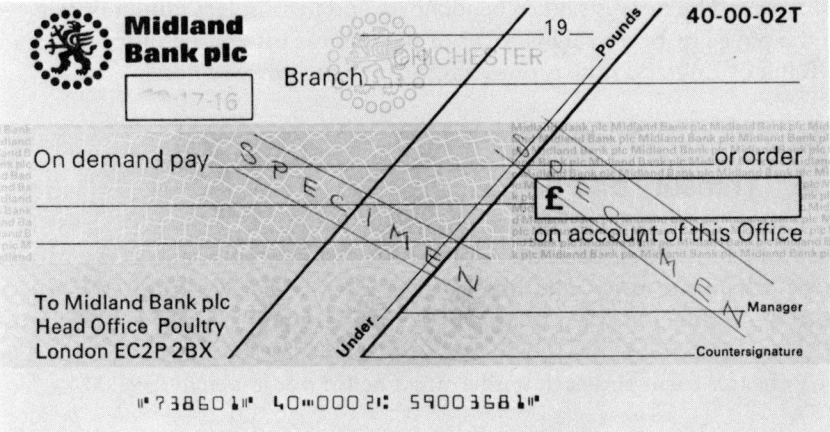

Fig. 7.7 Banker's draft

2 What are three main differences between a bill of exchange and a cheque?

7.42 Promissory notes

These are defined in the Bills of Exchange Act 1882 as: 'an unconditional promise in writing, made by one person to another, signed by the maker, engaging to pay on demand, or at a fixed or determinable future time, a sum certain in money, to or to the order of, a specified person or to bearer.'

Examples of promissory notes are shown in Fig. 7.8.

Chichester
1 January 19..

Ninety-one days after date I promise to pay Robert Smythe-Winde or order the sum of five hundred pounds for value received.

M W DOWNEY

Chichester
1 January 19..

Three months after date we jointly and severally promise to pay the A & B Insurance Co.Ltd or order at their Portsmouth office, the sum of six hundred pounds with lawful interest for the same the date hereof.

M W DOWNEY
G B FIELDER

Fig. 7.8 Two examples of promissory notes

As we can see from the diagrams a promissory note can be drawn by one person or by a number of persons jointly and severally according to its nature. The note is said to be inchoate and incomplete until it is delivered to the payee or bearer. This form of payment is often used in foreign trade. A Bank of England note is one example of a promissory note.

7.43 Treasury bills

Treasury bills are documents representing short-term loans to the government which are repayable ninety days after issue. We have seen the use of these in the classical money market in Chapter 4. They are for amounts of £5000, £10 000, £25 000, £50 000, £100 000, £250 000 and £1 000 000. They are in bearer form and each tender must be for not less than £50 000.

7.44 Bearer bonds

These are bonds payable to bearer. The company does not keep a list of the holders so that attached to each bond are a number of coupons which can be torn off by the holder at the right time to show that he is entitled to the interest. Title to these bonds passes by mere delivery with the added intention to transfer. The transferee must take these bonds in good faith, having given value and not having any knowledge of the transferor's defective title. In this case title proclaims right of ownership.

7.45 Bearer debentures

Debentures are acknowledgement of a debt by some person or persons. Usually issued by companies, they can be secured against the assets of the firm. This means that if the company does not meet the interest payments, or repayment, the holders of these debentures can sell the asset and take their monies from the proceeds.

7.46 Warehousekeepers warrants

When goods are placed in a warehouse for storage the depositor is given a receipt or warrant. Some of these latter are documents of title which are transferred by endorsement if they have been issued by a recognised warehouse keeper. Such powers are granted by Act of Parliament. The effect is to make these documents negotiable instruments.

7.47 Quasi-negotiable instruments

These are instruments which possess two of the characteristics of negotiability but not the third. An example of this type of instrument is a **bill of lading**.

These are documents signed by the ship's master or his agent and given to the person loading the goods on board a ship. A similar document for air transport is the **airway bill**. These instruments perform three functions:

(1) to show the terms of the contract for the enshipment of goods;
(2) to show that the goods have been shipped;
(3) to provide evidence that the holder has ownership of the goods, and they will only be released from the hold of the ship on presentation of this document. As we will see in a later chapter they form part of what is known as documentary credit.

They lack the third characteristic of negotiability in that the person receiving these documents cannot gain any better title to the goods than the person giving it.

Self-assessment exercises

1 Draw up a promissory note payable for £3000 from I M Grast to V Johannes for the purchase of toys.
2 What is a Treasury bill?
3 How can the holder of a bearer debenture receive the interest due? How does a bearer debenture differ from a bearer bond?
4 Explain the use of a bill of lading. Why is this document not a negotiable instrument?

7.5 Parties to a bill of exchange, their rights and responsibilities

We have already discussed in Section 7.4 of this chapter, in simple terms, the parties to a bill. We now need to consider, in greater detail, their nature and their responsibilities.

7.51 Drawer of the bill

This is the person who makes out the bill or sends the instructions. The drawer's liability only becomes an actual liability when the instrument is dishonoured. That is, when it is presented for payment and this is refused. Until that time no one can successfully bring an action against him. If it is dishonoured the drawer must compensate the holder or endorser who is compelled to pay on it. There are exceptions to this rule when a person can offer one of the following defences:

(1) absence or failure of consideration;
(2) failure to present the instrument at the proper time;
(3) no notice of dishonour was given;
(4) the defendant did not have the capacity to contract;
(5) instrument incomplete when signed;
(6) a condition was attached when drawn;
(7) there is evidence of a forged signature;
(8) there has been a material alteration of the instrument;
(9) a fraud has been perpetrated against the instrument;
(10) duress or undue influence was placed upon the drawer;
(11) the instrument is overdue;
(12) the instrument had been dishonoured previously.

In the case of a cheque, the drawer might be liable to one person but not to another. Thus if a cheque was drawn by Brown and paid to Smith, who had promised to dig Brown's garden but did not do so, Brown could instruct the bank not to pay Smith. He could not successfully sue Brown for a dishonourable debt as the action would fail because of the lack of consideration. If, however, Smith had used this cheque to pay Jones for a service that Jones had carried out for Smith, Jones could sue Brown and the fact that Smith had not done what he should would be no defence for Brown.

Section 5(1)b of the Bills of Exchange Act 1882 provides that the drawer of an instrument is precluded from denying to the holder in due course the existence of the payee and his capacity to endorse the cheque. This is known as the doctrine of estoppel.

7.52 Drawee/acceptor of the bill

The drawee is the person on whom the instrument is drawn and who is required to pay the money. This will be in accordance with the terms stated on the instrument. A bill of exchange is presented for acceptance, until and unless the drawee accepts the bill he is not liable on it. Once it is accepted he becomes the party primarily liable to the bill. Section 54 of the Bills of Exchange Act provides that the acceptor of a bill by accepting it thus agrees to pay on it. He is stopped from denying, to a holder in due course, the existence of the drawer, the genuineness of this person's signature and the drawer's capacity to draw the bill. If the drawer's signature is forged the drawer is not liable, but the drawee is still liable by operation of the doctrine of estoppel.

7.53 Payee of a bill

The payee is the person to whom the instrument is drawn – that is, the person to whom it is paid. In some cases the payee endorses the bill (signs it on the back) and transfers it to another person called the **endorsee**.

The payee has the right of payment provided he has given legal consideration, has not perpetrated a fraud, presented it on time, given no notice of dishonour and made no material alteration. He also has the right to endorse and transfer the instrument. If the payee's signature has been forged then the acceptor must still pay.

7.54 Endorser of the bill

The endorser is the person who endorses an order bill so that it can be transfered to another person. Endorsing means signing the bill on the back, by the payee, or any subsequent holder of the bill. Under Section 55 of the Bills of Exchange Act 1882 the endorser by endorsing the instrument engages:

(1) When the bill is presented it will be accepted and paid according to its terms. If it is dishonoured, he will compensate the holder or subsequent endorser who is compelled to meet it, as long as the proper procedures have been followed.

(2) He is also estopped from denying to a holder in due course that the signature of the drawer is not genuine, or that it was irregular in all respects.

(3) He cannot deny to any immediate or subsequent endorsee that he did not have good title. Thus in the event of a forged endorsement, a bill can become valid between parties transferring the bill after forgery.

7.55 Holder of a bill

This is the person who is either the payee or the endorsee of the bill, or note, who is in possession of it or the bearer thereof. The holder may be someone who is an unlawful holder such as a thief, or finder of a bearer bill, or someone who fraudulently transfers a bill to himself. Such people obtain no rights against the parties to a bill and any claims which may be brought will fail because of defective title. The rights of a lawful holder are as follows:

(1) He may sue in his own name.

(2) Where a holder in due course holds the bill free from any defect of title of the prior parties, he is also free from the more personal defences which are available to prior parties among themselves. He may enforce payment against all parties liable on the bill.

(3) If he has defective title and obtains payment on the bill, the person who pays him in due course obtains a valid discharge of the bill. If, on the other hand, he has negotiated a bill to the holder in due course, that holder receives good and complete title to the bill.

A holder's responsibilities are to see that if the bill has not been properly accepted that this is done, and that the correct procedures are carried out for presentation. This is also necessary if the bill is dishonoured.

7.6 Conversion and its consequences

This defined by Winfield as: 'any act in relation to goods of a person which constitutes an unjustifiable denial of his title to them'.

This is basically concerned with chattels, but it can be applied to cheques as a cheque may be a chattel, the value being the money into which the chattel can be converted.

A collecting bank would be guilty of conversion if it presented a cheque for payment and consequently obtained the money on behalf of a customer who was not entitled to it. There is some belief that conversion takes place on receipt of the cheque. This was seen in the decision in *Fine Art Society v. Union Bank of London* (1886). However, it is also held that the bank in such a case is merely holding onto the cheque, is acting as an intermediary and not interfering in the property of the drawer.

There is also some doubt as to whether a drawer who has been induced by fraud to draw a cheque can be said to have an immediate right to possess it sufficient to bring an action for damages for conversion. Thus where a thief sold stolen goods to a dealer who drew a cheque to pay for them and the thief then paid this cheque into a bank account and withdrew the money, the question is who was liable on the cheque – thief or bank?

It is not always possible to decide if a prospective plaintiff has a sufficient interest in chattels, including cheques, to enable him to bring an action for damages for conversion. The plaintiff must prove that he had an immediate right to possession of the chattels at the time.

Where the drawee's bank pays the proceeds of a cheque to someone who is not entitled to it and this person has acted in such a way that would amount to conversion, then the drawee's bank, unless protected by statute, is liable on an action for damages due to its conversion by the person who is lawfully entitled to the money. It is likely that the drawee bank is protected by Sections 6 and 80 of the Bills of Exchange Act 1882 and Section 1(1) of the Cheques Act 1957. One area where this protection is not afforded is under Section 79(2) of the Bills of Exchange Act which holds that when a cheque is crossed and the bank does not carry out the instructions regarding crossings, then the drawee sustains loss by this action.

Self-assessment exercises

1. When is the drawer of a bill liable on it? Give three exceptions to this liability.
2. What is the 'drawee on a bill'? When does such a person become liable on the bill?
3. List the conditions which give the payee on a bill the right to payment.
4. What legal obligations rest on the endorser of a bill?
5. What are the rights of a legal holder of a bill? Give an example of an illegal holder.

7.7 Conversion and safe custody

You are probably aware that customers of a bank ask it to look after various valuables like jewellery, share certificates, life policies and title deeds. This forms the **safe custody** service of the bank. The property is either kept in a box with the customer holding a key, or in the strongroom of the bank from whence the customer can request its return at any time during normal bank business hours. When these valuables are handed to the bank the customer receives a receipt detailing the items. Return of the items is on presentation of this receipt.

A liability for conversion arises if it can be proved that the bank delivered up these articles to a third party without the customer's authority. Any person who wrongfully disposes of another's goods so depriving him of possession is guilty of conversion. This applies even if the wrongful conversion was made bona fide and without negligence. In one famous case *Langtry v. Union Bank of London* (1896) an out-of-court settlement was reached with the result that no precedent decision was forthcoming. In this case Mrs Lily Langtry deposited jewellery in a bank. A thief obtained some of her headed letter paper and forged her signature requesting the bank to deliver up the jewellery. This the bank did. Until a case is decided in the courts there is no clear answer to this question. One of the underlying factors relating to safe custody is how careful should the banker be? The standard of care in these circumstances depends upon whether the bank is paid for this service, or if it is carrying it out for free (gratuitously). Where a payment is being made then there is no doubt that the standard of care should be greater than if it were giving a free service. However, if a bank receives a request to deliver up property to a third party it should take steps to discover the genuineness of the request.

Self-assessment exercises

Advise Smalltown Bank plc of its position in the following:
1. James Brown received a cheque from William Smith for £300. It was stolen

by Frickle who used the cheque to open up an account with the Closedown branch of the Smalltown Bank in the name of William Smith and then withdrew the money. The thief gave the name of a friend, who was known to Smalltown Bank, for a referee in the opening of the account. The cheque was crossed 'A/c Payee'.

2 George Loid had deposited, for safe keeping, some bearer bonds with the Rushton branch of the Smalltown Bank. A thief stole notepaper belonging to Loid bearing his address. The thief then presented a letter on this notepaper to the bank purporting that Loid requested the return to the thief. Loid is now complaining to the bank.

7.8 Agents, their unlawful acts and the effects of these on banks

An agent is defined as: 'a person who is employed by a principal for the purposes of bringing the principal into contractual relationship with third parties'.

Banks have dealings with agents when they do business with people who have power of attorney, who are partners in firms and directors of companies. On occasions, the banks themselves are agents for their customers, for example, when a customer instructs a bank to sell some shares on his behalf.

The unlawful acts of agents which are of interest to a bank are when an agent acts beyond his power, either to draw cheques on the principal's account, or to borrow money. When someone holds out to be the authorised agent of a principal and they are not, they are personally liable to anyone who has relied upon this action and has suffered loss thereby. This also applies to an agent who has limited authority and exceeds it – this is known as a **breach of warranted authority**. However, it is possible for a principal to subsequently ratify these unlawful actions of the agent. If this is done, the ratification is backdated to the time when the contract was originally made. A bank is, therefore, interested in this point of law, for if it lost by some unauthorised act of an agent, it could receive compensation if such an action was subsequently ratified by the principal.

There are also occasions when a principal is stopped from denying the actions of his agent on his behalf. This may be where the actions of the principal, either expressly or impliedly, are such that he cannot deny that the agent/principal relationship exists. This principle comes under the doctrine of estoppel. Thus where a business uses an employee acting as its agent to collect items from a bank, and then the employee is dismissed but continues to collect these items and the bank has not been informed of the dismissal, the firm may be estopped from denying an agency relationship. This is discussed further in Chapter 10.

7.9 Negotiability

Negotiability is that quality which enables a person who receives a negotiable instrument to gain good title to the instrument even though the transferor has a bad title. This is demonstrated in the following example.

Jones works in a particular capacity where he can draw cheques on behalf of his employer. Finding himself short of money, he draws a cheque in favour of his wife drawn on the firm's account. His wife then endorses it over to a trader in payment of an outstanding bill. The question is – has the trader the right to the money? The answer is that, provided the trader has fulfilled certain conditions, he has good title to the money for in these circumstance the cheque is a negotiable instrument.

You may wonder why this legal benefit is conferred in such an easy way. If one purchases land there is a long procedure to go through before transfer of title is effected; this procedure is outlined in Chapter 9. Obviously, commercial transactions would be slowed down considerably if all transfers of property necessitated checking the transferor's legal title to the property. Thus there developed in the courts the recognition that if a money instrument transferred was taken in good faith and for value by the transferee, he had a right of action to recover provided that order instruments were endorsed as well as delivered and bearer instruments were delivered.

In legal terms a negotiable instrument is a 'chose' in action. This means that the holder has a right or interest in property that does not physically exist. This contrasts with a 'chose in possession' which is an interest in an actual physical possession, such as land or a flock of sheep. The word 'chose' comes from the French which means 'thing'. Thus a person may purchase a crop of grapes from an Italian grower. If these grapes are in the stockroom then this is a chose in possession. If, however, the grapes are in a warehouse in Italy awaiting enshipment and a warehouse receipt is held then this is a chose in action. Examples of choses in action, in addition to cheques and bills of exchange, are patents, copyrights, insurance policies and shares in companies.

Negotiability exists if the following three conditions are present:
(1) the instrument is transferred by delivery or by endorsement and delivery;
(2) by such delivery all legal rights to the obligation outlined in the instrument are transferred as well;
(3) the transferee is seen to have received the instrument free from all defects in the title of the transferor or any previous party, and free from all counterclaims (equities) and from the rights of third parties.

In the case of (1) above there are specific times when an instrument needs endorsing so that a valid transfer is effected.

In the case of (2) this means the holder can sue in his own right, and if he wishes to transfer this on no notice of this transfer need be given to previous parties.

In the case of (3) the courts will only consider counterclaims in certain circumstances as it is believed that a bill of exchange must be similar to cash.

Self-assessment exercise

What do you understand by the term negotiability? What conditions need to be present for it to exist?

7.10 Acceptance, endorsement and discharge of a bill of exchange

7.101 Acceptance

Under Section 17(1) of the Bills of Exchange Act 1882 it is stated that this is the signification by the drawee of his assent to the order of the drawer. Section 17(2) of this Act states that in order for this acceptance to be valid it must comply with the following conditions:

(1) It must be written on the bill and be signed by the drawee. The mere signature of the drawee without additional words is sufficient.

(2) It must not state that the drawee will perform his promise by any other means than by the payment of money.

Where a bill is payable after a determined time after sight then the acceptor should put the date of acceptance on the bill. Often, after the bill has been accepted it becomes known in itself as 'an acceptance'.

Generally, a bill is complete when it is sent to the drawee for acceptance, but a bill may be accepted before it has been signed by the drawer or if incomplete in some other way. It can be accepted after the time it falls due for payment, or after it has been dishonoured, either by a previous refusal to accept, or by non-payment. Where a sight bill is not accepted at first it is automatically dishonoured. If it is subsequently accepted then the holder can have the bill treated as if it had been accepted from the beginning unless some different term is agreed.

Acceptance is either **general** or **qualified**. If it is a general acceptance it is accepted without any questioning of the orders of the drawer. Qualified acceptance, in express terms, is of five different types and varies the effect of the bill. These types of qualified acceptance are:

(1) *Conditional* – makes payment by the acceptor dependent upon the fulfilment of a condition therein stated. An example of a conditional acceptance is where the following statement was written on a bill: 'Accepted payable on surrender of bill of lading evidencing shipment of 3000 metric tonnes of wheat.'

(2) *Partial* – acceptance to pay only part of the amount for which the bill is drawn. An example of this is: 'Accepted for £350 only' (where the bill was for £500).

(3) *Local* – this is an acceptance to pay only at a specified place. An example of this is: 'Acceptable payable only at Eastland Bank plc, Poultry Lane, London.' If 'only' were omitted it would be a general acceptance.

(4) *Qualified as to time*. An example of this is: 'Accepted payable nine months after date' (where the bill is drawn six months after date).

(5) *Acceptance by one or more of several drawers but not by all*. An example of this is where a bill is drawn of Smith, Jones and Brown and it is accepted by Smith only. If Smith had the authority to accept on behalf of all the drawers this would not be qualified acceptance.

7.102 Endorsement

This is defined in Section 31(1) of the Bills of Exchange Act 1882 as being endorsement completed by delivery. In the *National Bank v. Paterson* a judge held that, with regard to a negotiable instrument, endorsement can have three meanings:

(1) In a general sense, this can be where every signature on the back of such an instrument is to act as a receipt or means of identification.

(2) Where it signifies that the endorser intends to take on the liability of the instrument. This is based on the legal premise of 'animo indorsandii'.

(3) Where it signifies delivery of the instrument. This is the meaning that falls within the Bills of Exchange Act.

Endorsement may be in **blank** or **specific**. If it is in blank this merely means the endorser signs the instrument on the back. This in effect makes the instrument payable to bearer and is negotiated only by delivery. Endorsement in specific specifies the person to whom, or to whose order, the instrument is to be paid. Thus where a cheque is made payable to John James or order it can be endorsed in specific to R Wells by James writing on the bank:

'Pay R Wells or order'
signed J James.

An order bill can be transferred as a bearer bill at one time and then subsequently changed back to an order bill. Where a bill has been through a number of transfers and there is not enough space on the back for further signatures, it is possible to attach a piece of paper to it for these further signatures. This is called an **allonge**.

A conditional endorsement is as follows:
'Pay William Brown, or order, on his attaining his thirtieth birthday'.

This condition may be disregarded by the payer, and the payment to an endorsee is valid even if the condition is not fulfilled. There are, however, two kinds of restrictive endorsements. The first restricts any further negotiation, and the second charges that the bill must be dealt with as directed. Sometimes a bank in one country endorses an instrument in this way for payment by another specific bank in another country. For example: 'Pay Eastland Bank plc or order for collection.'

The purpose of this endorsement is to prevent any wrongful dealings with the instrument. A restrictive endorsement gives power to the endorsee to receive payment and to sue on the bill any party who could be sued by the endorser but cannot transfer his rights as an endorsee. A restrictive endorsee cannot be a holder in due course.

Since the passing of the Cheques Act 1957 endorsements have become of lesser importance in the areas of cheques and bankers' drafts.

7.103 Discharge

This can be effected by:

(1) *Payment in due course* (Section 59) – this happens when the drawee or acceptor or an agent (including a banker) makes a payment at the time when the bill matures or after that to the holder, in good faith and without notice that the holder's title to the bill is defective. Sometimes a bill is renewed either by the original bill being accepted, or by the acceptor accepting a new bill payable in the future in exchange for the old bill. In either of these actions the holder must be aware that the drawee and endorsers are no longer liable unless, in the case of extending the existing bill, they consent to liability. It is best if this consent is in writing. In the case of a new bill they can be liable if they sign it as well.

(2) *Merger* (Section 61) – this is where the acceptor of a bill at some point becomes the holder of the bill at or after its maturity. This could happen where an acceptor receives the bill in payment of a debt from a subsequent holder. If it is received before maturity it is not discharged and it may go for negotiation, but payment cannot be enforced against any party to whom it was previously due.

(3) *Waiver* (Section 62) – this is where the holder of a bill at or after maturity either gives up the bill to the acceptor or renounces his rights unconditionally in writing. If, in the latter case, the bill comes into the hands of a holder in due course the acceptor is still liable.

(4) *Cancellation* (Section 63) – the holder or an agent must display an intention to cancel. If made in error it is inoperative. If a cheque is cancelled in the day's clearing, it should be inscribed 'cancelled in error' for it to be returned unpaid. Regarding a torn cheque, a drawee's bank will not pay on it unless the collecting bank confirms that the tearing was accidental. A torn cheque, not in two pieces, may still be paid.

Self-assessment exercises

1 What do you understand by acceptance of a bill of exchange and upon what conditions does it depend?
2 What must be done if a bill payable 'three months from sight' is accepted?
3 Explain the difference between general and qualified acceptance.
4 What is meant by 'endorsement' of a bill within the terms of the Bills of Exchange Act 1882?
5 Explain the legal difference between blank and specific endorsements on a negotiable instrument.
6 What is an allonge?
7 Give the two examples of a restrictive endorsement on a bill of exchange.
8 How is discharge of a bill effected by payment?
9 Explain the difference between discharge of a bill by waiver and discharge by cancellation.

7.11 Statutory protection for various holders of a bill of exchange

7.111 The holder

The interests of the holder of a bill are found in Section 2 of the Bills of Exchange Act 1882. We have already discussed earlier in this chapter (Section 7.55) the rights and powers of a holder. It would be of interest here to see how the wrongful possessor of a bill differs from a holder. A wrongful possessor is a person who takes a bill bearing a forged 'essential endorsement'. This person cannot be a holder as he is neither the endorsee of the bill nor the bearer of a bearer bill. There are two specific types of holder.

(1) *Holder for value* (Section 27(2)) – in this case a person can still be a holder even though he may not have given value for the instrument provided that some previous holder gave value. This type of holder has the right to enforce the bill against all parties who became parties prior to the giving of this value. This is against all parties who have actually received value. He can sue on the bill in his own name but obtain no better title than the transferee possessed. An example of a holder for value is as follows:

Jones sells goods to Smith who accepts a bill of exchange for £300. Jones endorses it and transfers it to Brown from whom he has purchased raw materials. Brown endorses it to Green as a gift. Green is a holder for value as both Jones and Brown have given value for the bill.

(2) *Holder in due course* (Section 29) – this is a holder who has taken a bill, complete and regular on the face of it, under certain conditions, namely:

 (i) that the bill was not overdue before he became the holder, and if the bill had been dishonoured that he had not been given notice;

(ii) that the bill was taken having given value and in good faith and that at the time when the bill was negotiated he had no reasonable doubt of the title of the person who negotiated it.

The face of the bill for this purpose includes the back of the bill also. Section 24 of the Bills of Exchange Act 1882 also provides that there must be no prior forgery on the bill as each person cannot be holder of a forged endorsement. Also, under Section 81 the bill must not be marked 'not negotiable' or have a specific endorsement such as: 'Pay J Brown only', nor must it be marked 'not transferable'. A holder in due course has certain privileges:

(a) he can sue on the bill in his own name;
(b) he can enforce payment against all prior parties;
(c) he holds the bill from all defects in title of other parties. Thus a holder in due course can gain perfect title from a person with defective title.
(d) he can pass on perfect title.

There are certain circumstances where a holder cannot set himself up as a holder in due course:

(i) if the payee;
(ii) where a holder knows of a fraud or has advice or constructive notice of dishonour.

(In these circumstances he is guilty of displaying lack of good faith.)

(iii) where he knowingly has the bill negotiated under circumstances which can be proved to have been fraudulent preference.

Self-assessment exercises

1   Who is a wrongful possessor of a bill?
2   Who is a holder for value and what are the rights of this type of holder?
3   What conditions must exist for a bank to be a holder in due course on a bill?
4   What are the privileges of a holder in due course of a bill of exchange?

7.12   Presentation for payment (Sections 10 and 45)

Within the terms of the Bills of Exchange Act 1882 a bill must be duly presented for payment. If it is not, the endorsee and the drawer are discharged from liability on the bill but the acceptor is not discharged.

Where a bill is presented in accordance with certain rules then it is said to have been duly presented for payment. These rules are:

(1) When not a demand bill it must be presented on the day it falls due.

(2) When a demand bill then, subject to the provision of the Act, it must be presented within a reasonable time after its issue so that the drawer will be liable and within a reasonable time of its endorsement, so that the endorser will be liable. This reasonable time will be determined with regard to the

nature of the bill, trade usage of similar bills and the facts of the particular case.

(3) Presentment must be by the holder or his authorised agent on a business day, at a reasonable hour and at the proper place to the person designated by the bill as the payee or his authorised agent.

(4) The proper place is either the place specified on the bill or if no place is specified and the address of the drawee or acceptor is on the bill at this place so named. If there is no name or address given then at the drawee's or acceptor's place of business if either is known. If none of these circumstances exist then the bill is said to have been presented to the drawee/acceptor if found, or at their last known place of business or residence.

(5) If the bill is presented at the proper place and, after the exercise of reasonable diligence, no one can be found authorised to pay on the bill or the payment is refused then no further presentment to the drawee or acceptor is required.

(6) If the bill is drawn or accepted by two or more persons who are not partners then if the place for payment is not specified it must be presented to them all.

(7) If the drawee or acceptor of a bill is dead and again it is not specified on the bill as to where it is to be presented then it must be presented to the personal representatives if, after reasonable diligence, they can be found.

(8) If, through usage or agreement, presentation can be through a Post Office.

It is possible for presentation of a bill to be specifically delayed if it is the result of circumstances beyond the control of the holder and it is not due to his default, misconduct, or negligence. Once the cause of delay has gone then presentation must be made with reasonable diligence.

Presentation can be dispensed with if:

(a) all conditions for presentation under the Act have been carried out and it still cannot be put into effect. If the holder of a cheque believes that it is likely to be dishonoured he is not excused the necessity of presentation;

(b) the drawee is a fictitious person;

(c) in the case of the drawer where the drawee or acceptor is not bound as between himself and the drawer, to accept or pay the bill and the drawer has no reason to believe that the bill will be paid if presented. For example, this would be where a bill was made for accommodation of the drawer who cannot then expect payment;

(d) in the case of an endorser where the bill was accepted for the accommodation of that endorser and he has no reason to believe that the bill will be paid if presented.

An example of (c) and (d) above would be where:

A seeking financial support borrows money from B and draws, in reserve, a postdated cheque payable to B for the money but intends to repay the loan in cash before this cheque falls due. In this case either the drawer or any subsequent endorser would not expect the cheque to be presented for payment.

(e) where presentation is waived, either expressly or impliedly.

Self-assessment exercises

1 If a bill is not presented for payment how does this affect the drawer and the acceptor?
2 What will determine a reasonable time for the presentation of a bill?
3 Under what circumstances can presentation of a bill be dispensed with?

7.13 Position of the collecting banker with regard to statutory protection

There are three possible protections available to the collecting banker; which protections apply depend upon whether the bank is collecting for itself or for another person.

(1) Protection under the Bills of Exchange Act 1882.

The purpose of this Act was to 'codify the law relating to bills of exchange, cheques and promissory notes'. The following is a guide to its main sections:

Part 1	Preliminary	Sections 1–2
Part 2	Bills of exchange	
	Form and interpretation	Sections 3–21
	Capacity and authority of parties	Sections 22–6
	Consideration for a bill	Sections 27–30
	Negotiation of bills	Sections 31–8
	General duties of holder	Sections 39–52
	Liabilities of parties	Sections 53–8
	Discharge of a bill	Sections 59–64
	Acceptance and payment for honour	Sections 65–8
	Lost instruments	Sections 69–70
	Bill in a set	Section 71
	Conflict of laws	Section 72
Part 3	Cheques of a banker	Sections 73–5
	Crossed cheques	Sections 76–82
	Promissory notes	Sections 83–9
	Supplementary	Sections 90–100

The first protection to the collecting banker is as the holder for value or as a holder in due course. To gain the latter, the banker must satisfy one of the conditions of a holder in due course as set out in Section 29 of the Act (*see* Section 7.11). In the former case the bank is seen to have given value if it:

(a) cashes a cheque drawn on another bank. This does not include cashing a cheque with a cheque guarantee card;

(b) has taken a cheque specifically to reduce a loan or overdraft. An example of this is where the proceeds from a maturing life policy are used to pay off a loan;

(c) is expressly or impliedly agreed to pay against uncleared effects. This means allowing payments in anticipation of cheques which have been presented but not yet cleared. There must be some agreement for this protection to be gained;

(d) is seen that the bank has a lien on the cheque. A bank's claim of lien may be upheld in two main collecting situations. Firstly, where the account is overdrawn. When a cheque is then paid into a bank, the banker has a lien on that cheque to reduce the overdraft. Secondly, where an account has insufficient funds or no funds and is overdrawn and a cheque for collection is returned unpaid, the bank has a lien for the amount which cannot be debited to the account. The bank should keep the cheque and give notice to all interested parties of its dishonour.

(2) Protection under the Cheques Act 1957.

The purpose of this Act was to 'amend the law relating to cheques and certain other instruments'. Its main provisions are:

(a) protection of bankers paying unendorsed or irregularly endorsed cheques, etc. (Section 1);

(b) rights of bankers collecting cheques not endorsed by holders (Section 2);

(c) unendorsed cheques as evidence of payment (Section 3);

(d) protection of bankers collecting payment of cheques, etc. (Section 4).

Section 2 of this Act provides: 'A banker who gives value for, or has a lien on a cheque payable to order which the holder delivers to him for collection without endorsing it, has such (if any), rights as he would have had if, upon delivery, the holder had endorsed it in blank.'

This section had to be included in the Act since the Act aimed at removing the need for endorsements. Unless this section was included the bank would not have been a holder for value within the necessary requirements for endorsing a cheque. As a result of this section, it is now possible for a bank to retain its right as holder in due course on cheques which have not been endorsed by the current holder.

Section 4 of this Act provides where a banker:

– in good faith and

– without negligence

– receives payment for a customer on any instrument covered by the Act

– or after crediting the account of the customer with the amount of such an instrument and then receives payment

– he will not be liable to the true owner merely by reason of the fact that the customer had no or a defective title to the instrument

– and that the banker will not be regarded as negligent even though the instrument was irregularly or not endorsed.

The effect of Section 2 of the Cheques Act 1957 is seen in the case of *Westminster Bank v. Zang* (1966).

The instruments included in this Act are crossed and uncrossed cheques, dividend warrants, bankers' drafts, paymaster general warrants, Queen and Lord Treasurer's remembrancer warrants and any other instruments which are issued by a bank's customer to enable payment to be obtained from a bank, but not bills of exchange.

Under Section 90 of the Bills of Exchange Act 1882 'good faith' is defined as anything which is in fact done honestly whether it is done negligently or not. A 'customer' is any account holder so that the opening of an account with the intention of permanency creates this relationship. The Judicial Committee of the Privy Council in *Commissioners of Taxation v. English, Scottish and Australian Bank Ltd* (1970) saw the test of negligence to be: 'whether the transaction of the paying in any given cheque, coupled with circumstances antecedent and present, was so out of the ordinary course that it ought to have aroused doubts in the bankers' mind, and caused them to make inquiry'.

The onus is on the bank to prove the absence of negligence and, while courts have been strict in calling for high standards of care, the situation now is that this duty of care must be interpreted in the light of modern practice.

(3) Protection under other statutes.

(a) For a plea of contributory negligence – the Law Reform (Contributory Negligence) Act 1945 was used for the first time in *Lumsdon and Co. v. London Trustees Savings Bank* (1971) where it was claimed that it applied to banking transactions. In this case judgement was given against the drawer of a cheque with regard to 10 per cent for his contributory negligence. The position of banks with regard to contributory negligence and conversion has been inconsistent in recent years. In the Torts (Interference of Goods) Act 1977 this defence was abolished. However, it was reinstated by Section 47 of the Banking Act 1979.

(b) With regard to negligence – there have been many different acts and omissions by banks which have been held to be negligent under Section 4 of the Cheques Act 1957. These cases fall into three main areas, namely:

(i) the opening of an account for a stranger without satisfactory references being taken up. This includes failure to obtain or follow up references, failure to obtain the name of the customer's employers, failure to obtain the name of the husband's employer in the case of opening an account for a married woman, failure to enquire as to proper registration under the Business Names Act 1916 where a customer wishes cheques to be paid into an account which is not in his name but in one under which trading takes place;

(ii) where the relationship between other customers of the bank and the drawee or payee of a converted instrument is such that it warrants enquiry;

(iii) all other cases where enquiry into the proposed collection would be thought by the courts to be necessary. Cases in this area have included:

– collecting of those instruments payable to a limited company for any account other than that of the company

– collecting cheques, etc. the amount of which is inconsistent with the station in life or business of the customer

– collecting cheques, etc. payable to a third party in circumstances which warrant enquiry

– collecting cheques, etc. crossed 'A/c Payee' for any other account than that of the payee. An example is the case of *Lloyds Bank Ltd v. Chartered Bank of India, Australia and China* (1928) where the bank was seen to have been negligent in the collection of cheques for agents or employees where the principal or employer was the drawer of the cheques. Negligence may also refer back to the opening of the account by the bank as seen in *Marfani & Co. Ltd v. Midland Bank* (1968).

This is not an exhaustive list of areas of negligence but they give an indication of the dangers that face the collecting banker and, as we have seen, the banker must exercise a strict duty of care on many occasions.

(c) With regard to endorsements – as we have seen the Cheques Act 1957 Section 1 removed the need for a cheque to be endorsed. However, the Committee of the London Clearing Banks Memorandum dated 23 September 1957 listed the following instruments as still requiring endorsements:

(i)   cheques with a receipt attached;
(ii) bills of exchange other than cheques;
(iii) promissory notes;
(iv) HM paymaster drafts;
(v)   cheques cashed over the counter;
(vi) a cheque which has been negotiated.

Self-assessment exercises

1   Under what circumstances would a banker have been seen to have given value on a cheque?
2   What was the purpose of the Cheques Act 1957? Give the main clauses included in this Act.
3   Explain, in your own words, the protection given to a bank under Section 4 of the Cheques Act 1957.
4   What is the position of a banker with regard to contributory negligence on the part of his customer?
5   List three areas where a banker could be considered to have been negligent in collection of cheques.

6   Give two examples of instruments that still need to be endorsed.

7.14   Position of the paying banker with regard to statutory protection

7.141   Under the Bills of Exchange Act 1882

(1) Section 59. Payment in due course – this section provides that the bill is discharged by payment in due course by or on behalf of the drawee or acceptor. This section provides that 'payment in due course' means payment made at or after maturity if it is in good faith without notice of the title to the bill being defective. This payment must be in accordance with the customer's instruction and in the ordinary course of business.

With regard to open cheques then the paying bank:
– must pay only to drawer or a known agent if drawn to 'self or cash'
– must not pay to presenter if they are drawn to bearer or to a third party
– must not pay if requested by a non-bank customer by post to pay cash on a cheque drawn on a customer. It might be helpful to try to get the customer's permission to settle this way.

With regard to crossed cheques:
– they must be paid only through a banker and strictly within the instructions of the crossing
– a bank cashing a crossed cheque will do so at its own risk as it may not be paying to the true owner and, if it does not, it is still liable to him. Thus payment is usually made to drawee or to his agent.

(2) Section 60. Where cheques are paid which have a forged or unauthorised endorsement the paying banker is protected provided he has paid in good faith and in the ordinary course of business. An example of a bank not acting in good faith is if it knew an endorsement was forged. This section applies to forged endorsements and not the drawer's signature. It also applies to open or crossed cheques but no other bills of exchange. For cheques cashed over the counter, only the endorsements must appear to be in order. Only the drawer's bank is protected and there is no protection for a bank cashing a cheque of another bank. Even if a bank acts negligently in paying on this type of cheque there may still be protection. This protection, after Section 1 of the Cheques Act 1957, is really only valid in certain cases such as the cashing of open cheques which still require endorsement.

(3) Section 80. A paying banker is also protected if he pays on any crossed cheque provided he pays in good faith, without negligence and in accordance with the crossing. Also if the drawee bank has paid in accordance with Section 60 and the cheque has reached the payee, the drawer ceases to be liable to the true owner.

7.142 Under the Cheques Act 1957 Section 1

There is protection afforded to the paying banker on cheques where there is no endorsement or on an irregular endorsement, provided the cheque is drawn on the banker and is paid in good faith and in the ordinary course of business. This section applies to open and crossed cheques, dividend warrants, bankers' drafts and any other instrument not a bill of exchange issued by a customer to enable a person to receive payment. But this must be considered in connection with the Memorandum of the Committee of the London Clearing Houses dated 23 September 1957 (*see* Section 7.133): 'Banks have decided that they will still require endorsement of open cheques paid out over the counter when drawn to a named payee or order or drawn to self or order. This does not apply to cheques drawn to bearer or cash.'

Self-assessment exercises

1 When is a bill discharged by payment?
2 How must a bank treat payment on an open cheque differently from payment on a crossed cheque?
3 In what ways is a banker protected when paying on a cheque which has a forged endorsement attached to it?
4 When is Section 1 of the Cheques Act 1957 valid?

7.15 Revocation of a banker's authority

A paying banker acts on the authority of the customer, the drawer of the cheque. This authority can be revoked by:
 (1) Countermanding of payment by the customer or what is called stopping a cheque. A banker requires both written and signed authority to do this. He also needs full details of the cheque such as date, number, amount and payee's name. If he is notified by telephone, he requests this written authority to be sent and, until it is received, only delaying of payment can be operated if it is presented. A customer has until the close of business on the day that the cheque is presented, either through the clearing house, or through the post, or over the counter for credit to another customer's account. Thus 'stops' will not be possible if the banker has already specified that the cheques have been paid.
 Even though a drawer of a cheque has put a stop on it he cannot deprive the holder of his rights to the cheque. As we have seen, a holder has good title to the proceeds of a cheque and the drawer must pay if the bank returns it stopped. If the drawer refuses, the holder can sue and compel him to pay direct or remove the stop to enable the bank to pay. Two cases show that countermanding of payment is only effective when it is brought to

the notice of the banker, and if it is unambiguous: *Curtice v. London, City and Midland Bank* (1908) and *Westminster Bank Ltd v. Hilton* (1926).

(2) Death or lunacy of the customer – it is not the event of death or lunacy of the customer which ends the banker's authority to pay, but reliable notice of this event. The balance in the account in each case is held by the bank and can be dealt with by the personal representatives of the deceased or the Receiver or the Committee in Lunacy. What is important for the protection of the bank is that the notice must be reliable.

(3) Notice of presentation of a bankruptcy petition against the customer, then a bankruptcy receiving order or, in the case of a company, notice of its winding up.

(4) Assignment of his balance by a customer.

(5) Serving of a garnishee order attaching the whole of a balance.

(6) Notice that the customer is a discharged bankrupt.

(7) Notice of a breach of trust.

(8) Notice of a defect in the presenter's title.

(9) Where the account has insufficient funds or the paying of the cheque would increase the size of the overdraft above the amount agreed, the banker has discretion to pay or to dishonour the cheque.

If a bank refuses to pay on a cheque without adequate reason it is possible that it will be liable for any damage caused to the customer's creditworthiness as a result of the refusal to pay. There is no privity of contract between the banker and the holder of the cheque.

Self-assessment exercises

1   What are the major requirements of a bank if it is required to put a stop on a cheque?
2   What rights has the holder of a cheque that has been stopped?
3   Give three other reasons why a bank may refuse to pay on a cheque.
4   Smalltown Bank plc received a telephone message from A Jones putting a stop on a cheque for £50 payable to Wellford Co. Ltd. By coincidence it received for payment a cheque for a similar amount to the same firm from another of its customers Mr A R Jones which it wrongfully put a stop answer on. What do you think is the legal position of the bank? How should it be advised to deal with this situation?

7.16   Material alteration of a bill

These consist of material alteration to the amount, date, time of payment, place of payment, where the bill has been accepted and the addition of the place for payment without the acceptor's assent. This is not an exhaustive list. With regard to cheques, we have to add alteration of the crossing, though not all alterations of a crossing are seen as material alteration. For example, changing a blank crossing to a special crossing has been held as immaterial alteration.

The general rule, laid down in Section 64 of the 1882 Act is that where an instrument has been materially altered it has become void unless it has the assent of all the parties to the instrument. An exception to this is where a party made, authorised or assented to the alteration as well as subsequent endorsers to the bill.

The Act affords protection to a holder in due course, if the alteration is not apparent he can avail himself in the value of the instrument as if it had not been altered and so enforce payment according to its terms.

The most common type of material alteration to a cheque is the fraudulent increasing of the amount payable. Thus if a cheque payable for £30 is altered to £130, unless this is apparent, or is in the hands of a holder in due course, any person prior to the alteration is not liable on the cheque, while assenting parties and those who become parties after the alteration are liable for £130.

7.17 Forgery

Forgery is the act of falsely making or altering any document with the intention of defrauding or prejudicing another person. This includes altering a cheque for £90 to £900 as well as forgery of the drawer's signature.

Section 244 of the Bills of Exchange Act 1882 states: 'where a signature on a bill is forged or placed thereon without the authority of the person whose signature it purports to be, the forged or unauthorised signature is wholly inoperative and no right to retain the bill or to give discharge therefore or to enforce payment thereof against any party thereto can be acquired through or under this signature, unless the party against whom it is sought to retain or enforce payment of the bill is precluded from setting up the forgery for want of authority'.

It is not necessary for the forged signature to be similar to the genuine one in any way so long as the forger intends it to be accepted as the genuine signature and that someone will suffer thereby. There are many occasions when a signature is unauthorised but is not forged, for example, if someone in a company signs bills and it is not obvious from his position that he is not authorised to do so. The firm may be prepared to ratify these signatures in certain circumstances, but there is no way in which a firm can ratify forged signatures. This section in the Act makes forged and unauthorised signatures inoperative. Thus for the purpose of transfers of title it is as if there were no signature at all, and the place that the forged or unauthorised signature occupies on the instrument may be treated as being blank.

The signatures on a bill can be by three different persons:
(1) the drawer;

(2) the drawee or acceptor;
(3) the endorser.

It is necessary to consider the effects of forgery of any one of these.

7.171 Forgery of the drawer's signature

This makes the instrument invalid against the drawer. Thus a bank will not be able to debit the customer's account if the signature has been forged. However, the customer is estopped from denying the genuineness of his signature even if it is forged if he has led others to believe that it is genuine. He is then fully liable on the instrument. The judgement in *National Westminster Bank Ltd v. Barclays Bank International and Another* held that a bank having paid out on a forged drawer's signature could recover from the payee.

7.172 Forgery of an acceptor's signature

In this instance, the acceptor incurs no liability but the holder has full rights against other persons where the signatures are genuine.

7.173 Forgery on endorsement

Transfer of an order cheque or one with a special endorsement is nullified if the endorsement is not correct. The receiver of such an instrument receives no title and has no claims on parties prior to the forgery. But, as we have seen, parties after the forgery are concerned with a valid and enforceable instrument. An endorser is precluded from denying to his immediate or subsequent transferee that the bill was a valid bill at the time of transfer and that he had good title to it. A forged instrument has no effect on bearer bills or on order bills endorsed in blank.

7.18 Dishonour of a bill

A bill is dishonoured by non-acceptance or non-payment. Dishonour by non-acceptance occurs within a customary time of the person presenting it. If this is not done, the holder loses his rights against the drawer and endorsers.

Both of these types of dishonour occur when:
(1) bills are presented for acceptance or payment at the proper place and the acceptance or payment is refused or cannot be obtained; or
(2) where a bill presented for acceptance or payment is overdue, or in the case of non-payment it is unpaid as well.

We have seen that if a bill is dishonoured the holder has the right of enforcement against the drawer and all the endorsers to the bill. For this right to operate there must:

(a) in the case of inland bills, be notice given to all parties;

(b) in the case of foreign bills, as well as notice the bill must be noted and protested.

7.181 Notice of dishonour

This can be in any form provided the bill is clearly identified, the form of dishonour is stated (non-acceptance or non-payment), it is given immediately or within a reasonable time to the drawer and each endorser. There are strict rules as to the time when notice of dishonour should be given. Notice of dishonour is not required:

(1) where notice cannot be given after reasonable diligence;
(2) when notice is waived;
(3) where drawer and drawee is the same person;
(4) where the drawer is fictitious or has no legal capacity;
(5) as in the case of a cheque where the drawer and the payee is the same person;
(6) where a stop has been put on the instrument;
(7) if the endorser knows that the drawee is a fictitious person, or has no legal capacity to contract;
(8) where the endorsee and the payee are the same person;
(9) where the bill was accepted or made for the accommodation of the endorser.

7.182 Noting and protesting

Foreign bills need, in addition to notice, **noting** and **protesting**. Noting is the presentation of a dishonoured bill to a notary public, who notes on the bill or on an attached piece of paper the answer obtained from representation for acceptance or payment and the date. The notary cross references the bill in his record books. Noting must take place on the day of dishonour or the next day's business. Notaries are found mainly in London, where no notary can be found a **householder's notorisation** can be used. In this case, the bill can be noted by any householder or substantial resident of the place, who may, in the presence of two witnesses, give a certificate, signed by them, attesting the dishonour of the bill.

After noting, at any time later the bill can be protested. This can be carried out by a notary public or by a householder and two witnesses. A formal notice is drawn up containing a copy of the bill stating who has requested the protest, the place, the date, reason for protest and any answer obtained. This is signed by the notary. Protest is usually at the place of dishonour and can be made even if the bill is not available. The time of protest is either on the day of dishonour, the next day, or at any time after the bill has been noted.

Self-assessment exercises

1 What is the general rule of law relating to material alteration of a bill of exchange? Give two examples of such alterations.
2 Define forgery and state what the general effect to a cheque is of a forged signature of the drawee.
3 When might a signature be unauthorised but not a forgery on a cheque? Is there any difference in the legal effect of these two types of signature?
4 What is the position on a bill where:
   (a) the endorser's signature is forged?
   (b) the acceptor's signature is forged?
5 When is a bill dishonoured?
6 When is notice of dishonour of a bill required, and give two instances when it is not?
7 Explain the noting and protesting of a bill. Under what circumstances are these required?

Assignments

1 In preparation for a training course your bank is sending you on, you have been sent the following tasks to complete:
   Task 1. Say to what the following definitions refer and when the instruments are likely to be used:
   (a) 'An unconditional order in writing, addressed by one person to another, who must be a banker, signed by the person giving it, requiring the banker to pay on demand a sum certain in money or to the order of a specified person or to bearer.'
   (b) 'An unconditional promise to pay in writing, made by one person to another, signed by the maker, engaging to pay on demand, or at a fixed or determinable future time, a sum certain in money, to or to the order of, a specified person or to bearer.'
   Task 2. What do the following statements mean in relation to cheques and what effect do they have on the cheque?
   (a) The back of the cheque is signed by the payee.
   (b) The front of the cheque has two parallel straight lines on the face of it and within these is written 'limited to £40'.
   (c) The back of the cheque is signed by the payee and has the words 'Pay John Smith only'.
   (d) The front of the cheque has two parallel straight lines with the words 'Not Negotiable' written between them.

(e) The back of the cheque is signed by the payee with the words 'Pay William Brown & Co. Ltd'.

(f) The front of the cheque has two parallel straight lines across it.

Task 3. Draw up a cheque showing the most safe form of crossing and all other details payable to R J Berrington-Smythe for the sum of £150.

Task 4. The following three cases involve cheques, give their major details and the important principles found therein:

(a) *London Joint Stock Bank Ltd v. Macmillan and Arthur* (1918)

(b) *Davidson v. Barclays Bank Ltd* (1940)

(c) *National Westminster Bank.Ltd v. Barclays Bank International Ltd and Another* (1975).

2 Give a detailed account of the development of crossings on cheques. Give three examples of different types of crossing and say what their effects are.

3 Say what would be the legal position in the following regarding cheques.

Situation 1. The ABC Co. Ltd are holding a bill for £1200 accepted by the XYZ Co. in payment for goods sold. It is stolen by Reeves, an employee of the ABC Co. and he endorses it over to the Acme Toy Co. who supplied him with aeroplane models. The Acme Toy Co. endorses it over to the Histon Engineering Co. for goods received.

Situation 2. Robert Raydock purchases a suit for £59.95 with a cheque backed by a cheque guarantee card. When the bank received it it was obvious that the card number was written by Raydock himself.

Situation 3. Braines, a minor, steals a £50 cheque from Innocent's pocket. He then uses the money to purchase a wrist watch from the Emerald Jewellery Co., although he has a perfectly good watch already.

Situation 4. John finds a cheque for £20 crossed 'not negotiable'. He forges a blank endorsement and then cashes it at his sailing club bar.

Situation 5. A thief steals a video tape recorder from Battle and then sells it to a second-hand dealer, who gives him a cheque. The thief then uses this to open up a bank account with a clearing bank and then draws cheques on this account.

4 Define and say what the rights and duties of the following are with regard to bills of exchange:

(a) A holder for value

(b) A holder in due course

(c) An endorser ofa bill

(d) The drawer of a bill

5 The following are typical inquires received by the Sussex Bank PLC at their Brightsea branch in one day. Say how they would be dealt with.

(a) The Eastlands Bank PLC requested a status enquiry for one of its customers regarding a Mr Williards, one of your customers.

(b) Miss Rednum has just bought her own house and is aware that she will have a number of bills to pay over the year, like mortgage, rates, gas and electricity. She knows that those will not occur evenly over this period so she makes an enquiry as to the ways in which the bank can help her to meet these payments.

(c) The Chiminster Engineering Co. Ltd has received payment of a debt from a customer by cheque for £10 500. It needs these funds to be paid into its account the same day. Advise.

(d) Mr and Mrs H Patrick are going abroad on holiday and wish to have flexibility and convenience for making payments while they are away. How would you advise them?

(e) John Astrix presents himself at the enquiry desk and asks you to explain the difference between an Access card and an American Express Card.

6 You have been asked by a marketing journal to write an article entitled 'The why and the way in which banks market their services'. Write this article.

8 Banking Services to Personal, Business and Corporate Customers

Before we look in detail at the various types of customer service it is perhaps useful, at this point, to consider the ways in which banks help in the making of payments both at home and abroad.

8.1 Cash

This not only includes one of the major functions of banks, the provision of coins and notes to both personal and business customers, but also those non-cash services such as operation of the cheque system, use of the credit clearing systems such as standing orders and direct debits as well as the provision of foreign payments systems.

To begin with our cash needs, this starts with the Bank of England printing the notes and the Royal Mint minting the coins. As we saw in Chapter 3 the Bank of England sees to the supply of cash through its Threadneedle Street branch and also through its provincial branches. Customers of the banks use these to satisfy their cash needs and it is up to the chief cashier of the branch to forecast the demands for cash on his branch in the coming weeks. From these forecasts supplies of cash are built up in the vaults in anticipation of the expected demand. It is very rare for branches to run out of cash but it has been known on occasions. There are times in the year, like Christmas and Easter holidays, when the banks need to hold higher stocks of cash than at other times. In recent years, the clearing banks and some building societies have had automatic teller machines (ATMs) installed on the outside to enable customers to get cash outside banking hours. For this purpose, the customer is supplied with a cash card and a personal identification number (PIN number) which he keys into the computer terminal to get cash sums from the bank. Customers, by this method, have an agreed limit which they can draw out in any one week. In addition, the customer receives other services from the terminal such as his current balance or he can make an order for a new cheque book or bank statement. Moves have been made to allow customers of different banks to obtain cash from each other's machines. For example, it is possible for customers of the Midland Bank plc to use their cash cards for cash withdrawals from the National Westminster Bank's machines and vice versa.

Self-assessment exercise

How does the Bank of England ensure an adequate supply of coins and notes in the country?

8.2 Cheques

Customers of banks make up to 3000 million non-cash payments a year. By far the largest non-cash payment is by means of the cheque. As we have seen in Chapter 1, the cheque is not money in itself but is merely evidence of the drawer's access to funds in a bank account, and it is an instruction to the bank to transfer an amount from one account to another. A cheque presented for collection from another bank has to go through the Clearing House. Millions of cheques are paid into the clearing banks every day for collection. These are paid in by personal and business customers, government departments and large financial institutions.

In the early days of banking these were cleared by hand, and clerks walked between banks to collect on the cheques which had been presented. The growth in the use of the cheque meant that some form of official clearing system had to be introduced which dealt efficiently and quickly with clearing. This growth can be seen in the figures in Table 8.1.

Table 8.1 Growth in bank clearing

Year	Value of cheques cleared (£m)
1839	954
1871	4526
1971	843 626
1981	4 835 412

Today the banks in the Clearing House are Barclays, Coutts, Lloyds, Midland, National Westminster, the Trustees Savings Bank and the Co-operative Bank and the National Giro Bank. Discussions are proceeding to allow some foreign banks into the Clearing House. It is managed by the Committee of the London Clearing Bankers which consists of representatives from the first six of the above institutions. The Bank of England is a member of the Clearing House as are the Scottish banks, but it does not participate in its administration.

Cheques, when drawn, are of three types:

(1) Drawn by a customer of one branch payable to a customer of the same branch.

(2) Drawn by a customer of one branch payable to a customer of another branch of the same banking group.

(3) Drawn by a customer of a particular branch of one banking group payable to another customer of a branch of another banking group.

In the case of (1), there is no need for the cheque to leave the branch. When it is paid in it will be seen that it is payable to and drawn on customers of the same branch so the debiting and crediting will be carried out at once.

In the case of (2), these cheques are processed in the branch as outlined below and then sent with other cheques to the collecting branch. Here, they are sorted out from the other cheques which need to go to the Clearing House and are retained by the collecting branch to be returned to the relevant branch the next day.

In the case of (3), these cheques need to go through **general clearing**. This, as such, came into operation in 1939. If we look at Fig. 8.1 we will see how such cheques are processed.

This process generally takes three working days to complete – let us consider what happens each day.

Day 1. The paying in customer fills out a **paying-in slip** and hands this with the cheque over the counter, some banks have the facility for paying in by machine. The counter clerk checks the details on the form and hands back a counterfoil from the paying-in slip, at the same time specially crossing the cheque with the bank stamp. The counter clerk places these with other **remittances** (hence the abbreviation 'rems'). Some banks also call these **waste**. These are collected by a clerk from the machines room and taken back to this place where they are electronically sorted into the different banks upon which they are drawn. Cheques are encoded with the amount in magnetic ink character recognition numbers which are similar to the numbers already on the bottom of the cheque and allow the electronic machines to read all the details of the cheques. These cheques are now processed by the terminal operator in order to credit the customers' accounts and to debit the head office account of the bank. Some banks microfilm the face of the cheques for future reference. These cheques and other remittances are totalled and this figure is agreed with the total for all waste. The cheques are parcelled up with a listing imprinted on control vouchers in magnetic ink which can also be read by computers. After the close of business and when all remittances have been processed and parcelled, these parcels are taken to the collecting branch of the bank in London by courier service. Some banks hire this service from firms like Securicor while others have their own service.

Day 2. By the start of business on this day the collecting branch will have received all of the cheques paid into the bank's branches the previous day. As they arrive, the parcels are checked and amalgamated and placed on trolleys to be taken to the collecting branch of the paying bank. All parcels are listed and so is each trolley.

The Clearing House opens for deliveries every weekday from 9 am and

206 Banking for Students

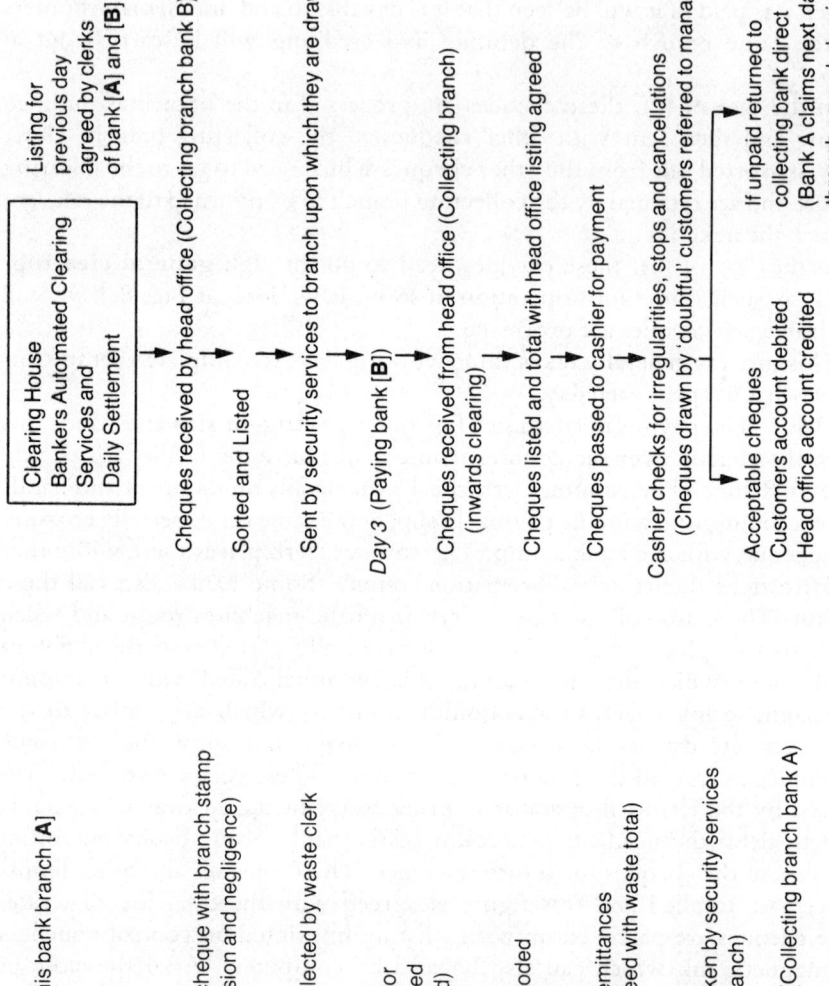

Fig. 8.1 General clearing

stays open to 11.15 or later depending upon the rules or *ad hoc* changes authorised. These cheques are delivered in plastic containers to the Exchange Centre. Representatives of each bank meet and exchange cheques. Also the listings from the cheques exchanged the previous day are agreed, and if one bank has a short fall compared with another bank a cheque for the difference drawn on its account in the Bank of England is completed so that the amounts passed over cancel each other out. (See Fig. 3.1.)

The cheques are taken to the paying banks' collecting branch where the amounts are totalled and agreed by the computers using the control voucher figures. The banks have invested millions of pounds in high speed reader sorters to help speed up this clearing. They can read over 2400 cheques every minute, collecting information to debit customers' accounts, sorting the cheques into branches, listing these totals and then putting them on computer tape. This tape is then put onto a printer and the information is put onto 'hard copy'. Each bank is also given a copy of this print out. The cheques for each branch are then parcelled together and sent, at the end of day 2, to these branches.

Day 3. During this day the paying branch lists and totals the cheques received from head office for inwards, clearing that these are agreed with the listings from the collecting branch. They are now debited against the customers' accounts and the total is credited to the head office account. During this process there is a check for irregularities, stops and cancellations. Cheques which are not to be paid are returned direct to the collecting bank with the appropriate answer, and claims are settled the next day.

The reason for the agreed value of cheques exchanged being carried out the day after exchange is so that the paying banks have the opportunity to refuse payment.

Self-assessment exercise

Miss Welsh purchased a hifi system for £324.95 from the Chiminster Electrical Co. and paid by cheque. Explain fully the process by which the cheque will eventually be paid out of her account.

8.3 Credit cards

These were introduced first by Barclays Bank in 1965 with Barclaycard, now called Visa – although this is not just a credit card. The other banks introduced their version, Access, in 1971. Customers with a current account are provided with a credit limit and a plastic card for identification purposes. This card has raised numbers on it in order to identify the customer's account, the date on which the card will expire and the name of the customer. A typical card is illustrated in Fig. 8.2.

Credit Cards

Fig. 8.2 Facsimile of credit cards (Reprinted by permission of the Banking Information Services)

Customers holding these cards can make purchases by using these cards so building up credit on their account. The system is as follows. The customer hands the card to the retailer who places it into a machine along with specially designed documents and, by impression, these pick up the details from the card. The customer signs these documents and receives the top copy as a record of the transaction. A specimen of the customer's signature is found on the card. For large amounts, the shopkeeper telephones the credit card company to find out if the customer is authorised to spend the amount required. At regular intervals, monthly, the customer receives a statement of account with a request to repay any amount above the minimum required. This depends upon the size of the balance outstanding. Thus the customer receives interest free credit for almost a month on any purchase made just after the settlement date if he pays the full amount by the next settlement date. Rates of interest range from up to 2 per cent per month on the amount outstanding. It is now possible for customers to make payments with these cards by telephone or for mail order by quoting their card number. The most popular use of these cards is to purchase petrol and electrical goods.

These should not be confused with charge cards like American Express or Diners Card where the holder is charged for the privilege of holding a card and is expected to clear the account when it is due and, therefore, cannot really get credit over the maximum of twenty-eight days.

Loss of the credit card should be notified to the credit card company as soon as possible so that a stop can be put on it. For this purpose, it is important for the customer to have the number recorded in a safe place. Fraud on cheque guarantee and credit cards is now reaching high proportions. It is believed that in 1985 £40 million was stolen by this method. A system is being developed using anti-fraud techniques to try and counteract this. This counterfeiting has reached considerable proportions in the USA and it is expected that this will develop in the UK. Here the banks offer a reward to shop assistants who spot a stolen card. Barclays paid out £600 000 in 1984 and Access £500 000. The banks feel that these payments could increase in the future and the card user now faces a new liability. Barclaycard, which operates British Visa, is to introduce a clause in its conditions of use which allows it to charge the cardholder for fraudulent misuse. Access consider they would have to prove that the cardholder had been negligent before they could refuse to cover such bills.

Self-assessment exercise

What is the difference between Access and American Express?

8.4 Credit clearing

8.41 Bank Giro

In 1960 the banks introduced a system of clearing by credit called **credit transfer** which really increased the practice they had already developed of transferring money from one bank to another by means of credit slips. This service was made available to non-bank as well as bank customers. It operated by means of instructions given to banks to place payments directly into a bank account on behalf of a debtor without the need to use postal orders or cheques. The customer, wishing to use this service, filled in a credit voucher which has become known as a **bank giro slip**. Delivery of this slip with the amount in cash or cheque to the bank enabled this service to operate. At the same time that this service was offered the banks extended the clearing system to include what is called **bank giro**. The bank giro slip goes through a similar process for clearing as do cheques. They are bundled together with a listing and sent to the collecting branch of the bank where they are processed and taken to the Clearing House for exchange. On receipt of these credit transfers, the receiving bank credits them to their customers' accounts. The use of this system can be seen for the payment of such bills as gas, electricity and rate demands of local authorities, an example is shown in Fig. 8.3.

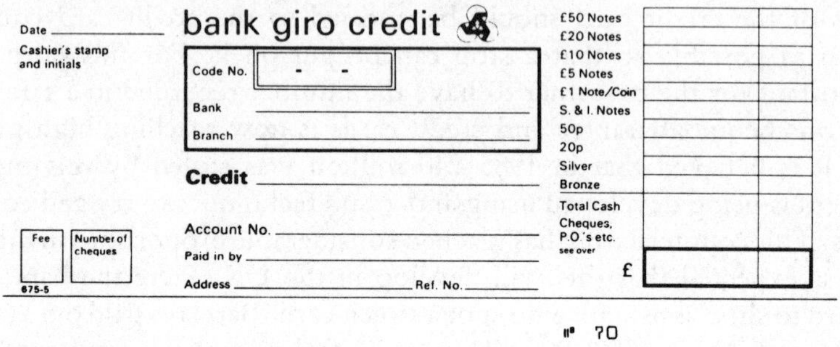
Date
Cashier's stamp and initials
bank giro credit
Code No. - -
Bank
Branch
Credit
Account No.
Paid in by
Address
Ref. No.
Fee
Number of cheques
675-5
£50 Notes
£20 Notes
£10 Notes
£5 Notes
£1 Note/Coin
S. & I. Notes
50p
20p
Silver
Bronze
Total Cash
Cheques, P.O.'s etc. see over
£
⑈ 70

Fig. 8.3 Bank giro payment slip

In such cases the customer pays his account through the bank by completing the bank giro form and this saves time and effort as a number of these payments can be made with one cheque. This could save the customer bank charges on his cheques.

8.42 Bankers' Automated Clearing Services (BACS)

This was formed to provide an automated money transfer service for the credit clearing system. Its function is to operate and develop a highly efficient computer-based time and labour saving automated service to be used by customers of the banks for the transfer of funds within the banking system. In the past twenty years there has been a rapid growth in the use of banking services with an enormous increase in credit transfers. These include such things as standing or bankers' orders, salary payments, pension payments, batch purchase ledger settlement, as well as other remittances like interest dividends, gifts and benefits, business expenses and savings deductions (SAYE). As well as the credit voucher which is used when paying into one bank for the account of another, the system uses computers, magnetic tape and telecommunications. BACS does not handle cheques. The operation of this system is best seen in the following transactions:

(1) *Standing orders* – these originated before the BACS system was set up. This is a service offered to customers who have regular payments to make such as mortgage repayments, monthly rate demands, club subscriptions or membership fees to professional bodies. By completion of the standing order form giving the bank details of the payment – amount, to whom payable, the bank branch to be paid, the account to be credited and the date of payment – then, provided sufficient funds are in the customer's account, the bank meets this payment. If the customer regularly neglects

to keep sufficient funds in the account, the bank is justified in not meeting these payments. Prior to the BACS system, standing orders were processed by the bank completing a credit transfer voucher and remitting these through the clearing system. This was a manual processing system. Although this may still operate, most standing orders are paid through the BACS centralised computer system. All the standing order payments of a bank for a given day are recorded on magnetic tape. This is sent to BACS where the items are sorted by the BACS computer and entered on tapes to be sent to the receiving banks. The tapes are then used by the latter to credit their customers' accounts. No vouchers are necessary with this system. The process, unlike general clearing, takes about four working days to complete. The difference being that on day 2 the amounts to be debited are communicated to the paying branches so that they can check to see if their customers have sufficient funds, and can give authority to pay even if this is not the case. If the amount is cancelled, or there is a technical reason for non-payment, there is a recall system whereby the remitting bank can contact the receiving bank direct and ask for return of payment. Recall is a standard letter which must be received before or on the day of credit. It is possible for a telephone call to be used provided it is for amounts over £100 and the telephone call is before 12 noon on the fourth day. The repayment is by manual transfer with the repaying bank completing a credit transfer voucher. It has been agreed that the recall of standing orders for less than £10 will not be for lack of funds but only if the paying customer withdraws his authority.

(2) *Salary/Wage payments* – at one time credit vouchers were prepared by employers and handed over to the bank for distribution through the credit clearing system. Use of the BACS system means that a magnetic tape can be prepared by the employer, either on his own computer or a bureau computer, and then handed to BACS. The same procedure is then followed as for standing orders. Employees' accounts are credited and the employer's account is debited.

(3) *Direct debiting* – this is a means of carrying out credit transfers in reverse. Whereas standing orders are instructions by customers of the banks to pay bills on their behalf, direct debits are agreements between businesses and their customers that allow the former to instruct their banks to collect on their behalf the amounts due from the customers' accounts. In this case a supplier, with the agreement of the purchaser, instructs his bank to collect the money due from the purchaser's account. These are useful where payments are to be made at regular intervals as with standing orders. These suppliers prepare magnetic tape of these collections which are passed on to BACS. The tapes are then processed and sent out by BACS to the relevant banks for the amounts to be deducted from their customers' accounts.

The advantages of BACS to the user are:
– improved cash flow;

- a saving in stationery and clerical labour;
- increased security;
- in the case of direct debiting, knowing that the funds will be paid on a specific day which suits the firm's accounting period. It also affords an easier system of credit control.

BACS is located in Edgware and is governed by a board which is made up of non-executive directors from a shareholding of Barclays, Lloyds, Midland and National Westminster. There are also two executive directors and it has four departments – operation, systems and programming, planning and external liaison and administration.

One of the biggest breakthroughs in 1983 was the introduction of telecommunications links. This, known as the BACSTEL service, enables data to be input direct on-line to Edgware. The delivery or posting of magnetic media to BACS takes time. Now this is saved by transmitting data by ordinary telephone lines, a leased circuit on British Telecom Kilostream or Packet Switch Stream. This allows some companies a distance away from London to use the BACS system. It allows for instant acceptance or rejection advice that BACS transmits on-line as well as the normal printed input report that is posted to all users after submissions have been validated.

Two-thirds of all UK monthly salaries now go through BACS and 40 per cent of occupational pensions. Direct debits through BACS now make up 80 per cent of all life insurance premiums. BACS' share of weekly wages payments is only 7 per cent but this is likely to grow.

8.43 Clearing House automated payments system (CHAPS)

Described as the world's most sophisticated interbank settlement system in *Banking World* February 1984 it is the 1980s version of town clearing. Town clearing was a system which covered financial operations in the City of London which included all of the banks, the Stock Exchange, all of the insurance companies, shipping companies and other large financial institutions. This was a method of clearing for amounts in excess of £5000 which were drawn on and paid into over one hundred 'town branches' of the clearing banks. This allowed these cheques to be cleared on the day paid in so that the payee could be sure of his money. This has now been replaced by CHAPS which allows this same day clearing to take place amongst all of the banks in the banking sector. This is because it uses a ring of powerful computers in tandem with the twelve settlement banks and the Bank of England. The system operates as follows. Each bank sends instructions of the payments to be made to the other banks through a so-called 'gateway'. This uses common software and there is no central executive on computer. Once the messages have been accepted in the system as being authentic they are not able to be revoked. This allows same day transfer throughout the clearing system. Larger companies may be able to link their own technology into the system and operate payments and receipts electronically. Small companies can instuct their banks to make these payments in the usual way – by telephone call. CHAPS also means that the expensive telegraphic transfer need no longer be used. At the same time, treasurers of companies are able to monitor their cash positions more easily.

8.44 Future developments

We cannot overlook the influence that computers and the new technology are having on banking. For example, the French have developed and have in limited use a credit card which incorporates a micro-chip so that transactions on the card can be recorded as they occur. Thus a customer can return home after a shopping expedition, put the card into a computer terminal and recall all of his purchases.

Another development, pioneered by the French, is the electronic funds transfer at point of sale (EFTPOS) system. This uses a plastic card identification system. The customer of say a large store selects some goods to purchase. At the cash desk an electronic reading device reads off a description of the goods, the department involved and the amount of the purchase. When the final bill is reached, the customer places a plastic card in the machine and keys in his personal identification (PIN) number. This identifies the customer's account and the bank to be debited. The assistant keys in the business's PIN number and this identifies the account to be credited. Thus by computer link the two actions are completed at once. Hence the transfer of funds electronically at point of sale.

Self-assessment exercises

1 Explain 'bank giro'.
2 For what do the initials BACS stand?
3 What kinds of payments can be made through the BACS system?
4 Give two advantages of the BACS system.
5 Explain the BACSTEL system.
6 The financial director of a large corporation is holding a cheque for £255 000 which is drawn on the account of an engineering firm in Sheffield. Explain fully how he could have this cheque cleared the same day.

8.5 Foreign currency and travellers cheques

Any branch of a bank will obtain foreign notes and coin needed for a holiday, or to buy foreign goods and services. Not all branches keep a till for foreign currencies, but those that do not can obtain currencies quickly if required.

Those branches which have a foreign till hold most European and North American currencies. A customer ordering foreign currencies is charged a commission for this service.

Travellers' cheques are provided for customers going abroad or on holiday in the UK. They are safe to carry around for, if they are stolen and the customer has taken the necessary precautions, the bank will make good the money. They are not only issued in pounds sterling but can also be supplied in other currencies. The customer completes an application form detailing the amount and type of currency required. Sometime later he collects them from the bank; on receipt the cheques have to be signed by the customer in front of the clerk supplying them and then countersigned when the cheques are cashed. It is a good security measure to record the number of the cheques on receipt in case they should be lost or stolen and reclaims are made. The customer is charged commission for these cheques by the supplying bank and sometimes by the encashing bank.

8.6 Eurocheques and cheque cards

This is a particular service offered to personal customers going abroad on holiday. Originally customers of banks were able to use their ordinary cheque books with their cheque guarantee cards to get cash from a foreign bank where the Eurocheque sign was displayed. They were rarely used for direct transactions. In 1984 a new Eurocheque and cheque card system was introduced which allowed customers to pay bills abroad; and to remove the possibility of fraud.

A new idea has been introduced from Europe in the form of a unified Eurocheque card. This came into operation in 1985 and has replaced the old system which will be phased out. As well as a new card new cheques have been introduced which have a wider application. Both the cheque card and the cheques can be used at home as well as abroad. To come into line with European practice the current £50 limit has been raised to £100. The banks are allowed to charge for the card (between £3.50 and £4.00) and its issue will be more tightly controlled than was the old card, with the possible use of some credit scoring system being employed to evaluate applicants (see Chapter 9). When used abroad, the foreign bank will make a charge on the value of the cheque and an additional charge (around 30p) is to be made by the British bank. Even though the new card does not use a hologram it has been made more fraud-proof.

8.7 Mail and telegraphic orders

The most common form of non-documentary payment is this instruction to transfer money by airmail or by telegraph. By the first method this is a slow process, the latter is quicker but more expensive. The UK sender has his account debited in pounds sterling and the foreign receiver has his account credited in the foreign currency. Actual transfer of funds is through what is called **nostro** (our) and **vostro** (your) accounts. These are accounts held by the banks in this country with corresponding accounts abroad. Nostro accounts are foreign currency accounts of UK banks abroad and vostro accounts are sterling balances held by the counterpart foreign banks in the UK banks. The procedure for making a payment in this way is as follows:

(1) a bank application form is completed stating the beneficiary and method of remittance. In addition to mail and telegraph order a banker's draft can be used;

(2) the bank debits the customer's account and credits the vostro account of the foreign correspondent bank it is going to use;

(3) the remittance is made and the account of the foreign beneficiary is credited in the foreign currency;

(4) the foreign bank debits the equivalent amount of sterling against the UK bank's account on its books (its nostro account).

8.8 Banker's draft

This is really a form of banker's cheque, similar to a banker's order, but instead of being drawn on the head office by a branch it is drawn by a bank's overseas department on one of its correspondent bank accounts. The customer has his account debited and then shortly afterwards receives the draft to be sent to the foreign business. Its procession through the banking system is as is outlined in Section 8.6 but in reverse, with the foreign bank effecting the credit first and then passing it back to the British bank through the nostro and vostro accounts.

8.9 SWIFT

The initials stand for the Society for Worldwide Interbank Financial Telecommunications. It uses the computer systems of over thirty countries as an international communications network to speed up the transfer of international payments and other business. It can achieve same day transfers. A system of coding is used to verify the authenticity of the instructions for payment.

8.10 International money orders

These were introduced by Barclays Bank in February 1974. They give the advantage of direct payment to the recipient rather than to a specific branch of a bank. They can be purchased by cash from any branch of Barclays and cashed at most banks throughout the world. The amount is limited and a charge is made when purchased. The recipient may also be charged when they are cashed in the foreign country.

Self-assessment exercises

1   Explain how the following foreign payments are processed:
   (a) Mr and Mrs Reid wish to pay the ground rent of 6000 French francs on their caravan in France into account 612/325 in the Société Général Bank in S. Raphael.
   (b) Simon Ride wishes to pay his hotel bill at the Hotel Continental in Paris for 330 francs.
   (c) Rita and Roland Barkus wish to purchase a hotdog from a vendor in 44th Avenue, New York.
2   What is the meaning of SWIFT? Explain how it works.

8.11   Banking services

Anyone making enquiries with a local bank will soon discover that it offers a wide range of different services. Some of these have already been discussed in this and other chapters. It would be useful at this point, however, to consider the other services offered. Classification of these can take many forms and, for the purposes of this book, the reader will be given a simple guide to the basic services offered to personal and business customers, in what ways they are the same and how they differ. This gives us a threefold classification.
   8.111 Services of banks which are generally applicable to a broad range of customers. Some of these are specifically relevant to one type of customer and not to others. Where this is the case, it will be outlined in the text.
   8.112 Services which are solely applicable to personal customers.
   8.113 Services which are solely applicable to business customers.

8.111   Services applicable to a broad range of customers

Accepting deposits

There are three basic types of accounts offered to customers by banks. These are:
   (1) *Current accounts* – these are usually for the operation of cheque payments. Therefore, they run from day-to-day with cheques and other money transmission orders being debited and credited depending upon the transaction being processed. Customers can arrange for overdrafts to be granted

on these accounts and, in some cases, cheques will still be honoured even if no prior agreement for an overdraft has been made. Generally, no interest is paid on these accounts although some banks and licensed deposit-taking institutions do offer a nominal rate of interest. At the present time major banks offer free banking to customers who keep their account in credit.

(2) *Deposit accounts* – these are the banks' original savings accounts. Customers holding these accounts generally have to give a period of notice of withdrawal, or the deposit is for some fixed period of time. However, banks will waive the period of notice if customers wish to have an immediate withdrawal in a case of urgency and so long as it is not for a very large sum, but the customer forfeits the interest due on the money. Customers are not allowed to go into debit on these accounts. They do, however, receive interest for these deposits at a rate which is related to the bank's base rate (*see* Chapter 5). Interest is credited to the account every six months. Since April 1985 banks have been treated similarly to building societies with regard to interest paid on deposit accounts. There now operates a **corporate rate tax system** for this interest so that depositors now have tax deducted at basic rate before the amount is added to their accounts. Non-taxpayers cannot reclaim the money.

(3) *Savings accounts* – as outlined in Chapter 5, competition between banks and other financial institutions has developed considerably in the past twenty years. Originally, savings accounts were for children to encourage thriftiness and also to try and secure a future customer. Nowadays, all kinds of incentives are offered to people of all ages to save their money for longer terms. A study of this market will show that saving schemes are available for children and young persons with a wide range of attractions from ceramic pigs and holdalls full of 'goodies' to vouchers for special offers for rail and bus travel at reduced rates. There are savings schemes for people with large sums of money to save offering free cheque banking with added interest, and also savings schemes of particular interest to retired customers. Basically, the schemes are for longer terms than the ordinary deposit accounts and usually offer higher rates of interest. Each one has its own terms and conditions and they vary among the different banks so it would be a very complicated task to detail every scheme available.

(4) *Safe custody and safety deposit* – these are two schemes which allow customers to deposit valuables other than money.

Safe custody is offered by most branches. This is a facility whereby customers can hand over valuables such as share certificates, deeds for property and insurance policies for the bank to look after in its vaults. The customer receives a receipt detailing the item(s) in safe custody and the bank only returns these on production of this receipt. Where the items are large and complex, such as deeds to property, the bank places these in an envelope sealed either with sealing wax marked by the customer's own seal or sealed all over with Sellotape with the customer's signature over the Sellotape.

The bank accepts the customer's word for the contents of the envelope. Generally, banks make no charge for this service for, as we have seen in Chapter 7, to do so could make the bank a bailee for reward and so give it a stricter duty of care than as a gratuitous bailee.

Safety deposit is offered by those branches which have sufficient room in the vaults to store the boxes of deposit. The customer is allocated a box which is placed in a compartment which usually has two keys. One is held by the customer, the other by the bank. The customer enters the vault with the bank employee, the locks are opened, the customer removes the box, places in it or takes out the valuable item(s), relocks the box and places it back in the compartment. These services are available to all customers of the bank but are mainly used by personal customers.

(5) *Night safes* – this service is offered mainly to business customers. Such safes are available to customers wishing to deposit money at times when the bank is closed. An extension of this system has been brought about by one bank in particular enabling customers to deposit cheques through machines like the ATMs. With the night safe system, the customer is given a wallet in which to place the money to be deposited in the safe. In addition, he receives two keys – one for the wallet and the other for the night safe. The customer enters up the paying-in slip and puts this in the wallet along with the money. The wallet is then placed in the night safe. This is generally a shute which takes the wallet into the vault of the bank. When the bank opens the next day two systems for dealing with the wallet operate. With the first, the bag goes into a locked room in the bank in which two clerks work. They open the bag and check the contents to see if they agree with the paying-in slip. There are two clerks so that one can confirm the value of the contents counted by the other. In this case, the customer agrees to accept their reckoning of the money's worth. In the second case, the customer returns to the bank, redeems the bag, takes out the contents and pays them over the counter. In this latter case, there is no possible doubt as to how much is in the bag.

(6) *Sterling and dollar certificates* – these have been discussed in Chapter 2. This is a special form of deposit usually for large amounts (in excess of £50 000 in UK). The customer receives a certificate as evidence of the deposit. He may keep this until the term of the deposit is up, or it can be taken to a bank or discount house before this time and be discounted. In the latter case, the customer receives a sum of money less than the face value of the certificate. The certificate can also be used to pay off another debt.

Lending

As we have seen in Chapter 3, the early banks soon discovered that they could lend out part of their money on deposit. This has now developed into a whole variety of lending facilities.

(1) *Overdrafts* – these are available to both personal and business customers. As we have seen, this facility allows customers to draw cheques on their accounts for sums in excess of that credited in their current account. Thus, by arrangement, I can draw a cheque for £200 even though my current account has only £100 in credit and the bank will still honour this cheque. Every weekday the computer in the bank branch produces a list of those customers' accounts that are overdrawn at close of business on the previous day. A bank clerk has the task of checking this list against the customers' records to see if they have permission to overdraw and, if this permission has been granted, whether the amount of overdraft is above the stated limit. If permission has not been given or the amount is greater than agreed, these customers are brought to the attention of the manager or other clerk who has the power to grant these excesses or who will take some action. This may be to write a letter to the customer requesting the clearing of this overdraft or that the customer visits the bank to discuss his financial affairs. If the customer persists in maintaining an overdraft against the bank's wishes, the bank may refuse to honour any cheques drawn and take whatever steps it can to recover any monies outstanding. The customer is charged interest on the balance overdrawn at the end of each day. Thus any reduction in the overdraft reduces the interest payment. Overdrafts are generally agreed for the purpose of allowing customers to improve their short-term cash flow shortage.

(2) *Loans* – these are given for longer terms and usually for specific purposes which are detailed to the bank. Personal customers seek these to buy consumer goods such as cars, boats, electrical goods, etc. while business customers seek to purchase machinery, buildings, equipment – those items which are known as investment goods (*see* Chapter 5). As we will see in Chapter 9, banks lend 'against the proposition' so that there are many different arrangements made with customers to meet their borrowing needs. Once agreed, the bank opens up, in the customer's name, a loan account which is in debit and credits the customer's current account so that cheques can be drawn on it for the amount of the loan. Generally, interest charged on these loans varies as the bank base rate changes, but sometimes a bank offers a fixed rate of interest over the term of the loan. The interest charged is usually on the total amount of the loan over its term although some contracts charge interest on the balance outstanding. If the former applies, this makes a bank loan more expensive than an overdraft. We will be discussing loans in more detail in this chapter.

(3) *Bridging loans* – these are loans to allow customers to bridge the gap between the purchase of one property and the sale of another. Usually these are requested by personal customers who are in the process of moving house. These loans are necessary because it is not always possible to have contracts completed on the same day. In order that the customer does not suffer by either losing the house purchased or facing a financial disadvantage,

the bank lends money to close the purchase with a guarantee from a solicitor that the proceeds from the sale of the house will be used to pay off the loan. The bank charges an arrangement fee for this loan and also interest on the amount lent. From the customer's point of view, this kind of loan can be expensive. This facility can also be used by the business world should the need arise.

(4) *Bills discounted* – this is a service which is offered mainly to the business world but personal customers may request it as well. As we have seen in Chapter 4, the classical market operates by the discounting of all kinds of bills. Discounting is the purchase of a bill at a price which is below its face value. The discount houses operate predominantly in this market, however, it is inconvenient for people who do not live in and around the City of London to have to travel to this market to have their bills discounted. Therefore, the banks offer this service in the same way as the discount houses. The interest is charged for what is, technically, a short-term loan and relates to that charged on the London discount market and depends upon the type of bill, the amount and the length of time left before maturity.

Foreign services

There are a number of services which the banks offer to all types of customer which are concerned with promoting foreign trade and travel. These are:

(1) *Forward exchange* – this is the buying and selling of foreign currencies in advance by means of the forward exchange market. This allows customers to cover the risk of uncertainty, because of the fluctuations in rates of exchange, of payments to be made and received. For example, a business may be receiving a payment in two months in another currency for goods sold to a foreign buyer. It needs to be certain of the value of this foreign currency in terms of pounds to be able to calculate the profit. If, in two months time, it were to take the foreign currency to the bank to change into pounds and the pound had risen in value, it would find the pounds received to be less than the amount needed even to cover the costs of production and so a loss would result. If, however, a forward exchange contract had been entered into, a fixed rate of exchange would have been agreed, resulting in certainty of income. The same protection is afforded to a customer seeking to purchase foreign currency in the future. We have talked about this facility with regard to business customers, but we can easily see how a personal customer who has payments to make on property abroad, say rent on a villa in Spain, can make use of this service as well. The rate offered for the currency by the bank depends upon what the forward exchange market thinks is going to happen to the currency in the future. Once a contract is agreed, the bank takes out a matching contract – thus a contract with a customer to buy a currency is matched at the same time, by a contract by the bank to buy this currency.

Forward exchange rates are quoted at **premiums** or **discounts** on present prices. These present prices are known as **spot prices**. A **premium** is at a price which is below spot so that the purchaser of the currency receives less than the spot rate – that is less of the currency than at the present time which means it is more expensive. A discount is the opposite – above spot, so that the purchaser receives more currency as it has become cheaper. Rates are quoted forward for one, two and three months although some major currencies (dollars, deutschemarks, Swiss francs) are quoted forward for up to five years or over, less important currencies for up to one year and some others are not even quoted. If the date forward is known it is called an **outright forward contract** with date so specified. If the date is not known then an **option forward contract** is made and the customer has a choice of completion between two fixed dates.

(2) *Letters of credit* – when a customer of a bank is going abroad for a period of time and wishes to be certain that he can get money wherever he may be, he may be offered this service. The total sum involved is agreed in advance and the bank debits the customer's account with this amount. It then provides the customer with a letter of credit which he will be able to present to the agent bank when each withdrawal is made. At the same time, the bank writes to the correspondent bank or agent authorising them to pay on any cheques or drafts which the customer may present and to charge the debit to the British bank. A specimen of the customer's signature is sent to the agent bank. There are two types of letter of credit. Where only one bank abroad is being used as an agent this is a **direct** letter of credit. If the customer is visiting several countries then it may not be possible to send individual letters so a **circulating** letter of credit is issued. The letter is issued with a **letter of indication** which bears a specimen of the customer's signature and which should be kept separate from the letter of credit. The letter of indication may be in a number of languages so that it can be used in different countries.

(3) *Letter of introduction* – this is a letter from a bank or other financial institution to its agents abroad in which a customer is introduced formally to them. It is useful for customers travelling or going to live abroad, and it enables them to have the facility of assistance from the agent bank. This assistance may take the form of introductions to the local businesses, identifying possible markets, or giving information about local economic, commercial, or legal situations.

Miscellaneous services

(1) *Credit established* – this is a facility offered by the banks whereby customers moving away from their home branch can arrange to make withdrawals from their accounts at other branches of the bank, or associated

banks at home or abroad. The bank needs to know the dates that the facility is required, the amount required and the places where this money is to be withdrawn. It sends particulars to the relevant bank along with a specimen signature. Obviously, with the development of the cash dispenser and the Eurocheque system the need for this service is diminishing.

(2) *Rail and airport banks* – these are very simply banking branches which are situated at international rail stations and airports to offer services to travellers. One of their features is the fact that they operate at hours which are outside the normal banking hours.

Self-assessment exercise

Complete the following table:

Customers' Requirements	Bank Services
1 The Ranger Exporting Co. will receive a payment of $300 000 in three months' time and wish to be certain of the pounds they will receive.	
2 John Raleigh wishes to keep his share certificates safe.	
3 William Brown was made redundant and has set up his own building firm. He knows his cash flow will not be easy and wants to make certain that he can meet his bills.	
4 Jane Rush is going to university and wants to be able to operate payments from her grant.	
5 The XYZ Co. have £350 000 available for the next three months and wish to gain a good return, but at the same time retain some liquidity.	

8.112 Banking services specifically to personal customers

(1) *Personal loans* – these can be viewed as direct competition by the banks with the hire purchase/credit sale market. They are loans to personal customers to enable them to purchase such items as motor cars, boats, caravans, furniture, carpets and other consumer durables. The bank manager considers the customer's proposition and decides whether or not to lend. The loan is for a fixed term, up to five years, and usually at a fixed rate of interest. Thus the monthly repayment includes repayment of capital and an interest element, that is, the interest charged in the final year is calculated on the

value of the loan on the day that it was taken out as the capital repayments reduce the amount outstanding.

The Consumer Credit Act 1974 requires the agreement to show both the actual and nominal rate of interest. When a customer borrows on these terms, the nominal rate of interest is the one quoted at the interview while the actual rate is the rate that the customer will pay on account of the reduction in the capital outstanding over the duration of the loan. Thus a customer may borrow £5000 for five years at 10 per cent, the nominal rate being 10 per cent and the actual (real) rate being around 25 per cent.

Such loans have a different legal basis from hire purchase. With the latter, the borrower does not become the owner of the goods until the final payment or some part is made. Up to that time he is the hirer of the goods. With a personal loan, the customer becomes a debtor of the bank and is given the facility to purchase these goods outright – the shopkeeper need never know that the customer has borrowed the money.

The bank offers these services to customers with a current account as, from the operation of this account, the bank manager can view the financial prowess of the customer, and this acts as some form of security for the loan. Usually a free insurance policy is attached to the agreement to enable it to be repaid should the customer be unable to do so, perhaps because of loss of income as a result of unemployment or sickness.

(2) *Budget accounts* – most customers have to pay a wide range of bills regularly over the year such as electricity, gas, rates, insurance, club fees, car repairs and mortgage. Unfortunately, these bills do not arrive at periods which are evenly spaced out. In order to help banks offer a budget account (although this facility may not be called this specifically). This allows the customer to spread these payments over the whole year and to meet the bills as they fall due. The operation of this account is as follows. The customer lists the payments to be included in the account. Some of these are known payments, like membership fees, others are estimates, like electricity bills. These payments are totalled and a contingency amount is added and then the total is divided by twelve. This twelfth amount is paid into the budget account every month by means of a standing order on the current account. The customer is given a special cheque book with this account with which to meet the payments listed above. If the budget account goes into debit in any month, the customer's current account is debited with the interest due. There may also be an arrangement fee charged by the bank against the current account each year that the budget account is operated as it is an annual agreement. At the end of the year, if the customer has estimated the payments correctly, the account will either be zero or at a small credit. The customer then re-estimates the payments and arranges for a different amount to be paid into the account each month for the following year. The advantage to the customer of this account is the certainty of being able to meet necessary payments as they fall due.

(3) *Probate advances* – these are loans to administrators or executors of the estates of deceased persons to enable them to meet any payments out of the estate before probate, for example, to pay burial expenses. Loans may even be extended to beneficiaries who seek to make some purchase before probate and distribution of the estate. In this case, as with a bridging loan, the bank seeks a solicitor's guarantee that the loan will be repaid from the estate and that the customer is a beneficiary in the estate to an amount which will more than cover the loan. These loans can be expensive to the borrower.

(4) *Executor and trustee business* – before discussing this, it is useful to explain that banks will help customers to draw up a will. The customer is interviewed by the bank manager who discusses with him the details to be included in the will such as bequests. The manager may also give advice as to how the customer can best indicate these wishes. The will is drawn up by the bank's legal department which is experienced in these matters and can use the correct legal language to make proving and implementation of the contents easier at the relevant time. Sometime after the first interview, the customer returns to the bank to see the completed draft. If all is in order, the will is signed and witnessed as required by the law. The customer may then keep the will or hand it over to the bank to be held in safe custody.

At some time during the making of the will the customer is asked to give the names of any executors of the will. An executor is the person who is responsible for seeing that the will is proven, that any taxation due is paid and that the estate is distributed as per the instructions in the will. The manager will let the customer know that the bank has a department especially experienced in these duties and, even if the customer has a personal friend he wishes to have as an executor, he might suggest that the bank also be included. One of the dangers of having individuals as executors is that they might die before the customer and so there will be no one to execute his wishes. As the bank is a company this problem does not arise. If a person dies without leaving a will he is said to be intestate, and the bank can take on the administration of his estate, if necessary.

Sometimes the terms in the will include a request that some or all of the assets in the estate be put in trust for a beneficiary. Banks have developed expertise in the managing of these trusts. The legal duties placed on a trustee are quite strict and it is, therefore, better to have (the benefit of) this expertise.

(5) *Income tax management* – banks offer taxation services to personal customers. These services range from basic advice to the bank looking after all of the customer's tax affairs including completing the annual tax return, claiming the relevant allowances, paying the tax and receiving any repayments of overpayments of tax. This service applies not only to income tax but also capital gains tax and inheritance tax management. These services are operated by the executor and trustee departments of the banks.

(6) *Investment management* – banks have also developed an expertise in investment advice and management for personal customers. Customers who have funds to invest can go to the bank for advice as to the best possible investments for their money. Banks, since the case *Hedley Byrne & Co. Ltd v. Heller Partners* (*see* Section 8.113), have tended to be cautious in their advice. Safe steady investments are recommended rather than the higher risk higher return ones. Banks offer these services particularly to customers who do not wish to manage their own investments. They take over the whole portfolio, make changes in the holdings, take up rights issues for the customer and collect on the dividends. An annual statement of the portfolio is sent to the customer. To make its job easier, the bank asks customers to sign over the investments to the bank so that, on paper, the bank owns these securities and can dispose of them swiftly. It is possible for the customer to give the bank complete control of the portfolio without reference back to him, however, the customer can request that the bank consults him before going ahead. Speculators are not encouraged to use this service as the banks are not interested in frequent purchases and sales.

(7) *Passport services* – customers travelling abroad and requiring a passport can ask their bank to carry out the necessary arrangements. The bank sees to the completion of the necessary forms and then despatches them to the relevant passport office, either Liverpool or Newport depending upon where the customer lives. One of the advantages of using the bank is that the certification signature of details and photograph, which has to be by a professional person, may be carried out by the manager.

(8) *Revolving credit account* – this is really a savings and credit account combined. It allows the customer to save a certain sum of money, usually on a monthly basis, and to have the facility of borrowing up to thirty times this amount for special purchases. A standing order is made against the customer's current account for the amount to be saved in the new account and a cheque book is provided for purchases up to thirty times the limit. When the new account goes into debit the monthly savings go towards paying this off. The customer can go on 'topping up' the loan to the thirty times limit with further purchases before the complete loan is paid off. Interest is paid to the customer if the account is kept in credit while a higher rate is charged for debits.

(9) *Unit trusts* – we have already seen the operation of unit trusts in Chapter 5. Here we saw that banks act as agents offering different kinds of unit trust to their customers in which the banks are managers with separate trustees of the funds. Like all unit trusts, they are ideal for people with small savings who wish to invest in companies. The wide range of trusts available show the great variation in success of these funds.

(10) *Home banking services* – a development which started with the building societies, now offered by one bank, is the home banking service. This is a system which links a home computer, a television information service,

like Prestel, and the bank. It enables customers to get information about their accounts immediately, to help them to make changes in their operation, such as changing standing orders, ordering cheque books and information about other banking services. At the moment the scheme is still in its experimental stage and, therefore, expensive to operate, but as more homes get computers and the facility for receiving the television information service then it will become more used and costs may come down. It does give an indication of the way banking may develop in the future.

Self-assessment exercises

1 Explain the difference between budget accounts and revolving credit accounts.
2 What is the difference between a personal loan and a probate advance?
3 Home banking has only just been introduced. What is it?

8.113 Banking services specifically for business customers

(1) *Farming advances* – farmers need to borrow from banks for three purposes. Firstly, for the short term to meet any short fall in operation income and payments. At particular times of the year farmers find outgoings exceed income, particularly spring and early summer when crops must be planted and cultivated before the harvest is ready for sale in late summer and autumn. For this purpose, the bank allows overdrafts on the current account. Secondly, there is a need for medium-term loans to purchase smaller machinery and equipment. Again banks provide this finance, or sometimes the farmer seeks hire purchase funding. Thirdly, long-term finance is necessary for the purchase of land and its development. Bank finance may be either direct or indirect, through such institutions as the Agricultural Mortgage Corporation (*see* Chapter 4). In the case of a direct loan, the bank lends the money from its own funds, whether it will do this or not depends upon the proposition put forward by the farmer.

(2) *Factoring* – this is a way in which business can raise funds using the money owed to them from sales, these being identified from the invoices. The factoring service, however, is more correctly described as a sales ledger accounting and bad debts collection service. These services are usually offered by companies who are subsidiaries of the banks. The types of service differ but they mainly cover three areas:

(a) discounting the value of the invoices, usually up to 80 per cent with the debts approved by the factoring company. A charge is made for this service;

(b) the taking on of all aspects of sales accounting within the business which includes keeping accounts of all debtors, issuing regular statements of account and collecting payments. This service obviously relieves the business of its administration and expense;

(c) guaranteeing full payment on approved sales even if they are eventually bad debts.

These services are usually offered to firms with large sales ledgers, £100 000 plus. Charges are made according to the service supplied being 1.5 per cent to 2.5 per cent for sales ledger and bad debt collection. Interest is charged on any loans made at current rates of interest.

(3) *Bills for collection* – this is a service offered by the banks where payment between a British exporter and a foreign buyer has been arranged by bill of exchange. The British exporter passes the bill onto the UK bank. The bank sends the bill to an agent or correspondent bank overseas; this is called the collecting bank. It presents the bill for payment if it is a sight bill or for acceptance if it is a term draft. On completion of the term, the collecting bank represents the bill for payment. If no documents are attached it is called a **clean bill** collection. These have become popular in some European countries where they may be used for internal trade as well as external trade. There are variations on this system. The acceptance may be completed by direct communication between the exporter and the foreign buyer. If documents of title are to be included it is called a **documentary** collection. In this case the customer seeking a banking service for collection must instruct the bank if the documents are to be released on acceptance or payment. In the former case the bill is inscribed with the letters D/A and in the latter D/P. The bank charges a small percentage of the value of the bill plus mail and other transmission charges. The foreign bank, on receipt of the funds, transfers them to the UK bank which credits the amount, usually after conversion into sterling, to the customer's account. On the other hand, a foreign currency account can be opened if requested.

The bank usually asks the customer to complete a **bank lodgement form** so that it will be clear as to what the exporter wants from the particular collection and what action should be taken if the overseas buyer does not meet the payment terms of the contract. This form is simply a systematic checklist which ensures that all the instructions are remembered so that a successful collection will be carried out. If an overseas buyer goes bankrupt or deliberately defaults on a term bill, the bank can arrange for legal action or act on instructions to start protesting the bill (*see* Chapter 7).

(4) *Bills for negotiation* – if a customer wishes to have cash before any bill for collection falls due he can negotiate for the bank to buy it. It is similar to discounting but it is called negotiation. In order to cover its position on the bill the bank might negotiate it with recourse to payment from the customer if the acceptor defaults. The banker may even ask for security as well, although where documents are included these will be seen as part of the bill's security. After negotiation the bank collects on its own behalf.

(5) *Computer services* – in the days of large main frame computers, banks very soon saw the advantages of this technology in the operation of their services. Smaller businesses could neither afford these computers nor, if they had bought them, would they have had sufficient work to keep them occupied. It was not long before banks began to sell time on their machines to businesses to carry out some of their activities. They were useful for keeping personnel records, stock records and for operating wage and salary payment systems. With the development of micro-chip technology, mini and micro computers have become available at prices which can be afforded by the small business. Thus we can assume that this service will decline over the years but that bank systems will develop to handle the locally-based software raised by businesses.

(6) *Documentary credit* – under bills for collection above we discussed the use of documents attached to the bill and saw that these afford greater security to the bank when lending. An even more secure system is a **documentary letter of credit**. This is also a way in which an exporter can receive payment in advance of the credit given to the foreign buyer. The system works as follows:

(a) The exporter and foreign buyer enter into a sales contract with an agreement that payment will be by documentary letter of credit.

(b) The foreign buyer issues instructions to his bank (the issuing bank) to open a documentary credit in favour of the exporter.

(c) The issuing bank instructs a UK bank to advise and/or confirm credit giving the types of documents to be used and the details to be included.

(d) The UK advisory or confirming bank then sends a letter of credit to the exporter.

(e) The exporter despatches the goods to the foreign buyer and then,

(f) presents the shipping documents to the confirming or advising bank.

(g) This bank then checks the documents and, if in order, credits the exporter's account.

(h) The confirming/advising bank forwards the documents to the foreign bank. This is known as 'advising'. Usually duplicate copies of the documents are sent by an alternative post.

(i) The issuing bank checks the documents and reimburses the UK bank and then,

(j) debits the customer's account in the agreed way.

(k) The issuing bank then releases the documents to the foreign buyer.

(l) The foreign buyer can then use these documents to claim the goods.

The documents used in this type of transaction may include: insurance certificates, bills of lading or airway bills and invoices or consular invoices.

Documentary credit can be revocable or irrevocable. A revocable letter of credit, rarely used these days, means that the terms of the credit can be amended or cancelled by the foreign buyer at any time without prior notice to the exporter. An irrevocable letter of credit is one where the terms cannot be altered or revoked without prior agreement between the parties.

A way to achieve better security is to ensure that these irrevocable credits are confirmed by the advising or UK bank. If the documentary credit is confirmed, the UK bank stands fully in place of the issuing bank and, provided all terms and conditions of the contract are fulfilled by the exporter, payment is assured. An extra payment is made for this service.

There are many different variations in documentary credits but the most common form is the **confirmed irrevocable letter of credit**.

(7) *Leasing* – this is an area in which banks have become heavily committed in recent years, particularly through subsidiaries. Leasing is a system whereby a firm is able to obtain the use of an asset without having to buy it outright but is able to hire it. What happens is that a firm identifies the plant, equipment or vehicles which it wishes to use. A leasing company purchases them and then the firm enters into a contract to hire these assets over a period of time. At no time during the contract does the firm own these assets. The hiring firm pays a regular instalment either monthly, quarterly or annually which covers capital repayments, administration costs, rental and profit for the leasing firm. At the end of the contract the hiring firm may be given the option to purchase the asset outright. Included in the hiring contract will also be a maintenance contract. Many firms now acquire computers, cars and heavy plant by this method. The service can be adopted by exporting companies. The advantage to the hiring firms lies in the saving of time and costs from administration, depreciation and maintenance.

(8) *Intelligence reports* – often businessmen wishing to export abroad are not always certain about markets and their potential. Banks provide intelligence reports about these markets giving details about potential growth, credit facilities, economic conditions, details about possible competitors, currency regulations and local commercial law and customs. Banks may also give introductions as well as credit and financial assistance to these exporters. These services are also supplied to producers for the home market.

(9) *Merchant banking services* – as we have seen in Chapter 3, this century has witnessed the development of competition between the banks. There were always some services which the banks offered in common. Just as the merchant banks compete against the clearing banks for the deposits of the general public, these clearing banks have developed what can clearly be seen as merchant bank services. These are:

(a) Acceptance credit facilities – these have been discussed already in Chapter 3 with reference to merchant banks. This is a service offered by acceptance houses whereby they lend their name to a bill of exchange to make it more acceptable for discounting. A customer wishing to have a bill discounted which does not have two good names on it will find that this is not possible unless it is accepted. It then becomes a bank bill and is more acceptable. As well as the merchant banks, some clearing banks offer this accepting service. If the original acceptor of the bill defaults, the accepting house will meet the payment.

(b) Equity financing – commercial banks often offer this service through their subsidiaries. This takes the form of providing loans for new ventures and taking security in the form of ordinary shares in the business. It involves the subsidiary in taking part in the management of the new firm, an aspect that deters would-be customers as they do not wish to surrender control.

(c) Issuing house business – certain merchant banks offer services to business in the form of assistance in raising capital for business development. Other commercial banks also offer this service.

The sale of shares is a complex business and some firms may feel that they have neither the time nor the expertise to carry this out properly. Therefore, they can enlist the help of these issuing houses. This help ranges from giving advice as to the correct procedures and the type of share to issue, to the complete management of the issue. The issuing house may also guarantee to underwrite the issue so that should all of the shares not be sold it will provide the finance and take on the shares itself. We must consider their services in relation to two types of issue. The first is when a company is entering the market for the first time. The firm may wish for a full quotation and the issuing house will help to arrange this. Then it will see to the publication of a prospectus with the shares being offered for sale or by tender. Small issues may be subject to a **placing** or **introduction**. It is the work of the issuing house to fix the price of the share at the correct level so that the issue is not 'oversubscribed', or possibly 'stagged', or 'undersubscribed'. The second is with regard to a placing on the unlisted securities market. This is a less formal quotation and is better for companies that have just started trading or wish to test the water before going for a full quotation.

The issuing house also assists an existing quoted company to raise additional capital through a rights issue. Shareholders either take up their issue or sell them on the market.

(d) Lending to business in the medium term – this developed as competition by the banks with other firms which could accept longer terms for deposits and so give longer term loans. Banks have been able to enter this market by setting up subsidiaries through which these services are offered. They became heavily committed in the Eurocurrency market. Since the deregulation of the banks which allowed them to accept longer-term deposits at higher interest rates, these subsidiaries have been merged into the bank's everyday business but have been kept separate in some respects. There is expected to be an increase in this type of business.

(10) *Guarantees and indemnities* – these are services which are provided to both business and personal customers. Personal customers might seek a banker's guarantee if they have lost a share certificate and seek a duplicate. On the other hand, a business may seek a bank's guarantee, for one of

its customers, to ensure that the financial terms of some future contract will be met.

(11) *Performance bonds* – these are used particularly in exporting. A bond is a written instrument issued to a buyer by a bank or insurance company stating that a customer will comply with the terms of the contract and, if not, the buyer will receive compensation for any loss which results. The terms of the bond do not relate to the terms of the original contract. The types of bond are:

(a) Tender or bid bond – this is issued by a prospective seller to a buyer to cover any loss where the seller does not comply with the terms of the tender.

(b) Performance bond – this is a guarantee that the seller will comply with the terms of the contract.

(c) Advance payment or repayment bond – in the event of the supplier failing to deliver goods under a contract the buyer can 'call' a bond to recover any advance payment made to the seller.

(d) Release of retention monies bond – issued by the seller to a buyer against release of any money held pending the final completion of the contract, or at some mutually agreed time.

A bank always takes a corresponding counter **indemnity** so that the monies that have been paid out on the bond may be reclaimed from the seller. The security of this indemnity is only as good as the resources of the customer.

Bonds of all types are available to all kinds of people but particularly to two types of customer – builders and exporters.

(12) *Status enquiries* – this is a service which the bank offers to business customers who seek to discover the financial position of their customers, whether they be individuals or businesses. This service either consists of answering status enquiries from other banks or similar institutions, or instigating such an enquiry on behalf of one of its customers. In order to maintain the necessary secrecy, the bank operates these status enquiries within strict lines:

(a) It only answers enquiries which have come from other banks or known trade organisations with a good reputation. It does not answer private enquiries, although the Mark Thatcher affair in 1984, whereby a newspaper was able to obtain the balance in the bank account of the Prime Minister's son, caused quite a stir.

(b) The replies to these enquiries are carefully considered and phrased with tact. This follows the case of *Hedley Byrne & Co. Ltd v. Heller Partners Ltd* (1963) which established a duty of care on banks answering status enquiries, and this duty comes into being when the bank gives such answers and it is foreseeable that the people receiving the information will act upon it. In this case a merchant bank Heller Partners Ltd were asked by an advertising firm, Hedley Byrne & Co. Ltd to answer a status enquiry on a firm,

Easipower Ltd, as they were thinking about taking a substantial order from the firm and committing themselves to considerable cost in preparing a campaign. Easipower had their account with the merchant bank which appeared to give a favourable report on the firm, thus causing the plaintiffs to book advertising space. Easipower went into liquidation and as a result Hedley Byrne lost £17 000. It was held that the merchant bank had made a negligent statement but that it was protected by a disclaimer it had issued that it would not be held responsible.

The Unfair Contract Terms Act 1977 changed the position whereby banks put disclaimers on their status enquiry forms in order to avoid liability. This Act excludes or restricts a businessman's liability for negligence arising in the course of business which results in another's loss or damage. Any such exclusions are now subject to the test of reasonableness. Thus a bank relying on a standard written disclaimer to evade its liability for a statement in a status enquiry which is reckless or negligent could find itself open to challenge in the courts. If, however, it were proved that the bank had acted with diligence and careful consideration but the report was not correct then the bank is protected.

(c) When a customer has requested an enquiry, the name, address and bank account of the person or company to be enquired about must be supplied. The reply will go to the enquiring bank and not the enquirer.

(d) The bank replying to the enquiry will not give specific information about the customer's account such as the balance, the customer's name and address, or specific payments made from the account. There are some standard statements used in these reports which give an adequate reply without disclosing these specifics. If it cannot give a good report, its statements must be couched in terms which do not damage the creditworthiness or character of the customer.

(e) The Consumer Credit Act 1973 (Section 148.8) requires that all credit reference agencies when requested are to disclose the subject of any enquiry and what is contained within the report. Banks are not subject to these provisions as they are not classed as credit reference agencies. Therefore, a bank will not give details of any enquiry or of the reply it has given.

Self-assessment exercises

Explain, fully, the services that would be supplied to the XYZ Co. Ltd by a bank in the following circumstances:

(a) It has a total sales income of £1.5 million and wishes to liquidate the money earlier than it would under the invoice system.

(b) It wishes to secure payments for its exports without relinquishing some control over the goods.

(c) It is holding a bill of exchange from a debtor for £15 000 and wishes to get cash for it.

(d) A new customer, from Gloucester, wishes to purchase goods from them and has asked for three months' credit. They are not certain of this firm's creditworthiness.

(e) A local building firm is going to build an extension to their factory. There are some rumours that it is not so good at completing its contracts. It is important for the XYZ Co. for the factory to be completed on time in order to meet a foreign order. They could lose money if it is not. How can they cover themselves if this event takes place?

8.12 Marketing the banks' services

Any bank manager today will tell you that one of the major roles he has to perform is that of marketing expert. Competition in the financial market has become so intense that if banks wish to survive they must learn to market a complete range of financial services. The aim is to produce a kind of departmental store of banking with one-stop banking being offered. Thus banks wish to produce a complete range of products. One of the strongest points regarding marketing is for banks to provide products which are well designed, constructed and delivered. Use of marketing strategies and techniques are now part of the banks' organisational structure. Banks would, however, deny that the 'hard sell' is now part of their philosophy and state that customer care and service is still the cornerstone of their aims.

The overall aim of marketing is firstly to attract new customers, people who, as of yet, do not use banks, but as banks have financial relationships with over 70 per cent of all households in the UK the peak of this market seems to be past. However, this brings in the second aim – to offer cross-services to existing customers. Thus banks seek to offer a wide range of financial services and products that are required by customers and can be supplied at a profit. A customer coming to the bank for one service may be attracted to an allied service. It is up to the bank staff to promote these additional services by identifying the need and highlighting the way in which the bank can help.

Part of the marketing policy of the bank will be its advertising and promotional techniques. We can look at these both from the point of view of the activities of head offices and those of the branches.

8.121 Head office advertising techniques

No matter how big a market is available this must be attacked and this involves spending large amounts on advertising. Head office advertising and promotions take the form of promoting an overall bank image, the development of new services and the advantages of the particular bank in relation to the others. Thus the banks use the major media techniques such as television, newspapers and magazines to advertise the benefits of banking with a particular bank. We are all aware of the black horse or griffin; advertisements about the advantages of certain banking services, such as credit cards, 'free' banking, business services, exporters' services, services to students and pensioners. Banks, obviously, try to use the medium which will reach the largest number of people. Banks also use promotions, such as competitions, which keep the bank's name alive.

8.122 Advertising techniques of the branch

Traditionally bank managers were not regarded as salespersons, but this has changed. Increased, sophisticated research and development techniques and computer technology now leave managers in little doubt as to what is the exact potential of their particular area. Some banks are now appointing marketing managers whose role is specifically to promote the branch services and image in a local area. This advertising and promotion is seen in the following areas:

(1) traditionally through the manager's connection with local organisations and clubs, visiting local schools, mother's unions and professional bodies. By the development of these connections, the benefit to the bank may be considerable;

(2) opening the bank to visits from local citizens either in special interest groups or individually outside opening hours. Showing videos about banking services, behind the counter activities, using staff to promote good relations all help to provide a good image and inform the public about what the bank has to offer.

(3) Banks, being placed in most high streets in our towns and cities, are ideally placed to advertise their services in their own windows.

(4) Banks can also supply information about their services in their normal communications with customers. Sending out statements, replacement credit and cheque guarantee cards can include advertising material about these services. This encourages the cross-servicing of customers' needs, at the same time offering a whole financial package.

(5) Setting up information points and promotional stands at exhibitions, fairs and agricultural shows so promoting the bank's services.

This is neither an exhaustive list nor is it unlikely that new methods of marketing will develop in the future. Banks may not have to manufacture all of the services they promote themselves, as seen with insurance services and the Amex gold card where the bank acts as an agent retailing a service manufactured elsewhere.

Self-assessment exercise

With examples, explain the difference between head office and branch marketing of the various banking services.

Assignments

1 The following situations involve some method of payment at home or abroad. Say how these will be made detailing the accounts that will be debited and credited.
   (a) Chiminster Engineering Co. Ltd wish to export their manufactured products abroad but are worried about losing control of them before they are paid.
   (b) Miss C Brean goes shopping at Harrods, purchases a dress for £109.99 and pays by cheque drawn on her account in the Eastlands Bank plc at the Reayley branch.
   (c) Mr and Mrs Snips wish to pay the ground rent on their Italian villa to Salvatori Estates to their account in the Banca di Firenze.
   (d) George Cane wants to pay the hire purchase instalment on his motor car of £120.88 a month to Hampshire Credit Co. in Gosmouth. His account is with the Eastland Bank plc at their Reayley branch.

2 Write about *four* of the following banking services:
   (a) Executor and trustee business
   (b) Merchant banking services
   (c) Personal loans
   (d) Factoring
   (e) Forward exchange
   (f) Accepting deposits

3 John Belt was made redundant from the local steelworks. With his redundancy money he has bought a small grocery business in a nearby village. He has written to your bank asking for details of the services you could provide him both as a business and personal customer. The manager asks you to write the reply.
   When he reads it over he feels that this information would be of interest to other customers or prospective customers. He asks you to prepare a memorandum outlining the ways in which these could be marketed. Prepare this memorandum.

4 What services can a bank provide to local exporters? Describe these fully.

9 Understanding the Basic Principles of Bank Lending

9.1 General principles of lending

We are all aware that banks give loans either in the form of an overdraft or a full loan. An overdraft is a facility to draw cheques over and above the amount shown in credit on our current account. By this method the bank does not know exactly how much it will be asked to lend but it usually puts an upper limit on the overdraft facility in the interest of the bank and the customer. There are many occasions when a customer takes his account into overdraft without first having secured the bank's permission. When this happens the customer is acting illegally and the bank is not aware of its lending commitment until it has happened. When a loan is arranged the bank adds the amount to the customer's current account and opens up a loan account in the name of the customer with the balance in debit.

When considering whether to lend money to a customer the bank manager bases his decision on a number of principles which have evolved over the years. Very basically the manager is lending to the **proposition**. This is the proposal the customer brings to the manager in order to secure the loan. As we will see this is not just the use to which the money will be put. The manager listens to the proposal and then using these principles and his experience decides whether or not to grant the loan. He does not apply these principles strictly all of the time but has the power to grant a loan even if it is seen as an extremely high risk. It may be that he/she wishes to foster a very useful connection. This is where the art of lending comes in for he needs to be able to know just when to accept a risk with the hope that it will end up profitable for all concerned. However, in the nature of banking, more often than not bank managers are very careful about lending so that generally only reasonably safe and secure propositions are accepted.

We can classify the basic principles upon which bank lending is based in general terms in three ways. First, all of these loans are based on the principle of **safety**. This means that the bank manager will generally lend to a reliable borrower who will be able to repay from sources of funds which are reasonably certain and that this repayment will be within a relatively short term. Ideally this loan should be supported by the customer depositing an approved security which the bank accepts as an insurance against non-repayment by the customer.

The second basic principle is **suitability**. Thus the loan must be in the interest of the economic health of the nation. This places upon the manager the responsibility for looking after the well-being of the community. In addition to this the manager must be aware of any restrictions in lending which may be part of the overall economic strategy of government. For example, it might be that the current government's aim is to reduce the money supply which is causing excess demand for consumer goods. A directive may have come from the Bank of England requesting banks to restrict their lending to the personal sector. Under these circumstances a bank manager would possibly refuse a request for a loan from a customer wishing to buy a car. At the same time it might be that the government wishes to encourage exports so that a request from an exporter may be received favourably. In addition to the suitability of the loan to the economy, the loan must be suitable to the lending policy of the bank and must be used for a purpose which the bank feels is compatible to its lending policy. The loan must also be regarded as suitable for the customer regarding his circumstances.

The third basic principle upon which lending is based is **profitability**. This is a most important aspect since interest received on advances is the main source of revenue for the bank, and banks are not in the habit of financing projects which can be classed as gambling. It is obvious that banks would soon go out of business if they were to lend money for less than the interest paid to their deposits customers. However, to enable the bank manager to take some kind of risk, interest rates charged will vary generally depending upon the security or safety of the borrower and the use to which the money is being put.

Borrowing from banks can be divided broadly into two categories. Firstly, there is the personal sector who borrow to purchase such items as food, clothing, cars, furniture and holidays. Secondly, there is the business sector who borrow to buy goods or raw materials; pay bills for power, wages or rates and rent; or purchase new plant and equipment.

When considering propositions from all types of customer, the bank manager must take a number of factors into consideration. First of all there is the character of the borrower. What is known about his ability, integrity and experience? Have previous dealings with the customer shown him to be of sufficient standard to inspire confidence? If the borrower seeks a business loan, what are the prospects of the business? Is it likely to experience growth or decline? If the borrower is a personal one what has been his record of financial dealings? How has the account been handled in the past? A satisfactory answer to these questions will encourage the bank manager to consider favourably any request for a loan. In the case of a long-term customer, the manager will be able to discover considerable information before the interview. If the customer is reasonably new to the bank, the manager may wish to ascertain some relevant information from people who know the customer better. For this purpose he may take up **references** from these people before the final decision is taken.

Secondly, the bank manager will want to know how much money is required. This is not just so that he can find out the extent of the bank's involvement and if this is in excess of what he would wish to lend, but so that the bank manager can appraise the adequacy of the loan from the customer's point of view. Is it sufficient for the borrower to achieve his purpose? Will the borrower be supplying his own funds towards the project and from what source is the money coming? Will the borrower still have sufficient funds available to meet unexpected demands? Once again, it is a satisfactory answer to these questions that will help the bank manager to decide whether or not to grant the loan.

As stated the bank manager needs to know if the funds are sufficient for the borrower to achieve his purpose, he must, therefore, know the purpose of the loan. In addition, this will enable him to establish that the money lent is not going to be put to an unsuitable use. For example, a bank manager would not normally grant an overdraft in order to purchase a motor car or some capital equipment. By knowing the purpose the bank manager can direct the customer to the correct form of loan, which may not necessarily be from a bank.

A bank manager is interested in short-term lending. This is because the money deposited by customers is only provided on a short-term basis. Money in current accounts can be demanded at once while deposit accounts are on seven days' notice. The bank manager is not absolutely certain what the demand for withdrawals is likely to be, so he must keep money available. In practice depositors do keep their money in the bank for longer terms so that banks have learned, through experience, how much money and for how long they can lend. It is, therefore, important for the bank to know what source of income will be available from which the borrower may repay the loan. For a personal customer this is likely to be from his income, and if this is paid into a current account the bank manager will know from the operation of that account how realistic that source is likely to be. With a business the bank manager may be able to identify some major source of income which the business may be able to tap in the future to repay the loan. This may be some contract which is maturing or the production of goods by the machinery which the loan has helped to finance.

There is also the possibility that the customer is able to supply some form of security which will act as an insurance to the bank against non-repayment. Very simply, if a security is offered the bank manager will be interested in its possible value if it were converted into cash, if the value will be maintained over time, if the value is sufficient to cover the loan and if the bank can successfully gain a right to the security.

Finally, the bank manager will discuss with the customer the rate of interest to be charged for the loan, the method of repayment and any other matters which may be relevant to the whole proposal. During the interview the bank manager will be assessing the whole proposition and will be in a good position, after he has progressed some way, to know if the loan can be granted. The bank manager will generally be able to grant or refuse the loan by the end of the interview but in some cases he may need time to consider the proposal more fully. In the case of a business advance, further analysis of the business's financial position may be necessary. Sometimes a bank manager may be asked for a loan which is in excess of his discretion. It does not mean that the customer will not get the loan but that the application will be passed up through the system, to district, area or head office branch, to the level which can deal with it.

Once the advance has been given and the money used by the customer, there must be some form of supervision operated by the bank system to see that no problems occur. The system varies according to the bank, and within different branches of the same bank, to the manager. In order to follow the system of supervision it is necessary to differentiate between overdrafts and loans. The reason for the differentiation is because the extent of a bank loan is known before the customer uses the money, but overdrafts are often taken without the bank's permission. Even when a customer has arranged an overdraft beforehand the bank is not certain that the full amount will be taken up. Thus the bank needs to monitor who goes into overdraft and by how much.

In order to supervise overdrafts banks need to set up some system whereby the accounts which become overdrawn are brought to their notice daily. From this can be discovered those customers who have permission to overdraw and if they have kept within their limit, and those customers who have overdrawn without permission. The manager must decide what to do about these offenders. In some cases customers will be asked to repay the money as soon as possible, in others the manager might overlook the withdrawal knowing that funds will come in very soon.

During the period of a bank loan the bank needs to operate some system of supervision. This will include monitoring the various trading concerns in the community to try and identify customers who may have difficulty in repaying loans. The bank will also want to know if the customer has failed to supply any information requested or has failed to comply with certain arrangements. It will be necessary to keep a check on the value of securities to see if they are maintaining their value. Finally, it will want to know if repayment dates are being met. If a major capital development has been financed by a bank loan, the manager may even visit the site as it progresses to see how the project is developing. Obviously, the bank managers cannot monitor all the lending by their branch so will delegate various responsibilities to their staff. No doubt they will have to inform him if any problem clients emerge or any major decisions have to be made. Such staff as the assistant manager and chief clerk will deputise for the manager in his absence so they will need to know about the lending arrangements within the branch. The securities clerk will supervise the securities held by the branch, and a good securities clerk can relieve the manager of considerable worry over the validity and value of securities. The same person or another clerk will be responsible for the analysis of the accounts of a business wishing to negotiate a loan.

Self-assessment exercises

1   What is meant by 'the proposition' in bank lending?
2   In what ways must a loan be secure in the manager's world?
3   For whom or in what ways must the loan be seen to be suitable?
4   List any other considerations in the mind of the manager when considering a loan application.
5   Outline the system of monitoring for (a) overdrafts; (b) bank loans.

9.2 Credit scoring

What we have looked at so far are the traditional methods of appraising a customer's request for a loan. In today's banking world, it is a more practical proposition to use some form of statistical system to improve the process by which credit decision making is carried out. These systems take the knowledge of experts in this particular field and then organise it into facts and rules which can be stored on a computer. The system of analysis is often developed to meet the specific needs of the institution concerned. These systems, however, have a number of common features:

(1) Post behaviour is analysed and a model or statistical representation compiled.

(2) This model is used to predict and improve future decisions.

(3) These models themselves are received and amended in the light of experience.

9.21 A general explanation

One of the best known of these statistical systems used by the financial section in decision-making is **credit scoring**. These systems have been in use for over twenty years, but there has been a growth in their use in the past ten years. Much of the development comes from the USA where firms in this field are now instrumental in the installation of these systems in the consumer lending areas of banks, financial companies and other lending institutions.

A typical system is operated by means of a table which evaluates the financial and non-financial aspects of the person applying for the loan. This table and the relevant points for each aspect on the table come from the lender's past experience of similar borrowers. The total of the points awarded to the applicant is compared with some predetermined cut-off point, and if the score is lower than the cut-off point then the loan is refused. Setting up the credit scoring process follows a series of steps, as many as twenty-seven have been listed by one writer, which enable the lender to develop a realistic and useful system. They involve identifying the type of system required, identifying the right type of people to operate the system, the degree of training required, the type of information needed to be stored in order to help appraise future credit scores, the systems necessary to re-appraise the system of credit scoring and the decisions made by the system.

There will not be instant success with the system and it may take two or three years before any benefits from its use are realised. A properly thought out and implemented system must be operated for worse problems arise from the operation of a crude credit scoring than from the system based mainly on personal judgement.

9.22 The advantages of credit scoring

(1) It enables a more efficient method of credit appraisal to operate.

(2) It helps to reduce the number of bad debts. Indeed, improvements of between 10 to 40 per cent have been achieved in lending portfolios by firms operating this system.

(3) A much wider information system for lending comes into operation which will be available for the whole organisation.

(4) Eventually the system will lead to the organisation being able to operate a low cost, high volume credit system.

(5) The system, itself, can be made self-revisionary.

(6) A greater use of data-based and statistical systems which are applicable to the new technology is possible.

(7) It enables banks to compete with other financial institutions more effectively.

9.12 The disadvantages of credit scoring

(1) It is difficult to make the system work for it needs considerable expertise by technical staff such as statisticians, operational researchers and computer specialists.

(2) Managers need to be convinced of the effectiveness of this system for they often feel that the existing methods work satisfactorily for them.

(3) It may cost money and time to introduce.

9.24 Future developments

(1) The application of credit scoring techniques to the analysis of customer account operations so that banks and financial institutions will be able to predict future customer behaviour regarding use of accounts. Banks will be able to improve decision-making with regard to collection strategies, increases or decreases in credit limits, purchase authorisation and credit card renewals.

(2) Information about the effectiveness of mailshots for the marketing of the bank's services. Discovering the types of customers who respond to such overtures and those who do not.

9.3 Circumstances in which a security may be required for a bank loan

A bank manager, when considering a request for an advance, will take into account the character of the customer. This is the best form of security the bank manager can have, for it is upon the reliability of the customer that the whole proposition will be successful and the advance repaid. We have also seen that banks will, on occasions, ask for the advance to be backed by some form of security. This consists of a document or documents of title which show that the holder is the owner of some asset of value. For anything to be suitable as a security, it must fulfil four basic requirements. First of all, it must be able to be valued and this value must be easy to ascertain. Secondly, it must have a market so that if the bank were to sell it there would be a number of possible buyers. Thirdly, the bank must be able to gain some kind of ownership or interest in the security so that if the loan is not repaid it will have the right to dispose of the asset with the minimum amount of difficulty. Finally, the value of the security must be sufficient to cover the loan, and this value must be reasonably maintained.

There are certain circumstances when a bank will insist on some form of security. Obviously, where the venture is very risky or the finances of the borrower are not absolutely certain then the bank will ask for backing. However, it must be stressed that the bank views the taking of a security only as insurance and prefers to see the successful completion of the proposition.

9.4 Some important definitions and principles

(1) *Lien* – this is the right to retain the property belonging to another until the debt due from the owner is paid. The holder of a lien is said to have a nuisance value in that the owner cannot retrieve the property until he has repaid the debt. The possessor of the goods cannot sell the property as he is not the owner. There are different kinds of lien:
 – a carrier has a carrier's lien over the goods transported.
 – an innkeeper or hotel owner has innkeepers' lien over the luggage of a traveller or guest.
 – a warehouse keeper has a warehouse keeper's lien over the goods he stores in his warehouse.
 – a bank manager has a lien over anything that comes into his bank in the normal course of business (i.e. cheques) if the customer is overdrawn.

Although the holder of a lien does not have the right to sell, this could be given by statute. A lien differs from a pledge or mortgage as it arises in law, and these latter arise out of express agreements between borrowers and lenders. A bank does not have a lien over items in safe custody (*see* Chapter 10). The scope of a banker's lien is seen in the case of *Brandao v. Barnett* (1846).

(2) *Pledge* – a pledge is a deposit of goods with a lender as security for a loan. It differs from a mortgage as the lender gains possession of the chattel while the borrower retains ownership. For example, bearer bonds are pledged as security for a loan from the banks (*see* Chapter 10).

(3) *Hypothecation* – this is a legal transaction whereby goods may be made available as security for a debt without transferring either the property or possession to the lender. The law on hypothecation is complex. An example where this may take place is when a customer offers to hypothecate goods which are in a warehouse and they cannot be separated from others so that the bank is unable to obtain a pledge.

There are two risks facing a bank when lending against hypothecation. Firstly, it does not get actual or constructive possession of the goods, thus the measure of control is limited and a fraud by the borrower could be effected. The second risk stems from the complexity of the Bills of Sale Acts. These make it necessary for many instruments used in this connection to be registered and if not, they are void. It is not exactly known which instruments are to be included in these rules.

9.5 Various types of security that can be used to back a bank loan

If we consider the attributes of a 'good' security listed on 9.3, we will soon come to see that there are a limited number of assets which fulfil these conditions. The major types of security that do cover these attributes reasonably successfully are:

9.51 Land

Ownership of land is evidenced in two ways. Either land is registered with the Land Registry, so that it will have a **land certificate**, or the land will be unregistered and a file with relevant deeds and documents will be held.

Registered title is governed by the Land Registration Act 1925 and subsequent amendments. Title to the land is evidenced by a land certificate. This is a state guarantee of title subject to entries on the certificate and on the District Register. The land certificate is issued under the seal of the Land Registry and it is divided into three sections:

(1) Property Register – this describes the property, gives the title number, a description of the land (whether freehold or leasehold), a general map reference and an outline of any restrictive convenants.

(2) Proprietorship Register – this shows the class of title (whether absolute, good leasehold, possessory or qualified), name and address of registered proprietor, date of registration of title and any notices, cautions, inhibitions or restrictions.

(3) Charges Register – here are entered any matters relating to mortgages or restrictive convenants.

A certificate can be brought up-to-date by being presented to the appropriate District Land Registry. When this is done it is stamped on the front cover so that it can be seen when this document was last updated. For most areas of the country, the registration of land is compulsory. However, not all land is registered as it is only required to be so if:

(1) the freehold is sold, or

(2) on the granting or the assignment of a lease with forty years or more to run, or

(3) a grant of a lease for twenty-one years or more where freehold has been registered in absolute title.

The main register is kept at Lincoln's Inn Fields, London, but generally enquiries, notices and charges should be sent to the local District Registry.

One of the advantages of registered land is that the checking of the title to the land is simplified, as the land certificate is the title. Once updated it will provide good evidence of the correct title.

A bundle of deeds and documents is evidence of title to unregistered land. Whenever a transfer of title occurs, the additional documents must be added to the file. These documents will be evidence of discharged mortgages, assets and conveyances. As time goes on, and if the property is transferred many times, the bundle will grow in size so that storage becomes a problem. These documents must be retained secure so that bank security clerks and solicitors are able to check to see that the chain of title is continuous. Since title deeds are not negotiable, a complex system of conveyancing is effected to transfer title on sale. Thus the checking of title of unregistered land is complex. It is necessary to go back at least fifteen years to discover a conveyance for the land which represents a commercial sale and then to check the chain of ownership from that date. If no transfer within fifteen years has been effected, then the check must go back further.

The legal position as to the ownership of land now comes under Section 1 of the Law of Property Act 1925. This is of two types:

(1) *Freehold* – in legal terms this is known as 'free simple absolute in possession'. The person holding the property has absolute ownership capable of lasting indefinitely and he can deal with the land as he chooses. The owner has the right to dispose of it as he thinks fit and the land is automatically passed on to his heirs, unless sold or willed to someone else. (The term, in possession, does not mean ownership for the land could be leased out to a tenant until the lease expires.) Certain Acts of Parliament place restrictions upon owners of such land, for example, Civil Aviation Act 1949 allows aircraft to fly over land. Registered and unregistered freehold land is transferred by conveyance.

(2) *Leasehold* – in legal terms this is known as 'a term of years absolute'. A lease for six months falls within the statement 'a term of years'. This is a statement to describe a legal estate in leasehold land. It can be granted by any freeholder (or leaseholder in the case of a sub-lease) for a limited period. A long-term lease – 999 years – is as good as a freehold, for in this case, to all intents and purposes, the leaseholder is the owner. For this lease, the leaseholder makes an annual or biannual payment of **ground rent** as stated in the lease. A 'peppercorn' rent is one where no payment is necessary. The freeholder can impose certain terms on the leaseholder which may include:

– no swinging from the banisters,
– keeping the property in a good state of repair,
– keeping it adequately insured.

As long as the leaseholder keeps to the terms of the lease there will be little or no likelihood of ejection. Under the Leasehold Report Act 1967, certain leaseholders have the right to buy out the lease or have it extended by fifty years.

Unregistered land is transferred by means of assignment of the whole remaining term or by sale-lease if it is for a shorter period than the remaining term. In some cases the landlord's permission to transfer the lease is necessary. Where land is registered, a simplified form of assignment and sub-lease are supplied by the Land Registry.

Freehold ownership in land is said to be ownership in real property, whereas all other goods owned, including leasehold land, are classed as personal property. Freehold and leasehold interests are known as 'chattels real' so

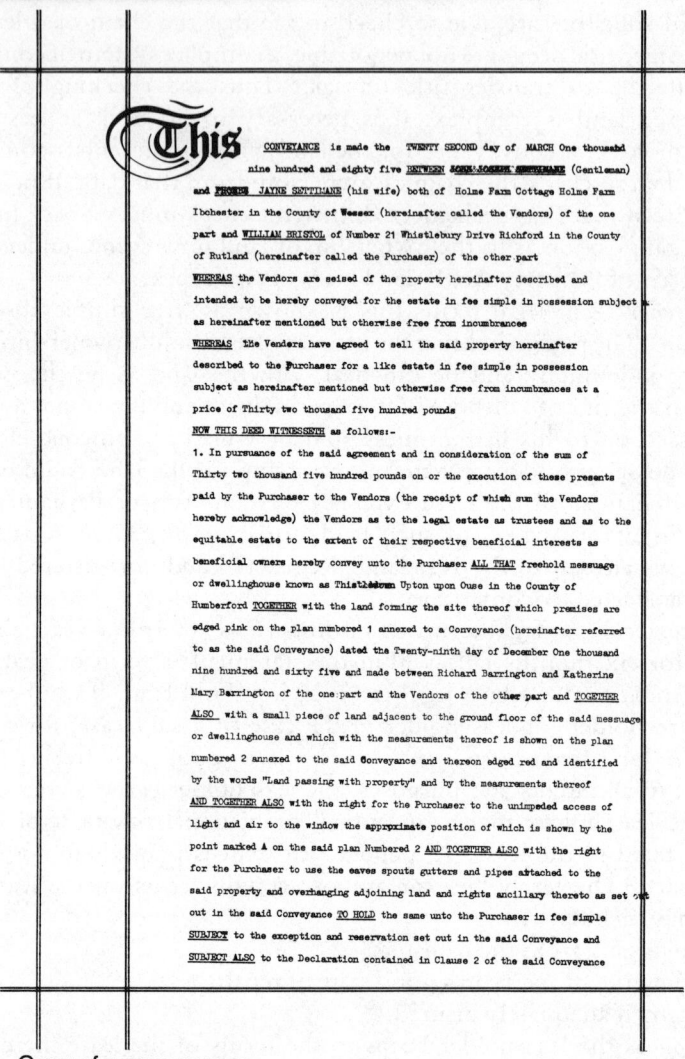

Fig. 9.1 Copy of a conveyance

that they can be distinguished from other forms of personal property which are known as 'chattels personal'. Cheques and personal belongings come under this latter category. This distinction is a legacy from the common law. If someone's freehold land was wrongfully taken, then an action could be initiated in the courts for the return of that land. No such claim could be made regarding other belongings and only an action for damages could be brought.

Where a bank takes an interest in land as security, this is said to have been **mortgaged**. A mortgage is the conveyance of a legal or equitable interest in real or personal property as security for a debt. A legal interest or right gives the holder an absolute right to do with the property as he thinks fit – sell it or destroy it. Thus a freeholder has a legal interest or right in land. An equitable interest does not mean ownership, but a claim against the property. A bank can take either a legal or equitable interest in land. It will take the former if it wishes to make absolutely certain that it can sell the land should the debt not be repaid.

On accepting the title to land as a mortgage, the bank manager needs to be reassured that the four basic requirements of a security are present. First of all that the security is of value. The bank manager should have some knowledge of property values in his area. Although this is not such an accurate valuation as can be gained for other types of security, it is satisfactory for this purpose. Secondly, is there a market for the land? Inspection of the local newspapers will give some indication. This will necessitate very careful appraisal of the potential buyers in case the land needs to be sold. Thirdly, can the bank gain the right to the land. The system of obtaining title to registered and unregistered land differs. With registered land the bank can take the land certificate as security either as a registered change or as a deposit. With the former, the customer signs a mortgage form, having deposited the land certificate with the bank. Both of these documents are sent to the Land Registry. The old land certificate is replaced by a charge certificate with the bank's mortgage form attached. If necessary, a search is carried out locally to see that no actions by the local authority will affect the land and, if leasehold, the bank will check to see that the ground rent is paid up-to-date and the reminder will be set up to check this every year. When the advance is paid back, the charge certificate is withdrawn by being returned to the Land Registry and a new land certificate is issued.

With a **notice of deposit**, the same initial procedure is carried out as above but when the mortgage form and the land certificate are sent up to the Land Registry, it is requested that the certificate is brought up-to-date. After comparing the certificate with its records, the Registry then makes any alterations that are required. The bank will include a special Land Registry form which gives the notice of deposit. This is recorded by the Registry, which enters up the bank's interest in the Charges Register section of the certificate. This is now returned to the bank. When the loan is repaid, the certificate is returned to the Registry. The bank's interest is removed and the certificate returned to the customer.

With unregistered land the system is slightly different. First of all a mortgage form is prepared for either a legal or equitable interest. The customer signs this and it is attached to the deeds. For a legal mortgage, the bank's solicitor will receive the deeds and prepare a report on the title and it is hoped, verify the customer's title to the land. In addition the solicitor will carry out a number of searches. The need for a local search has already been mentioned. With unregistered land, a search is made with the Land

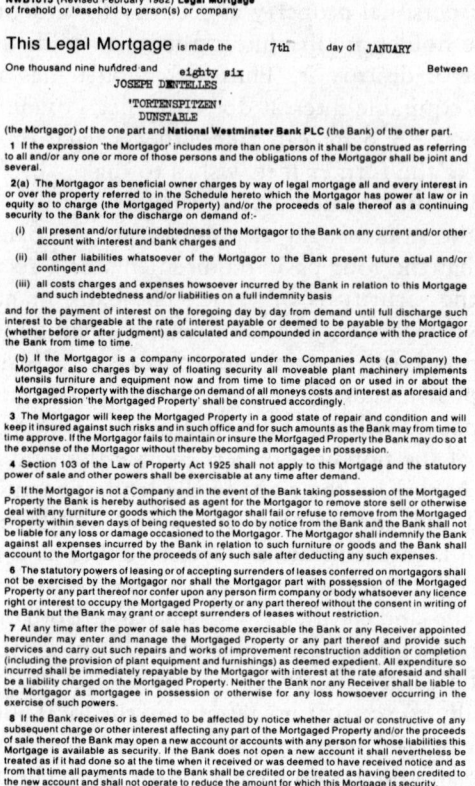

Fig. 9.2 Bank mortgage form

Charges Registry. This will show if there have been any outstanding related matters against the owner, for example, bankruptcy. Sometimes the securities clerk may carry out the necessary searches. On repayment of the loan, the legal mortgage is reconveyed to the customer and the deeds returned. With an equitable mortgage, the documents are filed away in the bank and on repayment they are returned to the customer.

The final requirement of a security is that it must maintain its value. There has been no doubt that land has retained its value over the years, but it will be up to the securities clerk to check this during the term of the loan. When taking land as a security the bank manager must be aware of the possibility of there being a second mortgage on the property. This is where the owner has negotiated an additional loan on the increased value of the land. This makes the land less valuable to the bank as a security.

The obligations of the mortgagee (the person giving the mortgage, i.e. the bank) are:

(1) To investigate the title.
(2) To value the land. This differs depending upon the type of land to

be mortgaged. With houses, a reasonably accurate valuation can be gained by the branch manager or securities clerk. The house must be viewed externally. The factors which are taken into consideration for the valuation are:
- whether leasehold or freehold,
- location,
- size of garden,
- state of repair.

Reference can be made to similar properties for sale in the area.

Agricultural land is also easy to value, but includes acreage and quality of the land as well as the condition of the buildings found thereon.

Factories and industrial premises are difficult to value for a banker, possibly because of a lack of special knowledge, and because of the complexity of the property. Therefore it is necessary to employ a professional valuer who will provide a detailed report which will take time:

(3) To carry out searches. These are important to discover any factors which may affect the title or value of the land.

(4) To take the mortgage. This is to get it completed, executed under seal with the parties signing the documents.

(5) To register the mortgage if necessary. When the deeds are held this is not necessary, but if not, there is a need to register a **puisne mortgage**. This is a legal mortgage of a legal estate in land where the mortgagee does not obtain possession of the title deeds. This type of charge is used by a bank when it takes a second or subsequent mortgage over unregistered land. In this case the deeds will be held by the first mortgagee.

(6) To take out a fire insurance. The mortgagor should be asked to deposit a relevant fire policy with the deeds. This should ensure full replacement cost, with any specialised cover required. This latter may be necessary for industrial buildings. It will also be necessary for up-to-date evidence of payment of premiums. It is only with property valued at over £70 000 that a duplicate copy of the bank's interest need be given to the insurance company. A receipted duplicate of the notice should be held with the deeds.

Returning to the position of the bank taking equities as security, in the case of *Coleman v. London County and Westminster Bank Ltd* (1916) it was held to be a maxim of equity that where equities are equal the first in turn prevails. In this case forty-five debentures in a private company were issued to a Mrs Coleman who settled them upon a trust for herself for life with the remainder to her three sons equally. The trustee did not register the transfer to himself. One of the sons assigned his share to his wife for value. Some years later the settler obtained possession and charged them to the defendant bank as security for an advance. The bank inspected the Company's register and found the settler registered there as the owner of the debentures. They then gave notice of their interest to the trustee of the debentures' trust deed, who was also trustee of the settlement. At this point the bank had no knowledge of the settlement. The trustee and the settler died and the action was brought by the wife of the trustee, to whom fifteen debentures had been assigned, claiming a declaration that the bank had no title to the debentures. The bank pleaded that the trustee had been negligent in not registering the transfer and for not disclosing the settlement. It was held that the omission did not debar the trustee's title but even if this was so the wife's equitable title must succeed. The operation of the rule in Clayton's case where payments into an account pay off the debits in chronological order, was seen by a decision of the House of Lords in *Deeley v. Lloyds Bank Ltd* (1912) where amounts paid into an account were sufficient to cover first, second and third mortgages and that subsequent withdrawals created fresh advances. The remedies of a mortgagee are as follows.

(1) *To sue* – bank forms omit the availability of this remedy but it is as of right in any case. This remedy is rarely used by the bank, since when the mortgagor is unwilling to pay it usually indicates that he is out of funds.

(2) *Appoint a receiver* – this power may be written into the mortgage contract. If it is not expressly stated, a right might be implied in all mortgages by deed unless a contrary intention is stated. Statutory power of sale arises if the legal date for payment has passed and the mortgage debt has not been paid. It may not be exercised until notice requiring payment of mortgage money has been served on the mortgagor and he has not responded within three months of the notice being served. Other factors are when interest is in arrears and is unpaid for two months after becoming due, or the mortgagor has broken some provision in the deed other than the repayment of money or interest. The receiver has the power to recover rents and profits by redress to the courts, and to give valid receipts. The receiver must use the money for the sale of the land to discharge the mortgage interest and reduce the mortgage debt. This is after meeting such payments as taxes, rates and other outgoings as well as his commission.

(3) *Right to foreclose* – the mortgagee must apply to the court for an order. The court will then set the date when the mortgagor has to pay the principal and interest. If the mortgagor fails to pay on that day, an order for foreclosure will be made by the court. This order extinguishes the mortgagor's rights to redeem the property. The bank, as mortgagee, now becomes the absolute owner of the property concerned.

If, after foreclosure, there is a wide divergence in the market price of the property and the debt, or if the mortgagor was prevented from carrying out the order by circumstances beyond his control, or the mortgagee sues for principal or interest, then the court may re-open the foreclosure and allow the mortgagor to redeem the property.

(4) *Right to take possession* – this is the physical possession of the land by either cultivating it or receiving rents from tenants. Such rents must be used to repay some of the principal or interest due. Caution must be

used in the exercise of this right as the mortgagee is liable for the rents which he could have received and not for the amount actually received.

(5) *Right to sell the property mortgaged* – the mortgagor may himself confer this power on the mortgagee. It can be exercised as soon as the mortgagor is in breach. If the contract does not give this power expressly, it may be implied by the nature of the deed unless it can be seen to the contrary. The power arises and becomes exercisable if the same events occur as stated for the power to appoint a receiver. When the property is sold, the mortgagee must pay due regard to the interests of the mortgagor. If the price on sale is less than the market value of the property, no payment would be liable. If the price is greater than the mortgage, then any balance must be paid over to a second or subsequent mortgagee, or if none, to the mortgagor.

Self-assessment exercises

1 List the contents of the Property Register section of a land certificate.
2 What is the purpose of the Proprietorship Register section of a land certificate?
3 Under what circumstances must land now be registered?
4 What is the evidence of title of unregistered land?
5 What are the rights of a freeholder of land?
6 What is a lease? How does it differ from a freehold interest in land?
7 What is the difference between a legal and an equitable interest in property?
8 When will a bank be prepared to take a legal interest in property rather than an equitable interest?
9 Explain in your own words the system whereby the bank can obtain a registered charge on registered land.
10 How does a system of obtaining a notice of deposit differ from a registered charge?
11 How does a bank make a legal charge on unregistered land?
12 What factors are there to consider when a bank manager estimates the value of a house?

9.52 Stocks and shares

These are also mortgaged to the bank. In this case they represent personal property, however, a legal or equitable charge may be taken on them. They are very acceptable to the bank as a form of security for they generally fit the requirements of a security very well. This does depend upon the actual security being offered by the customer. Shares in a 'blue chip' company are very acceptable, but shares in some less well known or less profitable company may not be acceptable. It is easy to discover their current value for, if they are listed on the Stock Exchange, then their trading value is quoted in the press every working day. The Stock Exchange Daily List encompasses even more shares. This means that there is a very clearly defined

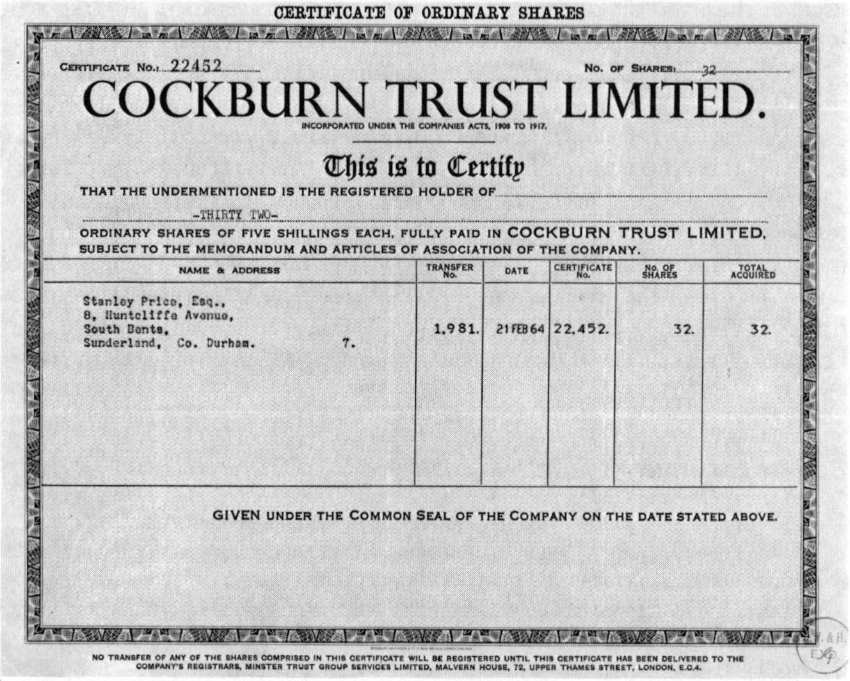

CERTIFICATE OF ORDINARY SHARES

CERTIFICATE No.: 22452 No. OF SHARES: 32

COCKBURN TRUST LIMITED.

INCORPORATED UNDER THE COMPANIES ACTS, 1908 TO 1917.

This is to Certify

THAT THE UNDERMENTIONED IS THE REGISTERED HOLDER OF

-THIRTY TWO-

ORDINARY SHARES OF FIVE SHILLINGS EACH, FULLY PAID IN COCKBURN TRUST LIMITED, SUBJECT TO THE MEMORANDUM AND ARTICLES OF ASSOCIATION OF THE COMPANY.

NAME & ADDRESS	TRANSFER No.	DATE	CERTIFICATE No.	No. OF SHARES	TOTAL ACQUIRED
Stanley Price, Esq., 8, Huntcliffe Avenue, South Bents, Sunderland, Co. Durham. 7.	1.981.	21 FEB 64	22.452.	32.	32.

GIVEN UNDER THE COMMON SEAL OF THE COMPANY ON THE DATE STATED ABOVE.

NO TRANSFER OF ANY OF THE SHARES COMPRISED IN THIS CERTIFICATE WILL BE REGISTERED UNTIL THIS CERTIFICATE HAS BEEN DELIVERED TO THE COMPANY'S REGISTRARS, MINSTER TRUST GROUP SERVICES LIMITED, MALVERN HOUSE, 72, UPPER THAMES STREET, LONDON, E.C.4.

Fig. 9.3 Share certificate

market in the London and provincial stock exchanges. In order to gain legal title to the shares, the bank will use the standard method of changing ownership – use of a stock transfer form. (See Fig. 9.4.)

Once again the system for a legal and equitable mortgage differs. With a legal mortgage the customer hands over the share or stock certificate and signs, having them witnessed, a bank mortgage form and a stock transfer form. The stock transfer form and the certificate are sent up to the company's registrars who produce a new certificate in the bank's name. This means that the bank is the new owner of the shares and is entitled to any dividends paid out on them. Generally these dividends are credited to the customer's account. When the advance is repaid, the whole process is reversed with a new share certificate being produced in the customer's name. With an equitable mortgage this system is not so complicated. The customer still hands over the certificate and completes the two documents. In this case the mortgage form is only for an equitable charge. All documents are held in the bank's safe until the mortgage is repaid in full. Thus the bank holds something of value on which it can obtain ownership, should the customer renege on the loan. On repayment, the mortgage form is retained in the files while the certificate is returned to the customer. With securities such as premium savings bonds, British savings bonds and national

Understanding the Basic Principles of Bank Lending 253

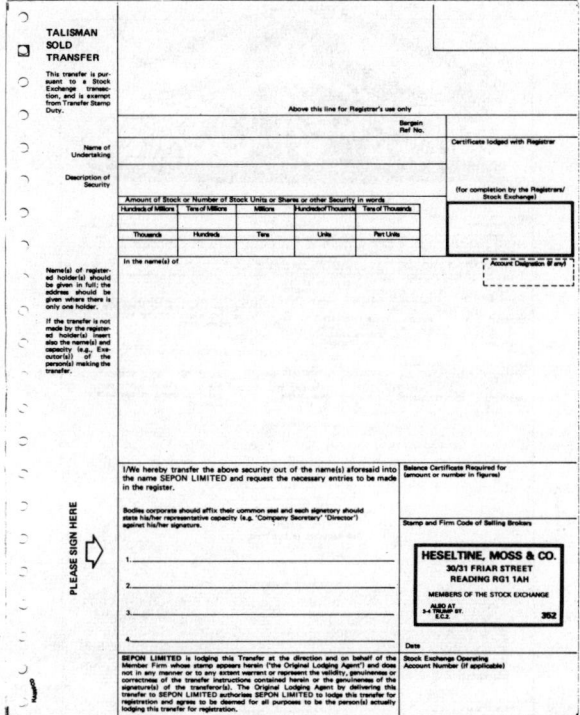

Fig. 9.4 Stock transfer form

savings certificates, only an equitable mortgage may be held since they can easily be duplicated. With these, an encashment form is signed by the customer rather than a stock transfer form, but in other respects, they are treated the same as stocks and shares.

9.53 Life policies

There are various types of life policies, the main ones are:
   (1) *Whole life* – payable on death.
   (2) *Endowment* – payable at some date in the future. (See Fig. 9.5.)
   (3) *Family protection* – aimed at providing for a wife and/or children. When looking at life assurance the bank manager will examine a number of factors relating to the insurance policy. First of all, is the insurance company one which is well known and UK based? Secondly, what type of policy is it and is it suitable as security? Thirdly, is it a policy that can be assigned so that the bank can obtain legal title to the proceeds? Fourthly, are there any restrictive clauses written into the policy which may affect any claim on it, such as a restriction on the insured from participating in

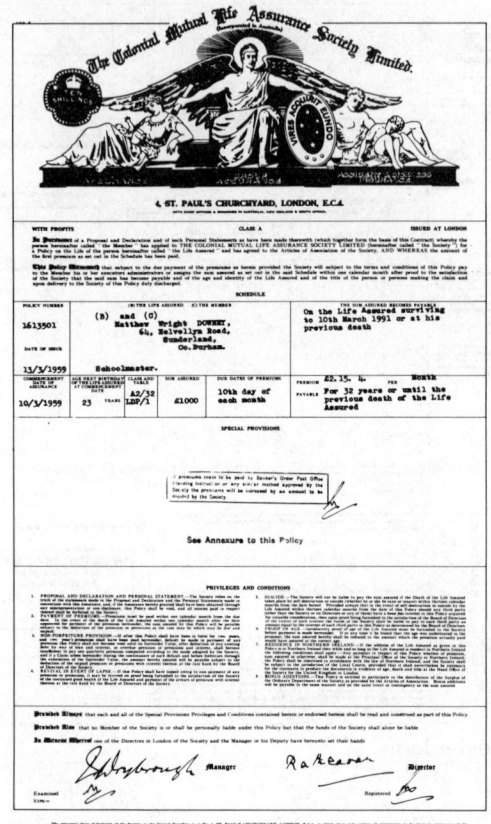

Fig. 9.5 Copy of a life policy

dangerous occupations or pastimes? Fifthly, have all the parties with an interest in the policy been consulted and has their agreement been obtained?

The value of the policy can be ascertained from the insurance company which is prepared to quote its surrender value at any time. This is the value of all the premiums paid to-date plus any profits which may have accrued. Obviously, the longer the policy has been in existence the greater its surrender value. The bank is given an interest in this value by means of assignment. This is the transfer, by a creditor to an assignee, of the right to receive a sum of money or some other benefit from a debtor. The assignment of rights is not allowed under common law, but the Judicature Acts 1873 make it lawful to assign rights under equity. To comply with the law, the assignment must be made in writing and must be unconditional. Thus a bank will accept the assignment of life policies and book debts. Before a bank can sue for the policy value it must have given written notice to the insurance company, at its principal office, of the date and purpose of the assignment. When notice is received all other claims are relegated to a lower priority. The insurance company must acknowledge receipt of the notice. Life assurance, therefore, proves to be a very acceptable security, and the value in money terms remains the same. The bank will have discovered if the surrender value is sufficient to cover the loan before the loan was granted.

9.54 Bearer bonds

As mentioned in Chapter 7 these are negotiable instruments and as such when they are taken as security for a loan are **pledged**. A pledge is where goods, documents of title or bearer securities are delivered by one person to another to be held as a security for the payment of a debt or the performance of some other obligation. There is an express or implied understanding that if the debt is repaid then the pledge will be returned to the owner. The person giving the pledge is called the **pledgor** and the person receiving the bonds the **pledgee**.

The difference between a pledge and a mortgage is as follows:

(1) The courts recognise that a pledgee has a special property in the thing pledged, allowing him to sell the pledge item(s) if the debt or obligation is not discharged. When a time is fixed for discharge and the pledgor is in default, there is an implied right for the pledgee to sell the items pledged. Where there is no agreed time the pledgee can demand discharge and if the pledgor defaults the items can be sold provided notice is given of the intention to do so. Any surplus on sale must be accounted for.

(2) A pledgee has no right of foreclosure.

(3) A mortgagee of land is not permitted to take an absolute conveyance of the legal estate subject to the mortgagor's right to redeem. However, a mortgagee of life policies or registered or inscribed stocks and shares obtains more than a special property in the subject matter of the mortgage. A bank, for example would obtain full legal title subject to the mortgagor's right to redeem.

(4) Another difference is that a pledge must be actually or constructively delivered to the pledgee, while the property involved in a mortgage does not necessarily pass to the mortgagee. The mere deposit of these items gives notice of the intention to pledge them so that a bank has the rights of a pledgee.

The bank obtains a perfect title provided the bonds are taken in good faith and for value without notice of defect in the depositor's title. When accepting deposits, the bank must ensure that they are not defaced and that all necessary coupons are attached. It is not really necessary but the bank will ask the pledgor to sign a **memorandum of deposit**, which outlines the bank's specific rights. Since the relaxation of exchange control in December 1979 these bonds no longer need to be deposited with an authorised depository. Some of the terms included in the memorandum are:

(1) To give the bank an express power to sell the bonds if an overdraft is not repaid when demanded.

(2) To make the bonds or warrants deposited a continuing security. This will exclude the operation of the rule in *Clayton's* case.

A memorandum of deposit which is executed 'under hand' instead of seal does not require stamp duty.

A pledgee of a negotiable instrument is entitled to some favourable treatment as a **transferee for value**. In *Lloyds Bank Ltd v. Swiss Bankverein* the former lent money to bill brokers against a bearer bonds security. Subsequently Lloyds called in the loan which was repaid with a cheque drawn on a third bank. They then released the bonds which were pledged to the Swiss bank before the cheque was cleared. The cheque was dishonoured and Lloyds tried to reclaim the bonds. However it was held, by the Court of Appeal, that since the Swiss bank had taken these negotiable instruments in good faith they could retain them. This decision, therefore, makes such bonds taken as security in such circumstances a good risk for any bank.

Another advantage to the banker in taking these pledges is that the formalities of taking other securities are removed. The formal system of transfer is not necessary. A possible disadvantage is that some bank clerks might be tempted to sell these illegally, since they are bearer securities.

9.55 Guarantees

A guarantee is defined in the Statute of Frauds Act (Section 4) as: 'a written promise by one person to be responsible for the debt, default or miscarriage of another person incurred to a third party'.

The three parties to an agreement are:

(1) Creditor – usually a bank.

(2) Principal debtor – the customer who wishes to borrow the money.

(3) Guarantor – a third party who is, in effect, saying to the bank, 'If X does not repay the debt to you then I will.' Although guarantees do not have a particular form they are unenforceable in law unless they are in writing and signed by the guarantor or his agent. For this purpose banks have special forms which seek the guarantor's signature and also detail the terms of the agreement.

Guarantees are of three types:

(1) Specific – these cover one debt only and are used for things such as personal loans. Banks are reluctant to accept these since they do not allow for further loans to be covered by the guarantee particularly those,

like overdrafts, which arise in the normal course of dealing with the customer.

(2) Continuing (but with limited amount) – these contain a statement which covers all money loaned now or later but for a specified limited amount.

(3) Continuing (but for an unlimited amount) – this is the same as in (2). but no limit is stated.

There is a system that has developed where companies in the same group cross-guarantee the debts of each other.

The advantages to a bank of guarantees as a security are as follows:

(a) The administration is easy as there is no need to search for title or to register the documents.

(b) The value of the guarantee remains stable. In the case of a strict guarantee the financial stability of the guarantor is relevant. Therefore, the bank will continue to carry out status enquiries, on an annual basis in these cases. With a secured guarantee the value is relevant to the security offered and to its maintaining its value.

(c) Legal action on the guarantor's default is easy to initiate.

(d) A guarantee, being collateral, can be ignored in any claim against the principal debtor.

(e) The standard guarantee form of the banks can give maximum security to them as well as maximum power.

(f) With regard to companies, where a bank seeks a guarantee from the directors, the latter may feel it incumbent on them to be more successful in their business activities.

(g) With business accounts, a customer may be more likely to obtain a loan when he has a number of guarantors backing him than on his own personal security.

(h) The guarantor's liability is fixed unless this is specifically stated.

The disadvantage of guarantees as a security are as follows:

(i) Unless a security backs a guarantee its financial stability will rest upon the stability of the guarantor.

(ii) It may be necessary to take court action to enforce payment.

(iii) Some people regard the giving of a guarantee as a matter of form only and do not consider that they will ever be called upon to meet it.

(iv) If guarantees are called up the customer may be upset and the bank may lose a valuable customer.

The considerations of a bank when taking a guarantee

(1) The guarantors should not have had undue influence put upon them by the bank. It is up to the bank to prove that this was not the case in any event of an action against the guarantor. For this reason the banks prefer the offer of a guarantee to come from the guarantor or the principal

debtor. This was seen in *Lloyds Bank Ltd v. Bundy* (1974). In this case the bank took guarantees totalling £11 000 from a Mr Bundy, a farmer, to cover the liabilities on the son's business. In addition, the guarantees were supported by a legal mortgage on Mr Bundy's farm for £10 000. In 1970 the bank called up the guarantees and, on default, took action for the sale of the farm. Mr Bundy claimed undue influence. It was held that his relationship with the bank was one of trust and confidence in which Mr Bundy had relied upon it for proper advice. The bank had a special duty of care and should have advised him to take independent advice about the supply of the security. It was found that the mortgage and the guarantee should be set aside.

(2) Non es factum – the bank should ensure that the guarantor knows what he is signing or this defence might be raised. This was seen in *Saunders v. Anglia Building Society* (1970) where an old lady, without her glasses on, thought she was signing a lease to her nephew, whilst really she was signing an assignment to another party. She later tried to remove her liability but it was held that her plea would not succeed as she had acted negligently and carelessly. This decision, in effect, reversed the standard case *Carlisle & Cumberland Banking Co. v. Bragg* (1911).

(3) The bank must obtain the signatures of the parties to the agreement, for if one party is prevented from signing then the other parties are discharged. At the same time, any alteration in the terms without the agreement of the other parties also means that they are discharged. Joint and several guarantees are not effective until they are executed by all the parties. This was seen in the case *National Provincial Bank Ltd v. Brackenbury* (1906).

(4) The bank does not have to disclose any material fact and its failure to do so does not render the contract voidable.

(5) The bank must not deliberately or negligently mislead the guarantor, for if it does so the latter can avoid liability. If a bank is aware that a customer is under a misapprehension, it should not accept the guarantee unless it enlightens the customer in the matter. It must be aware of its need to maintain secrecy and could, if the circumstances warrant it, arrange a tripartite agreement.

(6) Requests for information – with regard to requests by the guarantor for information about the balance on the amount of the principal debt the bank may divulge:

(a) Where the account is in debit for a greater amount than the guarantee that the guarantor is being relied upon for the full amount of this guarantee.

(b) Where the account is in debit for less than the amount of the guarantee what the debit balance is.

(c) Where the account is in credit that he is not being relied upon.

(7) Sometimes the rule in Clayton's case does not operate for guarantees. This was seen in the case *Westminster Bank Ltd v. Cond* (1940) where in the case of an unbroken account, payments made into the account, after

the bank's request to the guarantor to honour his guarantee, were able to clear the account.

Requests for sight of the principal debtor's statements or specific cheques will not be given. In the interest of the guarantor the bank might seek a tripartite meeting to discuss those matters which it knows are relevant to the guarantor.

The procedure for taking the guarantee as security

(1) The bank will seek some statement on the financial standing of the guarantor.
(2) Once satisfied as to (1) the bank will ask all the guarantors to sign its standard form at its own branch.
(3) A copy of the guarantee will be sent to the guarantor.
(4) An annual enquiry will be made regarding the financial status of the guarantor.
(5) The bank will send regular reminders to the guarantors reminding them of their liability.

When accepting guarantees from companies there are various steps that must be followed. The bank must see if the memorandum of association gives the company clear power to carry out this service. Unless Section 9 of the European Communities Act 1972 is claimed, any action in this situation will be *ultra vires*. The company may have to have its objects clause altered by special resolution. The articles of association must be examined to see how the guarantee is to be executed. If it is by resolution of the board of directors the bank will require a copy of this resolution certified by the chairman and secretary. It will also need to consider the borrowing limits of the directors; possibly the accepting of the guarantee may affect the interests of the directors, perhaps reducing their liability to the company.

9.6 Effect of the Consumer Credit Act 1974 on banks

9.61 The general background

This is a major piece of consumer legislation applied to the credit industry. It applies to all businesses that provide credit facilities up to £5000 to all groups of people, from private individuals to unincorporated bodies such as societies and associations. It includes all such businesses as banks, moneylenders, pawnbrokers, hire purchase and rental companies, debt collection, debt adjusters, credit and mortgage brokers and credit reference agencies. The aim of the Act is to provide an effective way of controlling this wide range of consumer credit agencies and transactions, and it does this through the regulating of the contracts drawn up between borrowers and lenders.

9.62 Major provisions of the Act

(1) Licences (Section 21) – these are required for the purpose of carrying on hire purchase agreements, credit and conditional sales, businesses to supply personal loans and mortgages, banking, the issue of credit cards, cheques and vouchers, and traders' shops and stores providing credit. The exceptions are those credit facilities outside the £30–£5000 limit and those providing credit under certain exempt agreements such as building societies, credit or hire companies.

(2) Advertising (Section 44) – regulations are made from time to time to ensure that advertisements give a fair and comprehensive indication of the nature of the credit or hire facilities, and that the true cost to the users is also given. This enables people to know the true rate of the total charge for the credit.

(3) Prohibition of canvassing off trade premises (Section 48) – an individual may not deliberately canvass for credit agreements off the trade premises by making oral representations to prospective customers or other persons unless this has been requested previously in writing. Under Section 51 it is an offence to give a person credit if he has not asked for it. With regard to banks this not only applies to any type of advance which does not exceed £5000 but also to certain brokerage, debt adjusting and debt counselling services. In the case of the latter, a credit card is seen as a credit token but not a cheque guarantee card or cash dispenser card. Restrictions apply to canvassing minors. It is an offence to send any material to a minor which can be seen as an invitation to borrow money, or to use other credit facilities, or to apply for information or advice on obtaining credit or credit services.

(4) Total charge for credit – this must include all other charges as well as the interest payment. Nowadays credit agreements give what is known as the annual percentage rate of charge or APR. This is calculated by equating the sum of the present value of all advances with the present value of all payments. It is useful to all customers who wish to compare the different lending charges proffered by the various financial institutions.

(5) Regulation of credit agreements (Section 60) – this deals with the form and content of agreements. These provisions ensure that the debtor or hirer is aware of:
(a) his rights and duties from the agreement,
(b) the amount and rate of the total charge for credit,
(c) protection and remedies available to him,
(d) other specified information that may be required by the regulations.
These apply to overdrafts, or budget accounts of shops.

Credit agreements with banks may be cancelled if two conditions are satisfied.

(i) The agreement was not signed by the borrower at the bank's premises or the trade premises of any other party involved in the whole agreement.

(ii) if, in the borrower's presence, oral representations were made by or on behalf of the bank.

Usually banks make certain that agreements cannot be affected by these regulations. There are some exempt agreements which do not come under this section of the Act. Two of these are advances at low rates of interest, and advances to finance export of goods and services. These latter are of possible interest to the banks.

The banks must be wary of situations where they might be involved in a debtor–creditor arrangement. This can exist where a bank agrees to finance a customer for the purchase of a particular supplier's goods or services. In this situation the supplier may be acting as a credit broker and should be licensed, if this is not the case the bank may be placed in a dangerous position.

Self-assessment exercises

1 What is a guarantee when used by a bank?
2 Under what circumstances would a bank use a guarantee?
3 William, who is 17 years of age, is able to arrange a loan from a bank for £500 and have his uncle act as guarantor. He uses the money to purchase a second-hand motorbike. He defaults on the repayment and by this time he is 18 years of age. The bank contacts the uncle and asks him to meet the repayment but he replies saying that now that William is 18 years of age he feels he is no longer liable. What do you think is the bank's position?
4 Outline the bank's position under the Consumer Credit Act 1974.

Assignments

1 Answer following questions.
   (a) What points does a bank manager bear in mind when considering a request for a loan from a customer?
   (b) Explain the difference between an assignment, a pledge and a mortgage.
2 *Situation:* Rita Hellier has set up in business running a boutique in the London suburb of Haxton. She has found premises in the High Street with an annual rental of £6000. She estimates that the fixtures and fittings required will cost about £4000 and that she will need a loan of £10 000 from the bank to be repaid over a period of five years.

She is 30 years of age, divorced, with a young daughter of 9 years of age. She is living in rented accommodation costing about £100 a month. After her divorce she had a settlement from the family home of £8000 and in addition she has £2000 in savings of her own.

Banking for Students

Tasks

(a) Acting as a bank manager produce notes to help you with the interview with Ms Hellier when she requests this loan.

(b) At the end of her interview you tell her that you need more time to consider the proposition and that you will be in touch with her. You have considered it fully now and would be prepared to lend her the money but not over 5 years but 4 years. Write a letter to her informing her of the decision and listing any information that the bank would require over the period of the loan which would help to monitor it.

(c) State and describe any security you might request to cover this loan.

10 The Banker and Customer Relationship

Before looking at the relationship of the banker to various types of customer we need to consider what is a banker and customer.

10.1 What is a banker?

To discover any valid answer to this question we need to look at statute law, case law and eminent writings. Under the Bills of Exchange Act 1882 (Section 2) a banker is described as: 'any body of persons whether incorporated or not who carry on the business of banking'. This is not very precise as we need to know what the business of a bank is to understand what a banker does. The 1946 Bank of England Act states that a banker means any such person carrying on banking for the purpose of Section 4, which allows the central bank to request information from and make recommendations to the commercial banks.

In his fourth edition of the *Law of Banking* Dr Hand gives the following definition: 'a banker or bank is a person or company carrying on the business of receiving moneys and collecting drafts for customers subject to the obligation of honouring cheques drawn upon them from time to time by the customers to the extent of the amounts available on the current accounts'. This gives a very clear guide to the activities of a bank and hence to what a banker is. A somewhat similar view of a banker's activities is demonstrated in the case *United Dominions Trust (UDT) v. Kirkwood* (1966). In this case UDT loaned money to Lonsdale Motors accepting bills of exchange as security. These bills were endorsed by the managing director, a Mr Kirkwood, which made him personally liable. When UDT sued the endorser for the money after Lonsdale Motors had gone into liquidation, Kirkwood claimed that UDT were unregistered money lenders so that the only way they could claim the money was if they were covered by Section 6 of the Moneylenders Act 1927. Under this section it had to be established that they were bona fide in carrying on the business of banks. Lord Denning, Master of the Rolls gave these characteristics of banks:

(1) They accept money from and collect cheques for their customers.

(2) They honour cheques or orders drawn on them by their customers when presented for payment and debit their customers accordingly.

These give rise to a third:

(3) They keep current accounts or something of that nature, in their books in which credits and debits are entered.

Although their Lordships were not satisfied that there was sufficient evidence that UDT's business fitted these definitions there was, however, subsequent evidence presented that the City of London regarded UDT as a bank, and this was so impressive that the case was decided in their favour by the narrowest of margins. The decision was so arbitrary that it is believed that any future case would be decided differently if the evidence were different.

Lord Denning quoted from Paget from the *Law of Banking* sixth edition is which it is stated 'no one and nobody, corporate or otherwise can be a banker who does not (i) take current accounts, (ii) pay cheques drawn on himself (iii) collect cheques for customers'.

Up to 1979 the use of the word 'bank' in a business title was not restricted. The Banking Act 1979 now restricts the use of this word to institutions which meet certain requirements about size of deposits and the types of business carried out. Other institutions that do not fulfil these conditions but accept deposits have to be licensed and are known as Licensed Deposit-taking Institutions (LDTIs). These rules were introduced to bring us into line with EEC regulations.

Self-assessment exercise

From the various statements above make a list of the activities that can be seen as part of the role of a banker.

10.2 What is a customer?

There is no statutory definition and we must resort to case law to discover the answer to this question. To give a commercial definition, a customer is someone who has habitual or continual dealings with a shop. An isolated purchase or transaction does not make the purchaser a customer. However, with a bank this is not the case for it is generally believed that a customer of a bank is an individual or company which has some sort of account with the bank and that this relationship starts when the account is opened. The two cases below show how the facts involved in the relationship can influence the nature of that relationship.

(1) *Woods v. Martins Bank Ltd and Another* (1959). In this case no account existed but the bank manager gave advice to the customer prior to opening an account. It was held that the bank held a duty of care to the customer even before the account was opened.

(2) *Stony Stanton Supplies (Coventry) Ltd v. Midland Bank Ltd* (1966). In this case the bank opened up accounts in the name of a company when the person the bank was dealing with did not have the power to act on the company's behalf. The court held that in these circumstances there was no customer relationship between the bank and the company.

(3) *Ladbroke v. Todd* (1914). In this case a thief opened an account with a stolen cheque. The drawer of the cheque claimed that the thief was not a customer of the bank, and the court found in favour of the plaintiff in view of the bank's negligence in not taking precautions to safeguard the interests of the true owner of the cheque.

10.3 Opening up and operating a bank account

As the existence of a bank account is seen as an important part of the customer/banker relationship, it is useful to consider the procedure for opening up and operating a bank account.

10.31 Opening the account

Usually, on receiving a request from a customer to open an account, the bank will wish to have the prospective customer interviewed by a member of the branch who is responsible for new accounts. This interview will enable the bank to find out the full requirements of the customer, and at the same time to answer any queries and to satisfy itself on four major points regarding the customer.

(1) whether the person is who he claims to be;
(2) whether he is a proper person to operate this type of account;
(3) whether, in the case of someone opening an account for a third party, he is authorised to do this;
(4) whether the person is employed by someone else and, if so, the name of his employers;

Banks must show that they have exercised extreme care in offering their services to the right and correct type of persons. Actions in the Courts have been lost where it was proved that a bank did not take a sufficient level of care over this matter. To safeguard itself a bank will ask a customer to complete an application form. An example of one bank's form is given in Fig. 10.1.

The applicant may have been introduced by another customer of the bank. This is a very good way of discovering the true identity of the applicant since the recommendation comes from someone known to the bank. If not, then the bank will ask for two referees. One will be, if relevant, the applicant's employer; this gives an answer to the fourth question. If the

266 Banking for Students

Application to open a new personal account

Identification details to signature card.
Type of Account C/A ☐ D/A ☐ HICA ☐
Other

Date _____

Midland Bank plc

Surname _____ Mr/Mrs/Miss/Ms
Forenames _____

Address for statement
_____
_____

Post Code [| | | | | |]   Number of years at this address [| |]
Previous address - *if resident at present address for less than 18 months*
_____

Date of birth [| | | | |]

Are you:
- Married ☐ Single ☐
- A houseowner ☐ A tenant ☐ Living with parents ☐
- Employed ☐ Self-employed ☐ Receiving a grant ☐ Receiving a pension ☐
- Unemployed ☐

- Paid weekly ☐ Paid fortnightly ☐ Paid monthly/4 weekly ☐ Paid at irregular intervals ☐
- Paid by bank transfer ☐ Paid by cheque ☐ Paid by cash ☐

Will all of your income be paid into your bank account?   Yes ☐   No ☐

Occupation _____
Employer _____
Number of years with present employer _____
Business telephone number _____
Home telephone number _____

Account Description - *if any*
e.g. Number two account _____

Account Transferred - *specify source* _____

If from another bank complete Access account transfer - *if appropriate*

Cheque card held   YES/NO

Recover unused cheques/paying-in book/cards - *if applicable*

For Bank use only

CRS

VRS

Initials

Checked

Details of Cheque Book/Paying-in Book

Account Title _____   Account number [| | | | | |]

Cheque Book   **Paying-in Book**

Pocket with record slips ☐   Crossed ☐   Paying-in book required Yes ☐ No ☐
Pocket with counterfoils ☐   Open ☐

Part 1

2465-2

Fig. 10.1 A typical bank's application form for opening an acount

referee is unknown to the bank then this referee might be asked to supply the name and address of his banker so that reference can be made to him. A bank may also make an enquiry with a credit agency. These enquiries will enable the bank to receive an answer to the second question as to the

National Westminster Bank PLC

Chichester Branch
5 East Street
Chichester
West Sussex PO19 1HH

Please address your reply to the Manager

Your ref

Our ref

Telephone Chichester (STD 0243) 787031

Date

Dear

Our prospective customer

whose address is

has given your name as a referee for the purpose of opening a bank account. I shall be grateful if you will answer the questions below and return this letter to me. A stamped envelope is enclosed.

I thank you in anticipation of your reply.

Yours sincerely

Manager

Is he/she, in your opinion, a person to whom the usual banking facilities may be safely afforded?

How long have you known him/her?

Can you confirm that the specimen signature below appears to be that of our prospective customer?

SPECIMEN SIGNATURE	Referees Bankers:
	Bank:_____
	Address:_____
	(This information is required by us to conform to accepted banking practice for completion of references and thereby afford us the protection of the Cheques Act.)

Please return to:

The Manager
National Westminster Bank PLC
Chichester Branch
5 East Street
Chichester
West Sussex PO19 1HH

Please Note:
If you are signing on behalf of a Firm, Company, Public Authority or other Official Body, please give the name and address of the organisation's bankers and arrange for an official stamp to be impressed hereon and add the capacity in which you sign

Signature _____

(Please fold this letter so that the return address appears in the window of the envelope provided)

Date _____

NWB12 Rev Feb 82-2001   Registered Number 929027 England   Registered Office 41 Lothbury, London EC2P 2BP

Fig. 10.2 Bank reference form

fitness of the applicant to operate this account. The reason for seeking knowledge of the customer's employment and employer is that if enquiries of this nature are not made and the customer pays into the account cheques payable to the employer or cheques drawn on the employer payable to third parties or in the case of married women payable to or drawn on their husbands' employers, then the bank will almost certainly be liable in damages for the conversion of the cheques if the customer is not entitled to them. The bank will not receive the protection of Section 4 of the Cheques Act 1957. This particularly applies to customers who are clerks or who, by virtue of their position, are likely to handle the cheques of their employer. A bank, if suspicious, should make careful and painstaking enquiries.

For an account which is to be operated by an individual, the bank will require a copy of the customer's signature to keep on its records. An example of this is given in Fig. 10.3.

Where the account is being operated by more than one person the bank will require the customers to sign a **mandate**. This is a written authority which is signed by the bank customer authorising another person to carry out certain acts on behalf of the customer. Figure 10.4 gives an example of a bank's mandate form.

Mandates will be used for accounts with corporate bodies, churches, clubs and societies. Indeed, any organisation which might have legal identity but not physical identity so it needs to have its financial transactions carried out by members or servants. In order that only authorised persons operate the account the bank needs to know who these authorised persons are and if they have been given this authorisation by people who, themselves, have the power to give it.

One practical example can be seen in the operation of its current account by a local Methodist church. The chairman and secretary of the Leaders' Meeting sign a mandate authorising the bank to pay cheques out of the account which have been signed by certain named persons. These will be the treasurer, the assistant treasurer, if there is one, or the church secretary and probably the senior society steward. When these people leave office then a new mandate should be raised. As well as giving authority to draw cheques the mandate can include a number of additional items, such as:

(1) to receive cheques, statements and vouchers relating to the account;

(2) to draw, accept, make and endorse bills of exchange and promissory notes on behalf of the account;

(3) to pledge on deposit securities with the bank and type of security against any loan negotiated on the customer's behalf;

(4) to negotiate advances by loan, overdraft or discounting;

(5) to withdraw from the bank any securities or property held by the bank for the customer.

The mandate stands until written notice to the contrary or the death of the customer, or mental capacity diminishes, or the customer is bankrupt. In the latter case the bank must be informed.

The banker will issue a cheque book for the new account when he has found out from the references that the customer is reliable, and that any cheques paid in to open the account have been cleared successfully. A cheque guarantee card will also be issued when the banker is certain that the customer can operate the account in satisfactory manner. In order to avoid future

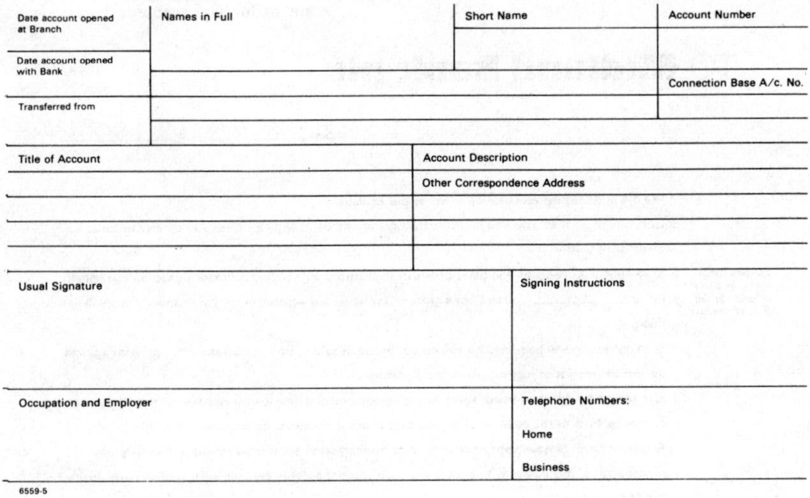
Date account opened at Branch
Names in Full
Short Name
Account Number
Date account opened with Bank
Connection Base A/c. No.
Transferred from
Title of Account
Account Description
Other Correspondence Address
Usual Signature
Signing Instructions
Occupation and Employer
Telephone Numbers:
Home
Business
6559-5

Fig. 10.3 Specimen signature form

problems, the bank should inform the customer of its right to make charges and apply commission to the account.

Self-assessment exercises

1 Why is it good practice for a bank to interview a prospective customer who wishes to open up a bank account?
2 What is a mandate? Who might use it and for what purposes in banking?

10.32 Operating the account

The major areas of interest in the operation of the account by any type of customer are:

(1) Drawing of cheques and the seeking of overdrafts.
(2) Ending of the banker's authority to pay on cheques drawn.
(3) Operation of standing orders and direct debits.
(4) The issuing of statements by the bank.

(1) Drawing of cheques and the seeking of overdrafts

One would assume that if a bank issues a customer with a cheque book and a cheque guarantee card it would expect the customer to draw cheques on the account. Also that it would, within certain conditions, meet these demands for payment. One or two factors are relevant to this situation.

Mandate for joint accounts

TO Midland Bank plc

Date_____

1 We the undersigned request you to act as our bankers.

2 Until any of us shall give you notice to the contrary (to be in writing unless you otherwise consent) we authorise you:—

Insert 'either,' 'any one/two' 'both' or 'all' as desired

a) to honour all cheques and other orders or instructions authorising payment signed on our behalf by _____ of us ("the signatory") whether any account in our joint names is in credit or debit;

b) to deliver up any item held by you on our behalf in safe custody or for any other purpose against the written receipt or instructions of the signatory;

c) to accept the signatory as our agent for any agreement from time to time with you for the withdrawal of monies from or the debiting of any account in our joint names by the use of any AutoBank Card, Cheque Card or other card or mechanical or automated means and despite any cancellation of this authority to charge any such account accordingly until such card or other device has been returned to you; and

d) to accept the signatory as fully empowered to act on our behalf in any other transactions with you.

3 We agree that any indebtedness or liability incurred to you under this mandate shall be our joint and several responsibility and in the absence of any express written agreement by you to the contrary be due and payable on demand.

Personal signatures of all the joint account holders

_____   _____

_____   _____

_____   _____

Names of account holders	Addresses	Business or Profession

Fig. 10.4 Bank mandate form (Source: Bank Education Service)

First of all, the very fact that the customer completes a cheque as required does not make it operative as a valid cheque. Holden in *Law and Practice of Banking* Vol. 1 states that this cheque must then be 'delivered to a person who takes it as holder'. Delivery means that possession is transferred from one person to another. This delivery can be actual delivery or constructive delivery. The Bills of Exchange Act 1882 (Section 2) defines the holder 'as the payee or endorsee who is in possession of it or the bearer thereof'. As we have seen in Chapter 7, the payee is the person named on the cheque while the endorsee is the person to whom the cheque is subsequently signed over. One of the most important duties of a banker is to honour cheques drawn upon the customer's account. There are a number of reasons for non-payment. The customer does not have an automatic right to draw cheques for amounts in excess of the amount in credit in the account. However, if the banker responds to the customer's proposition and grants an overdraft facility, then the customer can draw cheques which will not exceed this overdraft. On occasions a banker might allow an account to go into overdraft without taking action if this is seen as not being a regular practice and that, from the previous operation of the account, funds to cover the overdraft are likely to be paid in. This may be the case a few days before the customer's salary cheque is due to be paid in. This is a service given by the bank in the interest of good customer relations. What happens when a banker dishonours a cheque is discussed in Section 10.7.

(2) Ending of the banker's authority to pay on cheques drawn.

We have already discussed these in Chapter 7 but it will be useful to list the major areas where this authority can be terminated.
  (a) Countermand of payment (**stops**).
  (b) Notice of customer's death.
  (c) Notice of customer's bankruptcy.
  (d) Reliable notice that the customer is suffering from mental disorder.
  (e) The operation of the legal process usually in the form of service upon the banker.
  (f) Reliable knowledge or notice that the customer is committing a breach of trust.
  (g) Notice that a customer has assigned a credit balance.
  (h) Notice that the person presenting the cheque has a defective title to it.

(3) Operation of standing orders and direct debits

The operation of these has been discussed in Chapter 8.

(4) Issuing of bank statements

It is believed to be an implied term of the contract between a bank and a customer that the banker is careful in the operation of the customer's statement and that he provides the customer with information at regular intervals. Therefore, banks maintain a high standard when writing up a statement or pass book. It is, however, in the best interests of the customer to inform the bank of any errors found on these statements. Banks do make errors and it is necessary for them to know what the customer's position is when they are made. First of all, when a bank credits a customer's account with too much money, the action taken depends upon the way the customer has reacted. If the customer believes that the entries are correct and alters his position in reliance on them, then the bank is prevented from claiming that it has made a mistake. Thus in *Lloyds Bank Ltd v. Brooks*, the Honourable Cecily Brooks was due some income from preference shares in a colliery. The bank, on a number of occasions, credited amounts for a greater number of preference shares than she had. The bank claimed £1108 in overpayment. The customer claimed she had relied upon the bank's representations, had been led to believe that the entries were correct and had adjusted her spending to meet these. The bank lost the action as the judge said he believed the defendant when she said she had acted to her detriment as a result of the bank's mistaken action. However, if the customer does not change his position then the bank will be able to claim. Thus in *British and North European Bank v. Zolstein* (1927), a customer was unable to disregard a debit on the account and a subsequent claim for credit. In this case a bank manager added a sum to the customer's overdrawn account, which was in excess of the agreed amount, in order to disguise the fact from the auditors. These funds were from another source and they were returned to that source some time later. The judge disallowed the customer from gaining benefit from this when the bank eventually sued Zolstein for repayment of his overdraft. However, it has been suggested that a commercial customer would find it difficult to prove that he had acted upon information of inaccurate entries in his account, particularly for large sums. This difficulty was seen in the case of a Ugandan in *United Overseas Bank v. Jiwani* (1958) when he had received wrongful information about an amount credited to his account in a Swiss bank. In this case the defendant had to satisfy three conditions laid down by the judge, and this he was unable to do.

Where a bank debits a customer's account there is also room for error particularly when there are two customers of the same name in the branch. Obviously, a banker must guard against this as he could be open to a charge of negligence.

On the other hand, a bank may debit an account because of forgery of the customer's cheques. The banker must take care that forged cheques do not get passed but even with the most careful of bankers forgeries slip through. We could imply from this that there is, therefore, a duty on the customer to check all debit entries on their statements to discover any mistakes. In England this duty does not exist. In some countries agreements exist between the banker and the customer that entries will be checked and mistakes notified within a set time, and after this all entries are deemed correct.

Before leaving the operation of the customer's account we need to consider, in some detail, a famous case and its implications for the banker. Although it has become known as the rule in Clayton's case its full title is *Devaynes v. Noble* (1816). In this case a Mr Clayton had an account with a bank which was a partnership. At the time of death of one of the partners Mr Clayton had a credit balance. Sometime later the bank failed, but between the death and the failure of the bank Mr Clayton continued to operate the account drawing cheques which took the account into overdraft, but also paying in sums which could have covered this overdraft. The customer claimed that the payments in should have been used to cover the payments out, and that he could claim the credit balance from the deceased partner's estate. It was held that the credit balance was passed on to the remaining partners who had continued trading after death and that the withdrawals extinguished this balance for when operating an account 'payments in are presumed to be appropriated to payments out in the order in which they occur'. Thus as a result of this case it is now the situation that, in the case of a current account, the sums are paid out in the order in which they are paid in and the first item on the debit side is discharged or reduced by the first item on the credit side. The judgement has great practical importance for a bank. Unless a bank, when granting overdrafts and taking security, makes these charges a continuing security by specific instructions signed by the customer then the rule in Clayton's case applies so that payments into an account are treated as payments which would discharge a secured debt and payments out as unsecured advances.

Self-assessment exercises

1 When does a cheque become valid?
2 What is one of the most important duties of a banker?
3 Give three reasons why a banker may legally refuse to carry out this duty.
4 What is a bank's duty with regard to statements? Under what circumstances would a bank be liable for crediting more money to an account than it was supposed to?
5 State, in your own words, the rule in Clayton's case.

10.33 Closing of the account

As the banker/customer relationship is a contractual one then the termination, like all contracts, may be by agreement between the parties. The effects of either party, the customer or the bank, wishing to close the account are discussed below.

(1) Closure by the customer

With current accounts the customer can demand, immediately, the return of any credit balance, less any bank charges. It is however important for the bank to discover whether the customer wishes to close the account or merely wishes to reduce it down to zero. If this is not clear then the bank may find itself in trouble if it acts as if the account is closed and this was not the intention of the customer. To make it clear, when the account is to be closed the bank should request that the customer makes out the cheque in the following way: 'Self to close the account'. If this is not done then a clear written statement of intention to close the account should be sought by the bank. In *Wilson v. Midland Bank Ltd* (1961) it was held that the bank was liable when it acted on a telephone conversation in which the customer intimated that he would close the account. The bank refused to honour a cheque, stating that the customer had no account with them. At the same time, a credit to the customer's account paid in at another bank was credited to another customer's account with the same name. The judge awarded nominal damages for breach of contract and damages for dishonouring the cheque.

When the account is closed the bank should seek to remind the customer to leave sufficient funds for any cheques not yet presented for payment. If this is not done, these cheques may be dishonoured with a suitable statement that the account is closed. The bank should also take back any unused cheques. All other contractual relationships on this account will end when the account is closed. Other accounts are closed according to their terms – thus with a deposit account closure the bank would seek the seven days' notice or, in certain circumstances, might waive this notice. The customer will, of course, lose a certain amount of interest.

(2) Closure by the bank

A banker must give a customer reasonable notice of closure, and also reasonable time to allow the customer to make alternative arrangements. This time will depend upon the circumstances surrounding the situation. Even if the bank is aware that the customer is using the account for unlawful purposes, the time period is not necessarily a nominal one of twenty-four hours. In *Prosperity Ltd v. Lloyds Bank Ltd* (1923) McArdle J said, obiter dicta, that a banker had a right to close an account which was in debit. We may consider this as strange, for we can understand a bank asking a customer to pay back an overdraft but not then closing the account without sufficient notice to allow that customer to make alternative arrangements. Even if the bank were to dishonour later cheques it might find the customer was going to pay cash into the account to cover them. A bank would be very imprudent to upset customers in this way and so give itself a bad reputation.

The effect of closing an account is to end the contractual relationship but it does not end the bank's duty to keep the affairs of the customer secret (*see* Section 10.5).

Self-assessment exercises

1 In order to close a current account, what should the customer be asked to write across any cheque reducing the balance to zero?
2 Mr Jones was upset with his bank as it had made charges against his account which he felt were unrealistic. He telephoned it and, in a heated moment, said he would close the account. That same day he paid into his account, at another branch a cheque for £500, but this was credited to another customer's account with the same name. His branch refused to pay on a cheque saying that there was no account and, consequently, Mr Jones lost an important contract. He has written a letter to the bank manager threatening legal action. What do you think is the bank's position? Give reasons for your answer.
   Write a reply letter to Mr Jones acting as the bank manager.
3 What is the normal period of notice a bank gives if it wishes to close a customer's account?

10.4 Basic legal relationships between banker and customer

Before looking at certain specific legal relationships it is useful to consider the general relationship between banker and customer; other studies will no doubt introduce you to the law of contract. In these particular studies you will have learned that six factors need to be present constitute a valid contract. These are:

(1) there must be an intention to create legal relations by the parties;
(2) there must be offer and acceptance;
(3) there must be consideration;
(4) the parties to the contract must have the legal capacity to contract;
(5) the thing contracted for must not be illegal;
(6) there must be genuine consent between the parties.

Although the actual relationship between the banker and the customer is complex we can see from the above that this relationship falls within the basic area of the law of contract. The opening up of an account is a good example of the operation of offer and acceptance. Consideration is given and received in those cases where a customer is able to use the many services a bank offers, some free and some which have to be paid for. The parties to the banking contract have to have legal capacity to make such contracts and, as we will see, the bank can be constrained by any limitations in this capacity. At all times, the bank should ascertain the actual wishes of the customer so that it is acting correctly and cannot be charged with negligence. We have already noted the reaction of banks to the operation of an account where the customer is acting illegally. As we can see from these few examples a contractual relationship exists between customer and banker, and we could give many other examples.

The bank also has a special relationship with its customers regarding financial activities in that it must deal with these in a careful and prudential manner. We have mentioned various occasions where the bank has been asked to give advice and it has been necessary for it to act prudently. Three such occasions are:

(1) *Lloyds Bank Ltd v. Bundy* (1975) where it was held that a bank had been negligent in not advising a farmer to seek independent advice when mortgaging his property for the benefit of his son's business.

(2) *Hedley Byrne & Co Ltd v. Heller and Partners Ltd* (1964) where a bank was charged with giving a negligent reference about a customer. In this case the bank was covered by an exclusion clause. However, we must consider the decision in *Box v. Midland Bank* (1979) where a judge did not freely interpret the implications of the Hedley Byrne decision.

(3) Regarding married women, when they are considering acting as guarantors for their husband or a company, they should be advised to seek independent advice.

L C Mather, in *Banker and Customer Relationship and the Accounts of Personal Customers* states that the 'general relationship between banker and customer is one of debtor and creditor, subject to a number of superadded obligations'. These superadded obligations consist of the bank acting at times as the agent of the customer, as mortgagor and, when it holds a customer's valuables, as bailee. A case illustrating this contractual relationship is *Burnett v. Westminster Bank Ltd* (1965) which related to automated payments and a notice to customers on cheques and paying-in slips with magnetic code to use these only for transactions on the account with MICR numbers. In this case, a customer had two accounts, one with MICR numbers at one branch and one without at another branch. He altered an MICR cheque so that it would be drawn from the account without numbers. The bank automatically paid out of the MICR bank account despite the fact that a stop had been put on the cheque. The court held that the notice did not constitute sufficient notice by the customer to the bank, thus illustrating the need to adequately inform the other party of any terms or conditions existing in a contractual relationship. It is useful to consider these legal relationships in some detail.

10.41 Debitor/creditor relationship

This relationship revolves around the question of whether the money deposited in a bank belongs to the banker to do with as he likes, or whether the money belongs to the customer and the banker acts on the instructions of the customer. In other words, is the banker an agent or trustee for the customer. The early goldsmiths, accepting deposits, were really in the relationship of bailor or bailee. If they lent the money without the customer's permission it was in breach of their contract of bailment. In 1848 in the case of *Foley v. Hill*2 HL a customer claimed that the banker was really his agent and that he (the customer) had the right to know what had happened to the money and what profits had been made from it. It was held that this was not the position and that the money paid in was the property of the banker to do with as he thought fit. A subsequent case, *Joachimson v. Swiss Bank Corporation* (1921) gave a clearer view of the contract between the banker and the customer and the fact that the monies deposited were not held in trust but were the property of the bank. As Lord Goddard C J said in *R. v. Davenport* 'when the banker is paying out, whether in cash over the counter or whether by crediting the bank account of somebody, he is paying out his money not my money...'

So it would appear that a bank on receipt of money is gaining a loan. The customer is a creditor of the bank and the bank is a debitor of the customer. Although the contract allows for payments and repayments to be made, the banker is free to do with the money what he wishes, facing the full force of legal liability if he acts negligently.

10.42   Principal/agent relationship

An agent is a person who acts on another's behalf; the other person is known as the principal. The main feature of this relationship is that the agent is able to alter the principal's legal position in relation to third parties by making contracts for the principal. In doing so the agent is not personally liable on these contracts nor does he have any rights. Even if the agent, himself, does not have legal capacity, as long as the principal has this capacity the contracts are valid. Thus an agent who is a minor can act for a principal.

The relationship of principal and agent may be created in four ways:

(1) By means of a specific contract which sets up this relationship and where the authority is expressly stated. There may, however, be an implied agency set up within the terms of the relationship whereby the agent has to carry out specific tasks. Thus a banker has an implied authority to collect on cheques paid into the customer's account.

(2) In a situation where a person is dealing with two other parties, his actions may be regarded as being the actions of one of the other parties and this other party may be prepared to ratify (confirm) that this person is acting as his agent. It is even possible where an agent acts outside his powers that the principal will subsequently ratify these acts and so make them legally binding. Certain circumstances must exist before this ratification can take place.

(3) Sometimes a person is stopped from denying that another person is his agent – if a third party relies on a relationship that appears to be a principal/agent relationship and so contracts with the purported agent. Three things must exist for estoppel to take place. Firstly, there must be

no doubt as to who is the principal. Secondly, the third party must have relied on this representation and, thirdly, altered his position.

(4) By means of the operation of the law; there are two types:

(a) Agency of necessity – this occurs where, in order for someone to carry out some other contractual agreement, the agent has to carry out acts which are not part of this agreement but it is necessary to do so to safeguard the principal's property. Thus animals delayed while being transported by railway may need to be fed and the railway company might be seen to operate as an agent of necessity in feeding them if the principal cannot be obtained to give the company instructions. It also occurs where an agent needs to act to protect perishable goods.

(b) Agency of cohabitation – where the wife or mistress can pledge her husband's or partner's credit to purchase those necessaries which are seen as part of her domestic relationship. This type of agency may be of interest to the banker.

One type of agent is the **universal agent**. This is a person who is appointed to handle all the affairs of the principal. For this relationship to exist, a deed must be set up and the agency created by **power of attorney**. There are two main types of power of attorney. Firstly, there is the special power of attorney which is given to an agent to act for a principal for a specific purpose. Secondly, there is the general power of attorney which gives very wide powers to the grantee. Both are executed under seal hence the reason for their formation by deed.

A general power of attorney is seen in the Powers of Attorney Act 1971, an example of this is shown in Fig 10.5.

A power of attorney consists of four basic parts:

(i) *Preamble* – this gives the names and addresses and occupations of the parties and states the reason for the existence of the power.

(ii) *Authority* – this gives the extent of the power – general or specific.

(iii) *Ratification* – this usually states that the donor will ratify any act of the attorney.

(iv) *Attestation* – the signatures of the donor and witnesses.

When a bank is presented with a power of attorney it needs to satisfy itself on a number of matters. Firstly, is it a valid execution of the power. The mental state of the customer granting the power is important. If old or near senile it might affect the understanding of the nature of the document. Subsequent mental incapacity of the customer revokes this power. Secondly, whether the person named in the deed is the person claiming the power. Thirdly, whether the bank can acquire a copy of the deed after it has been appropriately stamped. Fourthly, whether the Law of Property Act 1925 Section 125 (1) has been complied with so that the power of attorney has been filed with the Central Office of the Supreme Court and, in some cases,

```
THIS GENERAL POWER OF ATTORNEY is made this            day of

19      by    AB of

    I appoint CD of                    (or CD of

and EF of                     jointly or jointly and severally)

by my attorney(s)  in accordance with Section 10 of the Powers of Attorney Act 1971

In witness, etc.
```

```
Two witnesses are necessary if the power is executed not by the donor himself but
by someone else on his behalf.
```

Fig. 10.5 Proforma general power of attorney

with the Land Registry. This latter applies when the power allows the disposal of or deals with any interest in or charge upon land. Finally, all powers sought by the holder must be covered by the deed. Often the courts narrowly interpret these powers so it is in the interest of the bank to have all possibilities covered in the deed and, if not, for a standard form of mandate to be signed to cover all possible services.

The powers conferred by the deed can be revoked in the following circumstances:
 (1) when the period of time stated in the deed has elapsed;
 (2) when the donor revokes the power;
 (3) when the attorney revokes the power by giving notice to the donor;
 (4) by the death, bankruptcy or mental incapacity of the donor or donee;
 (5) when the aims or objectives of the power have been achieved.

Under Section 5 of the Powers of Attorney Act 1971 a third party relying on a power of attorney, not knowing of a revocation, is protected. The attorney is also given similar protection in the same circumstances. Under Section 4 of the Powers of Attorney Act 1971 the power cannot be revoked by the donor or by his death, bankruptcy or mental incapacity as long as an obligation to the attorney remains outstanding.

A power of attorney is useful in cases of illness, infirmity or long periods of absence from the country. A bank may take on a power of attorney for itself when it takes an equitable interest in land.

In the case of the *Midland Bank v. Reckitt and Others* (1933) it was shown that a banker was not free from responsibility in his dealings with an agent when the latter acted under power of attorney. In this case, a fraudulent solicitor drew fifteen cheques to the value of about £18 000 on the account of Sir Harold Reckitt. They had been signed

'Harold A Reckett Bt.,
Tennington, his attorney'.

The House of Lords agreed with the Court of Appeal that the bank had been negligent in not questioning the drawing of the cheques.

There are also times when a banker acts as an agent for a customer without this formal legal arrangement. As well as considering the position of the banker when he is acting as an agent, we must also look at the position when he is dealing with agents of other principals. The banker acts as the customer's agent in the following transactions:

(a) collecting on cheques;
(b) paying standing orders;
(c) investing money on the Stock Exchange;
(d) receiving payments other than cheques, for example, rents.

This is not an exhaustive list and as the banks' services continue to grow there will be many occasions when the principal/agent relationship will be seen to exist.

A bank manager is an agent for his bank. He has the implied authority to represent his principal in all matters which are relevant to the business of banking.

When a bank deals with the agents of other principals then the following matters must be considered:

(i) The nature and the extent of the authority of the agent – with companies, as we will see later, the bank should call for sight of the memorandum of association and the articles of association as these give indications of which agents are likely to be able to act for the company and what their powers are likely to be. With partnerships this information may be contained in the deed of partnership, if it exists. A power of attorney may be in operation in the case of some agents.

(ii) The operation of the principal's bank account by the agent – where a mandate is called for the agent might be a specific agent and the bank has to make certain that the agent does not exceed his powers.

(iii) Bills of exchange and agency – an agent, when signing a bill, must clearly show that he is signing on behalf of someone else by signing 'Per Pro' otherwise he is personally liable on the bill. Where the signature indicates the possibility of an agency relationship the bank should exercise care. An agent collecting bills must show skill and care in presenting them for acceptance and/or payment. This also applies for notice of dishonour. As a cheque is a bill of exchange, this care and attention applies to the collecting banks too. There may be occasions when an agent exceeds his authority when drawing cheques for the principal and a bank must guard against this. If it does not take this care and attention, it could lose the protection given to it under Section 4 of the Cheques Act 1957.

(iv) Agents exercising borrowing powers for the principal – banks should seek to ascertain that an agent has such power. The signing of a mandate to this effect could well give the bank the right to bring actions against the principal for such loans to the agent. If the agent has not got this authority a bank's action will fail unless the principal ratifies the loan or he is estopped from denying the authority of the agent in these matters. We shall be looking later at the position of the bank when it lends money to companies, partnerships, clubs, churches and other bodies where agency is likely to exist.

10.43 Bailment

As we have seen when discussing safe custody a banker is a bailee for the items held in these circumstances. A banker is obliged to take such care as an ordinarily efficient and prudent banker would take in similar circumstances. The banker must show that he has not been negligent in the handling of these items left for safe custody. Thus if a banker left valuables outside the strongroom and these were stolen, it could be classed as being negligent, similarly if the bank did not inform the police or the customer that this had happened. The bank may not be regarded as negligent if it had locked these valuables away and the safe was broken into and the valuables stolen. It might be able to make use of any disclaimer of such liability if the customer had been informed of this exclusion. Under the Unfair Contract Terms Act 1977 this limitation of liability must be set against a test of reasonableness.

The standard of care exercised by a bailee depends upon whether he is a gratuitous bailee or a bailee for reward. The duty of care for the former is not as strict as it is for the latter. Thus when banks keep articles of value in safe custody free of charge they are regarded as gratuitous bailees.

With regard to safe custody, a bank is in danger of a charge of conversion in certain circumstances. This has been discussed in Chapter 7 Sections 7.6 and 7.7.

Self-assessment exercises

1   Take each of the six conditions of a contract and give examples of the banker/customer relationship where these can be seen to exist.
2   What is the legal position of a banker when receiving and paying out money to customers?
3   Describe the position of an agent. When is a banker acting as a customer's agent?
4   What is the purpose of a **power of attorney**?
5   On what matters must a bank assure itself when receiving a power of attorney?
6   Under what circumstances is a bank interested in the relationship with agents of other principals?

10.5 Obligations of banker and customer

10.51 Obligations of a banker to the customer

These are as follows:

(1) To pay customers' properly drawn cheques on their branch where the account is held. This is where there are sufficient funds in the account or an overdraft has been negotiated to cover these cheques. This is seen in the case *Tassell v. Cooper* (1850).

(2) To maintain secrecy about their customers' financial affairs. The guiding authority on this is the case *Tournier v. National Provincial and Union Bank of England Ltd* (1924). In this case the plaintiff was overdrawn at the bank and agreed to pay back £1 a week. At the time of the agreement, he gave the name of a firm with whom he was to take up temporary employment as a sales representative for three months. He fell behind with the payments and the branch manager revealed to one of the directors of the firm the position of the overdraft and also the fact that some of the cheques drawn on the account were payable to bookmakers. As a result of this information, the firm did not take the plaintiff on for an additional term of employment. The rulings in the Court of Appeal provide the basis for future dealings of this type. The bank was regarded as being guilty of breach of secrecy of its customer's affairs. Thus the duty of secrecy is a legal one which comes from the law of contract and is a qualified duty rather than an absolute one. The banker must still maintain secrecy after the account has been closed, and this also applies to information which comes to the banker from sources other than from the operation of the account. There are, however, a number of occasions when disclosure is justified. These are:

  (a) where the disclosure is compelled by law;
  (b) where disclosure is seen as a duty to the public;
  (c) where it would be in the interests of the bank to disclose the information;
  (d) where the customer, either explicitly or implicitly, gives his consent to the disclosure.

(3) To observe due care and attention in the customer's affairs. This duty covers all activities of the bank from handling of cheques as either collecting or paying banker to the giving of advice on possible investments and handling status enquiries.

(4) To give reasonable notice to the customer before closing the account or ending the relationship.

(5) To inform the customer of any charges he is likely to make against the account or for services offered.

(6) To keep accurate statements of account and to provide the customer with copies of these as and when the customer requires them.

10.52 Obligations of the customer to a banker

These are as follows:

(1) To draw cheques carefully – the main case is *London Joint Stock Bank Ltd v. Macmillan and Arthur* (1918). In this case an employee of a firm fraudulently raised a cheque drawn on the firm. It was incomplete when the partner of the firm signed it. The employee later added the numbers and words and presented it to the bank where it was drawn and received payment. It was held that the person signing the cheque should have taken more care in drawing the cheque and, therefore, as a result of this negligence the bank should not be the loser.

(2) To disclose forgeries – in *Greenwood v. Martins Bank Ltd* (1933) it was held that the plaintiff had a duty to disclose the forgeries on his cheques and that failure to do so gave rise to estoppel.

(3) To pay any interest or charges made by the bank in the operation of the account or services.

Self-assessment exercises

1 What are the obligations of the customer to a banker?
2 What are the banker's obligations to his customer?

10.6 Considerations of the different types of bank customer

10.61 Minors

Under the Family Law Reform Act 1969 a person reaches the age of majority at 18 years of age. This is at the first moment of the day on which the birthday occurs. Thus anyone below this age is known as a minor. When looking at contracts with minors we see that four types apply.

(1) Contracts which could be enforced against the minor by the courts. These are contracts for necessaries which are ordered and supplied to a minor and also contracts which could be deemed beneficial contracts of service. Necessaries are seen as goods and services which are needed to keep the minor at the standard of living which is regarded as his station in life. A beneficial contract of service might be an apprenticeship agreement entered into by the minor.

(2) Contracts which are absolutely void. These are of relevance to the banker as this applies to repayments of money lent to a minor as well as goods supplied which are not necessaries, as well as accounts stated. Thus if non-necessaries are supplied and not paid for, the trader is not able to recover the money and a banker is unable to recover money lent for these purchases. These contracts come under Section 1 of the Infants Relief Act

1874. Under the Betting and Loans (Infants) Act (1892) even if a minor, after attaining the age of majority, agrees to pay off whole or part of the void loan contracted as a minor, this new agreement itself is void.

(3) Contracts which can be repudiated by the minor. These are contracts of tenancy, partnership, or membership of a company. This repudiation must come whilst the young person is still a minor or at some reasonable time after coming of age. In these cases, the minor can repudiate the contract but cannot recover any monies which may have been paid.

(4) Contracts which are not covered by the other categories. Examples are where a minor contracts to have a house built. In such a case the minor has the right to sue but not to be sued. The rule in Section 2 of the Infants Relief Act 1874 also applies. Under this section any minor who, after attaining full age, accepts a bill for a debt which occurred whilst he was a minor cannot be held legally liable for payment. Similarly, no action may be brought against a person who during infancy drew and issued a cheque payable on a date after he attains full age.

There has been, as of yet, no court cases relating to the banker/customer relationship in connection with minors. It is believed that these would fall into the fourth group. Thus a minor can sue but could not be sued by the bank. If a bank acts in breach of its duty of secrecy or wrongfully dishonours a cheque, the banker would be liable as he would with any other customer. Under Section 22(2) of the Bills of Exchange Act 1882 a bill, including a cheque, drawn by a minor entitles the holder to receive payment so that a banker is not in jeopardy in these circumstances.

Generally, a cheque book is not given to a minor until he is 16 or 17 years of age. Where a minor is provided with funds from an account during minority it appears that he cannot make another claim when reaching majority. Children below the age of 7 can have an account opened for their benefit in the name of an adult, and this means that the adult is the customer and is the only one entitled to operate it.

Lending to minors

If a minor's account is overdrawn the position is as in the Infants Relief Act 1874. No action may be brought against the minor even if he claimed to be of full age. A promise by a minor to repay after reaching full age is void. Usually if a bank gives a loan to a minor it takes a guarantee from a person of full age. However, since the case *Coutts & Co. v. Browne-Lecky and Others* banks have included in their guarantee forms a clause which makes the guarantor liable as a principal debtor in the event of his liability as a guarantor proving, in any event, to be insufficient. If a loan is made for the purchase of necessaries the minor cannot give a binding security on it, but the bank stands in the position of the seller of necessaries and has the same right of recovery. Minors are given cheque guarantee cards which carry the danger of giving the minor an opportunity to overdraw. The banks' only action will be to call in the card and close the account. The risks in this area are thought to be so small that the banks are prepared to take a chance.

10.62 Married women

When a bank is asked to open an account for a married woman, a similar procedure is carried out as for an ordinary customer (*see* Section 10.2 of this chapter). In addition, enquiries are made as to her husband's employment and name and address of employer. The reasons for this are the same as enquiring about a husband's employment when opening up an account for him. When a security is deposited or a guarantee is given by a wife, there is thought to be a danger of undue influence being brought to bear on the wife. Before the bank accepts such an action from a wife on behalf of her husband, it must advise her that independent advice should be sought. This does not mean that it is presumed by the bank that in this particular relationship undue influence has been brought to bear by the husband, but only that in such relationships generally the danger exists. Where this independent advice is sought it should be from a solicitor who should explain the nature of the liability, witness the wife's signature and add a note that he has explained the full nature and implications of the transaction. When a single woman marries the bank asks for a sight of the marriage certificate. This is to remove the possibility of fraud by single women. However, since the Sex Discrimination Act 1965 it is now illegal to discriminate solely on the grounds of sex alone. Therefore, a bank in these circumstances must show other reasons as to why it is following these procedures, if it follows them at all.

10.63 Joint accounts

These are bank accounts which are held by two or more persons. These must not be partners, administrators, trustees, or executors. The parties need not be related. The most common form of joint account is one held by husband and wife. As with the opening of accounts for individuals, banks seek answers to the same four questions. As we have already stated in this chapter, the bank requires a mandate to be signed by the parties giving this bank an idea of how these parties require the account to be operated (*see* Fig. 10.4).

The printed format of the bank mandate includes a variety of clauses which give the parties a choice. One of the clauses in the mandate describes the liability of the joint parties to the bank as being 'joint and several'. The other option is just 'joint' liability. The differences between these two types of liability are as follows:

(1) A bank has only one right of action with joint liability while with joint and several liability the bank has as many rights as there are parties to the account. Thus with an account with joint liability only which is in debit for £1000 which is unsecured, any action by the bank for the balance against one of the holders which brings less than £1000 means that no other action can be brought against the other holders. With joint and several liability the bank can bring subsequent actions against the other holders to recover the remainder of the debt.

(2) On the death of one of the holders of the account where there is only joint liability the estate of the deceased is freed from liability. Only the survivors are liable for any debits on the account. With joint and several liability the estate of the deceased is also liable for any debits on the account.

(3) With joint and several liability the bank can set off any joint indebtedness against credit balances or private accounts. No such right exists for accounts with only joint liability.

It is not legally necessary for all parties to sign when cheques are drawn on the account; it is, however, in the interests of the bank to have clear instructions about the operation of cheques, the use of securities, safe custody transactions and to provide for joint and several liability if ever the account goes into overdraft. A bank is not protected if it pays a cheque on the instruction of one of the parties without the express permission of the other party unless clear instructions are given on a mandate. This states that either or both are to sign cheques in the case of two parties to an account. With a group of people on a joint account, an obvious difficulty arises if all are required to sign cheques. It is preferable to allow a lesser number, but not less than two, to sign. Stops put on cheques must be on the instructions of all the parties or authorised by the parties shown on the mandate. With the death of a joint account customer where the account is overdrawn, the bank should stop the account immediately when reliably informed of the death. If the bank is happy to trust to the indebtedness of the survivors this action may not be taken. This particularly applies where the parties are joint and severally liable. If the account continues, it is possible to use any payments in to offset against the liabilities of the deceased, while any further withdrawals are the sole responsibility of the survivors. Eventually, the deceased's personal representatives must be informed of any overdraft and some settlement arranged. Therefore, the bank must be absolutely certain that the survivors are able to meet any subsequent debits before it allows the account to continue in these circumstances. Where there is only joint liability the deceased's estate is automatically released from liability.

With regard to credit balances on joint accounts on the death of one of the parties, in *Shields Corbould Ellis v. Dales* (1912), it was seen as an implied term of the contract between a banker and a customer that any balance should automatically resort to the survivor. A mandate should clearly state this so that no doubt exists. Any claims by the deceased's personal representatives are regarded as resting with the survivors rather than with the bank, but the bank may interplead and leave it to the courts to apportion the balance in the event of any such claim against the bank.

With regard to items held in safe custody in joint names the position varies. With items which are in joint names like bearer bonds, share certificates, or deeds these pass to the survivors without reference to the personal representatives of the deceased. With other items, like valuables, it is wise to refer to the personal representatives before disposal.

Even where the joint account mandate authorises a bank to honour cheques drawn by either parties, it is not automatically agreed that any one of them is responsible for overdrafts created by the others on the account. If the mandate does not give specific power to overdraw, all parties must sign the cheques which will take the account into overdraft if they are to be liable for the debit. Again, for security purposes, the mandate should allow the bank account to be operated whether in credit or debit and also make all parties liable in either event. Where a party to a joint account faces bankruptcy proceedings, the account should be stopped immediately. If a stop is not placed on an account in debit, the bank's claim against the bankrupt's estate may fail. This is because the rule in Clayton's case operates against the bank. The bank may be prepared to rely upon the solvency of the other parties. If it is not prepared, it must lodge proof of the debt with the Official Receiver or the trustee in bankruptcy. Where the parties are jointly and severally liable on the account, the whole claim may be against the estate of the bankrupt and solvent parties can be ignored. Where the account is in credit and one of the parties is bankrupt, the account must be stopped as some of the balance will belong to the trustee in bankruptcy. Cheques presented for payment after this must be handled carefully. Those drawn by the insolvent party can be returned with 'refer to drawer' on them. Those drawn by the other parties must be returned and carefully marked that non-payment is not because of their lack of credit. Withdrawal of any balance must be under the instructions of the trustee in bankruptcy or the Official Receiver for the insolvent person's estate along with the instructions of the other parties. Similar conditions apply in these circumstances to the release of items held in safe custody on the joint account.

When the bank receives notice of the mental disorder of one of the parties to a joint account which is so serious as to stop that party from operating the account, a stop should be put on it immediately as the bank's mandate ends. The bank should wait for instructions from the Receiver and the other parties as to what should happen to the balance.

Holders of a joint account have a joint and several right of action against the bank as seen in the case *Jackson v. White and Midland Bank Ltd* (1967).

10.64 Partnerships

A partnership is defined in the Partnership Act 1890 as 'the relation which subsists between persons carrying on a business in common with a view to profit'. Your other studies will no doubt give you the details of the nature and organisation of partnerships.

The bank seeks answers to the same four questions, initially, when opening an account for a partnership. In this case the bank investigates the integrity of the partners. Some banks ask for a copy of the partnership deed if it exists. This gives the bank a guide to any provisions which may affect the partners' operation of the firm's affairs. Other banks merely rely for adequate protection upon a properly signed mandate. This mandate is usually signed by all of the partners and gives clear instructions as to the operation of the partnership account. All partners have an implied authority to open up an account in the partnership name but not in their own name where there is a danger of the other partners being made liable for overdrafts.

Dissolution of the partnership is brought about in the following ways:

(1) Death of a partner – the partnership deed may allow for the dead partner's share to be bought by the existing partners so that the business continues but in a different legal form.

(2) Bankruptcy of a partner – this is not the same as bankruptcy of the partnership. In the former case the deed can allow for existing partners to purchase this partner's share and for the money to be paid to the trustee in bankruptcy.

(3) When a partner is of unsound mind or unable to carry out his part in the partnership.

(4) When a partner is guilty of wilful misconduct.

(5) Where a partner has acted in such a way that impedes the operation of the partnership.

(6) Where the business will only be able to make a loss if it continues.

Instances (3) to (6) are specified in the 1890 Act which gives the courts power to dissolve the partnership.

In the event of dissolution by reason of (1) and (2) the account should be allowed to continue to help wind up the affairs of the partnership. If cheques drawn by the dead partner are presented, they should only be paid if the other parties agree unless the mandate gives specific instructions to the contrary. With a bankrupt partner, if the account is in credit it may be continued. If the account is overdrawn it must be stopped so that the bank can preserve its rights against the estate of the deceased person or the bankrupt partner. The rule in Clayton's case applies here also. A new account should be opened up to allow for the winding up of the partnership.

If the partnership is bankrupt all accounts, whether in credit or overdrawn, must be stopped. This applies to the partnership account and the private accounts of the partners. After this normal provisions apply as for bankruptcy.

If the constitution of the partnership changes, it may be necessary to have a new mandate. If a new partner is brought in then he may be asked to sign an assent to the mandate and the other partners to countersign this. If a partner dies and the mandate does not allow for the partnership to continue with its existing mandate, a new mandate must be signed.

The law allows for an incoming partner not to be liable for the debts of the partnership unless entry is conditional upon this. In this case, where an overdraft exists on the partnership account it requires a cheque from the partners to clear this and a new account will be opened with all of the partners liable.

An outgoing partner is still liable for the debts of the partnership incurred while he was a partner. In order to stop the rule in Clayton's case operating, the bank should make certain that this liability is against the retiring partner, the account should then be closed.

What has been said above is by no means a comprehensive view of the partnership/banker relationship but merely covers the major areas.

10.65 Companies

Most companies come into being by registering with an official of the Department of Trade and Industry called the **Registrar of Companies**. There are three types of companies basically:

(1) a company limited by shares;
(2) a company limited by guarantee;
(3) an unlimited company.

The unlimited company, up to 1967, was rarely formed but in 1967 the exempt private limited company was abolished so that these latter companies were no longer exempt from the filing of their annual accounts with the Registrar of Companies. However, unlimited companies were exempt with the result that, for some people, they became a more popular type of company to form. The company limited by guarantee is used by trade associations, charitable organisations, professional societies and clubs. One example of a company limited by guarantee is the Business and Technicians Education Council. This form of company is not uncommon.

Companies limited by shares may be either public or private companies. Private companies are defined in the 1980 Companies Act as those companies which are not public. Public companies are defined as companies limited by shares (or by guarantee and having share capital) being companies:

(a) in which the memorandum states that the company is to be public;
(b) registered or re-registered under the Companies Act 1980 as a public company.

For registration the company must provide the following documents:

(i) *Memorandum of association* – this is the basic document of the company and gives information to people who are external to the business whether dealing or intending to deal with it.

(ii) *Articles of association* – these make up the rules and regulations by which the company's internal affairs are governed. Under Section 8 of the Companies Act 1980 they must be printed and divided into paragraphs numbered consecutively. If they are adopted they must be signed by the people who sign the memorandum of association. If no articles are adopted then Table A of the First Schedule of the 1948 Companies Act or the amended version of the 1980 Act (the latter applying to companies formed after 22 December 1980) will be applied to the company. It should be noted that codification of the various Companies Acts begins in 1985, and that Table A will be formed by a separate statutory instrument. This is to allow Parliament greater flexibility to change its content as and when the need arises.

(iii) The statement, as required by the Companies Act 1976 (Section 21), giving particulars of the proposed directors and secretary and signed by them showing that they consent to acting for the company.

(iv) A statutory declaration made by a solicitor engaged in the formation of the company or by a person named in (iii) above as director or secretary.

(v) It is good practice (not required by law) to send the Registrar's letter of approval of the proposed name – this will avoid delay.

(vi) A statement relating to the payment of capital duty in compliance with the Finance Act 1973 Part V Section 47(3).

If the documents submitted are found to be correct and the fees and duty are paid, the Registrar issues a **certificate of incorporation**. This formally certifies the corporate existence of the company and contains its number, this latter must be quoted on all business letters. This certificate originated from an order under the European Communities Act 1972 Section 9(7). A private company can start trading straightaway but a public company must wait for a **trading certificate** to be issued. Once the Registrar is certain that the allotted share capital is not less than the authorised minimum and that the formal application and statutory declaration have been delivered, this certificate is issued.

Opening an account for a company

In discovering the identity of the company two factors are important. First of all, the legal status of the company and, secondly, the identity of the directors. To obtain answers to these questions the bank should ask for sight of the following documents:

(1) certificate of incorporation;

(2) trading certificate (if relevant);
(3) memorandum of association;
(4) articles of association.

Copies of the latter two should be obtained and retained by the bank. The bank must take care to ensure that the company has been formed legally, that its purposes are legal and that the powers of its representatives are not being exceeded.

Mandate and the paying and collection of cheques

The bank should also receive a certified copy of the resolution of the board of directors appointing the bank as bankers to the company. It includes detailed instructions about the operation of the account or accounts at the bank – this is the company's mandate. Banks can supply companies with proforma mandates which contain suitable provisions. The resolution should be passed by a meeting of the board and then the form should be signed by the chairman and secretary certifying that the resolution has been duly passed. The form usually contains specimen signatures of the persons who will sign on behalf of the company.

Banks have to be careful when collecting cheques drawn payable to a limited company, especially when a financial relationship exists with the person receiving payment, as there could be some danger of conversion on the part of this person. Banks, when they know of this relationship, should be cautious when they have to pay cheques to such people, and good practice dictates that enquiries should be made to the company for an explanation. A case in 1984 showed how a bank may not have to rely on two signatures on a cheque when paying to someone in this position. In the case, a company was formed and it was agreed that cheques drawn on the company were to carry two specific signatures. The bank, however, paid out to one of the promoters on cheques bearing only one signature. It was subsequently found that this person was entitled to the monies so paid and it was held that the bank was not negligent by not insisting on two signatures on the cheques.

Borrowing powers of companies

These are usually contained in the articles of association. In Table A this is in regulation 79 and is rather restrictive for some companies as the definition of borrowing under this regulation is very precise. It covers mortgages on the company's property, general charges on the undertaking as a whole and loans, secured or not, by such a charge and represented by debentures or loan stock. Under these articles of association the company's borrowing powers are exercised by the directors but their powers are limited to an amount equal to the nominal share capital, unless previously authorised by members of the company at a general meeting. Temporary loans obtained from a company's bankers in the ordinary course of its business are excluded from these limitations in Table A regulations, so this covers overdrafts. Acts by the directors or officers of the company which are beyond their powers are said to be 'ultra vires' and generally cannot be enforced by law. However, in the European Communities Act 1972 there is a modification to this rule in that third parties acting in good faith are not affected by any restrictions in the articles of association regarding the decisions of directors. Thus a bank may be protected if the directors exceed their powers in borrowing money provided it can be proved that the bank acted in good faith.

Winding up of the company

When the bank receives notice of the resolution of a company to voluntarily wind up its affairs, it should treat the mandate on the account as at an end. No cheques should be paid without permission of the appointed liquidator. Cheques should be returned with the answer 'refer to drawer, resolution to wind up passed'. If the company is insolvent the rules for bankruptcy apply. All accounts should be combined and the amount outstanding or due should be found. If there is a credit balance, this should be retained to pay any bills that have been drawn but not yet presented. Where the winding up is compulsory, it will have begun by a petition being presented to the court. When the bank learns of this petition it should stop payment of cheques drawn in favour of third parties. (If the account is in credit it could still pay cheques drawn for cash by an official of the company.) The practice of banks varies in this matter. There is no clear rule, statutory or otherwise, with regard to the collection of cheques payable to a company after a petition to wind up has been presented to the court.

10.66 Personal representatives

These are either **executors** or **administrators**. An executor is a person who is appointed by a will or codicil to administer the property of a deceased person (testator) and to carry out the provisions of the will. An administrator is someone who is appointed by an appropriate court to administer the property of a deceased person. These latter are appointed when a person dies intestate, that is, without a will.

Opening up of an account

Similar procedures operate for the opening up of an account for both executors and administrators. If they are unknown to the bank it is good practice to have them introduced by a solicitor. A mandate signed should give joint and several liability to all parties. Where the executors are to hold any residue of the estate in trust for other parties, it is good practice to have all cheques drawn on the account to be signed by all executors. Where a will is held in safe custody on the death of the customer, the bank will allow it to be released provided a receipt is signed by all the persons named in the will or by their solicitors. Other items in safe custody will be able to be inspected but not released until the will has been proved.

Advances to personal representatives

One of the major reasons for a loan to these persons is to enable them to pay taxes against the estate before probate or letters of administration are granted. As we saw in Chapter 9, these loans are generally made provided the bank can assure itself that the representatives have the power to borrow, and that there are sufficient funds in the realisable assets of the estate to cover the loan. Other loans may be made to pay debts or legacies or to continue the business of the deceased. The bank requires these personal representatives to be jointly and severally liable for the advance. The personal representatives also have the power to offer certain assets belonging to the estate as security for any loan.

If the advance is for the continuation of the business the bank should take into consideration three things. First of all, have the personal representatives the power to carry on the business? Secondly, have the deceased's creditors been paid off or have they assented to the personal representative carrying out the business? If they have assented, the bank is in a privileged position, as are any subsequent creditors, with regard to having a priority claim over these assenting creditors in the future winding up of the business. If this is not the position, the bank must take its place behind these creditors. This is even so where the testator has given specific permission, in the will, for the executors to carry on the business. Thirdly, what is the security for the proposed advance? The bank could rely upon joint and several liability. The executors cannot offer any assets outside the business as security for the loan, but they can give a valid charge upon the assets in the business.

On the death of a personal representative the account can still be operated as the representatives of the deceased representative can sign any cheques. A fresh mandate might be necessary. Where the account is joint and several and overdrawn it should be stopped and a new account opened. If a sole executor dies then, if the will is proven, the deceased's executors become the executors for the old will. A new mandate should be drawn up.

Bankers should beware of personal representatives who are in financial difficulties who may try to misappropriate any funds from the estate to their own use. Thus a bank should watch for and question any payments from the estate to the personal accounts of the executors.

10.67 Trustees

A trustee is defined as a person 'to whom property, real or personal, is committed, which is for the benefit of other people'. Banks are either given express details that the account is for a trustee where it is entitled 'Trustees of relationship in the activity that is being carried out'. Thus certain clubs and societies may be regarded as trust accounts although this is not specifically stated in the title of the account.

Opening up of an account for trustees

The bank may ask to see the **trust deed** but this is not necessary. Once again, the bank seeks the signing of a mandate covering all likely operations on the account. Generally, all trustees are required to sign cheques although some clubs and societies may delegate this task to no less that two of their members. If, in other cases, the bank is asked to allow delegation of signing, the bank should only do this if it is in no doubt as to the integrity of the trustees and an indemnity exists protecting the bank from possible loss. This indemnity is to be signed by all the trustees and any beneficiaries who are of full age. The bank should also ask the trustees to verify the balance of the account at least every six months. In these circumstances no less than two trustees should sign the cheques.

Advances to trustees

A bank must be aware of the problems of lending to a trustee. First of all, it must make certain that the trustee has the power to borrow. Secondly, if the trustee is offering security the bank must be certain that he has the power to do this. Power to borrow may be given to trustees in four ways:

(1) by the trust deed;
(2) by Act of Parliament;
(3) by the beneficiaries;
(4) by the courts.

Banks must be aware of any liabilities they may incur by knowingly or negligently acting in breach of trust by the trustee. They need to be cautious, for example, in accepting a cheque drawn on a trust account and payable to the personal account of the trustee, particularly where the personal account of the trustee is overdrawn and the bank is pressing for payment. This was illustrated in the case *British American Elevator Co. Ltd v. Bank of British North America* (1919).

10.68 Clubs and societies

When a bank operates such an account it is important for it to discover if the club or society is incorporated or unincorporated. Incorporation is in two forms, either under the Companies Acts, or under the Industrial and Provident Societies Acts. In the case of the former, this has already been discussed in the opening and operation of accounts of companies.

Industrial and provident societies include such organisations as working men's clubs and co-operative retail and wholesale societies.

Opening up an account

Opening up such accounts require banks to have sight of the society's rules for it is in these that the nature and limitations of the society are found. The committee of management or other ruling body should be asked to pass a resolution appointing the bank as bankers to the society, with power to draw cheques and with the names of the persons empowered to sign these cheques. A certified copy of the resolution must be handed to the bank.

Advances to industrial and provident societies

The rules of the society must give it power to do so. If it has not got this power then the management committee must be asked to pass a resolution to this effect. The Industrial and Provident Societies Act 1967 conferred wide powers on such societies. It provides that a society can create a fixed or floating charge on any of its assets in favour of any lender. A copy of the instrument making this charge must be sent to the Chief Registrar of Friendly Societies within fourteen days of its execution.

Opening accounts for unincorporated clubs and societies

These are not legal entities so they do not have legal capacity to contract. Accounts have been opened up in two ways. Banks have preferred to open up an account in the name or names of private individuals with some statement showing that they are not the actual beneficiaries. In this case, the named persons will be jointly and severally liable on the account for any overdrafts. Some bankers open up an account in the club or society's name despite the lack of legal capacity. If the society has rules these may give permission for such an account to be opened and operated. Banks receive a signed mandate which includes a draft resolution passed by the committee of the club or society authorising the bank to pay cheques provided they are correctly drawn – signed by two members with a counter signature of the treasurer.

Advances to unincorporated clubs and societies

Since these do not exist in law, lending to such bodies contains many difficulties. The only safe way of gaining any security is for the bank to lend against a guarantee in which the guarantor stands as the sole or principal debtor to the bank.

10.69 Churches

The various denominations operate differently.

Church of England

Individual parishes are controlled by Parochial Church Council. Under the Synodial Government Act 1970 this is a corporate body. This means it has legal existence in its own right. The account to be opened must be named the Parochial Church Council of – Parish. A mandate signed by the chairman and two other members must incorporate a copy of a resolution passed by the council authorising the opening of the account, appointing a treasurer to sign cheques. Some councils limit this one signature to cheques below a certain amount and have cheques of a higher amount drawn on two signatures.

Roman Catholic Church

The authority of the diocesan bishop must be sought for the opening of an account. Three priests' names appear on the application form with one of them being authorised to sign any cheques. The account is usually in the parish priest's name, cheques being drawn by him. Any borrowing by the church from a bank is negotiated by this individual.

Non-conformist churches

These are similar to trusts. The name of any account opened is in the name of the church or society, for example, 'Ellis Road Methodist Church Society Steward's Account'. The ruling council or body must pass a resolution appointing the bank as its bankers. This must be incorporated in the mandate and the people authorised to sign the cheques must also be identified with specimen signatures supplied. Usually it is the practice for there to be two signatures necessary to draw cheques. In some cases the bank will ask for sight of the trust deed.

Self-assessment exercises

1   What is a minor in law?
2   Give an example where a contract with a minor and a bank might be enforceable by the court:

(a) against the bank;
  (b) against the minor.
3   If a banker lends money to a minor to purchase goods which are non-necessities what redress has the bank for repayment of this loan? How can a bank ensure repayment of a loan to a minor?
4   Why is a bank interested in a husband's employment and employer when opening an account for a wife?
5   What is joint and several liability?
6   Jones and Brown have joint and several liability, and owe the bank £1000. If the bank is able to recover £750 from Jones, has it any further action and if so what? Would it have been different if only joint liability existed?
7   What must a bank do when one of the parties to a joint account dies?
8   Under what circumstances should a bank stop immediately any transactions on a joint account?
9   How differently should a bank act if the partnership is bankrupt than if only one of the partners is bankrupt?
10   Under what circumstances might a new mandate for a partnership have to be signed?
11   Which document gives us an idea of the external relationships of a company?
12   When opening an account for a company, which documents should a bank seek to inspect? Which of these should it retain?
13   What should be provided by a company to a bank which will detail the operation of its account(s)?
14   What is the position of a bank if it makes a loan in good faith to a director of a company who has not got the power to negotiate this loan?
15   If a company goes into liquidation and then receives cheques which are paid into a bank, what is the bank's position?
16   What is the difference between an executor and an administrator?
17   Why might personal representatives seek loans from a bank?
18   What problems exist for a bank lending to a trustee?
19   In what ways can a trustee be given power to borrow on behalf of a trust?
20   Give an example of an occasion when a bank will open up an account of a body that does not legally exist? What should a bank do for security when lending to such bodies?

10.7   A banker's legal liabilities

10.71   Breach of contract

We have seen earlier in this chapter that the relationship between the banker and his customer is a contractual one. Therefore, a banker has to carry out his business with such due care and attention as not to leave himself open to a charge of breach of contract. The way a banker can ensure that he is not in breach of contract is to act only under written instructions from the customer and to build checks and balances into his operations so that mistakes are not made or, if they are, they are rectified in good time. One area where a banker might be in breach of contract is where he dishonours a cheque wrongfully. A customer has to prove that actual damages were sustained in order to get compensatory damages. If these cannot be proved then the courts generally award nominal damages. However, this general rule does not apply in certain circumstances. If the customer is a trader then there is well established legal evidence that he is entitled to substantial damages. In the case *Robin v. Steward* (1854) the bank dishonoured three cheques and a bill which were presented. They were paid on presentation the next day and no actual loss was sustained but the jury awarded £500 damages. There was an appeal and the court held that the plaintiff was entitled to substantial damages. Were the customer not a trader then unless actual damage was sustained the plaintiff would not have been entitled to claim substantial damages. In *Gibbens v. Westminster Bank Ltd* (1939) a customer's cheques to her landlord were dishonoured as funds paid in earlier were credited to the wrong account. The bank claimed that as she was not a trader she was only entitled to nominal damages. This claim was upheld.

This distinction between a trader and non-trader is not relevant as non-traders are unlikely to claim damages.

10.72 Conversion

We have already seen in Chapter 7 the nature and effect of conversion. This, as far as the collecting banker is concerned, can be a danger when presenting a cheque for someone who is not entitled to it and obtaining the money. Some people hold the view that mere receipt of the instrument is sufficient for conversion to have taken place. Actions for damages resulting from conversion are statute barred after six years under the Limitations Act 1939.

10.73 Defamation

The definition of a libellous statement was given by Lord Aitkin in the case *Sin v. Stretch* and is as follows 'would the words tend to lower the plaintiff in the estimation of right-thinking members of society generally'. Thus the statement on a cheque when a banker refuses to pay could be important. The following are examples of words used and the decisions of the courts as to their libellous nature:

(1) 'refer to drawer' in *Plunkett v. Barclays Bank Ltd* (1936) du Pancq J held that these words were not libellous;

(2) 'not sufficient' in *Davidson v. Barclays Bank Ltd* (1940) Hilbery J held that these words were libellous;

(3) 'present again' in an Irish case these words were held to have no defamatory connotation. In a case in New Zealand a decision which though not binding in our courts could act as a guide to any similar cases, held that such a statement could be seen as reducing the customer's image in the eyes of right-thinking people. This case gave good guidance as to the assessment of damages in such matters;

(4) 'no account', to write this on the cheque when it is not true is also libellous. In *Wilson v. Midland Bank* (1961) the judge awarded nominal damages for breach of contract of £2 and substantial damages for libel of £200.

It is good practice for banks to carry out certain precautions to make certain that no mistakes are made by dishonour of a cheque. These are:

(a) Checking to see that all cheques paid for a customer have been drawn by the customer and that there is no likelihood of cheques of a customer with a similar name having been debited to the customer account.

(b) Checking to see that no postdated cheques have been paid in.

(c) Checking the account to see that no regular payments into it have been missed. This could mean that they may have been credited to another account.

(d) Checking to see that the cheque has not been drawn with a cheque guarantee card backing.

If a bank discovers that a cheque has been wrongfully dishonoured it should take steps to minimise the damage suffered by the customer. These should include telephoning the collecting banker, informing him of the mistake, following this up with a letter and sending a letter of apology to the customer. These actions will lessen any damages which may be awarded by the courts in the event of a case against the bank.

10.74 Negligence

There have been many acts and omissions where a banker has been held to have been negligent within Section 82 of the Bills of Exchange Act 1882 (replaced by Section 4 of the Cheques Act 1957). Three areas where the collecting banker has been found negligent are:

(1) Opening an account for a stranger without a satisfactory reference – this negligent act was recognised in *Lloyds Bank Ltd v. E B Savory & Co.* (1933). Where a referee is given and he is unknown to the bank it should make enquiries as to the standing of the referee. This point was seen in *Nu Stilo Footware Ltd v. Lloyds Bank Ltd* (1956).

(2) Collection of cheques payable to the customer – a bank is held to be negligent if it accepts cheques drawn by one customer say on the account of his employer for payment into his personal account without making

enquiries as to the customer's authority to do this (*Marquess of Bute v. Barclays Bank Ltd* (1955)).

(3) Collection of cheques payable to a third party – no simple test exists for determining whether or not the collection of third party cheques would be seen as negligence in certain circumstances. The following are circumstances where the courts have held that such actions were negligent.

(a) Collecting on cheques crossed 'Account Payee' not for the named payee. Where the bank did not ask for an explanation of this collection it was held to have acted negligently. (*House Property Co. of London Ltd. v. London County and Westminster Bank* (1915)).

(b) To stop a bank collecting on cheques which have been drawn on a customer's employer, the bank should seek the name of that employer. It would be negligent of the bank not to try and discover the name and address of the customer's employer. In practical terms, a bank will not be able to keep such a check on all cheques paid in but it must try and keep itself up-to-date as to the customer's present employer.

(c) Where a customer pays in cheques drawn by the customer's employer payable to third parties (*see Lloyds Bank Ltd v. E B Savory & Co.* (1933)).

(d) Collection of cheques payable to a limited company for the account of a director or officer of the company (*A L Underwood Ltd v. Bank of Liverpool and Martins* (1924)). If a bank seeks and receives an explanation for this payment it might be held that it was not acting negligently (*Penmount Estates Ltd v. National Provincial Bank Ltd* (1945)).

(e) Where the surrounding circumstances cast doubt upon the regularity of the transaction. The case illustrating this is *Baker v. Barclays Bank Ltd* (1955), where an insurance agent paid in nine cheques to the value of £1160 payable to Modern Confections, a partnership. These cheques had been handed over to the insurance agent by one of the partners who had misappropriated them. When the second one was paid in the bank enquired as to why the customer was paying in cheques payable to the partnership. It was told that this was a sole partner and that a business deal was being arranged. Other inquiries were made and at all times the manager was told the same story. The manager felt he had no reason to doubt this story and never asked to see the partner. The other partner discovered the misappropriations and brought an action for damages for conversion by the bank. The judge held that, although the bank manager had asked for an explanation, this was not satisfactory in relation to the total value of the cheques. The bank was held to be liable.

10.75 Vicarious liability

In criminal law the basic rule is that we are individually liable for the acts that we do. In civil law and tort, in particular, where someone is seeking compensation there are occasions where the wrongdoer does not have sufficient funds to provide adequate compensation. There is, however, an old legal mechanism which allows the plaintiff to fix responsibility upon someone other than the wrongdoer. This is called vicarious liability. In principle this is where a defendant (D) may be seen to be liable for the acts of a third party (X) to the plaintiff (P). For this to be possible the plaintiff must show that:

(1) X has committed a wrongful act which has caused damage to P;

(2) that some special relationship existed between X and D which is recognised in law, for example, where X is acting as D's agent or is employed by D;

(3) that the act was within the normal course of this relationship between D and X. In other words, was the act one that X would have normally expected to have done for D?

We can now see that an employer could be held vicariously liable for the actions of his employees in the normal course of his business. With regard to the position of banks, there are a number of occasions when they could be seen to be vicariously liable, but it will be beneficial for us to look at two aspects.

Banks are usually large organisations with head offices and many branches. Each branch manager is an employee carrying out the business of banking for and on behalf of the company. We have already noted a number of occasions when the bank manager has been seen to be acting negligently, sometimes resulting in actual damage to the customer. It is in the interest of the customer to sue the bank and not just the individual bank manager as the resources of the bank are much greater and, in this case, the bank bears vicarious liability for the actions of the manager.

The second example relates also to the actions of the individual employees of the bank. The nature of the relationship between the banker and customer involves the banker accepting at times articles of value into safe custody. The banker must ensure that a system of security exists. Thus if a bank employee wishes to get items of value from the safe, banks usually operate what is known as 'the two key system'. This is where one clerk holds one key to the strongroom and another clerk holds the other. Entry is only afforded by the use of these two keys so a clerk is always around to observe the actions of another when entering the strongroom. If a clerk steals an item of safe custody, this is a criminal offence and the thief is individually liable. However, the bank may be seen to have been negligent if its system of security had lapsed, or it had not insisted on its operation. This might also be so if a bank clerk had left these valuables lying around and so had put temptation in the way of another clerk.

These conclusions are not definitive as the position on the governing principle laid down by the House of Lords is not clear. This is that the employer is responsible for the wrongful acts of his employees which are committed in the normal course of business. It could be argued that stealing is not the normal course of business for the banker or his employee. There have not been any cases on this matter so this question has not been resolved by the courts.

10.8 Wills

A will is a written instrument whereby a person, the testator, indicates how his property will be handed down after death. Although it must be in writing, it does not have to be in any particular form, or in any particular words. It does not have to be in English, or in the testator's handwriting. Any instrument that has been properly executed may be submitted to probate, that is, as long as it could have been revoked during the testator's life, and was executed so that it was only intended to come into operation after his death. Thus if a person sends an order to a bank in a letter or direction to an executor and these are properly executed, they can be seen as testamentary dispositions. If a testator seeks to deposit his will in Somerset House for safe custody it cannot be withdrawn; any alterations or codicils should also be deposited.

Valid execution of a will occurs when:

(1) there is the signature of the testator or some other person in his presence and by his direction;

(2) this signature is made or acknowledged by him in the presence of two or more witnesses at the same time. The Administration of Justice Act 1982 introduced two new rules. The first releases the old law set out in Section 9 of the Wills Act 1837 and Section 1 of the Wills Act 1852. The latter act is repealed. It is now no longer necessary to comply with the previous conditions as to the position of the signature. It is now only necessary for it to appear from the face of the will that the testator intended to validate it with his signature. What is excluded from this provision is a scrawled signature, in pencil, on the backsheet of the will.

The second rule is a relaxation of the previous law relating to execution. It is now the position that each witness either attests and signs the will or acknowledges his signature in the presence of the testator, but not necessarily in the presence of each other. From the old law and as a result of the decision in *Re Codling* (1972), a will might be invalidated if either witness merely acknowledges his signature as opposed to subscribing after the operative signature an acknowledgement of the testator. It is now part of the new law that a witness can acknowledge his signature as an alternative to actually resubscribing. For example, if a witness leaves after he has signed a will but returns to attest the will, the witness who remained, by acknowledging his signature complies with the new law. He does not have to resubscribe. The new law has altered the need for each witness to a will to subscribe in each other's presence.

It is desirable for a will to have an attestation clause although it is not necessary. This clause appears at the bottom of the will declaring that the formalities of the Wills Acts have been observed. If no affidavit form can be obtained, the Registrar may want evidence or an affidavit of any other person he feels is acceptable and who can show that the signature or the will is in the handwriting of the deceased, or who can confirm any other matter which may be necessary to show that the will was executed.

Alterations, erasions or insertions between the lines must be identified in the attestation clause if made at the time of execution or, if afterwards, they must be attestated and executed by the testator and the two witnesses. Obliterations are inoperative unless attested.

A contingent will is one which is intended by the testator to be operative as a result of some event or non-event. If the condition is not satisfied the will is void. If the possibility of the event happening is stated as the reason for the will being made then it becomes operative if the event happens or not.

Wills of persons serving in the armed forces while on active service can be made without the required formalities; the same applies to seagoing naval personnel. These are known as privileged and noncupative wills.

Persons who are under no contractual disability and of sound understanding may make a will. The following are incapable of being testators:

(a) Minors – persons under 18 years of age cannot make a will unless they come under the category of privileged and noncupative wills. They can, if over 16 years of age, nominate somebody to receive any sums due at death in respect of national savings certificates, National Savings Bank deposits and any stocks and shares held on the National Savings Stock Register but not premium savings bonds. Nominations are to be in writing to the National Savings Bank witnessed by one attesting witness. Similar nominations can be made for deposits in the Trustees Savings Bank and for shares in any industrial and provident society. Revocation of the nomination is by subsequent marriage, or nomination, or by written notice of revocation.

(b) Persons of unsound mind, memory, or understanding – this is during the period of incapacity. This includes incapacity because of idiocy, general insanity, senility, excesive drunkenness which deprives a person of his reason and understanding. It is up to the person wishing to upset the will to provide the burden of proof.

Wills obtained by force, fear, fraud, or undue influence are void.

Self-assessment exercises

1   Explain the difference between a trader and a non-trader regarding a bank's liability in breach of contract.
2   What is conversion? When is a banker likely to be liable under conversion?
3   Give two examples of libellous statements which could be made by a bank.

4 What should a bank do if it discovers that it has wrongfully dishonoured a customer's cheque?
5 In what ways can a banker be seen to be negligent?
6 What is vicarious liability and give one example where a bank may be seen to have been vicariously liable for the actions of another person?

10.9   Personal representatives

Anyone who is authorised to deal with and distribute the property of a deceased person is classified as a personal representative. If a will is left then the persons named as the executors are the personal representatives. If no executor is appointed or the deceased did not leave a will, the personal representative is created when letters of administration are granted. It is the duty of personal representatives to collect the assets of the deceased, pay the debts, liabilities and testamentary expenses and distribute the remainder of the estate to the beneficiaries. If no instruction appears in the will then the personal representative is not entitled to any payment. The property of the deceased rests in the personal representative at death but his title to it is only proved by his obtaining probate of the will or letters of administration. The executor has a year's grace during which time he cannot be compelled to pay debts or distribute the estate. He has to account for all of the assets that have been gained hold of or could have been if through his negligence they are lost. Assets cannot be purchased from the estate by the executor, and personal liability must be avoided when dealing with any assets of the estate. A bank's relationship with personal representatives has already been discussed in this chapter.

10.10   Trustees

These can be defined as persons who hold property in trust for another. A definition more understandable to a banker was given by Sir Arthur Underhill who stated: 'an equitable obligation imposing upon a person (who is called a trustee) the duty of dealing with property over which he has control (which is called the trust property), for the benefit of persons (who are called the beneficiaries or cestius que trust) of whom he may be one and any one of whom may enforce obligation'. The trust is usually evidenced by means of a **trust deed**. Any individual who is capable of holding property is capable of acting as a trustee. A minor cannot be appointed as a trustee but a corporation can. There are many different kinds of trusts. Trustees are appointed to control and administer the assets in the interests of beneficiaries of the trust. A trustee has a duty to take as much care of the trust property as a reasonable man would of his own property. Unless specific instruction is given in the trust deed, he may not vary the investments which are held in the trust. He cannot make a profit out of the trust. A familiar form of trustee is a trustee in bankruptcy who has to take charge of the assets of a bankrupt, turn them into money and pay off the debts. Another is a trustee under a deed of arrangement where, with the agreement of the creditors, the trustee administers the property for the benefit of these creditors. The relationship of banker to trustee has, once again, been mentioned earlier in this chapter.

Assignments

(1) The following represents a potted history of the MBI Co. Ltd from its start in 1964 to its liquidation in 1982.

Situation
Martin Brown started a machine tool business in 1964 and registered it as the MBI Co. Ltd. During the 1960s the business prospered with orders producing a good return on capital invested in the firm. He started with a staff of ten and by 1971 this had grown to twenty-five. The 1970s found the business in a chequered situation. Martin managed to weather the oil price rises and the high levels of inflation of the first half of the decade by gaining a contract with a firm that was involved in the development of North Sea oil. The latter half of the 1970s saw a decline in the business along with the world recession. By 1980 Martin only had sufficient orders to last for eighteen months and no new orders came. In 1982 the company was put into voluntary liquidation with sufficient assets to cover the current liabilities.

Task 1 Outline the factors and procedures that the bank would follow when opening a bank account for the MBI Co. in 1964

Task 2 During the 1960s Martin was very busy building up the business and left the running of it to his chief clerk who had the job of drawing up the cheques to pay the bills. This chief clerk soon noticed that at times Martin did not look at what he was signing, so one day he slipped a blank cheque among others to be signed and then filled in the details later. This was payable to himself to the amount of £500. Later Martin discovered the fraud, sacked the chief clerk and wrote to the bank seeking some recompense for what he said was their negligence in paying out on the cheque. What do you think is the position of the bank? Back your answer up with other cases in law.

Task 3 In 1973, the new chief clerk, while Martin was abroad on business, negotiated a loan with the bank for £8000 to purchase a new piece of equipment. When the loan was due for repayment Martin refused to repay it on the grounds that the chief clerk had not had his authority to negotiate the loan, and that the articles of association, of which the bank had a copy, stated that no loan could be arranged without specific permission of Martin and his wife, co-directors.

Prepare a letter addressed to Martin stating the bank's position bearing in mind the European Communities Act 1972 and any other relevant law.

Task 4 Prepare a memorandum which could be issued to all bank managers providing a checklist of the items to bear in mind when dealing with a company customer which goes into voluntary liquidation.

2 (a) Outline the major obligations of a banker to his customer.

(b) George has an overdraft with the Warmington-on-Sea branch of the Eastlands Bank PLC for £600. He agrees to pay it off at £10 per week, and at the present time he is temporarily employed as a forecourt attendant at a local garage. The bank branch manager knows of this employment. One weekend the manager meets the garage owner and, in the course of conversation, lets it slip that George has defaulted on his repayment of the overdraft and is spending large amounts on clothes. The garage owner had been considering extending George's contract, but on hearing this information he decides not to. George hears of this and threatens to sue the bank. Advise the manager.

11 The Banker's View of a Customer's Balance Sheet

11.1 Introduction

We have seen in Chapter 9 that when a banker is asked for a loan some form of security is taken as an insurance against the default of the borrower. Sometimes a business customer will be asked to supply copies of current and previous final accounts so that the banker can analyse these and gain a greater understanding of the customer's business, its financial strength, whether the loan is reasonable for the size of the business and whether the money will be put to good use. These accounts also help the banker to discover if the source and timing of the repayments are practicable and as realistic as the customer claims. If the loan is for a short term, maybe the customer sees repayment coming from the income already generated in the firm. By looking at the final accounts, the banker can assess if this is a realistic viewpoint. On the other hand, a medium-term loan may have to be paid out of the income generated by the use to which the money is being put. Analysis of the final accounts aids assessment of this project by reference to previous projects, if any, and their profitability.

Before considering the ways in which a banker analyses these final accounts, we will look at briefly some general factors about them.

11.2 Nature and composition of final accounts

Businesses need to discover their financial position. Therefore, at least once a year, if not more regularly, the details from various accounts records are brought together and final accounts are prepared. In effect, the business tries to calculate its financial position at one point in time. Because transactions are continually going on, goods are being produced and sold, payments are being made into and by the firm by the time the accounts have been prepared the position will have changed considerably. To take a specific example, the firm will try to identify at that point in time all of the money that it is owed – this is its number of debtors. This money owed is relevant to the time period under review so it is identified as an asset of the business. What the firm does not know is exactly which of those debts are going to be unpaid – bad debts. Business accountants use their experience to calculate a possible figure for bad debts, and so provision is made in this area. However, the state of the country's economy may result in more or less firms experiencing financial difficulties so that the bad debts' provision may be too little or too much.

We might ask why firms carry out this complicated task of compiling final accounts. Apart from giving the people in the business an idea of their performance and viability, it fulfills, in the case of companies, the statutory right of shareholders to be given this information, and in the case of other businesses provides information for their income tax assessment.

We have so far talked in general about the final accounts of a business, now we will identify them.

11.21 Manufacturing account

These accounts are compiled by businesses producing goods and they show the cost of goods manufactured during the accounting period. A simple manufacturing account is shown in Fig. 11.1.

We can see the major items included in this account: during the year the firm purchased raw materials £20 000, these, with the stocks on hand, £1800, were available for processing into products and sale, but the firm did not use all of these as it had stocks of raw materials and work in progress at the end of the accounting period to the value of £1600. It, therefore, used stocks which had cost the firm £20 200. To this cost we must add the wages of the workers who produced the goods for sale, £10 000, and other expenses such as factory overheads (heating and lighting, insurance, rent or rates and any other salaries) and depreciation, £7800. This total of £38 000 can be identified as the cost of producing the goods for sale in that year (**cost of goods manufactured**). This figure is transferred to the account which deals with the trading of the firm to be compared with the money received from sales.

11.22 Trading account

The trading account helps us to calculate the gross profit of the business (*see* Fig. 11.2). It shows the cost of goods sold. This cost is calculated by taking the cost of goods manufactured and available for sale, £38 000, adding any stocks of finished goods left over from the previous period, £4100, and deducting any stocks that are still unsold from this period, £2500. This gives the total value in cost terms of the goods sold in that period. We must now deduct this from the income from sales, £58 000 to give us a gross profit of £19 500.

The Banker's View of a Customer's Balance Sheet 309

	£	£	£		£
Stocks (1 Jan 19...)				Cost of goods manufactured	
Raw materials	1 000			Transferred to Trading A/c	38 000
Working in progress	800	1 800			
Purchases		20 000			
			21 800		
Less stocks (31 Dec 19...)					
Raw materials	900				
Work in progress	700	1 600			
			20 200		
Factory wages			10 000		
			30 200		
Factory overheads			7 000		
Depreciation of machinery			800		
			38 000		38 000

Fig. 11.1 Manufacturing account of the MBI Co. for the year ended 31 December 19—

	£	£		£
Opening stock (1 Jan 19...)			Sales	58 000
Finished goods		3 000		
Cost of goods manufactured		38 000		
		41 000		
less Closing stock of finished goods		2 500		
		38 500		
Gross profit		19 500		
		58 000		58 000

Fig. 11.2 Trading account of the MBI Co. as at 31 December 19—

11.23 Profit and loss account

The gross profit shows us the relationship between the direct cost of producing the goods sold and the revenue from these sales. However, we should be aware that the operation of the business involves it in other expenses and these must be deducted from the gross profit to discover the profit or loss of the whole concern. A simplified profit and loss account is seen in Fig. 11.3.

Here we can see three kinds of expenses listed – selling, administrative and general. The items included under selling expenses are such things as advertising, transport costs on sales, salaries and commission to salesmen and any costs included in packaging. The items included in the administrative expenses are office rates and rents, office salaries, heating and lighting costs and insurance. The general expenses include an item such as depreciation of office machinery. This account could also include on the credit side any revenues from activities which are not the main purpose of the business. When all of these expenses have been totalled this figure is taken away from the gross profit to give **net profit**, in this case £10 650.

11.24 Appropriation account

If a business is a sole trader the net profit is the capital due to the owner and will be shown on the balance sheet as such. With a partnership, it is apportioned between the partners in the proportion agreed by the partnership deed or if not under Appendix A of the Partnership Act 1890. As our hypothetical firm is a company, the appropriation account looks like the one in Fig. 11.4.

This shows that the net profit is used (appropriated) to various items. These items may include taxation due on these profits, any amounts that might be put into a reserve fund and, of course, the dividends to be paid to the various types of shareholders.

11.25 The balance sheet

The balance sheet aims to give a fair and true view of the affairs of the company as at a particular date. It can also be said to show the sources of funds available to the business and the uses to which these funds have been put. Another way to look at it is to say that it shows what the business owns and what it owes. It is not an exact statement of the financial position of the business but it is a good guide. The double entry system where every recorded transaction in the accounts has a debit side and a credit side works on the principle that the total of these two sides should, if accounting procedures are correct, equal one another.

	£		£
Selling expenses	4 000	Gross profit	19 500
Administration expenses	4 750		
General expenses	100		
Net profit	10 650		
	19 500		19 500

Fig. 11.3 Profit and loss account for the MBI Co. for the year ended 31 December 19—

	£		£
Provision for taxation	4 000	Net profit	10 650
Proposed dividend	6 650		
	10 650		10 650

Fig. 11.4 Appropriation account of the MBI Co. for the year ended 31 December 19—

We have already seen, in Chapter 3, the way in which banks display their balance sheets. A traditional format is used; this shows the firm's assets on the left side of the account and the liabilities on the right. For our imaginary company this is shown in Fig. 11.5.

However a linear format is now used by many companies and businesses. For our company this would look like the one shown in Fig. 11.6.

It is useful to look at these items in detail.

(1) *Fixed assets* – these represent those assets which, in the main, have been used to produce the goods the company has for sale. They are classed as fixed as their value does not change greatly in the short term and are, therefore, seen by their owners as long lasting or semi-permanent. Our balance sheet in Fig. 11.6 shows that these assets do not keep their initial value throughout their life. It is good accounting practice to realistically appraise the current value of these assets as in the case of property, for example, its value can, and often does, increase in value so that the figure should be adjusted each year to take this into account. On the other hand, an asset such as machinery often depreciates each year so it would be wrong to show too high a value on the balance sheet as this would not reflect its true worth to the company. We have already seen the acknowledgement of this depreciation charge in the manufacturing and profit and loss accounts.

(2) *Intangible assets* – some balance sheets show assets which the firm can claim to own although they do not physically exist. One such is **goodwill**. This represents the reputation that the business has built up over the years it has traded. Sometimes it is only calculated when the business is sold so that the previous owner can be recompensed for the work he has put into building up this good reputation. Other items included in this classification include:

– preliminary (or formation) expenses
– expenses or discounts connected with the issue of capital or debentures
– suspense accounts
– patents and trade marks

These are also known as **fictitious assets**. Figure 11.7 shows an example of such assets.

(3) *Current assets* – these are also known as **circulating assets** for their value changes from day to day. For example, the day after the accounts are drawn up a debtor may have sent a cheque. Thus the debtor figure is reduced by this amount but the cash in hand goes up. It is useful to consider these in detail.

(a) *Stocks and work in progress* – the value of these as shown on the balance sheet is really an estimation. As we can see from the manufacturing and trading account, these consist of stocks of raw materials, partially finished products (known as work in progress) and finished products ready for sale. This valuation is a problem for the business. Does it use a system which tries to identify the actual cost to the business? Does it use a system which

Liabilities	£	£	Assets	£	£
Share capital			Fixed assets		
Authorised capital			Factory	45 000	
100 000 £1 ordinary shares		100 000	Plant and machinery (after depreciation)	26 000	
			Office equipment	18 000	86 000
Issued capital					
80 000 £1 ordinary shares		80 000	Stocks and work in progress	4 100	
Reserved		10 000	Debtors	100 000	
			Cash at bank	3 000	
Current liabilities			Cash in hand	550	17 650
Taxation provision	4 000				
Proposed dividend	6 650				
Creditors	3 000	13 650			
		103 650			103 650

Fig. 11.5 Balance sheet of the MBI Co. as at 31 December 19— (old style)

	£	£	£
Fixed assets			
Factory	45 000		
Plant and machinery (after depreciation)	26 000		
Motor vehicles	15 000		
			86 000
Current assets			
Stocks and work in progress	4 100		
Debtors	10 000		
Cash in hand and at bank	3 550		
		17 650	
less			
Current liabilities			
Creditors	3 000		
Taxation provision	4 000		
Proposed dividend	6 650		
		13 650	
			4 000
Net current assets			90 000
Represented by			
Share capital			80 000
Reserves			10 000
			90 000

Fig. 11.6 Balance sheet of the MBI Co. as at 31 December 19— (linear style)

shows the replacement cost to the business at current prices? Or does it, knowing that over the year concerned the price of these products has varied, try to calculate the average cost over that year? The business has to avoid either overvaluing or undervaluing its stocks in case it should have to either replace them quickly or to realise cash on them. It is important that an accurate figure for stock value is reached as this has a considerable effect on the final figures for gross and net profit.

(b) *Debtors* – this is the amount of money that the business is owed by its customers for the sale of its products. The business should attempt to identify those debts which might become unpaid. Although it will not necessarily be able to identify specific customers, it should calculate a realistic figure to represent bad debts that might occur. Again this helps to give a more realistic value of the business's worth.

(c) *Cash in hand and at the bank* – these items are really self-explanatory. For some businesses, cash in hand is very necessary as they deal with the general public every day and need to give change. For others, major payments are by cheque or credit transfer so that their base of cash is very small or non-existent. As we will see later there is a danger in having too much or too little cash.

(4) *Current liabilities* – these represent the demands on the business which are due to be met in the short term. As we can see from Fig. 11.6 these may consist of taxation, proposed dividends and creditors.

(i) *Taxation* – all income, earned or unearned of a sufficient level is subject

The Banker's View of a Customer's Balance Sheet 315

Liabilities	£	£	£	Assets	£	£	£
Share capital				Fixed assets			
Authorised capital				Factory			45 000
100 000 £1 ordinary shares			100 000	Plant and machinery at cost	30 000		
				less depreciation	4 000	26 000	
Issued capital				Motor vehicles at cost	20 000		
80 000 £1 ordinary shares		80 000		less depreciation	5 000	15 000	86 000
Reserves		24 000					
				Intangible assets			
				Goodwill			41 000
Current liabilities				Stocks and work in progress		1 400	
Taxation provision	4 000			Debtors		10 000	
Proposed taxation	6 650			Cash at bank		3 000	
Creditors	3 000	13 650		Cash in hand		550	17 650
			117 650				117 650

Fig. 11.7 Balance sheet of the MBI Co. as at 31 December 19— (adjusted)

to taxation. Sole traders and partnerships pay income tax, but under a different schedule than that operating under the PAYE system. Companies are subject to corporation tax. The size of the income has to be determined and this has to be agreed between the earner and the Inland Revenue. Since a business's financial year does not coincide always with the fiscal year, it is good practice to try and identify the liability for tax and to make provision for this out of profits. This should ensure that the liability will be met when it falls due. Some businesses pay tax in advance and receive certificates as evidence of this payment. These can be shown as assets and can be used to offset the future tax liability.

(ii) *Proposed dividends* – until shareholders meet and accept the final accounts and the proposed dividend payment, this latter must be shown as a future, short-term liability.

(iii) *Creditors* – on our proforma balance sheet this is shown as being £3000. This represents the money due to those businesses from whom our firm has purchased goods and services. These must be paid as and when the money falls due in order to maintain creditworthiness.

(5) *Long-term liabilities*

(a) *Capital* – in our proforma balance sheet this is shown as share capital of £80 000. This represents the money which has been subscribed by the owners (shareholders) of the firm for its use. In a sole proprietor business these funds are usually provided by the single owner, and in a partnership by the partners, sometimes in various amounts. In the traditional balance sheet (Fig. 11.5) we have shown both the authorised and issued capital. You will no doubt remember from your other studies that authorised capital is the amount that is itemised in the memorandum of association. The issued figure shows us if the company has used up its authorised amount, or if further funds can still be raised without recourse to the shareholders. Thus to increase the authorised amount, companies must seek permission from their shareholders by means of a special resolution passed at a meeting of these shareholders.

If the shares are sold over a period of time with what are known as **calls** for shareholders' money, any shares which are not fully paid up must be shown as being **partially paid**. Thus any future calls become liabilities on the company but they also enable the company to use these funds for development. In the event of the company falling into financial difficulties these funds can be used to meet any outstanding liabilities.

Sometimes this capital is subscribed for over a period of time and the company can sell the share at a value which is greater than the face value. For example, a £1 share may be sold for £1.25. Thus the extra money received is shown as a **premium**. At the same time, if the shares have to be sold at less than their face value then this **discount** must also be shown.

(b) *Reserves* – generally a business will try to plough back some of its profits into the business. This money still belongs to the owners and, should the business be liquidated and sufficient funds be left over after the payment of the other liabilities, then the owners are due this money. Although the Companies Act 1967 removed the need to distinguish between capital and revenue reserves the difference is still of interest. Revenue reserves are the result of the business not distributing profits. It would be wrong to think of these as a reserve of cash for, as we can see on our proforma balance sheet, revenue reserves stand at £10 000 while the cash on the assets side stands at only £2500. These reserves have been absorbed into the other assets of the business. The second type are capital reserves and these have been accumulated in various ways to include such things as share premiums, or the increase in the value of the fixed assets over their book value. Some balance sheets do not show the different types of reserves.

Self-assessment exercises

1 Why might a banker call for sight of a business customer's final accounts when the latter seeks a loan?
2 Which accounts would be included in these final accounts?
3 What items are included in a manufacturing account?
4 How can we discover the full cost of the goods produced for sale?
5 What is the difference between gross profit and net profit?
6 What kind of items might be found in the appropriation account?
7 Restyle this traditional balance sheet into a linear style.

Chiminster Engineering Co. Ltd

	£000		£000	
Ordinary shares	340	Fixed assets		
Share premium	60	Premises and equipment		160
Current liabilities		Fixtures and fittings		120
Creditors	100	Current assets		
Overdraft	20	Stocks	80	
		Debtors	160	240
	520			520

8 Define and give examples of intangible assets.
9 What is the difference between fixed and current assets?
10 What kind of items are contained in the stocks of a business which is manufacturing products?
11 How can a business build up reserves?

11.3 How a banker looks at the final accounts of a business

We have already stated that a banker, when asked for a business loan, may seek to look at the financial state of a business. In Chapter 9 we saw that the whole proposition is the important consideration.

What we must appreciate is that analysis of the final accounts does not just mean calculating a number of ratios. What is important is the ability to use these calculations to decide the viability of the business. Thus the banker must know the significance and implication of the results of the calculations. Thus as we calculate the ratios, we too must consider the significance and effects of these results. For the purpose of understanding these ratios we will consider the figures given in Fig. 11.8.

These ratios are as follows:

11.31 Rate of stock turnover

This is calculated by the following formula:

$$\text{RATE OF STOCK TURNOVER} = \frac{\text{COST OF GOODS SOLD}}{\text{AVERAGE STOCK}}$$

In our trading profit and loss account

$$1983 = \frac{360\,000}{90\,000} = 4$$

$$1984 = \frac{436\,000}{109\,000} = 4$$

We use the cost of goods sold rather than the full sales figure as the latter includes profit added and this is a variable figure. The average stock figure is calculated by finding the average of the opening and closing stock. If the monthly figures are available then these can be used. For 1984 the average stock is

$$\frac{95\,000 + 123\,000}{2} = 109\,000$$

This figure shows us the number of times the stocks changed over the year. It is important for a firm to carry adequate stocks so as to meet any sudden demands from customers; it is bad for its image if it runs out of stocks. Obtaining additional stocks quickly might be more expensive than the loss of revenue associated with maintaining higher levels of stocks. On the other hand, too high levels of stock can mean that money is not being used adequately or that the wrong goods are being stocked. We can say for our hypothetical company that its stocks are held on the shelves for an average of thirteen weeks (52/4). The quicker the stock turns over then generally the greater the profits. There is no standard rate applicable to all businesses – this depends upon the nature of the business. A grocer needs a quicker turnover than a business which can keep its goods on the shelves for a longer time. The amount of stock is decided by the ease with which the firm can obtain replacements. A fall in the rate of stock turnover is a sign

	1983		1984	
	£	£	£	£
Sales		600 000		700 000
Opening stock	85 000		95 000	
Purchases	370 000		464 000	
	455 000		559 000	
Closing stock	95 000		123 000	
Cost of goods sold		360 000		436 000
Gross profit		240 000		264 000
Variable expenses	40 000		64 000	
Fixed costs	170 000		180 000	
		210 000		244 000
Net profit		30 000		20 000
Interest on capital: Black	500		500	
Brown	4 000		4 000	
Salary: Black	10 000		10 000	
Profit: Black	6 200		2 200	
Brown	9 300		3 300	
		30 000		20 000
Balance sheets at 30 April		*1981*		*1982*
Fixed assets				
Premises at cost		250 000		250 000
Equipment at cost	120 000		150 000	
less depreciation to date	60 000	60 000	70 000	80 000
		310 000		330 000
Current assets				
Stock	95 000		123 000	
Debtors	120 000		160 000	
Bank and cash	15 000		—	
	230 000		283 000	
Current liabilities				
Creditors	38 000		44 000	
Overdraft	—		69 000	
	38 000		113 000	
Working capital		192 000		170 000
		502 000		500 000
Financed by:				
Capital A/c: Black	50 000		50 000	
Brown	400 000	450 000	400 000	450 000
Current A/c: Black	30 000		30 700	
Brown	22 000	52 000	19 300	50 000
		502 000		500 000

Fig. 11.8 Black and Brown Partners: Trading, profit and loss and appropriation accounts for the year ended 30 April

of overstocking, or falling sales, or both. A business is advised to consider both in such circumstances.

If the business is one that is common to the area, a banker will know what is an adequate rate of stock. If the business is not one with which he has experience, he can enquire of other branches which might have this knowledge. He will, therefore, be able to see if the figure is satisfactory.

11.32 Creditor ratio

This is calculated as follows:

$$\frac{\text{TRADE CREDITORS}}{\text{PURCHASES}}$$

For our final accounts these are as follows:

$$1983 \ \frac{38\,000}{370\,000} = 0.103$$

$$1984 \ \frac{44\,000}{464\,000} = 0.095$$

From these we can calculate the length of the credit period taken.

For 1983 this was 37.59 days or 5.36 weeks – 365 × 0.103
For 1984 this was 34.68 days or 4.94 weeks – 365 × 0.095

The position of the business is such that in 1984 it has not taken as long a credit period as in 1983. It might be that it has made more purchases in order to gain a price advantage. It must be remembered that a business does not have a right to credit, and if it runs into difficulties or economic conditions deteriorate then any credit given might be removed.

A high credit ratio might mean that a business is suffering from a shortage of cash so that it is unable to meet the bills as they come in. It might also mean that it is in such a strong position that it can dictate a long credit period to its sellers. The former is often the case, and the banker will often be asked to grant an overdraft, or for an existing agreement to be increased to cover cash flow shortages. The banker should consider the purchasing pattern of the business which may be subject to troughs and peaks. If a peak has occurred just prior to the compilation of the accounts then the true position may not be reflected.

11.33 Debtor ratio

This is calculated as follows:

$$\frac{\text{TRADE DEBTORS}}{\text{SALES}}$$

For our final accounts these are:

$$1983 \; \frac{120\,000}{600\,000} = 0.2$$

$$1984 \; \frac{160\,000}{700\,000} = 0.22$$

From these figures we can calculate the average length of time that the business gives credit to its customers.

For 1983 this was 10.04 weeks or 2.4 months – 52 × 0.2
For 1984 this was 11.44 weeks or 2.64 months – 52 × 0.22

This shows that the firm has allowed a slightly longer term for credit to its customers in 1984 than in 1983. The length of credit allowed debtors is different from business to business. Retail businesses are usually given longer periods of credit by wholesalers than the latter are by manufacturers.

11.34 Stock ratios

The object of calculating this ratio is to establish the length of time that the stocks on hand, at the time that the balance sheet is drawn up, will last out at current rates of production or sales. For the calculation of this figure we use the closing stock value rather than the average stock figure.

Our fictitious business is a retailer so that its stocks are final goods. Thus the stock ratio is calculated as follows:

$$\frac{\text{CLOSING STOCK}}{\text{SALES}}$$

and are seen as

$$1983 \; \frac{95\,000}{600\,000} = 0.16$$

$$1984 \; \frac{123\,000}{700\,000} = 0.18$$

This is equal to 8.32 weeks for 1983 (52 weeks × 0.16) and 9.36 weeks for 1984 (52 weeks × 0.18). In other types of businesses it is possible to calculate the raw materials ratio and the work in progress ratio. In these cases the stock figures are divided by the amount of production or work done. These are calculated as follows:

Sales plus/minus increase/decrease in work in progress

or

Sales plus/minus increase/decrease in finished stock.

These figures tell the banker how long the business is able to carry on if only it has the existing stocks available. Changes one year with another tell if the business is better or worse at being able to survive in the event of a drying up of suppliers.

11.35 Working capital

This is calculated as follows:

    CURRENT ASSETS *minus* CURRENT LIABILITIES

For our final accounts this is:

    1983 £230 000 − £38 000 = £192 000
    1984 £283 000 − £113 000 = £170 000

This shows that the business has sufficient funds in the current assets to meet current liabilities and still have sufficient stocks to carry on the business and also give its debtors an adequate length of credit. We can show these figures as a percentage of sales:

    1983 – 32 per cent
    1984 – 24.28 per cent

These show that for every £100 of sales in 1983 £32 of working capital was employed at the balance sheet date and in 1984 this was £24.28. The value of these two ratios lies in the fact that they show how much additional working capital is required for a contemplated expansion in sales.

In some cases, businesses start to ignore the importance of working capital as assisting the operation of the business, even though they are aware of the importance of fixed capital requirements.

11.36 Current ratio

This is calculated as follows:

    CURRENT ASSETS : CURRENT LIABILITIES

For our final accounts this is:

    1983 £230 000 : £38 000 = 6 : 1
    1984 £283 000 : £113 000 = 2.5 : 1

A ratio of 2:1 is seen as satisfactory. Obviously from the position of our hypothetical firm its current ratio in 1983 was too high and the business was either carrying too high stocks, allowing debtors too long in which to pay, or carrying too much cash with regard to assets, while on the liabilities side it may be paying its bills too soon. From the figures it appears that it is the liabilities side that has caused the major change with the firm taking on a large overdraft of £69 000. It might be the case that the nature of the business is such that the 1984 ratio of 2.5 : 1 is too small. It is always a good thing for a banker to look at the trend over a number of years to assess the implication of any variations.

One other ratio we can calculate is the **acid test** or **quick assets ratio**. This considers only those current assets that are near to liquidity such as cash and debtors. Stocks are excluded as these may become debtors before they are finally cash, and if they are sold for cash it may be for less than their value. The formula for this ratio is as follows:

CURRENT ASSETS − STOCK : CURRENT LIABILITIES

For our final accounts these ratios are:

1983 £230 000 − £95 000 : £38 000
= £135 000 : £38 000
= 3.5 : 1
1984 £283 000 − £123 000 : £113 000
= £160 000 : £113 000
= 1.4 : 1

This ratio is useful in showing the liquidity of the business. Once again a study over a number of years is a better indication of the viability of the business. A ratio of 1 : 1 is satisfactory but a ratio of 1.5 : 1 is much better. Any higher means that the business might have too much money lying idle in debtors or cash.

11.37 Gross profit to sales

This is a revenue account ratio. It is the most widely used and probably the oldest. It is calculated as follows:

$$\frac{\text{GROSS PROFIT}}{\text{SALES}} \times \frac{100}{1}$$

For our trading figures these are:

$$1983 \; \frac{£240\,000}{£600\,000} \times \frac{100}{1}$$

= 30 per cent

$$1984 \; \frac{£264\,000}{£700\,000} \times \frac{100}{1}$$

= 37.7 per cent

We can use this percentage to compare two businesses, or to compare different accounting periods within the same business.

It must be remembered that these figures are averaged over the whole year and that, because of the cyclical nature of business, a similar figure may not occur in future years. The firm needs to be aware that profits earned at the close of the financial year may be higher or lower than the average. There may be trends occurring towards the end which have been masked by the opposite trends in the early part of the year. If the bank manager is presented with a gross profit ratio of a certain size then his experience of other firms will help him to assess the favourability of this figure. If his experience does not cover this type of business, no doubt he can get advice from head or district office, or even from customers who are in a similar line of business.

11.38 Net profit to sales

This is similar to the gross profit ratio but we use the net profit figure as follows:

$$\frac{\text{NET PROFIT}}{\text{SALES}} \times \frac{100}{1}$$

For our trading accounts these are:

$$1983 \; \frac{£30\,000}{£600\,000} \times \frac{100}{1}$$

$$= 5 \text{ per cent}$$

$$1984 \; \frac{£20\,000}{£700\,000} \times \frac{100}{1}$$

$$= 2.8 \text{ per cent}$$

This ratio is not all that satisfactory when comparing results from year to year, as net profits are calculated by deducting all costs from sales not only those that are related to the sales. A more realistic ratio is the **gross profit to net profit ratio**. For our final accounts these are:

$$1983 \; \frac{£30\,000}{£240\,000} \times \frac{100}{1}$$

$$= 12.5 \text{ per cent}$$

$$1984 \; \frac{£20\,000}{£264\,000} \times \frac{100}{1}$$

$$= 7.5 \text{ per cent}$$

Comparing these figures over time the banker will be able to identify whether costs control has been exercised. A fall in this percentage could mean the business's indirect costs and expenses are rising at a greater rate than the direct costs.

11.39 Return on capital employed

This is calculated as follows:

$$\frac{\text{NET PROFIT BEFORE TAX}}{\text{SHAREHOLDERS STAKE + LONG TERM LOANS}} \times \frac{100}{1}$$

For our final figures these are:

$$1983 \; \frac{£30\,000}{£502\,000} \times \frac{100}{1}$$

$$= 5.98 \text{ per cent}$$

$$1984 \; \frac{£20\,000}{£500\,000} \times \frac{100}{1}$$

$$= 4 \text{ per cent}$$

This gives a view of the profitability of the business. It is useful to compare previous figures, and if they are falling it is important to investigate the matter further. This could indicate that the business is not using its capital as effectively as it once was. The banker may have had previous experience of other similar firms so that he should be able to assess how realistic these figures are. If he does not have this experience, no doubt enquiries can be made outside the branch.

11.310 Sales to net worth

Before considering this ratio we must look at the meaning and composition of net worth. When a business is liquidated its assets realise a certain value. From these funds the creditors and other short-term liabilities are paid. Any balance left over belongs to the owners. This balance is known as the **net worth**. It is calculated in a company by taking the paid-up share capital plus retained profit less any intangible or fictitious assets. These latter are deducted because they are unlikely to be realised at their book value if the business is liquidated. With our hypothetical balance sheet the net worth is easily extracted. For the two years it is:

1983 £450 000 + £52 000 = £502 000
1984 £450 000 + £50 000 = £500 000

Thus the ratios of sales to net worth are:

1983 £600 000 : £502 000 = 1.1 : 1
1984 £700 000 : £500 000 = 1.5 : 1

If the ratio is too high, this is an indication that the business is overtrading. This shows that there is too much activity going on from a very limited capital base. On the other hand, a low base might be an indicator that the business is not using the capital employed in the business fully.

Another area not shown on the final accounts is the nature of any loans made to the business. When asked for a loan, no banker is interested in becoming a major creditor nor will he wish to put more money into a business than the owners of that business. Therefore, the bank will want to know details about other loans. These details include the length of the loans, the nature of any security offered against the loan, whether the directors have made any loans. If they have the bank may require them to sign a **letter** of **postponement** in which they postpone their repayment until the bank has been repaid. Another aspect of loans in which the bank will be interested is the relationship of debt capital to equity capital. This is known as the **gearing**. Debt capital consists of loans from the bank, or directors, or debentures. These generally carry a fixed rate of interest. The equity capital includes ordinary shares, reserves and preference shares, although the inclusion of the latter, if they are not redeemable, is questionable as they form part of the permanent investment in the firm. If the firm has a high ratio of debt capital to equity capital it is said to be highly geared, if it is the other way around it has low gearing. High or low gearing affects the cost of capital to the business. A firm with high gearing faces a large demand for interest payments out of profits, whilst a firm with low gearing is not in this position. In the former case, it might be in the position that the interest payments on the debt capital take up all of the profits so leaving nothing for the equity capital holders. Also a firm with high gearing may not make sufficient profits to pay out the fixed interest dividends and so find itself facing a financial problem if these creditors foreclose on any security they may hold. It should not be assumed that a high gearing is a bad thing. In some cases such a firm may have a fairly stable and calculable return so that it is able to meet its fixed interest payments without any difficulty. For example, an investment trust company may have its funds invested in similar fixed interest securities.

Self-assessment exercises

1   What does the rate of stock turnover show us about a business and what do changes in this rate tell us?
2   How can we tell how much credit a firm is giving and how much it is taking?
3   What does the stock ratio tell us about a business?
4   How would you calculate the working capital for a business?
5   What is the value of calculating the working capital?
6   Explain, fully, the difference between the current assets ratio and the quick assets ratio.
7   How would you calculate the return on capital employed?

8 What is net worth and how is it calculated?
9 A business has the following:
   shareholders' capital – 100 000 £1 ordinary shares
   75 000 8.5 per cent non-redeemable preference shares.
   Discuss the gearing of this firm.

11.4 Bankers' use of future financial projections

The final accounts we have considered so far represent the activities of the businesses that have gone on in the past – what is called historical accounting. Since a loan represents a commitment to the future of the business then this is the time period which is of interest to the banker. The analysis of the past performance of the business acts as a guide to what may happen in the future but it is no guarantee. In the interest of the continuity of the business the management will seek to forecast what the future is likely to be. For this they use budgetary techniques. From these forecasts the management compile estimated final accounts on the assumption that these forecasts will materialise. This involves predicting the future sales, production costs, economic conditions and the influencing factors on these predictions; the accuracy of the projections reduces the further into the future the company forecasts. Another reason for compiling these forecasts and final accounts is to have a comparison with actual results as they occur and to try and analyse the reasons why they are not the same, if this is the case. A bank will wish to see these projections of a firm's future to try and discover the future viability of the firm. These, with the actual results when they happen, also give the bank manager some indication of the success or otherwise of the management's ability to predict future performance. This is useful with regard to any future requests for advances.

The three main areas of projected finance that a bank manager will be interested in are:

(1) the projected profit and loss and trading accounts for any time from six months hence.

(2) the projected balance sheet outcome for the same time period.

(3) the cash budget.

The banker considers any figures given as estimates; we will look at the cash budget in greater detail.

A typical cash budget is shown in Fig. 11.9.

This shows when the business is likely to meet a short fall in funds coming in, in comparison to payments out, and, therefore, likely to need an overdraft; and when it is likely to have a surplus. A banker must make certain that all expenses are included. The actual out-turn in the figures can be checked against these projections each month to discover their accuracy.

A banker may wish to find out if the business has sufficient funds to

Details	Jan £	Feb £	March £	April £	May £	June £	July £	August £	Sep £	Oct £	Nov £	Dec £
Receipts												
Cash sales	1 000	1 000	800	800	800	800	800	800	800	1 000	1 000	1 000
Credit sales			20 000	20 000	19 000	19 000	18 000	18 000	18 000	18 000	19 000	20 000
	1 000	1 000	20 800	20 800	19 800	19 800	18 800	18 800	18 800	19 000	20 000	21 000
Payments												
Assets	40 000											
Goodwill	10 000											
Stock	25 000											
Miscellaneous expenses	2 000											
Purchases												
Cash		800	800	640	640	640	640	640	640	640	800	800
Credit		16 000	16 000	15 200	15 200	14 400	14 400	14 400	14 400	15 200	16 000	16 800
Expenses	1 500	1 500	2 100	1 600	1 600	2 200	1 700	1 700	2 000	2 500	1 500	2 100
	78 500	18 300	18 900	17 440	17 440	17 240	16 740	16 740	17 040	18 340	18 300	19 700
Cash increase/decrease during month	−77 500	−17 300	+1 900	+3 360	+2 360	+2 560	+2 060	+2 060	+1 760	+660	+1 700	+1 300
Capital available	75 000											
Closing cash												
In hand (overdraft)												
At end of month	(2 500)	(19 800)	(17 900)	(14 540)	(12 180)	(9 620)	(7 560)	(5 500)	(3 740)	(3 080)	(1 380)	(80)

Maximum overdraft required for February 19—

Fig. 11.9 Cash budget for MBI Co. for the year ended 31 December 19—

meet any repayments on loans. For this purpose, a **funds flow statement** can be compiled. For this the banker makes use of the following calculation:

          RETAINED PROFITS
plus   PROVISION FOR FUTURE TAXATION
plus   DEPRECIATION FOR COMING YEAR
minus CURRENT TAXATION
minus INTEREST PAYMENTS ON PROPOSED LOAN

The retained profits are taken from the profit and loss account. The taxation provision will not be due to the Inland Revenue for at least one year so it is added back as is depreciation, for this is purely a bookkeeping exercise and no actual cash flows out of the business. Current taxation is deducted for this has to be paid before nine months is up. The interest on the loan is also deducted as this has to be paid within the next year. The final figure is an indication to the bank as to how successfully or otherwise the business is managing to maintain adequate funds to meet current commitments.

Self-assessment exercises

1   In which main areas of a business's projected financial statistics is a bank interested?
2   How can a banker find out if a business has sufficient funds to meet repayment of any loan it may be given by the bank. What calculations are necessary to discover this?

11.5 Business as a going/gone concern

One of the major concerns of a lending banker is the safety of the advance. There must be some kind of assurance that the business's affairs will go according to expectations and that the loan will return to the bank. Hence the reason for analysis of past and future finances of the business to obtain some guide as to its viability. However, all these figures have been prepared in the belief that the business is going to continue – in other words that it is a **going concern**. However, in reality, should the business fail and the assets have to be realised, they may not all realise the value shown on the books. Therefore, it is useful to appraise the balance sheet as if the business were a **gone concern** – that is if it had been liquidated. If this is done the result may be very revealing, for it may show that it is worth considerably less.

It is useful for us to consider just how the banker appraises the realisable value of the various assets held by the firm.

11.51 Land and premises

The banker should, if necessary, get a professional valuation as the book value will not be correct. The premises placed on the land may be of a specialised nature so that its value on resale may be very little, especially if the reason for failure is due to a fall off in demand for the use of the goods or service. If the premises are of general use then an alternative use may be found. With land, its resale value will depend upon whether it is freehold or leasehold, whether there are restrictive covenants attached to it, or local authority planning permission is easy or difficult to obtain. It also depends upon the ease with which the land can be put to an alternative use. It is often difficult to assess the value these assets would realise on liquidation. Generally, in recent years, their value has risen in the UK, but this is not to say that this will continue, or that if it does that the rise will be at the same rate as in previous years. In some cases the book value may not be realistic. Some firms may have been good at assessing the annual value of these assets while others may have been totally wrong so showing them as either over- or undervalued.

11.52 Plant and machinery

Generally there is a limited second-hand market for these assets. Their realised value depends upon their age and condition. If the business has been in a financially dangerous position for some time, it could well be that these are old and only worth scrap value. Once again the extent to which these assets are of a specialist nature is also important, for highly specialised plant and machinery may be difficult to resell. Also to be considered is their ability to be transported. If this is difficult then they may not be attractive to a new owner.

11.53 Vehicles

Their condition is an important factor in their resale value. If they have been maintained and if they have been depreciated realistically then they could achieve something very near to their book value. However, the danger is that a business in financial difficulties often neglects these aspects first in order to appear to be more financially sound. Thus if and when they are sold it may be for something much less than the value shown on the books.

11.54 Stocks

As we have seen, these stocks consist of raw materials, components, partially finished goods and finished goods depending upon the type of business.

Raw materials and components are generally easily resold so that the banker can take the figure on the books as being nearly correct as to the value.

Partially finished goods or work in progress do not realise their value so that this should be written down for resale purposes.

Stocks of finished goods may only sell at a reduced price as 'liquidated stocks' and a figure of at least 50 per cent of the book value should be taken as the realisable value.

11.55 Debtors

As these are debts owed to the business, they should be collectable. If the business has been realistic in its provision for bad debts then what is recovered should be very near to their value in the accounts. If, however, this debtor figure includes some debts which are considerably long overdue, the book figure will not be realistic.

11.56 Cash and bank balances

If the business is not in financial difficulties and the banker is only looking at it from that point of view as an exercise, these figures could well be positive and, therefore, realisable. However, if the business is really in difficulties then it uses up its cash reserves quickly so there is nothing in these assets on liquidation and indeed the business may have a sizeable overdraft.

As we have seen the valuation of a firm, should it need to be liquidated, is difficult. We have not discussed what the banker would do with intangible assets. Obviously, things like goodwill are completely discarded but it may be able to salvage something from the patents and trade marks it is holding. Generally these intangible assets are disregarded altogether.

If the business were liquidated, the funds gained would need to be applied to the liabilities in the prescribed order. It is a useful exercise for the banker to consider this application and try to determine where the bank stands in relation to repayment out of the realised assets. In the event of a short fall in funds in relation to its liabilities, the bank may only receive a percentage of any loan made. To be able to ascertain this position beforehand gives the banker greater insight into the viability, from the bank's point of view, of any loan asked for. Under statute there are certain preferential creditors

who are due payments from liquidated assets before other creditors and these include:
(1) within certain limits the wages due to employees;
(2) taxation due on profits;
(3) unremitted PAYE;
(4) VAT due to Customs and Excise.

Self-assessment exercises

1 What is the difference between a business as a 'going' and as a 'gone' concern?
2 Which assets, when realised, are likely to achieve near to their book value?
3 If a business is in financial difficulties which assets are likely to be of little value when realised? Why?
4 If a bank had made a loan to a business and the business has to go into liquidation which other creditors are likely to be given preferential treatment for payment from the realised assets?

11.6 Effects of a bank advance on the business balance sheet

In the interest of simplicity we will consider advances for specified purposes.

11.61 A loan to purchase some fixed asset

If we assume a customer has made a proposal to the bank for a medium-term loan to purchase a new piece of equipment then we could see the effect as follows:

Balance sheet of MBI Co. Ltd as at 31 December 19.......

Liabilities	£000	Assets	£000
Long-term liabilities	100	Fixed assets	80
Current liabilities	50		
–		Current assets	70
		–	
	150		150

Suppose MBI Co. Ltd negotiate this medium-term loan of £10 000 then the balance sheet will now look like this:

Liabilities		Assets	
	£000		£000
Long-term liabilities	100	Fixed assets	90
Medium-term liabilities	10	Current liabilities	70
Current liabilities	50		
	160		160

Although the balance sheet ratios of working capital, current ratio and acid test ratio have not been changed two areas could be altered. The first is the net worth of the company, although one would expect the fixed assets purchased by the loan to realise as near to their book value as is possible. At the same time the gearing of the business has now changed. We cannot state definitely whether this loan will be for a fixed or variable interest rate. This depends upon a number of factors. If it is fixed it is to be hoped that profits will be sufficient in the future to meet these repayments.

11.62 An overdraft given to pay off other creditors

Consideration of the effects of this type of transaction show that the nature of the current liabilities have changed. For example, if we itemise the current liabilities in the balance sheet of the MBI Co. Ltd we see the following effect:

Current liabilities and assets of MBI Co. Ltd (before overdraft)

	£	£
Current assets		
Stock		30 000
Debtors		35 000
Cash		5000
		70 000
less Current liabilities		
Taxation	10 000	
Dividends	10 000	
Creditors	30 000	
		50 000
Working capital		20 000

Suppose an overdraft of £15 000 is negotiated to pay off some of the creditors then the position is as follows:

Current liabilities and assets of MBI Co. Ltd (after overdraft)

	£	£
Current assets		
Stock		30 000
Debtors		35 000
		65 000
less Current liabilities		
Taxation	10 000	
Dividends	10 000	
Creditors	10 000	
Overdraft	15 000	
		45 000
Working capital		20 000

The working capital is still £20 000 but we have a considerable change in the structure of these assets and liabilities.

The current asset ratio has changed from 1.4 : 1 to 1.44 : 1.

The acid test ratio has changed from 0.9 : 1 to 0.99 : 1 – a slight improvement.

11.63 An overdraft used to purchase a fixed asset

If the MBI Co. Ltd were to use an overdraft to purchase a fixed asset then the revised balance sheet could be seen as follows:

Balance sheet of MBI Co. Ltd as at 31 December 19.......

Liabilities	£000	Assets	£000
Long-term liabilities	100	Fixed assets	90
Current liabilities	60	Current assets	70
	160		160

If we itemise the current assets and liabilities we see that these are:

Current liabilities and assets of MBI Co. Ltd (after overdraft)

	£	£
Current assets		
Stock		30 000
Debtors		35 000
Cash		5000
		70 000
less Current liabilities		
Taxation	10 000	
Dividends	10 000	
Creditors	30 000	
Overdraft	10 000	
		60 000
Working capital		10 000

Now our working capital has halved to £10 000.

The current ratio has reduced from 1.4 : 1 to 1.16 : 1.
The acid test ratio has reduced from 0.9 : 1 to 0.66 to 1.

The position is now worsened since the return on the asset purchased might be sometime in the future and the repayment of the overdraft might be soon. One fact should be stated – overdrafts should not be used to purchase fixed assets.

Self-assessment exercises

The following is a balance sheet of a business. Show how the following loans affect its structure:
1   A bank loan of £15 000 to purchase new plant and machinery.
2   An overdraft of £5000 to pay off all the trade creditors.

Balance sheet of New Images Co. Ltd as at 31 March 19.......

	£000	£000	£000
Fixed assets			
Factory	42		
Plant and machinery	22		
Motor vehicles	20		
			84
Current assets			
Stocks and work in progress	5		
Trade debtors	12		
Cash in hand and at bank	3		
		20	
less Current liabilities			
Trade creditors	8		
Taxation provision	2		
Proposed dividend	5		
		15	
Net current assets			5
			89
Represented by:			
Share capital			80
Reserves			9
			89

Assignments

1   The following are certain balances taken from the books of the Redrite Hydro Co. Ltd:

	£
Purchases	47 000
Debtors	15 000
Factory wages	19 000
Bank account	10 200
Factory overheads	11 000
Office equipment (*after depreciation*)	22 000
Depreciation of machinery	1 200
Sales	146 000
Plant and machinery (*after depreciation*)	61 400
Reserves	40 000
General expenses	2 000
Selling expenses	8 000
Factory	180 000
Administration expenses	15 000
Creditors	12 000
Authorised and issued capital	200 000

Notes

(a) Stocks

	01.01.1984	31.12.1984
Raw materials (£)	4000	5000
Work in progress (£)	2000	2500
Finished products (£)	2000	3000

(b) Taxation is 30 per cent of net profit and the remainder is to be paid as dividends.

Using the above figures compile the final accounts for the Redrite Hydro Co. Ltd.

2 From the above figures calculate any ratios you feel will help you in an analysis of the viability of the company seeking a loan of £50 000 from a bank and then go on to estimate its value as a 'gone' concern.

Index

Administration of Justice Act, 1982 302
Agents 182–3, 277–8
Agricultural Credit Act, 1928 96
Agricultural Mortgage Corporation 96
A. L. Underwood Ltd v Bank of Liverpool & Martins, 1924 300
Appropriation accounts 310
Assets 6

BACSTEL 212
Baker v Barclays Bank Ltd, 1955 300
Balance of payments 18, 146–9
Bailment 281
Bank accounts
  closing 273–4
  opening 265
  operating 269–73
Bank Charter Act, 1844 49–50, 61, 67
Bank clearing 63, 209–13
Bank customer
  defined 264
  obligations 283
Bank giro 209–10
Bank lending 219–20
  budget accounts 223
  farming advances 226
  general policy 236–40
  loans 219
  overdrafts 219, 239
  personal loans 222–3
  probate advances 224
Bank mandates 268
Bank of England
  history 59–62
  functions 62–6
Bank of England Act, 1946 60, 61, 263
Banker
  as agent 263
  breach of contract 297–8
  churches 296
  clubs and societies 294–5
  companies 275–81
  customer relationships 289–92
  defined 263
  joint accounts 285–7
  legal liabilities 297–302

married women 285
minors 283–5
obligations 282
partnerships 288–9
personal representatives 292–3
trustees 294
Bankers automated clearing services 210–13
Bankers draft 215
Banking Act, 1826, 1979 49, 64, 66, 192, 264
Banking ratios 67–9
Banking supervision 64–6
Banks
  assets 70–4
  balance sheets 68
  Bank of England 59–66
  British overseas 56
  consortium 57
  country 49
  early history 47–50
  for savings 99–123
  foreign 56
  liabilities 67–70
  merchant 53–5
  National Giro 57
  savings 58–9
  town 49
  trustee savings 58–9
Barter 1–2
Bearer bonds 176, 255–6
Bearer debentures 176
Betting and Loans Act, 1982 284
Bills for collection 227
Bills for discount 220
Bills for negotiation 227–8
Bills of Exchange
  acceptance 184–5
  allonge 185
  defined 172–4
  discharge 186–7
  dishonour 198–9
  endorsement 185–6
  forgery on 197–8
  material alteration 197
  noting and protesting 199–200
  parties to 177–80
  protection 187–93

338 Index

Bills of Exchange Act, 1882   64, 172–97, 270, 284, 297, 299
Blue chip rates   141
Borrowers and interest rates   135–7
British Technology Group   94–5
Building societies   87–8
  share accounts   107–8
  deposit accounts   108
  agency agreements   108–9
British American Elevator Co Ltd v Bank of British North America, 1919   29
British and Northern Bank v Zolstein, 1927   272
Burnett v Westminster Bank Ltd, 1965   276
Business Names Act, 1916   193

Capital bonds   86
Carlisle and Cumberland Banking Co v Bragg, 1911   258
Cash   203–4
Cash budgets   327
Certificates of deposit   82
Cheques
  and bills of exchange   174
  clearing   204–7
  crossings   169–72
  definition   164
  eurocheques   214
  travellers   213–14
  walks   166
Cheques Act, 1957   168, 180, 186, 191–5, 268, 280, 299
Circular flow of income   103–4
Civil Aviation Act, 1949   245
Claytons Case   272–3
Clearing house automated payment system   212–13
Coins
  changes   33–43
  early use   2
Coleman v London County and Westminster Bank Ltd, 1916   249
Colwyn Commission   51
Commissioners of Taxation v English, Scottish & Australian Bank Ltd, 1970   192
Companies
  borrowing   291
  opening accounts   290
  prospectus   85
  types   289
  winding up   292
Companies Act, 1967, 317
  1980   289, 295
Company final accounts   307–18
Competition and credit control   139
Consumer Credit Act, 1974   223, 232, 259, 260–1
Computer services   228

Conversion   180–1
  safe custody   181
Corporate Tax rate system   217
Credit cards   207–9
Credit clearing   209–13
Credit established   221–2
Credit creation explained   19–21
Credit creation multiplier   21
Credit scoring   240–2
Creditors   316
Curtice v London City & Midland Bank, 1908   196
Current/circulatory assets   312
Current liabilities   314

Davidson v Barclays Bank Ltd, 1940   298
Deeley v Lloyds Bank Ltd, 1912   250, 256
Defamation   298–9
Deposits
  bank   34
  certificates of   70, 80, 158, 218
  current accounts   100, 106, 216–17
  deposit accounts   100, 106, 216
  savings accounts   107, 217
  special   22
  supplementary special   43–4
Development agencies   95
Deveyne v Noble, 1816 (Clayton's Case)   272–3, 250, 287
Directives   22, 40
  discount
    houses   76–81
    liabilities   78
    assets   78–80
Disintermediation   43–4
Documentary credit   227–8
Drawn notes   164

EFTPOS   213
Eligible bills   72
European Communities Act, 1972   259, 292
European currency unit   7
Export Credit Guarantee Department   95–6

Factor incomes   103–4
Factor services   103–4
Factoring   226–7
Family Law Reform Act, 1969   283
Finance Act, 1956   112
Fine Art Society v Union Bank of London, 1886   180
Fiscal policy   38
Fixed assets   312
Foreign currency   213
Foreign Exchange Market   96–7
  premiums   221
  discount   221
  spot   221
  outright forward contract   221
  option forward contract   221

Index

Free capital 67
Freehold 245
Full employment 37
Funding 23, 44

Gibbons v Westminster Bank Ltd, 1939 298
Going concern 329
Gone concern 329–31
Goodwill 312
Government economic policy
  objectives 36–8
  present 44–5
Greenwood v Martins Bank Ltd, 1933 283
Gross profit 308
Growth 37

Hedley Byrne & Co Ltd v Heller Partners, 1963 225, 231, 276
Home banking services 225–6
House Property Co of London Ltd v London County and Westminster Bank 191, 300
Hypothecation 243

Income and Corporation Taxes Act, 1970 112
Income tax management 224–5
Infants Relief Act, 1874 283–4
Inflation 11, 19
Insurance companies 88, 114–15
  endowment 114–15
  annuities 116
Intangible assets 314
Intelligence reports 229
Interest rates
  balance of payments 146–9
  changes in bank's 141–2
  direct regulation 23
  government influences 138–40
  indirect regulation 23
  liquidity preference 128–33
  loanable funds 124–8
  minimum lending rate 23
  money market influences 141
  precautionary motive 129
  speculative motive 129–30
  theories 123–35
  transactions motive 128–9
International money orders 214–15
Investing in industry 96
Investment
  defined 103
  management 225
  of banks 73, 142–4
  trusts 90

Jackson v White and Midland Bank Ltd, 1967 287
Joachimson v Swiss Bank Corporation, 1921 277

Joint and several liability 286–7
Judicature Act, 1873 254

Ladbrooke v Todd, 1914 265
Land Registration Act, 1925 244
Langtry v Union Bank of London, 1896 181
Law of Property Act, 1925 245, 278
Law Reform Act, 1945 192
Leasehold 245
Leasehold Report Act, 1967 245
Leasing 86, 229
Legal Tender 12
Letter of Credit 221
Licenced deposit-taking institutions 264
Lien 243
Limitations Act, 1939 174
Liquidity 70
Lloyds Bank Ltd v Brooks 272
  v Bundy, 1975 276
  v Chartered Bank of India, Australia and China, 1928 193
  v E. B. Savory & Co Ltd, 1933 299–300
  v Lundy, 1974 258
  v Swiss Bankverein 256
Local authorities 122–3
London inter-bank offered rate 141, 159
London International Financial Futures Exchange 97, 160–2
London Joint Stock Bank Ltd v Macmillan and Arthur, 1918 283
Lumsdon & Co v London Trustees Savings Bank, 1971 192

Mail and telegraphic orders 214–15
Manufacturing accounts 308
Marfani & Co Ltd v Midland Bank Ltd, 1968 193
Marketing bank services 224–33
Marquess of Bute v Barclays Bank Ltd, 1955 300
Merchant banks 53
  functions 53–6
Merchant banking services 225
Metropolitan Police Commissioners v Charles, 1976 168
Midland Bank Ltd v Reckitt and Others, 1933 279
Monetary policy 38–9
  techniques 40–5
Money
  characteristics 8–10
  demand for 124
  evolution 1–4
  forms 12–14
  functions 4–8
  near 14–16
  overnight 71
  quantity theory 30–5
  supply 25–9, 125

340 Index

Monetarism 32–3
Moral suasion 40, 61
Moneylenders Act, 1927 263
Money markets
  short term 76–81
  classical 81, 83–96
  parallel 81–3, 151–2
  local authority 122–3, 152–4
  finance house 81, 123, 154–5
  Eurocurrency 82, 155–8
  interbank 83, 158–9
  inter-company 83, 159–60

National Bank v Paterson 185
National Investment Loans Office 94
National Provincial Bank Ltd v Brakenbury, 1906 258
National savings 118–22
National Westminster Bank Ltd v Barclays Bank International and Another 198
Negligence 299–300
Negotiability 183–4
Net profit 310
Night safes 218
Notes
  banks' holdings 62
  early forms 3
  fiduciary issue 4, 49
Nu-stilo Footwear Ltd v Lloyds Bank Ltd, 1956 299

Open market operations 23, 41–2
Orbit Mining Co Ltd v Midland Bank Ltd, 1963 164

Partnership Act, 1890 288, 310
Partnership Act, 1908 288
Passport services 225
Penmount Estates Ltd v National Provincial Bank Ltd, 1945 300
Pennington v Crossley & Son, 1987 169
Pension funds 88–9
  state retirement 110–11
  occupational 111–12
  personal 112–14
Performance bonds 231
Personal Representatives 304
Physical policy 36
Pledges 243
Plunkett v Barclays Bank Ltd, 1936 298
Power of attorney 278–80
Powers of Attorney Act, 1971 278–9
Preferential creditors 331–2
Profit and loss accounts 310
Profitability of banks 70
Promissory notes 175–6
Prosperity Ltd v Lloyds Bank Ltd, 1929 274
Protection of Fraud Act 117
Provident Societies Act, 1967 295

Prudential regulations 64
Public Sector Borrowing Requirements 35–6
Public Works Loans Act, 1875 94
Public Works Loans Board 94

Quantity of money theory 30–5

R v Davenport 277
Rail and airport banks 222
Ratios
  acid test 323
  credit 320
  current 322–3
  debtor 320–1
  gross profit to sales 323–4
  net profit to sales 324
  rate of stock turnover 318–20
  return on capital employed 325
  sales to net worth 325–6
  stock 321–3
  working capital 322
Re v Codling, 1972 302
Regulation 195–6
Regulator 155
Reserve requirements 22, 40–1
Reserves 316, 317
Robin v Steward, 1854 298

Safe custody 217–18
Safeguards Act, 1817 58
Safety deposits 218
Saunders v Anglian Building Society, 1970 258
Savings 99–123
  reasons for 101–2
  major funds 106–23
Savings banks 58–9
Securities
  land 247–51
  stocks and shares 251–7
  life policies 253–5
Sex Discrimination Act, 1965 285
Shares
  calls 316
  discount 316
  ordinary 84–5
  participating 85
  partially paid 316
  preference 85
  premiums 316
  rights issues 84
  stock transfer 92
Shields v Corbould Ellis & Dales, 1912 286
Sin v Stretch 298
Slingsby and Others v District Bank, 1932 174
Social Security Act, 1975 10
Special deposits 22, 41

Special drawing rights 7
Stable prices 37
Stamp Act, 1853 77, 163
Status enquiries 231–2
Stock Exchange 90–4
  bears 93
  bulls 93
  official list 91
  option trading 93
  stags 93
  unlisted securities market 93
Stony Stanton Supplies (Coventry) Ltd v Midland Bank Ltd, 1966 265
Supplementary special deposits 23
SWIFT 215
Synodial Government Act, 1970 296

Tassell v Cooper, 1850 282
Theft Act 168
Tournier v National Provincial Union Bank of England Ltd, 1924 282
Trading accounts 308

Treasury bills 35, 77–8, 176
Trustees 304

Unfair Contract Terms Act, 1977 281
Unit trusts 89–90, 116–18, 225
  advantages 118
  disadvantages 118
United Dominion Trust Ltd v Kirkwood, 1966 263
United Overseas Bank v Jiwani, 1958 272

Vicarious liability 300–2

Warehousekeepers warrants 176
Westminster Bank Ltd v Cond, 1940 258
  v Hilton, 1926 196
Wills 302–3
Wills Act, 1852, 302–3
  1937 302
Wilson v Midland Bank Ltd, 1961 274, 299
Woods v Martins Bank Ltd v Another, 1959 264